ALBERT A. NOFI is a frequent contributor to "Strategy and Tactics" magazine. He is a noted military expert in the modern, Napoleonic and ancient warfare.

Mr. Nofi has designed several historical simulation games and war games.

He lives and teaches in New York.

THE WAR AGAINST HITLER

THE WAR AGAINST HITLER

Military Strategy in the West

Edited by Albert A. Nofi

HIPPOCRENE
BOOKS, INC.

For information, address: Hippocrene Books, Inc.
171 Madison Avenue, New York, N.Y. 10016.

Manufactured in the United States of America.

Library of Congress Cataloging in Publication Data
Main entry under title:

The War against Hitler.

Selected articles previously published in Strategy & tactics magazine.
Bibliography: p.272
1. World War, 1939-1945—Campaigns—Europe—Addresses, essays, lectures. 2. World War, 1939-1945—Campaigns—Africa, North—Addresses, essays, lectures. 3. World War, 1939-1945—Naval operations—Submarine—Addresses, essays, lectures. 4. World War, 1939-1945—Naval operations, German—Addresses, essays, lectures. 5. World War, 1939-1945—Atlantic Ocean—Addresses, essays, lectures. 6. Tactics—History—20th century—Addresses, essays, lectures. I. Nofi, Albert A.
U740.W37 1982 355.4'8'094 82-15481
ISBN 0-88254-631-7

Contents

Preface vii

Introduction ix

Note on Usage x

The Blitzkrieg: Evolution of a Military Instrument, 1914–1940, by Albert A. Nofi 3

The Fall of France, 1940, by Albert A. Nofi 27

WolfPack: The German Submarine War in the Atlantic, 1939–1940, by Frank Davis 47

Panzerarmee Afrika and the War in the Desert, June 1940–December 1942, by Albert A. Nofi 69

Sicily: The Race for Messina, 10 July–17 August 1943, by Albert A. Nofi 95

Overlord: The Normandy Invasion, 6–26 June 1944, by Albert A. Nofi 114

Cobra: Patton's Offensive in France, Summer 1944, by John Prados 133

Highway to the Reich: *Operation Market-Garden,* 17–26 September 1944, by Phil Kosnett and Stephen B. Patrick 156

Patton's Third Army: The Lorraine Campaign, 19 September–1 December 1944, by Joseph Balkoski 178

The Ardennes Offensive: An Analysis of the Battle of the Bulge, December 1944 by Stephen B. Patrick 206

Operation Grenade: The Battle for the Rhineland, 23 February–5 March 1945, by Joseph Balkoski 225

Battle for Germany: The Destruction of the Reich, December 1944–May 1945, by Stephen B. Patrick 248

Recommended Reading 272

Preface

The War Against Hitler is a collection of studies on important aspects of the history of the Second World War in Europe as it involved the Western Powers, chiefly Great Britain and the United States. It is not, strictly, a chronological history of the war, although it does present a generally chronological account of the struggle in broad outline. Some of the studies are essentially analytic pieces examining particular technical subjects or certain key operations. Others are primarily narrative accounts of important battles or campaigns. Most of the materials incorporated in *The War Against Hitler* are drawn from the pages of *Strategy & Tactics* magazine.

Devoted to the intensive examination of historical events, *Strategy & Tactics*, or "*S&T*" as it is more commonly referred to, attempts to bridge the yawning gap between scholarly monographs which are often excruciatingly detailed and generally superficial "popular" histories which are so common. To accomplish this, *S&T* has developed and employs a number of unique approaches for the presentation of data to supplement the more traditional narrative treatment. Among these innovative techniques are an unusual "modular" system for presentation of information of an unusual or technical nature, an extensive use of graphics for the elucidation of confusing doctrinal concepts and data, plus considerably more "hard" technical, doctrinal, and statistical information than is normally found in historical literature. This technical and mechanical approach is essential for the kind of analytic view of cause and effect which has been the principal strength of *S&T* during its fifteen years of publication. In that period literally hundreds of articles have appeared using precisely this approach. The fall of Rome, the Battle of Trafalgar, the development of mechanized warfare, and the practice of war in the age of Napoleon have been among the magazine's numerous topics. By far the greatest proportion of the articles which have appeared in *S&T* have been devoted to the Second World War. In 1977 the Editors of *Strategy & Tactics* published a collection of articles largely drawn from the magazine which dealt with the titanic Russo-German conflict, entitled *The War in the East. The War Against Hitler* complements that work.

Only one article in *The War Against Hitler* is totally new. This addition was necessitated by the remarkable fact that, in some fifteen years of concentrating on the Second World War, *S&T* never once managed to treat of D-Day. This interesting and curious omission has been corrected by the preparation of "Overlord: A Summary Analysis of the Normandy Invasion," which gives the full *S&T* treatment to the "mighty endeavour." Reversing the history of all the other materials in this volume, "Overlord" will be published in *Strategy & Tactics* at the end of 1982.

In preparing *The War Against Hitler* for publication, every effort has been made to preserve the distinctive styles and approaches of the original authors. Only one article has been extensively rewritten, "Blitzkrieg: Evolution of a Military Instrument, 1914–1940." Originally a treatment of the development of mechanized warfare between the wars, this has been recast so as to provide an introduction to *The War Against Hitler* and a look at German military methods and institutions at the beginning of the Second World War. Another article, "Highway to the Reich," has been expanded through the incorporation of additional materials from a different article, "Westwall: Battles on the German Frontier," in order to include certain valuable information. In this instance, the authors of both articles have been credited with the conflated article.

Aside from these rather significant revisions, the Editor has confined himself to only a few small changes in the material. Save for the correction of minor errors, the updating or reworking of occasionally obsolete tables and charts, and the eliminations of repetitious passages where several articles treat of similar subject matter, each article has been presented substantially as it originally appeared in the pages of *S&T*. Of course, the opening of hitherto secret archives since the early 1970s has necessitated some minor revisions of, or additions to, the text at times. This has been done as carefully as possible. It should be realized, however, that *Ultra*, the special classification given information derived from the breaking of Germany's most sensitive codes, the *XX Office*, the agency responsible for "turning" virtually every German agent in Britain during the war, and similar revelations are hardly likely to be the final secrets of World War II. While an effort has been made to incorporate such materials, it must be understood that, as more and more secrets are revealed, many conclusions about the war may have to change.

The Editor wishes to thank the authors of the articles incorporated in *The War Against Hitler* and asks their indulgence for the occasional liberties he has taken with their materials. Thanks are also in order to the staff of Simulations Publications and that of Hippocrene Books, who made this volume possible; to J.F.D., Redmond, M.F.M., and M.E.M. for their assistance and advice in its preparation; and most particularly to M.S.N. and M.J.S., who suffered through that preparation.

Albert A. Nofi

Brooklyn
20 April 1982

Introduction

The roots of World War II lie deeply embedded in European History. Nationalism, imperialism, militarism, ideology, and history itself combined with human weakness to produce the brutalities of World War I. That struggle might have inaugurated a century of peace despite the rather harsh terms of the Versailles Treaty, given men of good will on all sides. But certain tensions remained unresolved and new ones arose. Economic crises in the post-war period exacerbated existing difficulties. And the rise of totalitarian dictatorships in Russia and Italy and Germany, plus a plethora of petty tyrannies in Eastern and Southern Europe, was hardly conducive to international cooperation based upon negotiation and agreement among just men. Perhaps if the United States and France and Great Britain had acted swiftly and concertedly against the Dictators, peace might have been maintained. The former power, however, had retreated into isolation in the early 1920s, content to enjoy its economic boom and suffer its Great Depression alone, while the two latter powers, mindful of the enormous cost of the Great War, feared a resort to decisive action which might lead to another conflict. So the West pretended that Hitler and Mussolini and Stalin were men of good will.

Thus, the dictators thrived. As Hitler rebuilt German military power and Mussolini raped Ethiopia, and all three dictators meddled in Spain's Civil War, the democratic powers dithered, putting their trust in pious words. Nevertheless, by the late 1930s they began to realize the futility of reliance on the words of dictators. But by then the military balance had begun to shift in favor of the totalitarian states. So, as France and Britain began to rearm, they sought ways to postpone the inevitable struggle until a more favorable time. Appeasement of the dictators became a necessity. Thus Ethiopia and Spain, Austria and Czechoslovakia were traded for time. Meanwhile the growing power of Nazi Germany began to cause Stalin uneasy moments. Efforts to secure Western cooperation against Hitler being rebuffed, Stalin threw in with him instead. On 23 Aug. 1939 Russia and Germany concluded a non-aggression pact. At the stroke of a pen Stalin gained Latvia, Estonia, Lithuania, and portions of Rumania and time in which to build his own strength in exchange for undertaking to do what he intended anyway, avoid war with Germany. And Hitler, at the cost of some real estate he didn't own, secured his rear for the coming struggle with the West. Barely a week later he invaded Poland. The Second World War had begun. And as a stunned world looked on, Poland was crushed in a campaign of such rapidity that it introduced a new word to the world, *blitzkrieg*.

Note on Usage

Certain conventions have been used throughout *The War Against Hitler* to facilitate a clearer presentation of the materials.

Nomenclature. Allied military formations are always given in ordinary type: thus "1st Armored Division" would be an American or British unit. German and Italian military formation names have been given in italicized type; "*1st Panzer Division*" would be a German unit. In the case of German units, the practice of retaining the German words "Panzer" for armored and "Panzergrenadier" for armored infantry has also been adopted. Standard military usage prevails in the way a unit designation is presented. Divisions are designated by ordinal numbers, "1st," "2nd"; corps by Roman numerals, "I," "II"; armies by written out ordinal number, "First," "Second"; and army groups by ordinal numbers again, "1st," "6th."

Abbreviations and Mapping Symbols. A modification of the standard NATO military mapping symbols has been used throughout.

Symbol	**Type of Troops**	**Abbreviations**
	Infantry	Inf
	Parachute Infantry	Para, Abn (Airborne)
	Mountain Infantry	Mtn
	Armored Infantry	Arm Inf; Mech Inf; *PaGr**
	Cavalry	Cav
	Reconnaissance	Recon
	Tank, Armored	Arm; *Pzr**
	Self-Propelled Gun	SP; AG
	Artillery	Art
	Anti-tank	AT
	Anti-aircraft	AA

Symbol	**Type of Troops**	**Abbreviations**
	Rocket Artillery	[none]
	Aircraft	[none]
	Signal	[none]
	Engineer	Eng
	Supply	[none
	Transportation	[none]

**PzGr*= panzergrenadier; *Pzr*= panzer

In the NATO system, formation sizes are indicated by symbols placed on top of the troop-type symbol, as follows:

Size Indicator	**Unit**	**Abbreviations**
I	Company	Co
II	Battalion	Bn
III	Regiment	Rgt
X	Brigade Combat Command	Bde, CC
XX	Division	Div
XXX	Corps	-
XXXX	Army	-
XXXXX	Army Group	-

Combining the size indication with the troop type symbol gives the full identification of the units as found on a map or an organizational diagram. Thus,

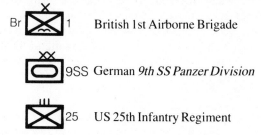

Br  1 British 1st Airborne Brigade

 9SS German *9th SS Panzer Division*

 25 US 25th Infantry Regiment

Time. All times given have been rendered in the 24-hour system. Thus, *0930* is 9:30 A.M., while *2130* is 9:30 PM.

Comparative Officer Ranks

Abbrev	American	British Commonwealth (Army)	British (RAF)
FM	General of the Army	Field Marshal	Marshal of the RAF
Gen	General	General	Air Chief Marshal
LG	Lieutenant General	Lieutenant General	Air Marshal
MG	Major General	Major General	Air Vice-Marshal
BG	Brigadier General	Brigadier[1]	Air Commodore
Col	Colonel	Colonel	Group Captain
LC	Lieutenant-Colonel	Lieutenant-Colonel	Wing Commander
Maj	Major	Major	Squadron Leader
Capt	Captain	Captain	Flight Lieutenant
Lt	First Lieutenant	Lieutenant	Flying Officer
Lt	Second Lieutenant	Second Lieutenant	

Officers will generally be referred to by the abbreviations at the left of this table. This is to permit some idea of the actual rank held relative to that used in the British or American service. Note, for example, that the literal translation of the *Generalleutnant* is "lieutenant-general," while the relative rank is actually that of a British or American Major-General. In certain cases, notably that of the Waffen-SS *Oberfuhrer,* there is no equivalent rank in the Anglo-American system. Other variations have been indicated by superscript digits referring to the notes below.

1. Brigadier is not a general-officer rank in the British service.
2. Strictly speaking the highest *rank* in the French army is *General de division*. *General de corps d'armee* and *General d'armee* are granted when an officer is serving in the indicated capacity, and *Marechal de France* is a title of distinction.

French	German (Army, AirForce)	German (Waffen-SS)[5]	Italian
	Reichsmarschall		Maresciallo del Impero
Marechal de France[2]	General-feldmarschall	Reichsfuhrer-SS	Maresciallo d'Italia
General d'Armee	Generaloberst	Oberstgruppen-fuhrer	Generale d'armata[6]
General de corps d'armee	General der . . .[3]	Obergruppen-fuhrer	Generale di corpo d'armata
General de division	Generalleutnant	Gruppenfuhrer	Generale di divisione[7]
General de brigade	Generalmajor	Brigadefuhrer	Generale di brigata[8]
		Oberfuhrer	
Colonel	Oberst	Standartenfuhrer	Colonello
Lieutenant-colonel	Oberstleutnant	Obersturmbann-fuhrer	Tenente-colonello
Commandant	Major	Sturmbannfuhrer	Maggiore
Capitaine	Hauptman[4]	Hauptsturm-fuhrer	Capitano
Lieutenant	Oberleutnant	Obersturmfuhrer	Tenente
Sous-lieutenant	Leutnant	Untersturmfuhrer	Sotto-tenente

3. Officers with this rank always bore an arm of service designation as well, thus *General der Panzertruppen* or *General der Artillerie*.
4. For all arms except cavalry, when *Rittmeister* was used.
5. Army ranks commonly used interchangeably.
6. A *Generale di corpo d'armata* designated to command an army was called *Generale di corpo d'armata commandate designato d'armata* and ranked between *Generale di corpo d'armata* and *Generale d'Armata*.
7. Officers of this rank not in the infantry or cavalry are *Tenente Generale* unless in command of a division.
8. Officers of this rank not in the infantry or cavalry are *Maggiore Generale* unless in command of a brigade.

THE WAR AGAINST HITLER

Blitzkrieg: Evolution of a Military Instrument, 1914–1940

by Albert A. Nofi

The *Blitzkrieg* shocked the world. It was a revolution in the conduct of war. The First World War had been characterized by fixed lines of battle stretching literally hundreds of miles across the face of Europe. In a frontal sector rarely more than twenty miles wide hundreds of thousands of men had fought and died for virtually imperceptible gains. Victory was attained only after years of almost continuous bloody combat. Barely twenty years later came the Second World War. And when Hitler unleashed the Nazi war machine the world stood in awe. Fronts shifted rapidly, decisive advances in the hundreds of miles were achieved in days, critical objectives fell at relatively small cost in manpower. So superior was this new method of waging war that for nearly three years Hitler stood supreme in Europe. The Allies required long years of hard experience before they could learn to cope with Blitzkrieg, and still more years before they could begin to practice it themselves.

Origins: 1914–1935.

In 1914 the armies of Europe had marched off to war expecting a few months of swift campaigning and an early victory. Instead, the power of the machine gun and quick firing artillery and barbed wire proved too much for the infantrymen of the age and the perverse form of siege known as trench warfare began. Supported by the inexhaustible productivity of the industrial revolution, the armies ensconced themselves behind endless lines of field fortifications. Try as they might, the generals of the time could find no solution to the stalemate beyond hurling mountains of men and shells at the enemy. Despite the resulting carnage, they tried repeatedly, each time to fail even more disastrously than before. But if the established leadership was unwilling to accept the fact that their methods were obsolete, others were not so stupid. In both the Allied and the German camps, well-placed thinkers sought innovative solutions to the problem. They were successful. In time, they even found acceptance.

For the Allies, the solution was technological, the *tank*. It was actually developed by the British at Winston Churchill's urging, but it was such an obvious solution that the French and the Italians and the Russians were working on something similar, and an Austrian officer, Gunther Burstyn, had presciently proposed it even before the war began. The basic idea was to take an ordinary track-laying farm tractor, equip it with armor plate to enable it to shrug off machine gun fire, and give it some weapons of its own to permit it to carry firepower to the enemy. With its tracks it could ignore the obstacles of trench and wire which had for so long frustrated the infantry. Basically, the tank was seen as a device for helping the infantry break loose from the stalemate of the trenches. And it worked.

The Germans came up with an essentially philosophical solution to the problem of trench warfare. Rather than resort to technology, they revised their tactics and came up with *infiltration*. This new tactical approach worked in a fashion completely counter to the prevalent tactics. Conventional wisdom dictated days or even weeks of heavy bombardment preparatory to an assault; infiltration tactics stressed a short, overwhelming "hurricane" barrage. And whereas conventional tactics packed enormous numbers of men into the attack, in massive formations, on broad fronts, infiltration utilized smaller formations on vary narrow fronts. The optimal trench defensive was a broad, thinly held frontal zone well-seasoned with machine guns and strong points. Infiltration tactics took advantage of this. The attacking *stosstruppen*— storm troopers, would advance in small groups, bypassing enemy strong points, leaving them for follow-up waves to cope with, as they strove to gain ground as rapidly as possible and cut the enemy"s lines of communication. Like the tank, infiltration worked. It was repeatedly successful, against Romania in 1916, against Russia and Italy in 1917, and in the Spring of 1918 it almost won the war for Germany. But, in desperate fighting on the Western Front, the German drives had been halted. As millions of fresh, tough, young American troops were beginning to arrive on the Continent, and as the Allied blockade of Germany finally began to tell, German morale began to crack even as their ability to carry on the war waned.

In the later portion of 1918 the Allies, using their growing manpower superiority and swarms of tanks, began to drive the Germans back all along the Western Front. By late September, the German High Command was looking for a way out of the war and in November an Armistice was reached. The Allies had won. The infantryman, supported by the tank where necessary, had proven to be the ultimate weapon.

But not everyone agreed that the way the Allies fought the final campaigns was necessarily the best way. One of the most vocal critics was J.F.C. Fuller, a British staff officer who had served with tanks. Fuller believed that tanks could find an independent role for themselves. In the course of his experiences with the tanks he had participated in the *Battle of Cambrai* (20–26 November 1917). At Cambrai, three brigades of tanks had gone "over the top" without preliminary bombardment, closely supporting six divisions of infantry. The results had been startling. In less than six days the troops had penetrated about four miles, perhaps the most significant change in the Western Front since 1915. A shortage of infantry caused the British to lose their gains within a few weeks, as the Germans skillfully counterattacked. Nevertheless, Fuller had seen what tanks could accomplish. In planning for future operations he proposed doing a Cambrai all over.

Fuller's *Plan 1919* envisioned heavy tanks as spearheading a breakthrough of the German trenches. With the front ruptured, light tanks would pour through followed by infantry in trucks and transport tanks, to permit them to keep up with the rapidly moving light tanks. These mobile forces would speed deep into the enemy's rear, disrupting his lines of communication, supply, reinforcement and retreat. In this fashion, Fuller believed that the Allies could rip off huge chunks of enemy controlled territory at relatively little cost. Fuller's proposal aroused considerable interest. Ferdinand Foch himself, Allied Supreme Commander, favored it with his blessings. But the war ended before Fuller's plans could be implemented. The radical idea that tanks should be considered the principal element in a combined arms tactical system was soon forgotten. The Allies had found a technique which worked, the tank-infantry combination, and intended to stick with it. But the matter didn't end there. For after the war, Fuller and other tank proponents produced copious writings in support of their positions.

Through the 1920s a considerable amount of ink was spilled over the question of what was the proper way to employ tanks. The net result of all this was that four schools of thought eventually evolved.

Pure Tank. This school held that the tank was the ultimate weapon and would sweep all other arms before it in massive frontal assaults. It generally ignored the possible contributions of the other arms in combat, even should those other arms be raised to the same level of mobility as the tanks. And when the pure tank advocates did concede some role to infantry and artillery, it was usually a minor one. One of the most vocal of the advocates of this school was Giffard LeQ. Martel, a British officer. In 1927 he proposed a division of 720 machine gun-armed two-man tanks and 120 light cannon-armed tankettes, without supporting combat arms. He seriously believed that this force would be able to overrun any other combination of troops in the world. This resulted in the highly unbalanced armored divisions of the prewar and early war period. It also created several notable disasters.

Infantry Tank. The advocates of this school represented the voice of conservatism, for they held that the tank was primarily an infantry support weapon. In combat, it would act as a sort of mobile pill box, helping the infantry overcome local obstacles. This was essentially the role performed by tanks during World War I, and it tended to dominate the theories of several armies. It eventually led to the infantry support armored forces of France, Britain, Japan and the Soviet Union. There was, of course, some merit to the idea.

Cavalry Tank. This school, advocated by such men as the U.S.A.'s Adna Chafee and France's Maxime Weygand, held that tanks would enable the old mounted arm to resume its proper role in battle, a role which the machine gun had frustrated. Thus, light armored forces would perform all the functions of the traditional cavalry: reconnaissance, screening, and strategic and tactical pursuit. The Italians, French, and British created sizeable armored formations much along these lines. The Americans, Germans and Soviets formed smaller armored cavalry arms, primarily as reconnaissance forces. In the outcome, this school was also found to have some merit.

Mobile Combined Arms. This was the voice of reasonand compromise, first clearly stated by Britain's B.H. Liddell Hart. Liddell Hart, a junior British officer, combined features of Fuller's *Plan 1919* and the German infiltration tactics. The idea was for a fully mobile combined arms force which could rupture an enemy front and then proceed to exploit that rupture by penetrating deep into the enemy rear area, thus isolating enemy forces at the front. Curiously, a German officer, Heinz Guderian, came up with very much the same concept independently. Guderian's background was somewhat different from Liddell Hart's. For one thing Germany had little experience with tanks in World War I. And at the end of the war Germany was prohibited from experimenting with such contraptions and her army reduced to but 100,000 men. Neither of these restrictions were taken seriously in Germany, but the German Army nevertheless moved cautiously. In the early 1920s Guderian was placed in charge of motor transport development, which was a front for tank development. One of his earliest actions was to consult the Cavalry as to the role which it believed mechanized forces should fill. The cavalrymen suggested reconnaissance and Guderian oriented his experiments towards the development of reconnaissance forces. Even his very earliest experiments, using simulated equipment, stressed a fully motorized combined arms approach. This is not to say that Guderian was given a free hand. He had his problems with extremists on both sides of the issue.

By 1930 all the major powers had experimented with tank forces, but none had ever gone beyond developing anything more than a brigade. The official doctrine in most countries was that the tank was auxiliary to the infantry. In some places, such as Britain and France, the idea of a mechanized cavalry was also considered reasonable. Thus we find two lines of development. This is much the situation which prevails for the next five years. But in 1933 something happened in Germany which was critically important—Hitler came to power with the intention of rearming Germany. One of his earliest acts was to examine Germany's military situation. In the course of this Guderian was asked to demonstrate his experimental combat techniques. Within a few days Guderian organized a combined arms reconnaissance team of motorcycle infantry, light anti-tank guns, armored cars and Pz I light tanks and led them in a demonstration. Hitler was impressed. He gave Guderian the official approval to go ahead. In 1934 Hitler agreed to permit the formation of armored divisions based on Guderian's principles and three of these were formed in late 1935. These were not, however, the first such formations in existence.

In 1934 the French developed their *Light Mechanized Division.* In many ways this resembled Guderian's proposed armored division as approved in 1935. Indeed, the mixture of tank and infantry elements was very similar, with a 4:3 ratio. But there was a difference. The difference was that whereas Guderian envisioned an independent role for armored divisions, the Light Mechanized Division was essentially an infantry support formation with pretenses of being cavalry.

Experience, 1935–1939

With the establishment of three Panzer divisions in late 1935, the focus of mobile warfare development shifts decisively to Germany. The principal reasons for this are twofold. First, Hitler liked the new weapons system and ran interference for Guderian whenever he got into difficulties with more conservative elements in the army. Second, there was Guderian himself, the only tank proponent to actually be given a fairly free hand by any country.

As organized, the 1935 armored division was a fairly balanced combat force of tanks, mechanized infantry and motorized artillery. Even the ratio of tank to infantry battalions was fairly good, 4:3, at a time when other armies were speculating on ratios of 3:1, as was the case in Russia, or 5:1 as proposed by Liddell Hart to the British Secretary of State for War. The infantry is necessary to hold ground and help keep enemy infantry off the tanks' backs. It also is useful in country relatively unsuited to tanks, and when there are lots of unfriendly anti-tank guns about. So the German 1935 organization was very well balanced indeed. One of the curious things about this formation is the fact that it greatly resembled Guderian's experimental simulated reconnaissance battalion of 1929. The ratio of forces was the same and even the tactical doctrine very much the same.

Guderian's basic idea was that the armored division was designed to achieve and exploit breakthroughs in the enemy's front. The French saw the DLM as an infantry support formation, designed primarily to help the infantry break a 1917-style front. Motorization was seen as an advantage in terms of mobility in a reserve situation, not to facilitate exploitation.

One of the best bits of evidence to demonstrate the essential soundness of the 1935 armored division is the fact that it lasted until after the 1940 campaign in France, when Hitler doubled the number of armored divisions by halving the amount of armor in them and using the surplus to raise new formations. But this is not to say that the formation as originally conceived was perfect. There was a great deal of minor adjustment made in its organization. Thus, the original engineer company soon was reinforced to battalion size. And the infantry contingent increased by the addition of another battalion, which produced a ratio of infantry to tank battalions of 1:1. This adjustment was made after maneuvers demonstrated that such a ratio was optimal. Each tank battalion was supported by (and gave support to) a single mobile infantry battalion. This is still considered standard doctrine by virtually all armies. The experience gained in simulated battle was incredibly useful. But even more important was that gained from actual combat, for in 1935 the tank went to war.

The perspective gained from the *Italo-Ethiopian War* (1935–1936) and the *Spanish Civil War* (1936–1939) was critical. In effect, the lessons helped prove what could *not* be done and what disadvantages tanks possessed. Among the most important such lessons was the relative ineffectiveness of the light machine gun equipped tankette. The Italians had used their C.V. 3/33 in both wars and the Germans had sent many of their more sophisticated but essentially similar Pz I to Spain. Both of these vehicles were very light, the Italian being about three tons and the German about six. They were very lightly protected, carried one or two machine guns, but were relatively maneuverable and able to make about 25 mph over roads. In effect, they were very much the type of vehicle which the British "pure" tank proponent Martel had proposed in the 1920s. But in action they soon proved highly vulnerable to even relatively primitive anti-tank methods of the day. Indeed, even improvised methods could damage or destroy such vehicles if employed by determined infantry.

Heavier vehicles, such as the Soviet *T–26, T–27,* and *B.T.* series, also proved vulnerable to anti-tank fire. These vehicles were far superior to the German and Italian tanks appearing in Spain. They were considerably heavier, usually eleven tons or more, carried a cannon/machine gun armament and were usually far better protected. But existing anti-tank guns could damage them severely, and experimental pieces, such as the German 88-mm. anti-aircraft gun, could destroy them with little trouble. Nevertheless, Soviet tanks were so superior to the vehicles supplied the Nationalists by the Italians and Germans that they strove to capture as many Soviet tanks as possible, and by the end of the conflict many Nationalist tank units were entirely equipped with Soviet tanks. This sort of thing tended to upset many tank proponents, particularly the "pure tank" people. But the hostile people, the ones who saw no merit whatsoever in tanks, ate it up. After all, they reasoned, if anti-tank weaponry was *already* capable of destroying any tank in existence, what would things be like in a few years, as anti-tank technology improved? One could never logically evolve tanks faster than anti-tank weapon systems, and therefore the tank could never be more than an interesting auxiliary. Perhaps, but Guderian seems to have found that the *Spanish Civil War* confirmed his early ideas about tank warfare. The fact that tanks could be destroyed by anti-tank fire did not make them useless. Properly supported, with infantry and field artillery of equal mobility, tanks would still be the principal arm. Adding in anti-tank elements would make a tank formation even more powerful. And Guderian seems to have come up with a new way to apply anti-tank fire. Rather than use anti-tank guns defensively, he proposed using them offensively, to seek out enemy tanks rather than await them. It gave the Germans a long-lasting edge. Standard British and French anti-tank tactics were purely defensive. Only the Americans and the Soviets thought about using this arm offensively, and they were not too clear on how to go about this. Curiously, although large numbers of tanks were sent to Spain by both sides, no tank battle of interest occurred there. This was because both the Nationalists with their Italian and German Allies, and the Republicans with their Soviet Allies, used tanks in an infantry support role. The few times something radical was attempted, it was usually in terms of massed tank frontal assaults. Against poorly equipped infantry these had some chance of success. But against determined troops moderately well equipped with artillery and anti-tannk weapons the "cavalry charge" tactic usually led to a serious defeat. It was one of the things which the Germans were fortunate enough to notice and the British and French unfortunate enough to miss.

Italian mechanized operations in Spain did have some effect on Guderian's thinking. While British and French and Soviet tacticians stressed the serious, but by no means disastrous, Italian defeat at Guadalajara in early 1937, Guderian noted that the attack had been undertaken in adverse weather, with road-bound equipment, and that the counterattacking Republicans had coordinated tank attacks with air support in beating back the Italians. He went on to observe the admirable advances attained by Italo-Spanish mechanized units in Catalonia in late 1938, when as many as 25 miles were gained in a single day. All this was as grist for the innovative tactical school which Guderian was fostering. But Spain provided still more. There was dive bombing.

Dive bombing was a technique pioneered by the U.S. Marine Corps. It necessitated sturdy aircraft, but was immensely useful in delivering bombs with pinpoint precision on selected targets. Experiments with dive bombing were conducted by both sides during the Spanish conflict. The famed *Stuka* was designed from experience gained in Spain, and a small number were used effectively in the closing days of the war there. Dive bombers soon became an important part of the blitzkrieg repertoire, serving as "flying artillery."

Spain also proved the necessity of having a radio in each tank. Although von Thoma, the German tank commander in Spain, didn't feel they were necessary this was another point about which Guderian was convinced. Then he spent the next two years trying to convince the rest of the army that radios were vital to successful tank operations. In the end he won, and was proven correct, for the rapidity of mechanized operations and the necessity of coordinating the different arms made them indispensable.

The impression may have been created that Guderian had no difficulties in organizing the tank arm and training it to his concepts of mobile warfare. Actually, nothing could be further from the truth. There were powerful interests in the German Army which objected to his concepts. Although Hitler was committed to developing a powerul mobile arm, his political power in the mid-1930s was too uncertain to permit him to behave cavalierly with the more conservative elements in the German Army. The net result was that there was a certain fragmenting of effort in the motorization of the German field forces. As early as 1936, one tank brigade was set aside for an infantry support role at the insistence of the Army High Command. Simiarly, the German cavalry demanded its share of motorized formations with the result that three "light" divisions were organized from the existing cavalry divisions. These were a mixture of mechanized cavalry and motorized infantry formations. In theory, they were supposed to replace horsed cavalry formations, but in battle they eventually proved relatively ineffective in terms of the outlay necessary to maintain them.

There were even problems with the traditional infantrymen, who wanted some motor vehicles of their own as well, with the result being the creation of four motorized infantry divisions. Here again, the diversion of tanks and other armored and cross-country-capable vehicles detracted from the development of the armored forces. However, the formation was more cohesive than the "light" divisions, which lacked an effective role. More motorized equipment was wasted in the mechanization of infantry regimental anti-tank companies. On paper, the creation of motorized infantry divisions and motorized anti-tank companies was not unreasonable. The problem was that the supply of useful motor vehicles, and in particular tanks and other tracked motor vehicles, was severely limited. The cost of a mechanized infantry division, in equipment, fuel, manpower and money, is virtually the same as for an armored division, with much less combat power. But if the diversion of vehicles displeased Guderian we can but speculate on his feelings about the concept of "massed cavalry charge" which continued to dominate the thinking of some German higher officers around 1937.

In the maneuvers of 1937 one regular army corps, with its normal contingent of heavy, field, and anti-tank artillery, was required to defend itself against two similar corps, each supported by a brigade of about 300 tanks. Apparently spectacular results were expected, for Hitler invited a host of foreign dignitaries to watch the operation with him, taking up positions with the defending troops. The two tank brigades made a massive frontal assault against the defenders, moving ahead of, and out of effective supporting range of their friendly infantry and artillery. The results were impressive. The attacking brigades were cut to pieces by the defenders. The incident must have been highly embarrassing for Hitler. But it had far reaching results for the development of German mobile troops. In 1938 Guderian was appointed inspector General of Mobile Troops and a general reorganization of armored formations commenced.

Guderian's new command supervised all armored and mechanized forces in the German Army. Thus, he controlled the three "light" divisions, the four motorized infantry divisions, the three panzer divisions, and the three "infantry support" tank brigades. Guderian quickly began to make changes. The tank brigades were gradually converted into proper panzer divisions over the next years, giving him five. Although he made no move to eliminate the "light" divisions, he made significant changes in their function, changing them from screening forces into exploitation forces. This command reorganization came about just as the Germans were to get some practical experience in the operations of large mechanized formations under virtual war time conditions, for in 1938 Germany annexed Austria and the Sudetenland.

The incorporation of Austria and the Sudetenland in Hitler's Reich was carried out without fighting, but was conducted in an operational fashion. Thus, troop units were assigned routes of march, regular boundries, and so forth. Nor was the possibility of combat nonexistent. Although the Austrians seem to have been fairly willing to be incorporated into the Reich, it was uncertain as to whether the Czechs would agree to the dismemberment of their country through the surrender of the Sudetenland to Germany. The Czech Army was large, apparently well trained and very well equipped. Thus, the operations had a semblance of live action which is usually lacking in maneuvers. For the German mobile troops both operations proved highly instructive. Although the road march of Guderian's inexperienced and ill-prepared XVI Corps (2nd Panzer Division and the SS Lieb Regiment) into Austria was not the disastrous mechanical failure which many British writers portrayed it as, neither was it the overwhelming success which Guderian said it was. As he diplomatically put it, losses "were certainly not as high as 30 per cent." After the *Anschluss* with Austria the techical problems of the tank formations were given considerable scrutiny, with attention being paid to improved maintenance techniques. One of the interesting lessons of the campaign was the improvisation of fuel supply through the use of local gasoline stations. It was one of the many improvisations which would become almost standard operational procedure in the armored formations of all countries later. By the time of the annexation of Czechoslovakia, just a few months later, the mobile forces seem to have solved most of their problems. The operation went off even more smoothly than Austria. It seems likely that, had things come to a fight, the Germans would have been able to make effective use of their mobile forces to overcome the Czechs, though the mountainous belt around Czechoslovakia would have slowed them up considerably. But the Czech Army had only a handful of tank battalions, and these were committed to an infantry support role. Their standard tanks, however, were particularly fine. In fact, one was so good that the Germans adopted it as the *Pz 38* (t).

With the acquisition of Czechoslovakia and the occupation of its remnants in early 1939 the stage was set for the outbreak of World War II. And Germany's mobile forces were well-prepared for battle. By September of 1939 Germany had five armored divisions, four "light" divisions and four motorized infantry divisions, plus one cavalry division. In Poland, Germany's mobile troops would undergo their baptism of fire.

Poland 1939

The Polish Campaign of 1939 was the first operational combat employment of Germany's new mobile forces. It is quite likely that the Germans would have won even without the mobile troops, though at far greater cost in men, materiel, and time. But the new tactics and weapons proved highly effective and the campaign helped the Germans further refine their mobile warfare doctrine, which was to prove itself so devastatingly powerful in France and Russia in 1941 and 1942. In addition, the campaign provided the spur which furthered the development of mobile troops in other countries. And in 1943, 1944 and 1945 these newly formed armored forces would repay the German war machine with interest for its efficiency in 1939–1942.

Frederick the Great once said, "He who would defend everything ends up defending nothing." This is probably the most accurate assessment which can be made about the Polish Campaign. The Polish Army attempted to defend everything. The Polish-German frontier ran to over 800 miles, with numerous salients of Polish territory abutting German territory, particularly the area of the "Polish Corridor" and Poznan. The best strategy for the Polish Army would have been to pull back to a more easily defended line, conserving troops. This would undoubtedly have delayed the German advance, and it might even have delayed them long enough to inspire the British and French to do something creative on the Rhine. But the Poles chose to defend everywhere. The result was swift defeat.

The Polish Army deployed some 39 regular and reserve infantry divisions, eleven cavalry brigades, and two mechanized cavalry brigades. Much of their equipment was obsolete or in short supply. Total armored strength was some 200 tanks of various types along with some 470 machine gun-equipped tankettes and perhaps 100 armored cars. In contrast, the Germans deployed about 45 infantry divisions, five armored divisions, four "light" divisions, four mechanized infantry divisions, and even a horse cavalry brigade, plus an *ad hoc* armored formation. These totalled about 2,000 tanks, roughly 60% of Germany's inventory at the time. Although the Poles fought bravely, inflicting relatively heavy casualties on the Germans, they were totally outclassed. German equipment, German air power and, above all, German tactics, were just too much for them. Poland fell within a month, in the first true demonstration of "blitzkrieg."

The most spectacular German success came in the north, where Guderian commanded two armored and two motorized infantry divisions in the *XIX Corps*. Moving aggressively, Guderian's troops managed to pierce Polish defensive lines, sweep around them and help bottle up the five infantry divisions of the Pomorze Army within a few days. It was a remarkable demonstration of the basic concepts of blitzkrieg. The integrated German armored formations had moved swiftly to concentrate against a particular portion of the Polish lines, had broken through at that point, and had swept beyond to exploit the victory. The result was the bottling up of an entire army. It was, as Guderian expressed it, "kiel und kessel—wedge and pocket." But the success of the *XIX Corps* didn't stop there. No sooner was the Pomorze Army isolated than the *XIX Corps* undertook a fast motor march across East Prussia and into the eastern regions of Poland, where it succeeded in aiding in the destruction of yet another Polish army. By the end of the campaign the corps had covered about 400 miles in 28 days. Not a bad performance for a motorized outfit by 1939 standards—in fact, the longest motor march in wartime up to 1940. It was a remarkable feat, and the only true employment of armored forces in accordance with the basic concepts of Guderian's blitzkrieg theory. Other German armored forces, although enjoying considerable success, were handled far more cautiously.

The Germans learned a great deal from the Polish Campaign, though in general the basic concepts established by Guderian proved fairly sound. But the performance of the "light" divisions had proved a disappointment, though not an unexpected one. In addition, the lighter tanks, *Pz I* and *Pz 2,* had not proven particularly useful, while the heavier *Pz IV* had performed satisfactorily. Neither of these developments had been unanticipated. The effectiveness of *Stuka*- tank cooperation could have been better, as indeed could army-air force cooperation in general, but that was to be expected considering that Poland was the first true test of such cooperation.

The net result was that, after the Polish Campaign, no earth-shaking changes were made in the German armored forces, although considerable refinements occurred. The "light" divisions were converted into regular armored divisions by the simple expedient of adding two or three tank battalions to each. Since they already had one such battalion, and had already been trained in Guderian's theories of rapid concentration, swift attack, and speedy exploitation, the changes were accomplished with a minimum of disturbance. Meanwhile, tank production was such as to permit the retirement of many *Pz I* machines. In addition, with the annexation of Czechoslovakia, the Skoda tank works came under German control and by late 1939 were turning out large numbers of the fairly sound Czech *Pz 38,* which permitted the new armored divisions to be equipped with these vehicles, and thus further reduced the number of *Pz I* s. Finally, the cooperation of air and ground units was studied and refined. And as always, an endless series of training exercises continued. In final analysis, the German training was just as important as their equipment and doctrine in explaining their victory in Poland. Later, in France, much the same thing could be said.

Afterwards, 1939–1945

The campaign in Poland put the finishing touches on the German war machine. Guderian's innovative mobile tactics were totally vindicated. All resistance to them crumbled. In less than a year France lay prostrate. In a little more than another year the Panzers were knocking at the gates of Moscow. But victory is never so good a teacher as defeat. The Germans, everywhere triumphant in 1939 and 1940 and 1941, began to falter in 1942. The German triumphs gave the British and the Russians a hard tuition, but by 1943 they were more than able to hold their own. And, aided by the Americans, in 1944 and 1945 they rolled back the Germans in blitzkriegs of their own, having learned war in the toughest school of all, the battlefield. In the end, blitzkrieg, which made possible Germany's remarkable march of conquest, was also responsible for its disastrous defeat. For without blitzkrieg Hitler and his henchmen could never have turned Europe into a charnel house and rouse the wrath of nations.

Blitzkrieg: Principles and Practice

The basic principles of *blitzkrieg* —"lightning war"—had been familiar to the German Army since the Franco-Prussian War (1870–1871). In that conflict the Prussian Army, under the direction of Helmuth von Moltke, had actually attempted to avoid battle unless absolutely necessary. Its smashing victory was attained by rapid movement of entire armies through regions undefended by the French, with the object of bottling the enemy up at the first opportunity: encirclement. World War I had begun with just such a plan on the part of Germany. But the environment was unfavorable. The enormous size of the armies, the overwhelming power of the machine gun and quick firing artillery, the endless multiplication of wired-in trench lines, and the lunar landscape of "No Man's Land," made rapid movement impossible. Then came the tank, with its remarkable survivability in a hostile environment and its high mobility under virtually any conditions of ground. Suddenly, the cherished battles-of-encirclement were once again possible. The new weapon was grafted on the older strategic concept, suitably modified.

The most fundamental concept of blitzkrieg was *einheit*, or "unity." Tanks were to be used as part of a combined arms combat force to include infantry, artillery, engineers, aviation, and all the necessary services, all suitably motorized and with some elements mechanized (i.e. in armored half-tracks) as well. But *einheit* did not merely mean that the different arms would operate in a coordinated fashion. It meant that they would operate in an integated fashion down to the lowest level. So a tank battalion in an attack might supplement its own three or four companies by two or three more of infantry, one of engineer special assault troops, perhaps a battery of anti-aircraft artillery—very useful for killing hostile tanks—and a liberal seasoning of signalmen, while a battalion or more of field artillery would be on call and a flight or two of Stuka dive-bombers as well, all covered by friendly fighters. Tactically, the engineers would supplement the field and anti-aircraft fire with chemical smoke to further confuse the enemy, while the Stukas took out defensive positions and artillery installations in the rear. Right in with the attacking tanks, on a platoon-for-platoon basis, would be the infantry, supplemented by small teams of engineers with flamethrowers and other devices useful for winkling defenders out of fixed positions. As soon as the objective was secured, the second and third waves of the attack would go forward, with the intention of pressing on as rapidly as possible and securing yet more ground.

Now, such an attack was not a trade secret with the German Army. Everyone could do it if they wanted. Indeed, Allied success in World War I had been based on essentially these tactics, less the dive-bombers. What was different about the German use of tanks was the employment of armor on a strategic scale: not merely to gain local success, but to break and unhinge the entire enemy defense in order to attain a swift, decisive victory.

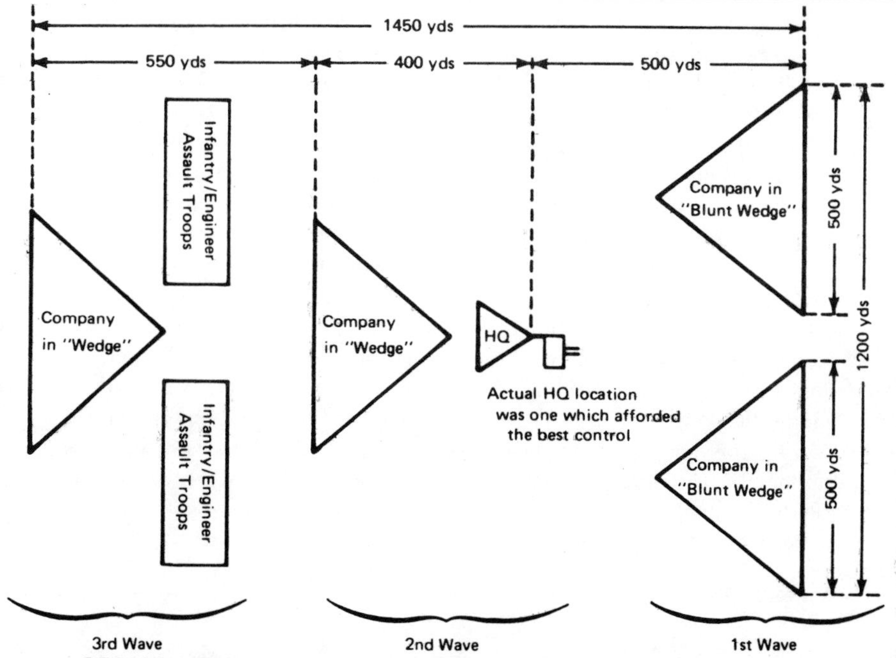

GERMAN TANK FORMATION, BATTALION IN "BLUNT WEDGE."

GERMAN TANK FORMATION, COMPANY IN "BLUNT WEDGE."

Alternatively, Company Troop Might Act as 3rd Wave.

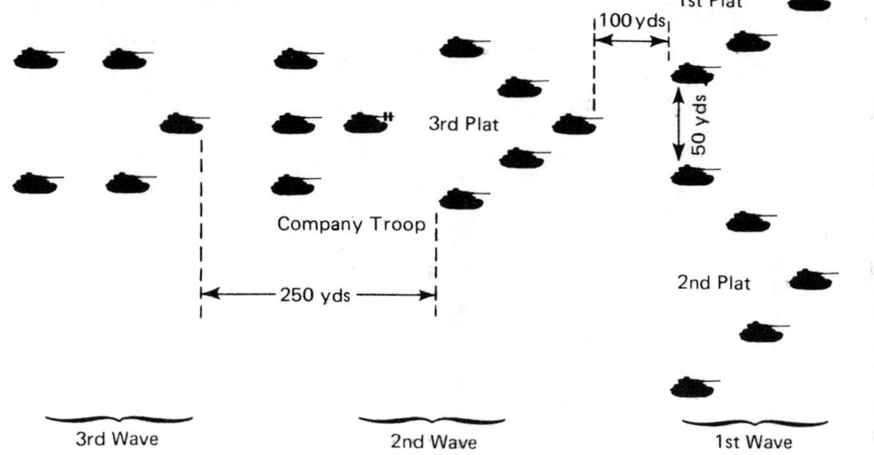

Strategically, a blitzkrieg operation had several fundamental principles. First was rapid concentration—*aufmarsch* —from a dispersed area to a narrow sector of the enemy front—*gefechtsstreifen.* This was the *Schwerpunkt,* or center of gravity, of the attack. The attack itself would be carried out with overwhelming force and decisive brutality for the purpose of achieving penetration—*einbruch* —of the enemy's line. As the initial assault forces drove into the enemy front, additional forces would pass through them in order to press on and gain ground for the achievement of breakthrough—*durchburch.* Once through enemy lines the important thing was to move and avoid his strength. It was the tactics of space and gap—*flächen und lückentaktik:* press on to gain control of the enemy's lines of communication. Meanwhile, additional forces would follow through the gap, motorized infantry to follow closely behind the spearheads, and other elements to undertake the rolling-up—*Aufrollen* —of the tattered ends of the enemy line and mop up isolated strongpoints and forces. Exploitation was now the mission of the spearheads. Pressing onwards with the object of encirclement. This was called *keil und kessel*— wedge and pocket. By moving rapidly on objectives far in the enemy rear, by avoiding his strength, vast envelopments could be achieved.

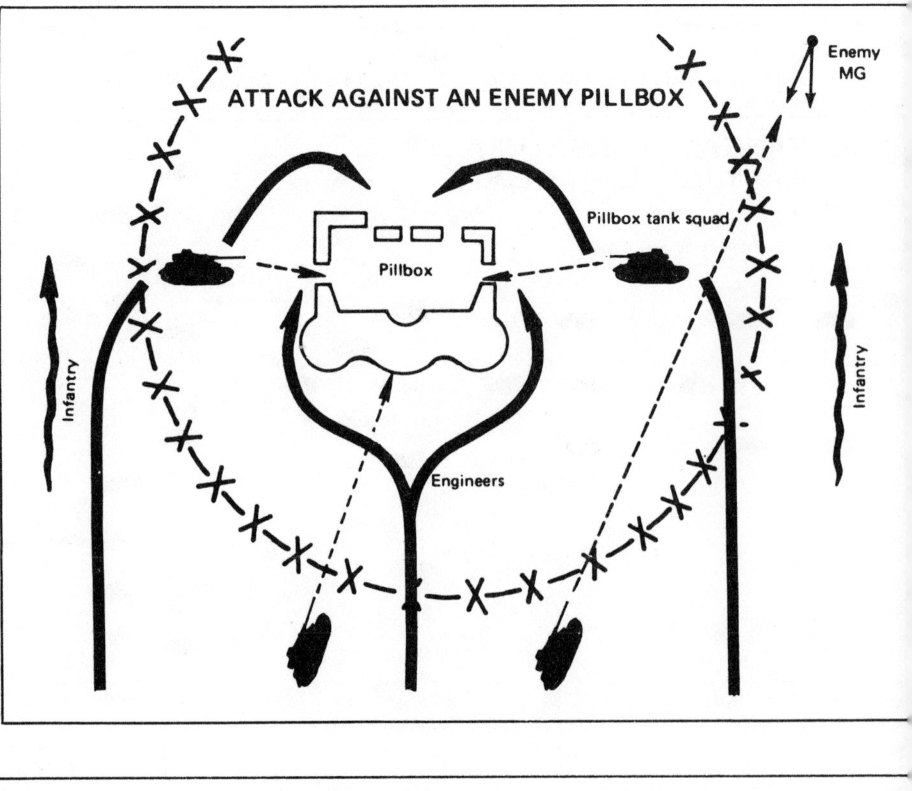

An attack such as described here might employ four or five armored divisions on a ten mile front, with each attacking on a 2000 meter front, with two reinforced battalions going in abreast and the rest of the division following behind. It required careful teamwork, excellent command control, and effective communications to execute such an offensive. And above all, it required careful timing and surprise. Only success was reinforced. Failures, dead ends, were abandoned.

But the success of blitzkrieg depended upon the enemy almost as much as upon the attacker. He had to allow himself to be surprised. He had to be unable to employ blitzkrieg-style counter-attacks. He had to be inferior in the air and in anti-tank equipment. And he had to quit when encircled. If any of these conditions were unfulfilled, the blitzkrieg attack might fail. Without surprise, the defender could make careful preparations; with strong mechanized reserves of his own he could drive into the flanks of the attacking columns as they began their exploitation, shattering them; with air superiority he could employ his aircraft as "tank busters"; with sufficient anti-tank equipment he could make the assault too costly at all points; and if he fought on when encircled he could gain time. In the end it was these very factors which defeated blitzkrieg. The Western Allies possessed overwhelming material superiority; the Soviets, endless manpower. First they employed these to halt blitzkrieg. Then, slowly and painfully, they began to learn. For blitzkrieg was a technique which could be learned. And once the Allies learned its secrets it was far less valuable as a tool of war.

Footnote: Panzers in Defense. German defensive tactics were very flexible, based generally on "defense in depth" tactics which they had developed during World War I. The most important part of defensive planning was to keep the armored forces, including motorized infantry, well in hand for use in counterattacks as needed. Normally a defensive front was thinly held in some depth. If there was sufficient time and resources, the position might be mined and wired. A liberal sprinkling of mutually supporting machine gun posts was established throughout the defensive zone. These were supplemented by light artillery, anti-tank guns, and anti-aircraft artillery—the latter were usually supplied with anti-tank and anti-personnel ammunition. Further back, heavier artillery was available on call, with pre-registration of targets, if possible to facilitate rapid, accurate delivery of fire when needed.

When the enemy attacked, he first had to cope with the thin "crust" defenses of the frontal zone. As he worked his way through this, the defenses tended to get thicker. If his attack succeeded in breaking through the defensive zone he could be taken in the flank by a mobile counterattack using standard blitzkrieg tactics or, in the absence of armor, more conventional infantry-artillery tactics. One or two sharp counterstrokes were likely to be sufficient to beat the attackers back provided numbers were not too disparate.

German Anti-Aircraft Artillery Stocks

Year End	Total	% in Ground Divisions			Mobile Share	
		All	Mobile	Other	% Divs	% Divl AA
1939	10.3	NA	NA	NA	14.0	NA
1940	11.3	37.2	7.2	30.0	13.8	19.4
1941	12.8	43.8	10.7	32.9	17.7	24.4
1942	15.5	33.2	9.0	24.2	20.9	27.1
1943	26.0	22.7	10.2	12.7	21.8	44.9
1944	29.9	25.8	14.1	11.7	24.1	54.7

The mobile divisions—panzers, panzergrenadiers, parachute, and similar motorized formations—consumed an inordinate proportion of Germany's available anti-aircraft artillery. There were two reasons for this. Anti-aircraft artillery was particularly useful in mobile combat, being fully motorized. Provided with anti-tank and high explosive as well as anti-aircraft shell, it was an important element in blitzkrieg. In addition, motorized formations were particularly vulnerable to air attack, due to the long "tails" they possessed: an army panzer division required 95 kilometers of road-space, the equivalent SS formation 124. This made for tempting targets. Note that the proportion of anti-aircraft artillery allocated to divisions generally fell, while that allocated to mobile divisions remained fairly constant. This was due largely to the stripping of non-mobile forces of their anti-aircraft protection as German cities became increasingly subject to aerial attack.

Key: *Total,* the number of anti-aircraft pieces on hand in thousands: these were mostly of calibers smaller than 75mm, but the proportion of larger pieces rose through the war—25.2% in 1939, 27.6% in 1940, 28.6% in 1941, 30.8% in 1942, 32.7% in 1943, and 35.8% in 1944, as the Allied air threat increased. *% in Ground Divisions* indicates that proportion of the anti-aircraft artillery pieces in the previous column found in field divisions, with figures then broken down for mobile divisions and other divisions. *Mobile Share* indicates the % of all divisions which were mobile *(% Divs)* and then the percentage of divisional anti-aircraft artillery assigned to these mobile divisions: Thus in 1940, the mobile divisions constituted only 14.0% of the army but held 19.4% of the anti-aircraft assigned to the ground divisions.

The Beginning: Armored Divisions, 1934–1940

Year		**1934**		**1935**	**1938**				**1939**		**1940**				
Power		Fr	Sov	Ger	Br	Fr	Ger	It	Br	Fr	Br	Fr	Ger	Sov	US
Type		DLM				DCR				DCR	B	DCR	Lt		
Tanks		240	463	561	600	250	266	330	321	158	342	158	200	341	345
Bns:	*Tank*	4	7	4	9	6	4	4	6	4	6	4	3	8	8
	Inf	3	4	3	2	5	4	3	1	2	3	1	5	2	2
	Art	3	1.3	4	2	3	4	2.6	1	3	3	3	4	4	2
	Recon	1	1	1	1		1	.3		1	1		1	1	1
	Engrs	1	.3	.3	.3		1	.3	1	1	1	.3	1	1	1
	Sigs	.6	1				1					.3	1		.3

The armored divisions organized during the 1930s were all essentially experimental. As this table indicates, the Germans were not the first to establish such a formation, both the French and the Soviets having done so a year before they did. French doctrine for the employment of their innovative *division legere mechanique* was poor, however, despite the urgings of their armor enthusiasts. The Soviets had ideas similar to those of the Germans—after all, the *Reichswehr* had been testing them in Russia for some years. But Soviet notions of how to wage mechanized war did not survive the Great Purges.

The most important organizational fact about armored divisions is not so much the number of tanks they contained—indeed too many tanks was found to be undesirable—but rather that there be a rough parity among the numbers of battalions of tanks, infantry, and artillery in the ratio 1:1:1. This greatly increases tactical flexibility and permits an armored formation to hold the ground it secures. Also important is the possession of an organic mechanized reconnaissance battalion, a formation sufficiently strong so as to be able to fight for information when needed. Ideally such a reconnaissance unit ought to be an armored division in miniature, with detachments of tanks, motorized infantry, artillery, and so forth. In a similar fashion armored divisions require considerable support from engineers and signalmen, the former to facilitate overcoming physical and tactical obstacles, and the latter to keep rapidly moving elements in very close contact.

Abbreviations: *DLM, division legere mechanique; DCR, division cuirassee de reserve* (i.e. armored reserve division); *B*, the second T/O&E adopted in 1940; *Lt*, light, a division converted from one of two motorized cavalry through the addition of some tank battalions. *Bns*, battalions: each digit indicates one battalion of the type shown, with .3 for a company.

General Summary of Divisions Available by Branch of Service, 1935–1945

	ARMY					WAFFEN-SS					LUFTWAFFE				TOTAL				
YEAR	*Add*	*ReD*	*Dis*	*Los*	*Tot*	*Add*	*ReD*	*Dis*	*Los*	*Tot*	*Add*	*Dis*	*Los*	*Tot*	*Add*	*ReD*	*Dis*	*Los*	*Tot*
1935	26	-	-	-	26	-	-	-	-	-	-	-	-	-	26	-	-	-	26
1936	14	-	-	-	40	-	-	-	-	-	-	-	-	-	14	-	-	-	40
1937	5	4	-	-	41	-	-	-	-	-	-	-	-	-	5	4	-	-	41
1938	10	-	-	-	51	-	-	-	-	-	-	-	-	-	10	-	-	-	51
1939	141	4	2	-	186	3	-	-	-	3	-	-	-	-	144	4	2	-	189
1940	102	25	33	-	230	1	-	-	-	4	1	-	-	1	104	25	33	-	235
1941	37	9	3	-	255	2	-	-	-	6	-	1	-	-	39	9	4	-	261
1942	47	2	5	-	296	4	-	-	-	10	22	-	-	22	73	2	5	-	327
1943	93	20	23	37	308	11	6	-	-	15	5	2	1	24	109	26	25	38	347
1944	154	31	88	68	275	16	-	1	-	30	5	12	3	14	175	31	101	71	319
1945	49	6	2	-	316	11	-	1	1	39	6*	-	-	20*	66	6	3	1	375
Total	**678**	**101**	**156**	**106**	**316**	**48**	**6**	**2**	**1**	**39**	**39***	**15**	**4**	**20***	**765**	**107**	**173**	**110**	**375**

The table gives a general overview of the divisions available to Germany at the end of each year, with 1 March being used for 1945. It excludes approximately 25 wartime training divisions and about 20 Landwehr divisions raised in 1939 and subsequently disbanded. Three naval divisions are included with the Luftwaffe figures for 1945 as indicated by an asterisk (*). *Add* is the total number of divisions raised in the course of the year; *ReD* indicates divisions redesignated, such as infantry divisions converting to panzergrenadier; *Dis* is the number of divisions formally disbanded during the indicated period, although from 1943 onwards these could readily be included with *Los*, divisions lost in combat; *Tot* is the total for each branch of the service. The *Total* columns to the right represent the general summary for each year.

This table should *not* be considered 100% accurate. There was enormous confusion in the German order of battle and it is unlikely that anyone ever knew the precise number of divisions officially in existence at any one time. In addition, many units were total losses in combat but were maintained in the order of battle and rebuilt, in one case as many as seven times. Similarly, certain units of elite status, such as SS-Panzer outfits or the Luftwaffe's *Herman Goring Panzer Parachute Division* were considerably over-strength. Nevertheless these have all been counted as single divisions. Great numbers of "divisions" were activated in the closing weeks of the Reich. Most of these were little more than brigades in actual strength. Some did not even reach that level. All of these have been excluded.

German Army Mobilization in World War II

In 1919, the Treaty of Versailles limited 100,000 long-service personnel in Germany to an army of ten divisions, seven of infantry and three of cavalry. Each infantry division supervised a military district, or *Wehrkreis,* and was responsible for recruiting, training, and record keeping within that district. The cavalry divisions were recruited at large. Over the divisions were two *Gruppenkommandos* to supervise their operations. Over it all was the *Truppenamt,* or Troop Office, which covertly carried out the functions of the outlawed Great General Staff.

With the rise of Hitler, the army, which had already secretly undertaken some expansion, began to increase rapidly and more openly. The first step in this process was the disbanding of the existing divisions. Thus, from 1934 through 1935, Germany actually had *no* army. In this period the existing divisions were overfilled, then subdivided into new units. The number of *Wehrkreise* were increased, and each became the recruiting ground for three divisions, the cadre being provided by the old *Reichswehr.* Thus, the old 2nd Regiment became the 21st Division. As Germany expanded peacefully in the mid-thirties, Austria was organized into new *Wehrkreise* and her army added to the existing cadre, and Czechoslovakia was divided up through the expansion of adjacent *Wehrkreise.*

Obviously, to command this horde officers were needed. The old army provided about 3,500 and the Austrians a further 1,000. Thousands of former officers were recalled and many NCO's promoted, so that about 100,000 were available at the start of the war.

The *Luftwaffe* was also created in secret and subsequently revealed once operational. The cadre was provided by some army officers, airline personnel, former Imperial Air Service men, and "private" flying club members. Similarly, the *Waffen-SS,* which began as Hitler's personal bodyguard, gradually expanded as well.

At the start of the Second World War, allocations of available manpower were fixed by Hitler so that out of each annual contingent the army received 66%, the Luftwaffe 25%, and the navy 9%, with the Waffen-SS getting a piece of the army's share, usually set at 6,000 men. To maintain a steady flow of manpower, the army proceeded to organize units in "waves," each to consist of a varying number of new or reorganized units having the same table of organization and equipment. In theory, the lower a division's "wave" number, the better trained it was. Eventually, 35 waves were created (the first 32 had numbers, the later ones names). This system was certainly orderly and rational. However, once the war really got started (i.e., 22 June 1941—Russia), it began to fall apart as a result of in-fighting among the services.

The Waffen-SS ran into manpower problems quite early. Himmler's desire to expand his private army, plus the very high casualty rates incurred by units under inexperienced officers, created problems. Restricted in his access to German manpower, Himmler turned to the *Volksdeutsch,* or overseas Germans, many of whom had lived in various parts of Eastern Europe for generations. He also began to recruit "Germanic" non-Germans, such as Swedes and Danes. Later he dipped into "non-Germanic Aryans," like Frenchmen and Italians. The pressure became so great that even *"untermenschen,"* like Slavs, black Africans, and Bosniak Muslims, soon found themselves in SS uniforms.

Most of the foreign "volunteer" units were not overly valuable, though acceptable for occupation duty and massacres. However, the true strength of the Waffen-SS lay in the fact that, although it never constituted more than 10% of Germany's total ground force manpower, it had 25% of the panzer and motorized formations in the Wehrmacht. Even some of the foreign formations were better equipped and motorized than most regular army outfits. This did not create good feelings on the part of the army. The situation was further embittered by the fact that, although SS recruiting in Germany was restricted, they got the pick of the available manpower.

The Luftwaffe also demanded the best manpower—this was true in the Allied nations as well—even for tasks not requiring physical and mental perfection. Germany's inability to maintain the air force's inventory of aircraft, however, soon led to the development of an enormous surplus of manpower in the Luftwaffe. By the fall of 1942, the army was eyeing this considerable pool for use as replacements.

Goring objected, not wishing to expose his good National Socialist personnel to the decadent army. The corpulent *Reichsmarschall* prevailed upon Hitler to permit him to organize his own ground forces—which he had been doing anyway in the form of anti-aircraft and parachute troops. Thus were formed 22 *Luftwaffe Felddivisionen,* completely under Luftwaffe control. When sent into action these outfits promptly disintegrated, having no operational cadre. Rather than disband them, Hitler maintained them and forced the army to provide officers and enlisted personnel.

The manpower problem was complex. At the very start of the war, Germany had overmobilized! Great numbers of men vital to industry had been taken. In the summer of 1940, nearly three dozen divisions had to be demobilized. Later, most of the men involved were called up again. To facilitate organization and training, the army was divided into two parts: The Army, or *Feldheer,* to conduct operations, and the Replacement Army, or *Ersatzheer,* to raise troops. However, the Replacement Army never had enough men in the pipeline to keep the Field Army at strength.

As a further complication, Hitler thought in shallow terms: to him a division was a division, which ignored the fact that it could be reduced to 20% of official strength. Thus, he favored the raising of new divisions over the reinforcement of old ones. This increased the number of divisions, but reduced the overall strength of each. Moreover, the increased number of cadres further drained useful manpower. *Richard L. DiNardo*

The Less Glamorous Aspects of Blitzkrieg

The tank, making spectacular advances with its unique ability to move and fight in circumstances and environments wholly unsuitable for unprotected men and machines, is the most obvious and impressive symbol of blitzkrieg. But tanks cannot do it alone, not even when supported by adequate numbers of infantry and amounts of artillery. For as warfare has become more sophisticated, the importance of non-combatant personnel and equipment has increased markedly. If necessary, blitzkrieg can be waged without tanks. But it cannot be conducted without motor transport, for blitzkrieg is a gluttonous consumer of munitions and fuel.

A single tank may be composed of as many as 30,000 separate parts. Maintenance is a perpetual task. Average vehicle endurance in the Second World War was no more than 500 miles between overhauls. Exceeding that limit would result in excessive breakdowns. Germany's most spectacular panzer victories all occurred at less than 500 miles from the start lines. When efforts were made to press beyond that limit without a pause for refitting, disaster resulted, as before Moscow in late 1941. So an armored unit must have extensive workshop facilities and spare-part inventories. All of this requires transportation.

Fuel is another drain on transport. The movement of 100 tanks of average available types 100 miles in 1941 required 13.8 tons of fuel; in 1942, 14.8 tons; in 1943, 19.8; and in 1944, 22.4. Roughly speaking, about 5% more than this would have to be supplied to the units to accommodate wastage during refueling. So the figures now read 14.5 tons, 15.5 tons, 20.8 tons, and 23.5 tons. This does not even account for fuel consumed in transporting this fuel. An armored division ran about 160 tanks in 1941, plus some 2600 other motor vehicles. Even if such an outfit were totally inactive its daily fuel requirements would run about six tons. Fuel supply as a problem had two sides. The more obvious was getting the fuel to the using units when needed and in the quantities needed. This the Germans were not always able to do.

As with fuel, so too with ammunition. Consider the accompanying table, which treats with artillery expenditure during the war:

Division Artillery Fire Power, 1939–1945
Deliverable Ordnance Tonnage Per 1000 Men Per Hour

Army	*1939*	*1945*	*%Change*
Br	14.7	11.9	–23.5
Fr	15.3	18.9	+19.0
Ger	15.1	22.6	+33.2
Sov	13.7	21.0	+38.1
US	9.9	18.9	+47.6

The model used in this table is the standard infantry division. Note that in all cases except the British—who reduced artillery but raised anti-tank 905%—the firepower increased. If non-divisional artillery is included the increases for everyone, including the British, would be even more marked.

Now, a division's artillery can fire off upwards of 300 tons of ammunition in an hour. This amounts to a requirement for 345 tons of "lift" if such a rate is to be sustained. Normally, of course, such a barrage would be rare. But in some blitz operations, notably on the Eastern Front, it was common for a division to fire off literally every round and then do without for days afterwards. Note, moreover, that this table represents only artillery ammunition, mortars, guns, howitzers, and the like. It omits small arms and anti-tank and anti-air ammunition, which can also be fired off in tremendous amounts. All of this also had to be moved. In an infantry division horses and mules could be used for some transport duties, despite the high inefficiency of such beasts: on a horsepower-per-pound-of-fuel basis, gasoline is considerably easier to store and transport than fodder.

Obviously horses and mules could not be used for all transport requirements. Highly inefficient above 50 miles from a supply point, animal transport is also quite slow and manpower intensive. Nevertheless, it was what most of the German Army moved by during the war. Ultimately, Germany just did not have enough motor transport. Certainly never enough to motorize more than a fraction of the armed forces, something which the Anglo-Saxon powers were able to accomplish fully given their remarkable economic base. Most of the time Germany endured a shortage of motor vehicles. Consider the accompanying table on "tons of lift" availability:

German Motor Transport Capacity
Thousands of Tons of Lift

Year	*On Hand*	*Prod*	*Conf*	*Lost*
1940	221	134	160	5
1941	510	134	75	30
1942	710	192	585	70
1943	1360	290	8	260
1944	1350	260	20	780
1945	850	?	?	?

This table gives some idea of the availability of lift—measures in tonnage capacity of motor vehicles—during the war. Increases were the result of Production and Confiscation, decreases were due to combat losses. Had the Germans not confiscated a significant proportion of all motor vehicles in Europe in 1940 they would have been virtually immobile for the Russian campaign in the following year. The enormous losses in 1944 could only be made up by taking practically every available motor vehicle in Europe, sending much of the continent back to animal traction.

Germany required roughly 750,000 tons of lift at any given moment for military purposes: about a third for infantry divisions, another third for non-divisional combat and administrative units, and the balance for the mobile divisions. Some 50,000 tons were required for the operations of the Replacement Army, which was responsible for training personnel. For most of the war Germany experienced a shortage of motor transport, averaging about 9% of requirements, roughly 70,000 tons of lifts, although there were times when the shortage ran as great as 56.6% (300,000 tons), before the great confiscation of motor vehicles in the Spring of 1942, and there was an occasional surplus, as 9.73% (110,000) after the confiscations of 1942.

The greatest obstacle to improving the motor transport situation was a lack of production facilities. Even before the war, Germany's motor vehicle production capacity was low. Only Italy, Japan, and the Soviet Union produced fewer motor vehicles per capita among the Great Powers. The degree of "motorization" in society was lower than in France, which had 23 citizens per motor vehicle compared with Germany's 37, Britain's 32, and America's remarkable 4.4. Not until 1942 were serious efforts made to rationalize German war production. Luxury goods continued in production, single shifts were still common, and women were not yet mobilized as industrial workers. When Albert Speer took over the armaments ministry he began to make great strides in improving production, despite serious economic and political obstacles. In the face of increasing Allied aerial attacks motor vehicle production rose by over 50% in tons of lift during 1943. Tank production went up a remarkable 206%. But it was not enough. Indeed, as bad as the shortage of motor transport was, the shortage of tanks was worse, and grew worse as time went on.

Ultimately, the Second World War was a war of attrition. The blitzkrieg was insufficient to bring victory by itself. A negotiated peace was out of the question given the nature of the regime which Hitler imposed on Europe. So the war had to go on. The Allies, fighting an unusually skillful and wily foe, expended men and materiel in greater amounts than the Germans were capable of expending them. Nowhere is this more readily evident than in tank production. During the war Germany produced approximately 52,000 tanks and other weapons on tank chassis. In 1943 alone the United States produced some 29,500 medium tanks, the Soviets over 23,000 tanks and assault guns. Once the Allies began to catch on to the ways in which to defeat blitzkrieg, they could out-produce Germany to insure final victory.

If Hitler waged "*blitzkrieg* —lightning war" against Poland, the Allies waged "*Sitzkrieg* —sitting war" against him. Despite thin German defenses in the West, the rapidly-mobilizing French and British failed to act while Hitler concentrated the bulk of his forces against hapless Poland. And so it remained through the Autumn and Winter and into the following Spring. But if the Allies wished to remain inactive, or contemplated intervention in the Russo-Finnish War which soon broke out, Hitler had other ideas. Even as his generals supervised the transfer of their forces from devastated Poland to the Rhine, he began to contemplate offensive action in the West. Planning and preparations proceeded through the winter, the operation actually being ordered but then postponed several times. Meanwhile, impressed by alleged British violations of Norwegian neutrality and irresponsible speculations in the Allied press, Hitler became convinced that the Allies intended to occupy Norway. Because such a move would make it more difficult for German submarines to sortie into the Atlantic and would also sever the vital iron ore supply lines to Northern Sweden, Hitler decided to move first. On 9 April German air, naval, and ground forces struck at Denmark and Norway. Tiny Denmark fell within hours to the rapid German advance. Norway proved a tougher opponent, though resistance was never properly organized. Preceded by the first combat use of parachute troops, German convoys sailed into vital ports all up the Norwegian coast. As the partially mobilized and ill-equipped defenders fell back, Britain and France scraped together miscellaneous forces and threw them into the struggle. By 1 May the Germans were in full control of the southern part of the country and were rapidly advancing to the relief of a beleaguered and isolated column at Narvik in the far north. The Allies might have been able to cling indefinitely to this precious bit of Norway but events elsewhere rapidly overshadowed operations in Norway and their troops were soon evaculated. For Hitler had finally struck in France.

The Fall of France, 1940

by Albert A. Nofi

It was the most stunning victory of the war. In a lightening swift campaign of not sixty days, France, one of the Great Powers since the Middle Ages, and the intellectual, cultural, and emotional heartland of the West, lay prostrate beneath the feet of her ancient foe from across the Rhine, a bare twenty years after her triumphant victory in World War I. As German soldiers marched under the *Arc de Triomphe* a stunned world wondered.

Between the Wars

France's triumph in 1918 was deceptive, to say the least. Vast armies of Britons and Russians and Italians had helped shoulder the burden of the long years of fighting, and, in the proverbial nick of time, the United States had thrown young, energetic armies of her own into the balance in 1917-1918. Though France always maintained the largest armies on the Allied side she would never have been able to survive and win without Allied help, and may well have lost even with that help had not the Americans arrived.

The victory had been a costly one. Roughly one out of four military age Frenchmen had fallen during it, or one in twenty-eight of the population, a higher loss ratio than any other state except Serbia. This loss, chiefly in young, vigorous males, had a serious effect on the birth rate, which never had been particularly high. During the war, with so many young men off at the Front, the birth rate fell off appallingly—indeed it fell off so seriously that the birth years 1915-1919, when called to the colors in 1935-1938, were termed "the empty years," and barely 65-70 divisions could be mobilized. After the war there was a brief "baby boom" but the basic trend remained unaltered and by the mid-1920's France's birth rate was the lowest in Europe.

Another great casualty of the war was France's morale. The finest manpower, the choicest lands, the greatest factories, the most historic shrines had all been destroyed in the long, bloody conflict. By a great effort of will France had set aside her partisanships, had met the enemy and repelled him, and had rebuilt her shattered industry, farmlands, and treasures. But the appalling memory still lingered, and Verdun, site of the greatest battle of the war, became the symbol of a weakening will to fight.

All of these factors had the net effect of demonstrating to the most far sighted statesmen that France was not, indeed, a major power any longer. As early as 1919 an American-British-French alliance for defense had been proposed by Frenchmen only to be rejected by isolationist minded Anglo-Saxons on both sides of the Atlantic. To compensate for the loss of major allies, France cast about for minor powers to join her. Thus Poland, a "natural" enemy of Germany, joined in alliance with France, as did Roumania, Czechoslovakia, and Yugoslavia in the Balkans and Belgium in the West. This coalition, it was felt, would be so greatly superior to Germany that Germany would never dare to raise the spectre of war again. Yet no real effort was made to maintain the alliances. In 1936 King Leopold of Belgium took his nation out of the alliance and "neutralized" it, failing to learn very much from his father's experience with the problems of neutrality in a great-power dominated world. France made but feeble efforts to convince him otherwise.

Likewise, France's political and military leaders frittered away chances to strike out at Germany's rising power by permitting Hitler to acquire the Rhineland, then a real army, then Austria, and finally Czechoslovakia. Meanwhile, France's other allies, Yugoslavia and Roumania, had more or less gone Fascist themselves. A feeble attempt to place Mussolini's Italy in the anti-German camp ended with the Ethiopian War (1934-1935), in spite of Pierre Laval's efforts to get France and Britain to ignore the minor tyranny to concentrate on the major. The fear of war, the revulsion against it, was just too great to overcome. It would even influence those who one would have expected would welcome the change for another go at Germany, the Army.

The French Army, 1918-1939

During World War I, France had evolved a very effective retirement and replacement system for her generals. An enormous number of inefficient people were sacked, and younger, more vigorous men commanded France's armies by 1918.

At the war's end, however, the effective and forward looking regulations for the retirement of officers were modified into virtual ineffectiveness. The age for retirement was raised until it became almost nonexistent. Thus, when Marshal Henri Pétain retired as head of the Armed Forces in the mid-1930s he was nearly eighty years of age. The younger, more vigorous men with forward looking ideas found it difficult to move upwards in such an army, while the old crocks at the top saw to it that little change was wrought in "their" glorious army of 1918.

The Theory of the "Continuous Front"

In 1914 the French Army had but one theory of war: attack. The troops went forward in droves, and were slaughtered in droves. This continued until 1917 when the more cautious influence of Pétain brought a halt to the senseless slaughter. By that time the French had a few new misconceptions. The chief of these was that a well organized defense line could not be broken, and that, in order to win a war, all one had to do was to sit tight behind the trenches and wait for the enemy to exhaust himself trying to break through. Once this point had been reached you could then go over to the offensive yourself and mop up the remains in a short time, with a minimum of effort and loss. This theory had the added advantage of meaning that no French general could ever again be sacked for ordering men to their deaths.

Actually, even by 1918 standards, the "continuous front" theory was out of date. Perhaps in 1915 or 1916 it had some validity, but by 1918 two techniques had been evolved which had both demonstrated their ability to break the deadlock of the trenches: tanks and infiltration tactics.

Tanks, a mechanical solution to a mechanically viewed problem, were essentially armored, mobile gun platforms. They could resist the fire of machine guns, the infantry killer *par excellance,* and carry their own machine guns forward to the point where they could reach the enemy's infantry. The French quickly adopted the idea of the tank from the British and used swarms of them in their 1918 drives against an already beaten enemy. The technique seemed an abberation, however, since even in 1918 German anti-tank arms had been able to knock out tanks.

Infiltration tactics, a philosophical solution to a philosophically viewed problem, were a German invention. Essentially they entailed short, furious bombardments followed by rapid infantry attacks which attempted to avoid any strongpoints. The troops would move forward as best they could and leave the strong points to be mopped up by troops in the rear. The Germans used these with great success during the early part of 1918, nearly winning the war in the process. Nearly is, of course, the key to all this. They had failed to break the front, ergo the front was unbreakable. The logic was impeccable and the French generals ate it up. Neither tanks nor infiltration tactics could break the continuous front.

Having decided that the continuous front was the way to do it, the French inevitably moved one step further: if earthworks and barbed wire were virtually impregnable, then how much more so would a reinforced concrete and steel fortified zone be?

The seeds of the Maginot Line had been sown.

The Maginot Line

The French have always been among the most accomplished fortification experts in the West. From Vauban in the Seventeenth Century onwards, their fortifications engineers were among the most talented in Europe. As the concept of the "continuous front" took hold of the imaginations of the French High Command and people, inevitably the possibilities inherent in an extensive, deep, heavily fortified defensive zone lying across Germany's main invasion route into France became more attractive. This would be "continuous front" on a grand scale and with a vengeance. No German Army could possibly break through with sufficient force as to resist well delivered, swift counter attacks from mobile reserve forces.

Thus it was that in the late 1920s and early 1930s the Maginot Line—named after a minister of war who lost an arm at Verdun in 1916—captured the imagination and pocketbook of the French nation.

The basic concept was not as regressive as it at first seems. The fortified zone was not considered impregnable, merely difficult to penetrate. Mobile forces held behind the line—in fact it was a fortified "zone" and not a line—would be able to contain any German breakthrough which might occur, though such were considered to be unlikely, and would form the basis for an eventual advance into Germany, after the Germans had exhausted themselves.

Ideally a defensive zone extending from Switzerland right across Europe to the sea would have perfectly sealed the country—insofar as the "continuous front" theorists were concerned—but France could not afford the price in either money or manpower. As a result the main defensive sectors were along the Lorraine frontier with Germany, roughly from Strasbourg to Montemedy in the Ardennes. The Rhine frontier was held by reconstructed German forts of pre-1914 vintage reinforced with some new positions, the river being considered a sufficient obstacle to any serious German advance. From the Ardennes to the sea there were the older fortified cities of Lille and Maubuege, though these positions were not reconstructed. Otherwise there was little in the way.

The line as built cost some seven billion francs, a portion of that being due to the rampant inflation plaguing France—and the world—at the time. To cover the additional 240 miles of frontier from Montmedy to the North Sea near Dunkirk would probably have more or less doubled the cost, even considering the considerably easier terrain the work would be done in. Roughly, the 87 miles actually built cost 80.5 million francs per mile. The actual investment of fortifications for the other, longer portion of the frontier was but 292 million francs—the cost of 3.6 miles of Maginot position.

Quite aside from the financial considerations there were questions of manpower which militated against any extension of the line to the sea. France was already short of manpower and any scheme of fortification on such a grand scale would have depleted her manpower reserves significantly. It must be borne in mind that in addition to manning the positions in the fortified zones, France had also to establish reserve mobile striking forces—just in case. Hence, unlike the wall of China, the wall of France could not completely cover the threatened sectors.

As built, the Maginot Line was a wonder to behold. Every position was carefully prepared after consideration of natural cover, suitability of observation, maximum arc of useful fire with minimal obstacles and dead ground, general suitability of the terrain for the construction of field fortifications and anti-tank obstacles, suitability of the terrain for the construction of hard surfaced roads for the rapid—and secret—transfer of reserves, and general all-round usefulness. Virtually everything was concealed below ground, and all fortresses were gas tight—just in case. Positions were mutually supporting yet capable of independent operation for an extended period. The entire system was linked together by an extensive series of subways and underground communications tunnels. Finally, the fortified zone was from five to ten miles deep, depending upon the sector, though the main line of defense only began between four and six miles from the frontier.

Due to the overwhelming expense, not all positions were ready in 1940. One area of the Lorraine frontier was but lightly fortified. Between Saaeguimines and Bouzonville was the Sarre Gap, some 30–35 miles of virtually unfortified positions, though plans did exist to flood several areas utilizing the Saare River and France's extensive canal system.

There seems but little question that, considering what the French expected, the Maginot Line would have been virtually impregnable. The heavily fortified zone would have made it virtually impossible for the Germans to penetrate it to any significant extent before the mobile reserve forces behind it would have been able to move up and deliver a telling and deadly blow. Unfortunately, what the French expected and what the Germans intended were not precisely the same.

The French Theory of Mobile Warfare

France had accepted the tank as a weapon since late in World War I, when it had proven useful in helping the infantry break the stranglehold of the trenches and restore a measure of movement to the war. In 1940 France actually had slightly more tanks than did Germany, albeit many of these were obsolete. And the French did believe in "mobile" warfare: they, of all people, did not desire a repetition of the 1914–1918 stalemate. As early as 1927, when asked what the French Army should do if the Germans attacked through Belgium rather than against the Maginot Line, Petain had replied, "We must go into Belgium."

The French Army thought of "mobile warfare" in terms of 1918, or even 1914; relatively rapid advances by primarily infantry forces supplemented by tanks in order to assist the troops in breaking particularly difficult resistance. In Germany by the mid-1930s a different idea was being developed. Men like Heinz Guderian had gained the support of Adolph Hitler in fostering an entirely new concept of warfare. The tank—whose main asset was great mobility and relatively high firepower—would be used in infiltration attacks on a vast scale, slipping through the enemy lines and running far ahead of the plodding infantry to disrupt enemy communications, supply lines, and retreat. This idea was not unknown to the French. Charles DeGaulle, a protege of Petain's, had developed some aspects of his own thought from DeGaulle. Both men were colonels in the early 1930s. But where Guderian had Hitler, the best DeGaulle could do was Gen Maxime Weygand.

Weygand was an old timer by the mid-1930s, not unlike much of the French High Command, but he was able to see possibilities in the somewhat radical ideas expressed by the armor enthusiasts. As head of the French Army in the mid-1930s he made a number of significant, but insufficient changes. For one thing, a number of the Army's infantry divisions were fully motorized. For another, he authorized the establishment of two "Light Mechanized Divisions," which were in reality rather well conceived armored task forces. But that was all. The primary purpose of these formations was not to wage truly mobile, "mobile" warfare, but rather to enable the reserves—as these troops were to primarily comprise—to move into battle more rapidly. No thought of infiltration or penetrating exploitation drives.

When the war broke out in 1939 the successes of the German panzer divisions and motorized infantry in Poland were received with considerable shock. The implications of the Polish debacle did not fully dawn upon the French, though they realized that apparently there was some merit to the rather radical ideas of DeGaulle and his ilk. As a result, in late 1939 another light mechanized division was formed and three horse cavalry divisions were dissolved, combined with odd lots of armored units and reformed as five new "Cavalry" Divisions. In early 1940 the organization of proper Armored divisions was undertaken as well. By then it was too late. Unquestionably, the French could have fielded an effective mobile force in 1940 only if they had begun to develop one in the mid-1930s—about the time the Germans did.

Organization, Training, and Equipment. The bulk of the French Army in 1939–40 was composed of unmotorized infantry divisions. These units were little changed either in organization, training, or equipment from those which went "over the top" in the closing days of World War I. To be sure, there had been some minor organizational adjustments to reflect the need for greater anti-aircraft and anti-tank protection, the rapid improvements in communications equipment between the wars, and the introduction of motorized transport of artillery and supplies. Likewise some adjustments had been made in equipment, with additional anti-aircraft guns being assigned, anti-tank guns making their appearance, and odds and ends like a new model of the Lebel rifle. Training had also not moved ahead particularly, although the problems of "tank busting" had been taken into consideration. Of course, these changes had not always been for the best and, in the areas of equipment, there were frequently shortages so that some divisions did not have any anti-tank guns when the war broke out. All in all, the French infantry in 1940 was pretty well prepared—for 1918. Unfortunately, circumstances had changed and a 1918 army was no longer what was needed.

On the other hand, the German infantry was not particularly different from that of 1918 either. Though some improvements had been made in weaponry, and although training had gone completely over to the infiltration technique for the offensive, there was but little that was different from 1918 and the *stosstruppen.*

Nevertheless, the Germans did have something unique in the world at the time, an effective mobile force. While this was by no means a perfect weapon system—indeed its significant flaws would only emerge as the Allies became more proficient—it was considerably superior to anything anyone else had. So superior, in fact, that the Germans would probably have won the Campaign of 1940 no matter what plan they followed or what the French did.

The French Air Force

Until 1933 the French Air Force had been a part of the Army. In that year it was made an independent and coequal arm of defense. As in all air forces, there existed a serious split between the Douhet—"air power will render all other arms useless"—theory and those who believed that the Air Force should remain as an adjunct to the ground forces. As usual, the voices of compromise went unheeded. Actually, this quarrel—which went far towards creating effective air forces in nations such as Britain and the United States—neglected one of the most important aspects of the entire problem. In order to be effective, whether as a strategic striking force or army cooperation force, an air force needs aircraft. And to build aircraft an aviation industry is needed.

The Aviation Industry

Between 1934 and 1938 France spent roughly 22.8 percent of her defense budget—exclusive of the Maginot Line expenses—on her Air Force. For this enormous investment she received relatively little.

In France, aircraft production was still not on an assembly line basis, as it was in most other countries. Aircraft can be mass produced like automobiles: they do not have to be handcrafted with the same kind of tender loving care that goes into ship or locomotive construction. Unfortunately, this hand-crafting was more or less what was going on in France during the 1930s.

In addition, relatively little capital investment—tools, dies, plants, and so forth—had been made in the French aviation industry after World War I. Thus the rather ludicrous spectacle of France, one of the major economic powers of the world, producing but 35 aircraft a month at a time when Italy, far and away a poorer country with a very weak industrial base, was turning out 200. In the mid-1930s, when the French began to get their heads together and look over their defense industries, aircraft production actually dropped for a time, due partially to the inevitable loss in production resulting from tooling up, and partially to the considerable confusion which resulted from the nationalization of the aircraft industry.

Thus, on the eve of the war in 1937 France produced only some 600 aircraft though in theory she could have produced 1,000. In the same year the Italians produced about 1,200 and the Germans something like 4,000! Nor was this all.

Because of the rampant confusion in the French aviation industry the unit cost for aircraft in France—aircraft in no way comparable to their foreign counterparts—was considerably higher. Thus, one of France's best fighters, the Morane MS.406, cost some 969,000 francs as against the much more efficient Hurricane's 1,247,000 francs. In addition, the Hurricane was in service nearly two years earlier than the MS.406.

Curiously, if the French had moved to improve their industry just a short time before they actually did, their Air Force would have been considerably more powerful than it was in reality. During the entire Campaign of 1940 the French Air Force actually increased in size as new lots of, for example, the D520 fighter were delivered. There were more of these modern aircraft in service at the end of the campaign than at the beginning. There was, in fact, nothing wrong with France's aviation industry that a good dose of Government scrutiny could not have cured. That that scrutiny was late in coming sealed the fate of the French Air Force.

Organization, Training, and Equipment

There is actually not much that can be said about the organization, training, and equipment of the French Air Force. Air Forces have displayed a marked tendency to copy from each other and the French Air Force was not very different in organization or training than most other air forces, with the notable exception of the Luftwaffe. The big hole in training and organization was in army cooperation.

Though the French Air Force had originated and existed for twenty years or so, as part of the French Army it had not developed any effective liaison with that army. Thus, corps and armored divisions were supposed to be assigned Air Force reconnaissance aircraft yet most such units lacked such support, and dive bombing was an unheard of technique, at least in the Air Force, as the Navy did have some dive bombers.

Of course, there were serious problems of status and morale between the two services. The French Army did not think of the Air Force as a decisive arm. On a number of occasions during the 1940 campaign Air Force commanders would place their aircraft at the disposal of the Army, only to find themselves sitting around waiting for orders which never came. The Air Force was extremely status conscious, being the junior service, and suffering from something of an inferiority complex in dealing with the older services. This does not seem to have adversely influenced the 1940 campaign but represents an interesting historigraphical problem: would Army-Air Force cooperation have been better if the Air Force had not been separated from the Army in 1933?

In terms of equipment the French Air Force was behind all the other major powers. Only by retaining considerable numbers of obsolete aircraft on the active list was France able to muster 1,350 aircraft in 1938. Of these only some 500–600 were what might be termed "first line." The rest were outdated, to say the least. The best bombers the French had were American, as was one of their better fighters. None of these was more than fair-to-middling when compared with Luftwaffe, or even RAF aircraft, and the bulk of French equipment was often of a still lower standard than that.

The curious thing about all of this is, however, that the French Air Force, for all its faults, put up a pretty good fight. It is difficult to say what motivates men to fight well under adverse circumstances, yet the case of the French Air Force during the 1940 campaign is an excellent example of precisely this. Though outnumbered and outclassed, the French Air Force did a credible job.

The Allies

Of the approximately 140 divisions confronting the Germans in the West in the Spring of 1940, about ten were Dutch, twenty-two Belgian, and ten British. Of these forces the most formidable were, of course, the British, but the others were forces to be reckoned with even if they did not reach the scale of importance of the French, or even the British.

The Dutch

The Dutch Army was not particularly powerful, nor well trained, nor well equipped. Holland had not fought a real war in nearly 150 years, the only things occurring during that period being in the nature of colonial ventures or serious civil disorders. Not surprisingly the Dutch treated their Armed Forces to a considerable amount of benign neglect. On the whole the Dutch seriously believed that they would be left alone in the event of another war and were quite ill-prepared. Holland's ten divisions were considered an inconvenience by the Germans, not a threat; her fortifications a hindrance, not an obstacle.

The Belgians

If the Dutch were not considered a serious problem by the Germans, the Belgians were another story. They had 20 infantry and two cavalry divisions, and were at least as well prepared for war—albeit 1918 style—as the French. Experience in World War I had shown the Belgians to be a tenacious foe.

The Belgians had been allied with France until 1936, when the new king, Leopold, had ended the alliance to trust in "neutrality." Still, the long influence of the French told and the Belgian Army held to the "continuous front" theory as faithfully as did the French. The Belgians even had their own fortifications in imitation of the Maginot line.

The area between the "impassable" Ardennes and the Dutch frontier was heavily fortified, using a combination of newly constructed position plus the remnants of the defenses of 1914, particularly in the vicinity of Liege. One of the more vital links in this position was the fort of Eban Emael which protected the northwestern approaches to Liege, through Holland. It was, in fact, "impregnable" to infantry attack. Unfortunately, the Germans did not attack it in the traditional way. Hitler, in addition to showing an interest in mobile warfare, had been also interested in the possibilities inherent in the use of airborne troops. Both the Dutch and the Belgians would be surprised by this "secret weapon."

In general, Belgian organization, training, and equipment was not unlike that of France, and it would seem that the Belgians were no less efficient than their friends. What the Belgians lacked—as did the French—was resolute, firm leadership.

The British

Man for man, or perhaps division for division, the BEF was probably the most formidable of all the forces in the 1940 campaign. Unlike the German or French armies, the enitre British Army was fully motorized and actually had higher scales of equipment than either of these forces. Thus, while only about 10 percent the size of the French Army, the British Army had the same number of mortars, 20 percent of the AFV's, and slightly more than 10 percent of the field artillery. In general, however, the British were no better prepared by their training or organization than were the French: basically, they were ready to fight 1918 all over again. To be sure, the total motorization of the force was a significant progressive step but it had not come accompanied by the mobile tactics so long advocated in Britain by men like Liddel Hart. However, and an important "however," within the British Army, particularly in the tank forces, were a number of officers who had a considerably fuller understanding of the possibilities of armored warfare than anyone else on the Allied side. These would prove a boon when things tended to get rough. Though not perfect, the British Expeditionary Force was far better prepared than the French.

The most important aspect of British participation in this campaign was not, however, their land forces, but rather their air forces. The RAF was definitely the superior of the Armee de l'Air in just about every category and was more or less able to meet the Luftwaffe on equal terms, with roughly equal aircraft, though a large portion of the RAF contingent was composed of obsolescent aircraft, which would prove virtual death traps in combat.

Only Britain, of the Allied powers, possessed an air force of consequence and it was more consequential than the French Air Force itself. Taken as a whole the British Expeditionary Force was by far the most effective, most well-balanced Allied contingent, at least in terms of equipment: British generals do not seem to have been any less obsessed by World War I than French ones.

Planning and Preparing for War, 1935–1940

Hitlerian Germany began open rearmament in 1935. Though many political leaders urged action, the French Government and High Command managed to find reasons to avoid taking military action right through the German attack on Poland—in all of this they were, of course, warmly supported by the British.

So anxious was the French Army to avoid operations against Germany during the period 1935–1938 that official intelligence presentations to the government were falsified on numerous occasions. Thus, the estimate of the number of properly trained men Germany could put in the field in the mid-1930s went from some 450,000 (a figure which had been used since the mid-1920s and included the 100,000 man "Versailles" Army, the militarized border patrol, and various paramilitary organizations)—a force which the standing French Army would have been adequate to deal with—to something near to a million—a force which would have required mobilization of the French reserves, which was precisely what the French government did not wish to do.

Actually, it is difficult to determine the precise degree of falsification which went on. It is certain that the High Command deliberately overstated the size and effectiveness of the Luftwaffe, which was depicted as some sort of monstrously effective force against which there was no defense. In this they were undoubtedly aided in their efforts by the outspokenness of many pro-German air power "experts," such as Charles Lindbergh, who continuously stressed the "overwhelming superiority" of the Luftwaffe even when that superiority was measured in a handful of superior aircraft. Thus, in their calculations the French High Command never seem to have noted the strength of the RAF, yet assumed that Germany had 14–16,000 aircraft! After the victory over Poland this vaunted air superiority became more entrenched—though at this point with considerably more reason, for by now the Luftwaffe was, at least marginally, superior to both the Armee de l'Air and the RAF in both quantity and quality.

The precise reasons behind the considerable lengths to which the French High Command went to deceive its government are not clear. It was charged—in the midst of defeat—that treason was afoot but the suggestions seem rather questionable from the present vantage. It may, however, be possible that the French Armed Forces—dominated by the Army—felt that any military action against Germany before France was fully "ready" would be ill advised. And France would not be "ready" before 1941, when the final stages of rearmament programs of 1936–1937 would have been reached. This would certainly seem the most plausible explanation, though it is also certain that the inactivity of the French during the late summer of 1939 is totally inexplicable.

To be sure, France had not acted during the Czech crises of 1938 and 1939, though the Czechs had some 20-odd well equipped and effective divisions. But then circumstances were somewhat different. For one thing, it was "peace" and neither France nor Britain wanted the onus of having "caused" the war on their shoulders. For another, many sincere people in both countries felt that the Sudeten Germans did, in fact, want to be part of Germany. Needless to say this was absolutely true. The Sudetenland had been forcibly incorporated into Czechoslovakia in 1919 to provide that nation with a "strategic frontier" against Germany. Somehow it seemed wrong to apply the principle of "self-determination of peoples" only to one's friends—though it did not seem wrong to deny it to the Arabs, Indians, and Africans.

Moreover, during all the earlier crises, right down to the Czech Crisis of 1939, France expressed no desire to act unless Britain committed herself fully.

Britain would not do so beyond "the Royal Navy and a couple of divisions," so France did not act. Perhaps if Albert, King of the Belgians, had been still about he would have cooperated, as he did in the 1920s, but his son was of different timber.

Given the military situation in September of 1939, however, we find no such problems. Both France and Britain were definitely at war with Germany and their ally, Poland, was in desperate need of succor as *blitzkrieg* was unleashed for the first time. A swift Allied advance to the Rhine was reasonable and, indeed, many Germans felt it to be inevitable.

Assigned to defending the Rhine frontier with France and the Rhineland provinces, were some 46 German infantry divisions, all but eleven of them composed of reservists, replacements, *Landwehr,* and trainees. Among them was not a single tank, only some 300 non-divisional artillery pieces, and scarcely an airplane. On the date the French completed mobilization, 4 September, they had 40 divisions in position opposing only 17 of the still assembling Germans. By the end of September there were some 70 French and two British divisions available, with over 3,000 tanks, 1,600 pieces of non-divisional artillery, nearly a thousand fighters, and over 700 bombers. The expected invasion of Germany never materialized, however, Why?

The answer will forever lie buried with the principals involved but certain points are evident. For example, neither the RAF nor the French Air Force wanted to get involved until they were better prepared for action. Indeed, it would seem that the Allies were, at this point, more interested in averting defeat than in achieving victory. Significantly, in both London and Paris there sat the governments of appeasement. More significantly, both Britain and France had made strenuous last minute efforts to get Poland to reconsider her position vis-a-vis Danzig and the Polish Corridor! Indeed, it was only with the advent of Churchill that British attitudes changed from viewing the war as an essentially balance-of-power conflict to that of the survival of nations.

Whatever the causes of the Allied inactivity during 1939, the lack of resolution proved to be anything but transitory, as their preparations for operations in 1940—when the whole weight of the German Armed Forces would be available against them—clearly demonstrate.

Evolution of Two Plans

With the subjugation of Poland, and the resultant transfer to the West of enormous German forces, the Allies began to prepare to meet what appeared to be an inevitable German offensive. This, in itself, is a key to their state of mind at this time: they prepared to meet a German offensive, not to take some positive action of their own.

Assuming the Germans would be foolish enough to attack the Maginot Line, the Allies calculated that they had nothing to worry about. The basic concept of the line seemed sound and with available mobile forces any breakthrough would have been rather handily repulsed by these. The assumption was, however, that the Germans would not be so cooperative as to take on the Maginot Line. Therefore there was but one other thing they could do: invade Belgium, and perhaps Holland as well. As early as 1927 Marshal Petain had set up the basic outline for such an eventuality when he noted, "We must go into Belgium".

Going into Belgium had several advantages for the Allies, as opposed to waiting for the Germans on the frontiers of France. For one thing it kept the fighting as far from France's vital industrialized northern provinces as possible. For another it shortened their front somewhat and enabled them to add the 22 Belgian divisions to their order of battle. The main disadvantage was that it thrust them very far forward and out of the way should the Germans drive through the Ardennes, but that was unlikely, for Petain had once noted that the Ardennes was impassable to armored forces. Of course the old marshal had added, "If adequately defended," but that part seems to have been ignored. At any rate it was into Belgium that the Allies intended to go if the Germans did. But how far?

There were several schools of thought as to how far the Allied armies ought to advance in the event of a German invasion of Belgium. The most aggressive proposal was for an advance to the Meuse-Albert Canal, just a few miles west of the Germano-Belgian frontier. Less daring individuals believed that the Dyle River line, just east of Brussels, was more reasonable, as this would probably be where the Belgian Army itself would attempt a stand. Still less daring generals opted for an advance only as far as the Escaut River in western Belgium. These were designated the D Plan and the E Plan respectively. The Albert Canal notion was ignored.

In the end Plan D was adopted. There were a number of reasons for this. Plan D permitted the Allies to cover Brussels and Antwerp, the latter desirous as a supply port for the BEF. It also seemed likely that the Belgians would fight east of Brussels, rather than give up the city without a fight. By advancing to join them a decisive battle might be brought about very early in the campaign. Then too, there was the problem of Holland. The Schlieffen Plan of 1914 fame had initially envisioned a German advance into that country, but this was later dropped. The Allies were laboring under the misconception that the Germans intended to use this plan again in 1940 and that Holland might therefore have to be aided as well. In this case, in addition to aiding Holland, the defense of Antwerp would be furthered by the occupation of portions of the southern Netherlands and of the islands of the Scheldt estuary. Thus, these areas were added to the Dyle Plan. Needless to say, the Escaut Plan provided none of these advantages, though it was considerably less audacious.

Looking backward, it seems more in keeping with the general lack of resolution on the part of the Allied High Command if they had opted for Plan E, rather than the somewhat daring plan D, which would have required energetic, heroic leadership to bring off. Both plans, E and D, were based upon one faulty assumption, however. This was that the Germans intended to repeat the Schlieffen Plan of 1914.

The Germans had entirely rejected the Schlieffen Plan as unworkable, considering that it had failed once and that the Allies would have some idea of how it was supposed to work. The plan devised by their Army High Command, though often termed a variant of the Schlieffen Plan, had very little resemblance to that remarkable operation. The OKH plan envisioned merely the occupation of Belgium, Holland, and France north of the Aisne and Somme, not the total encirclement and destruction of the Allied armies somewhere in the vicinity of Paris, as Schlieffen had envisioned. To implement this, a very strong drive was to be made across Holland and northern Belgium towards the Somme, pushing the Allies into the south of France. It was a conservative plan, but one which was extremely realistic.

Even as the plan was being completed, however, it was being questioned by everyone from Hitler himself on down to various staff officers. One of these, Erich von Manstein, drew up some general proposals for an entirely different operation, based on an advance through the Ardennes towards the sea, with the intention of cutting off the northern portion of the Allied forces. Hitler was let in on this, liked it and passed it on to OKH, which adopted it as its own, after some recrimination and a bit of modification. The driving force in this change of plan was Hitler, a point too readily forgotten in the light of his later failures as a military commander.

This was the plan adopted by the Germans: a diversionary advance into Holland and North Belgium, to lure the main Allied forces as far north as possible, and a main thrust toward the "impassable" Ardennes, using armored and mobile forces, with infantry to follow it up. To make sure that it would work, the entire Ardennes road movement was war-gamed out several times in advance, just to be on the safe side.

Thus, on the eve of the German offensive, a vague Allied plan of operations—it failed to outline what the Allies intended to do after reaching the Dyle—was about to be tested against a clearly stated, and carefully considered, German plan.

The Campaign of 1940

In general, the Germans were fully prepared for the operations which they launched on 10 May 1940. They achieved their victory within ten days: after that it was all mopping up and consolidation. The Allies, on the other hand, were considerably less well prepared, both materially and psychologically. The psychological failings were primarily confined to the higher levels of the respective Allied forces: the men were, with few exceptions, ready, willing, and able to put up ferocious resistance when called upon to do so. Their superiors, however, were indecisive and hesitant, defeated even before the first shot had been fired. When Gen Maurice Gamelin, French Commander-in-Chief, was informed of the German invasion of Belgium, his reply to theater commander Gen Alphonse Georges' "It is the Dyle scheme then?" was an uninspiring "What else can we do?"

The Allies therefore went forward at full tilt, towards a position which most of their unmotorized infantry had great difficulty in reaching, though the motorized forces had no problems at all. In some cases the Germans had gotten there first, in the form of reconnaissance units. The Allies needed perhaps five days to consolidate the Dyle position; they had barely two. Meanwhile the main German thrust was further south on the Meuse near the historic city of Sedan.

The front at Sedan was held by a handful of second-line reserve divisions and a pitiful collection of light field fortifications. During the winter of 1939–1940 a substantial line of concrete and earth field fortifications had been projected to stretch from the end of the Maginot Line to the North Sea but the extreme severity of the winter had prevented serious construction efforts and only very late had any real work been done. In the Sedan sector virtually nothing had been done. Of course, the Ardennes and the Meuse were considered sufficient obstacles as to prevent any German advance, and Petain had said that the forest was impassable, so there was no felt threat in this sector. To defend the Ardennes was the task of a Belgian light infantry division plus some French and Belgian horsed and mechanized cavalry. But their assignment was to impede the German advance through demolitions and to avoid combat. The initial Belgian demolitions actually slowed up the French more than the Germans. What would have been the case if the Belgians, and later the French, had offered serious resistance is moot, but a provable possibility exists that the German drive might have been seriously delayed. One Belgian battalion failed to get the orders to fall back and resisted bitterly, delaying the German advance in its sector for a day or so.

Whatever the case, by the fourth day of the campaign the Germans were over the Meuse in strength and France's only available counterattack force, comprising an armored and a motorized infantry division, with one cavalry and a fine regular infantry division, had been frittered away in holding an arc over 30 kilometers long, to prevent Germans from infiltrating to the Aisne. From then on it was all down hill.

As the German forces in northern Belgium kept up the pressure, their panzers in southern Belgium, along the French frontier, drove steadily westward. On 18 May, roughly four days after the Meuse had been pierced in strength, they were on the Somme near St. Quentin, two days later at Abbeville on the sea. The northern group of armies was completely isolated from the rest of France and only feeble counterattacks were undertaken to break out.

The sturdiest of these, the British counterattack at Arras and DeGaulle's armored attacks from the south, were eventually inflated into tremendous victories which failed but for the lack of sufficient reserves to follow up. In fact, neither operation seriously discomforted the Germans once they determined their actual extent.

The rest of the campaign was essentially anti-climactic. The high romance and heroism of Dunkirk, the ferocious defense of the Aisne-Somme position, and the final collapse of the French armies in the south all were more or less inevitable following upon the German success in crossing the Meuse on a broad front from Sedan to Namur.

Among the many generalizations made of this campaign is that pro-German "fifth columnists" were extremely active, that French traitors deliberately lost the campaign, and that the French troops had no desire to fight. In no case have these allegations been proven correct. Some fifth column activity did in fact occur but did not materially aid the Germans; there seems no real evidence of treason having occurred on anyone's part; and French troops, with a few exceptions (mostly among poorly led, over-40-years-of-age reservists) fought with remarkable tenacity. What is true is that the Allied High Command was extremely lethargic and uninnovative. Victory in 1918 had made them blind to the potential of the internal combustion engine. Defeat had done more or less the exact opposite for the Germans.

L'Envoi

The origins of the defeat of France in 1940 lie deeply embedded in the history of France over the previous century and a half. All of the forces working to bring

The Campaign in France
Deployment and Plans
9 May 1940

⊠ = Germans
⊠ = Allies

Scale in miles
0 25 50 75 100

← = Advance of Army Group A
▲▲▲ = Maginot Line

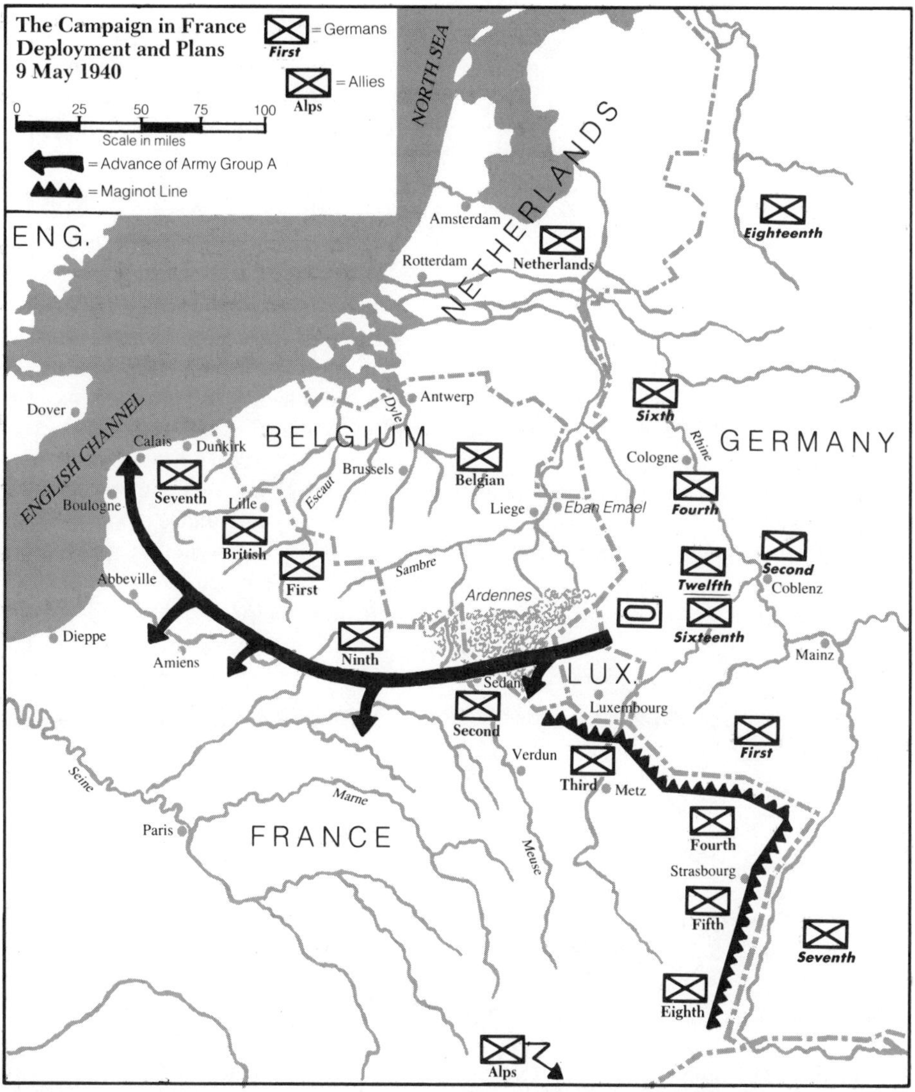

down the Third Republic, whether consciously or not, had been around for a long time. Nevertheless, France had survived the terrible ordeal of 1914–1918 intact and victorious. Despite a certain lack of will, the fall of France was engendered as much by certain military failings as by anything else. And these failings were rooted in the same soil from which the all-conquering Wehrmacht drew its nourishment, the Allied victory in 1918. The French, and to a lesser extent the British as well, clung to outmoded concepts in warfare, while the Germans, intent upon avenging defeat, sought new, more innovative ways of war. The German techniques were by no means perfect, but the imperfections of the French military establishment told far more when the test of battle came. If ever a nation prepared itself for defeat, it was France in the period between her triumph and her fall.

EQUIPMENT AVAILABLE: THE BATTLE FOR FRANCE SPRING 1940

Class	*French Army*	*British Army*	*German Army*	*Dutch Army*	*Belgian Army*
MG	153,700	11,000	147,700	3,400	3,600
Mortars	8,000	8,000	6,796	144	2,268
A/T Guns	7,800	850	12,830	88	144
Field Guns	8,265	880	15,969	192	390
Heavy Guns	3,931	310	2,900	242	152
AA Guns	3,921	500	8,700	182	600
Tanks	3,437	580	3,227	-	-

Notes: As can readily be seen the Germans had a significant quantitative superiority in terms of artillery pieces over the combined British and French arsenals. It should be noted, further, that some 60 percent of the French machine guns were in reality automatic rifles, thus giving the Germans the edge in this category as well. The figures for Germany and France represent total available equipment, while those for the British represent that equipment actually sent to France before and during the campaign, and in most cases lost there. Figures for the Dutch army include material in colonies (10–20%).

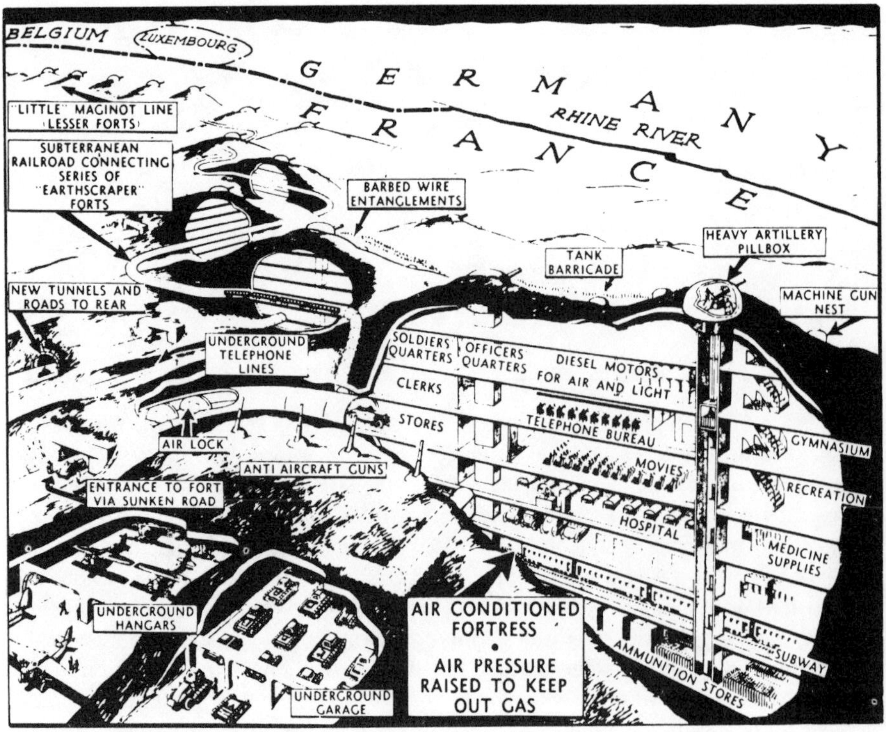

Forces Available: 10–25 May 1940

	Divisions					Brigades			Div Eq
	Arm	*Mtzd*	*Inf*	*Ftr*	*Cav*	*Arm*	*Inf*	*Cav*	*Total*
Belgium			21		2			1	23.5
Britain	1	15				1	2	2	18
Czecho-slovakia							2		1
France	7	7	79	5	5			4	105
Netherlands		1	8				2		10
Poland			1			1			1
TOTAL	8	23	109	5	5	2	6	7	158.5
Germany	10	7	118		1		3		137.5

This table summarizes the number of major combat formations—divisions and brigades—available to each side on the first few days of the German offensive. Units represented are those actually in or brought into the theater of operation during the period indicated. Sizeable French forces were available in North Africa and elsewhere, some elements of which were eventually committed during the campaign. In addition, the French improvised a number of formations from training personnel, recruits, frontier guards, and stragglers in the course of the campaign. Four or five of the British infantry divisions were incomplete, missing all or part of their artillery and other elements, but with full infantry complements. The Polish and Czech forces-in-exile were only partially trained, although eventually committed. It had been originally intended to form a Polish Corps of three infantry divisions and one DLM, plus a full Czech division. The Germans had most of their army committed to this campaign, though a number of divisions were on occupation duty in Poland and Czechoslovakia, a few were retained in the interior, and several had not yet completed training.

Abbreviations. *Arm,* armored formation, including the French DCR and CLM: *Mtzd,* motorized, an infantry division capable of fully mechanized movement without additional motor vehicles, a luxury which only the British could afford on a large scale [the Netherlands division indicated was actually partially bicycle]; *Inf,* all other types of infantry—the French had six different ones—including mountain troops; *Ftr,* fortress units, immobile outfits designed to occupy prepared fortifications; *Cav,* cavalry units, including French semi-mechanized divisions, German horsed troops, British mechanized reconnaissance units, and Belgian semi-mechanized forces. *Div Eq Total,* or Division Equated Total, is the number of divisions available assuming brigades are lumped together.

Their mastery of the blitzkrieg made the Germans unbeatable. No foe was capable of standing up to them unless he developed ways to beat this revolutionary form of warfare. To do so would take time. And with the fall of France in the Summer of 1940 it appeared that the Allies had run out of time. But there was one thing that blitzkrieg could not do. It could not defeat Britain. No panzer division, no matter how brilliantly commanded, could reach Britain, the

"... Precious stone set in the silver sea
Which serves it in the office of a wall,
Or as a moat defensive ...."

To subdue Britain would require crossing the 20 miles of sea separating it from France. Such an undertaking would necessitate a three-fold victory, for the Royal Air Force and the Royal Navy would have to be dealt with before a single man could be landed to engage the British Army. So Hitler laid plans for an assault on Britain while Sir Winston Churchill, the new Prime Minister, steeled the will of the British people with his promise of "Blood, toil, tears, and sweat."

The Battle of Britain was the first in history decided entirely by air power. Surface forces, whether armies or navies, played no direct role. Envisioned as merely the preliminary round of an invasion on Britain, the air battle became the totality of the struggle for the "sceptered isle."

Adlerangriff (Eagle's Onslaught)

by Frank Davis

The launching of the German invasion hinged upon the ability of the Luftwaffe to negate Britain's naval defense so as to ensure the landing force the opportunity to establish a strong bridgehead. Before tackling the Royal Navy, the *Luftwaffe* first had to gain superiority over the Channel by crippling or eliminating the Royal Air Force's Fighter Command. Reichsmarshal Herman Goring planned to destroy the R.A.F. in a swift two-stage battle. *Operation Adlerangriff* would require four days to destroy the fighter defense of southern England. Within a month, according to Goring's forecast, the ground installations and aircraft industries throughout the island could be eradicated. After this onslaught, the *Luftwaffe* could be made available to cover the invasion embarkation, crossing, and landing operations. Alternatively, Goring proposed to allow the air force alone to stampede Britain into capitulation and make the planned invasion unnecessary. By attacking population and food storage centers, the *Luftwaffe* could accelerate the original siege policy and force Britain rapidly towards submission. Throughout the summer, as the invasion forces were continually whittled to fit their barge accommodations, Hitler increasingly relied upon the *Luftwaffe* to singlehandedly smash Britain's resistance.

The Luftwaffe began rehearsing for the onslaught on 10 July 1940 when FM Albert Kesselring's *Luftflotte II,* newly based in Northern France and the Low Countries, and LG Hugo Sperrle's *Luftflotte III,* operating from Western France, began harassing Channel merchant shipping. Daily, the two airfleets were capable of airing about 800 medium and 250 Stuka dive-bombers supported by 800 fighters, two-thirds of which were short-ranged Me–109E planes, the remainder the newer twin-engine Me–110 fighters. Primarily engaged by Fighter Command's Groups Nrs. 10 and 11, flying less than 600 Spitfire and Hurricane aircraft, the Germans took a surprising licking during the month-long rehearsal—losing 181 bombers and 105 fighters to only 150 British fighter aircraft. The German losses were caused by a variety of errors and difficulties. Early in the battle, Goring erred by outlawing attacks against both the British radar chain which detected formations assembling over France, and the Fighter Command sector stations, the ground-to-air control bases which issued ample warning for British planes to scramble to superior elevation, and controlled the squadron trafficking and deployment which enabled the outnumbered British to meet the widespread German raids. The Germans were also seriously hindered by the short range of the single-engine Me-109E which could only escort bomber formations for a distance of about 125 miles, or just to the north of London. To conserve this fighter's brief endurance it was necessary to rendezvous fighter-bomber teams above the French coast with split-second timing and once united these formations remained limited to straight line sorties over England.

Between 13 August, Goring's *Adlertag* (Eagle Day), and 18 August when bad weather temporarily halted air operations, the Luftwaffe flew more than 5,000 sorties in the initial onslaught which Goring expected would eliminate Fighter Command's forces in southern England. The battle climaxed on 15 August when the Norway-based *Luftflotte V* coordinated its first mission against the northeastern coast with the heaviest raids yet flown over the south. This mission proved to be *Luftflotte V*'s first and last attempt to support the cross-Channel raiding. Having outranged their escorts, the Norway-based bombers encountered such stiff resistance from Fighter Command's Groups Nrs. 12 and 13 off the Northumberland coast, as to make further daylight operations from Norway impractical. The assault between 13–18 August cost the Luftwaffe 258 aircraft. During the same period the British lost 103 fighters.

Following the initial assault, Goring, influenced by the padded claims of his pilots and believing Fighter Command to be nearly broken, ordered the Luftwaffe to resume the dizzying attrition battle. On 24 August, flying sparse numbers of closely escorted bombers, the Luftwaffe rose again to press the British into further attrition. Finding their meager bomber bait refused, the Germans finally concentrated their attacks against the airfields and sector stations of Fighter Command's Group 11, defending London and the southeast. The British planes were forced up in defense of their vital ground-control bases at Tangmere, Kenley, North Weald, Biggin Hill, Hornchurch, Northolt, and Middle Wallop. In the next fortnight the Germans damaged six of these seven sector stations ringing London.

By patrolling Dover Straits in massive numbers and repeatedly feinting at the British coast, the Germans were finally able to turn the British radar network against its proprietors. The exhausted British squadrons were kept continuously aloft chasing phantom raids only to be taken at a disadvantage by a newly risen or previously masked German formation. By these tactics the Luftwaffe scored its most impressive losses-to-victories ratio of the battle. Between 24 August and 6 September, the Germans downed 277 British fighters for a sacrifice of 378 German aircraft. More importantly, 103 British pilots were killed and 128 wounded out of the Fighter Command's total pilot strength of under 1,000. While throughout the battle, British fighter production, averaging 450 aircraft per month, easily replaced the combat losses, the pilot drain seriously threatened Fighter Command's ability to continue fighting. At the beginning of August, Fighter Command mustered 1,434 pilots, but the loss rate averaging 120 pilots a week during the battle left Fighter Command with only 840 pilots (barely enough to man the available machines) by early September. Thus the Germans were unknowingly on the verge of crippling Fighter Command. Then they switched the emphasis of the assault to London in hopes of gaining even greater results, thereby granting the RAF a respite.

Throughout the battle Hitler had reserved terror attacks against London as his trump card which, when played, would force the British government to capitulate at the hands of a panic-stricken, perhaps even rebellious, British populace. On the night of 24 August, while breaking in the *Knickebein* radio-guidance system for night navigation, several German bombers strayed from other objectives to drop their payloads accidentally on central London. Retaliation came the following night by orders from Churchill. Twenty-nine British bombers struck Berlin, repeating the reprisal for four additional nights. Enraged, Hitler ordered Goring to prepare to switch the assault onto London. On 3 September, after being informed that Fighter Command had been reduced to 350 aircraft (there were in fact 650 operational British fighters), Goring ordered *Luftflotten II* and *III* to abandon their attacks against the Group 11 targets. On 4 September the London docks were ignited, and on 7 September the battle to burn London began in earnest. That Saturday the struggle to disarm the British air defenses ended and the battle to demoralize the British people began. By the end of September the Luftwaffe's losses since 10 July reached 1,408 aircraft. Fighter Command's losses over the same period totalled 697 planes.

Ten days after the switch to London, Hitler postponed *Sea Lion,* the proposed invasion of Britain, indefinitely. The invasion prerequisite of German air superiority was never gained. While the Luftwaffe might have broken Fighter Command's skeletal pilot force, they had no such chance to break the determined resistance of millions of Londoners.

Failure in the Battle of Britain did not put an end to Hitler's plans for the defeat of Britain. Rather it initiated an effort to defeat the defiant island kingdom through a submarine blockade. The result was the longest campaign of the war and one of the most critical, the Battle of the Atlantic.

Wolfpack: The German Submarine War in the Atlantic, 1939–1943

by Frank Davis

Even before the outbreak of World War II Hitler's U-Boats had taken up positions in the broad expanse of the Atlantic. When the war came, the onslaught began as, for the second time in a generation, Germany strove to starve a defiant Britain into submission. The toll mounted rapidly, three million tons in the first twenty months. And, with the failure of the Luftwaffe over Britain in the summer of 1940 and of the panzers before Moscow in the winter of 1941, it was with the underwater arm that Hitler's best hope for victory lay.

The Wolves' Debut

The submarine's debut in World War I was more impressive than that of the tank. Although rudimentary submersibles had been clumsily stalking warships ever since the American Revolution, it was the German U-boat which abruptly ended the slapstick pioneer exploits in submarine warfare.

Despite the handicaps imposed by their crude instruments and their own lack of experience, the first U-boat crews achieved ominous results almost immediately. On September 22, 1914, the *U–9* sank three British cruisers within one hour's time off the Dutch coast. Thereafter, the submarine's threat to warships was curbed by screening the heavy ships with swarms of destroyers. The most menacing role for the submarine, as a commerce raider, was now quickly exploited.

In early 1915, the British exchanged a blockade against Germany for a German proclamation which unleashed the U-boats against merchant ships entering the waters surrounding the British Isles. In early 1915, the British suffered a U-boat blitz which sank a quarter million tons of Allied and neutral shipping. The British responded to the threat by launching a massive propaganda campaign to vilify the German's potent use of submarine warfare. At the outbreak of the war, the belligerents still subscribed to international law which forbids a warship from attacking an unarmed merchant vessel without first stopping the merchantman to examine her cargo for contraband. If the ship was then found to be carrying war materials, she could be seized or sunk on the condition that her crew was ensured a safe means for reaching land, for which purpose the merchant ship's lifeboats were not considered sufficient. Clearly, this humane code favored Great Britain which possessed the world's largest mercantile fleet, but deprived the submarine of its *raison d'être*.

The U-boat had been designed to attack without warning from a submerged position. Her surface armament could not compete with that of a conventional warship nor even an armed merchant ship. Moreover, a U-boat could hardly accommodate the survivors of vessels which she torpedoed.

As British propaganda turned world opinion against the U-boat, the Kaiser was forced to choose between condemning his submarines to an impractical, if not suicidal, form of combat, or to continue the gradual escalation toward unrestricted submarine warfare even though this encouraged the wrath of neutrals like America which were eager to profit off trade with the belligerents. The latter course prevailed, leading to the sinking of the Cunard liner *Lusitania* on May 7, 1915. This, in turn, led to America's eventual declaration of war against Germany, ensuring her ultimate defeat. Before then, however, the free reign given to the U-boats almost produced a German victory. Overall, the U-boats sank some 5,000 ships for an aggregate total of eleven million tons between 1914–1918. In what was virtually her eleventh hour, Britain began convoying her merchant shipping and thus eluded a fast approaching defeat. After May 10, 1917, when the convoy system was adopted, only about 250 out of some 84,000 ships traveling in convoys were sunk.

Thus, two items of import surfaced from the submarine war waged between 1914–1918. The first was that independent ships suffered from submarine attack far more grievously than ships in convoy. The second fact was that of all the ships sailed in convoy attended by both *air* and naval escort, only *five* had been sunk by submarines. This was in spite of the fact that, owing to the lack of effective airborne anti-submarine weapons, only one submarine was sunk by aircraft during the entire course of the war.

Who's Afraid of the Big Bad Wolf?

By the terms of the Versailles Treaty, Germany was forced to renounce the use of submarine warfare for all time. Thereafter, until the signing of the Anglo-German Naval Agreement of 1935, the innocuous *Reichsmarine* forswore future conflict against the British, even to the point of prohibiting naval wargames with Great Britain as an opponent. By the 1935 agreement, however, Germany exchanged a promise to abide by international law for permission to construct a new U-boat fleet which might equal but not exceed Britain's.

Britain's curious acceptance of this treaty was based on her belief that any future U-boat threat could be countered by the rapid adoption of the convoy system. Also, agreeing to a German submarine fleet that might equal her own seemed a small risk since Britain planned little submarine construction for the foreseeable future. Most important, since the conclusion of the last war, the Royal Navy's development of *asdic,* an underwater radio-echoing device for detecting a submerged submarine, led the British to believe that the U-boat would now be far more vulnerable than had been the case between 1914–1918.

As events later revealed, Britain's complacency toward the potential U-boat menace was extremely foolhardy. By 1939, the United Kingdom had become even more dependent on sea commerce than she had been in 1914, for while the British population increased by four million between wars, the internal resources of the British Isles did not increase. Although sufficient coal and part of her iron ore needs were produced locally, Britain's survival depended on her ability to import about half her food requirements, plus eight million tons of timber to prop her coal mines and twelve million tons of petroleum products annually.

While in 1939 the British Commonwealth could still rely on the world's largest mercantile fleet, the 21 million ton capacity of this fleet was only one million tons greater than its 1914 capacity. Moreover, whereas in 1914 Britain had owned half of the world's tanker fleet, in 1939 her share had fallen to a quarter of the world's ten million gross tons, despite the fact that Britain's petroleum needs had increased tenfold between 1914 and 1939. Because oil became a strategic import of the highest importance in war, the inadequacy of the British tanker fleet would become one of Britain's major weaknesses, and one which the U-boat was particularly well suited to exploit. Altogether, the British Merchant Navy of 1939 registered about 6,000 ships of five hundred tons or more, of which only half were ocean going types. To this initial fleet, the long neglected British shipbuilding industry could add only about one million tons of new construction annually.

To defend her vital merchant trade, which on any day comprised up to 2,500 ships at sea, in 1939, the Royal Navy had only about 150 short-ranged, asdic-equipped destroyers, and virtually no aircraft specifically allocated for convoy escort work. By comparison, in 1918 the British were employing 257 warships on full-time escort duties, another 500 ships as part-time escorts, and about 500 aircraft and dirigibles. So, on all counts, in 1939 Britain was a great deal worse off regarding her ability to cope with submarine warfare than she had been twenty years earlier. If the U-boat was in fact more vulnerable in 1939 than in 1918, no less so was the British merchant ship.

The belief in the U-boat's greater vulnerability was based on a series of miscalculations. The Royal Navy's peacetime testing of asdic had been largely confined to hunting submarines whose initial positions were known within fairly narrow limits. These tests had only been conducted in daylight under favorable weather conditions. Despite these circumstances there were as many unsuccessful hunts as there were "kills" in these mock anti-submarine attacks due to a blindness which asdic developed as it approached too near the target. The British also failed to appreciate that the greatly increased endurance of contemporary submarines would allow them to operate far out in the Atlantic well beyond the range of their short-winded, asdic-carrying escort vessels.

The most damaging example of British myopia ws their assumption that the U-boats would behave like "true submarines," approaching and attacking only while submerged. The British held to this opinion despite their knowledge that the U-boat fleet's commander was an advocate of the technique of using groups of boats in night attacks on the surface. This technique, the so-called "wolfpack" tactic, had been developed by Admiral Karl Donitz during the 1935–39 period as a means by which the U-boat could overcome both asdic, which was ineffective against a surfaced submarine, and the tightly knit defense of a convoy, which would be distracted and dispersed by a U-boat pack assault involving up to thirty individual submarines. When the U-boat war began under Donitz' direction, British escort crews were forced to rely as much on eyesight to detect an approaching sub as on their asdic sets.

As it happened then, the sole safeguard the British were able to fall back on was the adoption of the convoy system. Although this time the decision to begin convoying merchantmen came quickly—the first convoy left Gibraltar the day *before* Britain declared war on Germany—it remained a controversial issue well into 1940. Britain's former First Lord of the Admiralty, Winston Churchill, was among those who begrudged the passive use of British warships as convoy escorts. He argued strenuously for dispersing the meager anti-submarine forces available into a number of "hunter-killer" groups whose function would be to patrol the sea-lanes like a cavalry reconnaissance force and persecute the U-boats in the same manner in which the German pocket-battleship *Admiral Graf Spee* was hounded to death off South America in December 1939. Churchill's error, which the Americans stubbornly repeated in early 1942, stemmed from his incorrect judgment that warships could profitably search out submarines in the vast grey wastes of the Atlantic. In fact, throughout the six-year sea war, the U-boat proved almost totally immune to detection by either surface or airborne search except in the immediate vicinity of convoys, or along congested U-boat transit routes such as in France's Bay of Biscay where the area to be searched was strictly confined.

The Z-Plan

Considering their dangerous disregard of the potential U-boat menace, the British owed a debt of gratitude to the fact that Hitler had little appreciation of naval strategy. Hitler first perceived Britain as his potential enemy during the Sudetan Crises of 1938. In the latter part of that year, Adm Raeder, C-in-C of the German Navy, ordered an examination of the problems involved in war with England. As a result of that examination, he submitted to Hitler two alternatives for the expansion of the German fleet. The first, more economical, plan emphasized production of U-boats and pocket-battleships to be used against the British merchant traffic in the event of war. The alternative, known as the *Z-Plan,* involved a long term commitment to construct a high seas fleet which could directly challenge the British Navy, whose strength would necessarily be dissipated to protect Britain's worldwide merchant trade. In offering Hitler this alternative, Raeder warned him that the battleship fleet envisioned in the *Z-Plan* would require a decade to construct and if Germany became involved in a premature war with England her chances for success would be minimal. As Hitler gave Raeder assurance that he would not risk any confrontation with Britain before 1946, the *Z-Plan* was adopted.

Throughout this planning period, Donitz, Commander-in-Chief of the German U-boat service, steadily opposed adoption of the *Z-Plan,* which was to provide only 129 completed U-boats by early 1944. Convinced that an early war with England was likely, Donitz repeatedly warned Raeder that the U-boat construction schedule envisioned in the *Z-Plan* was terribly inadequate. Because one-third of whatever number of boats were available would always be en route to and from the area of operations, and another third of the available fleet would have to be retained in home waters for refitting and training purposes. Donitz calculated that a minimum of 300 ocean-going U-boats would have to be on hand in order to wage an effective supply war against Great Britain.

Donitz also disagreed with the *Z-Plan* 's emphasis on constructing a large number of heavy (2,000 ton) U-boats. Believing that the number of "eyes" which could search for convoys would be more important than either armament or endurance, Donitz supported the medium-sized (500–700 ton) *Type VII* boat as the optimum weapon for the pack tactics he planned to employ. Although he repeatedly implored Raeder to modify the *Z-Plan* to produce the necessary numbers, and to construct *Type VII* boats in a three to one ratio to all other types, his efforts met with little success. For far longer than was prudent, Raeder remained convinced that Hitler would avoid conflict with England. Hitler himself strongly favored construction of the heavier, more prestigious surface combat ships. As a result, although during 1935–1939 German shipyards completed about 300,000 tons of warships, only 56 U-boats were produced. And, although the *Z-Plan* was modified in the Fall of 1939 to incorporate more submarines, with the object of producing 300 by mid-1942, the chances for an undersea victory had by then been diminished by Hitler's impatience, which plunged the German Navy into war with Great Britain seven years too soon.

Specifications of the Principal German U-Boats Employed in World War II

Type	Tons	Length Feet	Beam Feet	Speed in Knots Surf.	Speed in Knots Subm.	Torp. Cap.	Max. Range Miles	Years in Service	Total Built
VII-C	750	220	20	17	7.6	14	6,500	1940–45	660
IX-C	740	244	21	18.2	7.3	21-23	11,000	1941–45	146
IX-D	1,200	290	20	19.2	6.9	27	23,700	1942–44	32
XIV	1,600	220	30	14.4	6.2	9	9,300	1941–43	10
XXI*	1,600	251	21	15.5	17.5	23	11,200	1944–45	120
XXIII**	250	112	12	9.5	12.5	2	1,350	1944–45	63

NOTES: * Although 120 Type XXI Schnorkel-equipped boats were completed before the end of the war, only three actually departed on combat missions. They achieved nothing.

** Sixty-three Type XXIII boats were completed before the end of the war. These were actually a small, coastal version of the Type XXI boat. Both the Type XXI and Type XXIII were built in prefabricated sections. About ten Type XXIII boats made combat patrols in Britain coastal waters in the last few months of the war. Because of their small size and schnorkel breathing equipment they were extremely hard to detect and therefore were fairly successful.

Of the 56 submarines Donitz had on hand in August 1939, eight were *Type VIIB* boats of 740 tons, capable of operating as far from base as Gibraltar or the Azores. Another 18 were *Type VIIA's* of 616 tons, capable of operating only out to about 150 miles west of Ireland. The remaining 30 were *Type II* boats of 250 to 300 tons nicknamed "canoes" since they could only operate in British coastal waters or the North Sea.

The Opening Round: September 1939–June 1940

By September 3, 1939, when Britain declared war against Germany, thirty-nine U-boats had been deployed in positions bordering the principal British shipping routes. The first victim of the sea war was the British passenger liner *Athenia* which was mistaken for a troop ship and sunk by *U-30* on the first evening of the war. Although the *Athenia* 's sinking was, in fact, attributable to her misidentification, the British government immediately accused the Germans of resurrecting unrestricted submarine warfare. In fact, Hitler was still extremely anxious to avoid escalation of hostilities between Germany and Great Britain and he had expressly forbidden attacks such as that on the *Athenia*. Within a few weeks, however, the question of adherence to international law was forgotten. As soon as Hitler realized that Britain was unwilling to accept a compromise peace, he began lifting the restrictions on U-boat operations. Soon after, the British announced that their merchant ships were being armed and would henceforth attack U-boats on sight. By late October 1939, U-boat commanders had permission to attack without warning any ship sailing in convoy, steaming without lights, zigzagging, or acting in any suspicious manner. Although Hitler still forbade attacks on ships of certain neutrals, such as America, within a decreed war zone surrounding the British Isles unrestricted submarine warfare was permitted.

In the initial months of the sea war, the U-boats, of which there were rarely more than six or seven at sea at any time, acted individually in the eastern North Atlantic between Gibraltar and the Hebrides. Their patrols were focused west of the English Channel, where the Atlantic shipping lanes were most concentrated. In this period Donitz had little opportunity to test *Die Rudeltaktik* (the pack attack) because the number of boats at sea at any one time was so small. Although the revised *Z-Plan* now called for 29 boats to be constructed each month, actual construction fell far short of this quota due to the priority which Hitler granted for strengthening the German army and air force. Also weakening Donitz' ability to concentrate his forces was the fact that, following the losses of two boats to British mines in the Channel, all boats bound for the Atlantic were being forced to make a lengthy voyage around northern Scotland. This considerably shortened the amount of time a boat could operate, thus limiting the number of boats available for operations on the Atlantic to about 20, no more than a third of which could be expected to be on station at any one time.

Despite the small numbers of boats, excellent individual achievements were made. The enemy's use of "hunter-killer" groups received a sharp set-back on September 17, 1939, when *U-9* sank the British aircraft carrier *Courageous* which had been supporting the anti-submarine patrols in the Western Approaches to the Channel. As a result of the loss of *Courageous* and 518 of her complement, the

British withdrew carriers from all anti-submarine operations until well into 1942. The most noteworthy exploit of this period was the sinking of the battleship, *Royal Oak,* in the Home Fleet main anchorage at Scapa Flow. This daredevil feat, which considerably enhanced the morale of the U-boat service, was executed by *U-47* whose commander, Lieutenant Gunther Prien, went on to become one of the U-boats' greatest "aces." As a result of Prien's attack on October 14, 1939, the British Home Fleet had to be transferred to more remote anchorages in western Scotland while Scapa Flow's defenses were strengthened.

Although the British had readily reintroduced the convoy system, they at first failed to include ships capable of 15 knots or greater speed, or those unable to sustain at least 9 knots. These vessels were known as "independents" since they sailed individually or in small groups, never escorted by warships. The bulk of the U-boats' victims were always drawn from such "independents." By the end of 1939, 5,756 ships had reached their destination via convoys and of these only four had succumbed to attacks by U-boats. In contrast, 102 "independents" were sunk during the same four month period.

The vulnerability of the "independents," however, was far from the most serious problem which the British faced. The severe shortage of escort ships prohibited more than one or two warships being allocated to each convoy. What was worse was the fact that, due to the limited range of these escort ships, a "limit of convoy" was imposed about 100 miles west of Ireland. At that point the ships of a convoy would disperse, and make the remainder of the trans-Atlantic voyage as "independents." Incoming—U.K. bound—convoys were picked up by escorts at this point west of Ireland and escorted from there to the British ports. Later, as more long-ranged escort ships became available, the convoy limit was pushed farther out into the Atlantic from both the North American and British coasts, but it was not until June 1941 that it became possible to escort a convoy for its entire voyage across the Atlantic.

The availability of aircraft for convoy escort duties remained insufficient throughout the first two years of the war. The initial strength of the R.A.F. Coastal Command was limited to a few squadronsof twin-engined Anson aircraft. Because of the limited range of these aircraft, they could only be used for reconnaissance work over the North Sea thus leaving the Atlantic convoys almost totally neglected.

Fortunately for the British, Donitz possessed too few long-range U-boats to fully exploit this situation. Nonetheless, between September 1939 and June 1940, U-boats succeed in sinking 224 ships of approximately 1.3 million tons. This total might have been much higher were it not for Hitler's interference. In April, 1940, he ordered a suspension of the war against the British supply lines so the U-boats could be used to support the Norwegian invasion. For the U-boats, *Operation Weserubung* proved only an exercise in frustration. They launched no less than thirty-six attacks on British warships and transports with uniformly dismal results. Subsequent investigation revealed that their poor performance was due to a malfunction in the firing mechanism of the German magnetic torpedoes which was compounded by unusual magnetic fields in Scandinavian waters. The problem was partially solved in June 1940, when the U-boats began employing a new type of contact percussion torpedo.

The Happy Time: July 1940–December 1941

Following the Fall of France in June 1940, the danger to Britain's shipping routes became much more severe. By July, 1940, the Germans had established the first Atlantic U-boat base at Lorient on the Bay of Biscay in western France. Subsequently, the Germans established bases at Brest, St.-Nazaire, and La Pallice, which gave the U-boats direct access to the Atlantic and shortened the previous transit route from Germany by more than 1,000 miles. The possession of these bases permitted the U-boats to increase both their time at sea and the distance out into the Atlantic in which they could hunt. Because of the shortened transit route, more U-boats could be kept simultaneously at sea. A further advantage accrued when *F. W. 200 Kondor* long-ranged German bombers arrived in newly acquired bases in northern France. From these bases the *Kondors* posed a serious threat to British shipping anywhere within their extensive 2,200 mile range. Most serious of all, the British, menaced with the prospect of invasion, were forced to withdraw many destroyers from convoy escort duties and reassign them to the Channel ports as the principal deterrent to *Operation Sealion.*

While the fall of France shortened the U-boats' voyages, it lengthened that of the British convoys. The Western Approaches from the Atlantic into the English Channel had to be abandoned due to their proximity to the German airbases. Atlantic convoys now had to be routed through the Northwest Approaches which passed north of Ireland into the Irish Sea and thence to the Mersey ports. Coastal convoys had to be rerouted around northern Scotland. In general, the German occupation of France increased the convoy voyage times by 30–40% and imposed an impossible burden on the west coast British ports causing bottlenecks and further reducing the efficiency and speed of British shipping. Britain's troubles were severely compounded by her inability to use naval and air bases in Eire. Although air and naval bases in Northern Ireland were gradually improved, and Britain's occupation of Iceland in April 1940 eventually allowed invaluable bases to be established there in mid-1941, the lack of bases in southern Ireland diminished the security available for Atlantic convoys throughout the first two years of the U-boat war.

On August 17, 1940, Hitler declared a total blockade of Britain as a means of softening up the island's resistance prior to the planned German invasion. During the following autumn, later recalled as "the happy time" by the German submarine commanders, the U-boats had their greatest harvest of the war. Although the total losses they inflicted in the fall of 1940 were far less than the loss inflicted two years later, the tonnage sunk per submarine was much greater. Altogether, German U-boats sank 2,373,070 gross registered tons of shipping during 1940 when they had an average of only 21 boats at sea at any one time. During 1940, a total of 26 U-boats were lost. Thus, 91,271 tons of shipping were sunk for each U-boat. On average, during 1940, each U-boat sank 9,416 tons of shipping per month. In comparison, during 1942, with an average of 24 U-boats at sea at any given time, the total tonnage sunk was 5,819,065 tons. Thirty-eight U-boats were lost during 1942, giving a figure of 55,155 tons of shipping sunk per U-boat lost, and 7,537 tons per U-boat per month.

During the autumn of 1940, the U-boats began to move into the mid-Atlantic and make concentrated attacks against the weakly escorted convoys. In September

1940 a ten-boat wolfpack intercepted two convoys west of Ireland and sank a total of 16 ships. The following month saw the most successful U-boat convoy battle of the war, when a pack of 12 boats trailed convoys *SC-7* and *HX-79* for four successive nights, sinking 32 merchantmen for a total of 154,661 gross tons.

Despite these successes, Donitz felt that the opportunity for even greater triumphs was being hindered by the lack of effective long range air reconnaissance, which he desired so as to be able to spot convoys far out at sea and concentrate sizeable wolfpacks against them. Although for a short period in early 1941 the U-boats had received tactical support from the *40th Bomber Group,* flying *F. W. 200 Kondor* aircraft, the intense personal rivalry between Donitz and *Reichsmarschall* Hermann Goring, head of the Luftwaffe, prevented the development of effective air-submarine teamwork.

Donitz also tried to heighten the effectiveness of the tonnage war by accepting Italy's offer to send a number of U-boats into the Atlantic to cooperate with the German U-boats. Little came of this, however, as the Italians were totally unfamiliar with the German tactics and were unaccustomed to the horrendous Atlantic weather conditions. There was not a single opportunity to employ a pack attack against a convoy sighted by an Italian submarine. In December 1940, Donitz abandoned his attempt to organize tactical cooperation with the Italians and thereafter the Italians were assigned a separate Atlantic area of operations. Between September 1940 and July 1943, about 30 Italian submarines operated in the Atlantic and sank an aggregate total of 105 ships of 588,553 tons. Sixteen Italian subs were lost on Atlantic patrol, five were taken over by the Germans when Italy departed the war, and one surrendered to British forces at Durban, South Africa.

During 1940, the German shipyards completed an average of four and one-half U-boats a month. Although production was stepped up to nearly 17 a month during 1941, the bulk of the new boats did not become operational unti 1942 because of the lengthy training period required for the crews. One benefit of the accelerated production, however, was immediately appreciated. In early 1941, a number of large *Type IX* boats were put into commission. Between February and April, Donitz dispatched seven of these to operate along the coast of Africa in the South Atlantic, an area beyond the range of the normal *Type VII* U-boats.

For the British, the shortage of air and surface escorts remained the crux of the problem. To match the increasing number of U-boats entering the contest during late 1941–42, British shipyards were straining to produce a large number of new anti-submarine vessels, but most of these would not be available until mid-1942. Thus, the "Destroyers for Bases" deal between Churchill and Roosevelt was a vital interim measure. By this agreement, signed in September 1940, fifty over-aged American destroyers were transferred to the Royal Navy in exchange for the granting to the United States of air and naval bases in Newfoundland, Bermuda and the West Indies. In March 1941, the United States strengthened her commitment to Great Britain with the passage of the first "Lend-Lease" legislation. Thereafter, American food, supplies and arms necessary to sustain the British were given on credit. This ended the previous "cash and carry" policy which Britain could no longer afford.

In an effort to help relieve the strain imposed by the shortage of British escort ships, in April 1941, the United States assumed responsibility to protect all shipping in the Western Hemisphere (west of 26 degrees West Longitude). In July 1941, at Britain's request, an American occupation force was landed at Reykjavik. By this time, Iceland, which the British had occupied in April, 1940, had been developed as a vital airbase and refuelling station for convoy escorts on the North Atlantic convoy routes. For the remainder of the war, Allied aircraft based on Iceland would greatly hinder U-boat operations against the North American convoys.

The *Greer* incident of September 1941, involving an exchange between a U-boat and an American destroyer, initiated a *de facto* war between the United States and Germany. In October *U.S.S. Kearny,* a destroyer assigned to convoy duty, was torpedoed by a U-boat during the battle of convoy *SC-48,* though not fatally. Shortly thereafter, another American destroyer, *Ruben James,* was sunk by a German torpedo with the loss of 115 lives. Thus, America had been at war for several months by the time of Pearl Harbor.

The Golden West: January-July 1942

The American decision to render every aid "short of war" to Britain in 1941 had helped ease the pressure enormously. Ironically, during the first six months in which the United States was a formal combatant, Britain's position deteriorated sharply due to America's mismanagement of her own merchant shipping.

Throughout the autumn of 1941, Donitz had unsuccessfully tried to persuade Hitler to allow his U-boats to operate against the concentrated shipping on the eastern seaboard of the United States. Hitler, fearful of encouraging America to enter the war against Germany, steadfastly resisted Donitz, despite the *de facto* war which already existed. Hitler instead opted to retain a third of the available U-boats in the Mediterranean. As in the case of Norway in 1940, this Mediterranean diversion was a serious blunder. Because of the small volume of Allied shipping, the Mediterranean U-boats accomplished very little in comparison to the U-boats working the North Atlantic convoy routes.

In January 1942, however, Donitz was given permission to begin operations in the western Atlantic. The initial German operation, involving only five boats working between the Gulf of St. Lawrence and Cape Hatteras, began in mid-January and was codenamed *Paukenschlag* (Drum Roll). In two weeks, the five boats, manned by "ace" German crews, sank at least 20 ships of approximately 150,000 gross tons. It was the beginning of a six month massacre. American merchant ships were unarmed and no arrangements had been made to begin convoying the heavy American coastal shipping traffic. Ships sailed fully lit at night and broadcasted information about their schedules, air search patrols, etc. on a frequency regularly monitored by the U-boats. It took five months to enforce a black-out along the American coastline during which time merchant traffic was brilliantly silhouetted each night, inviting submarine attacks. By day, the U-boats stayed submerged beneath the congested traffic lanes. At night they surfaced amidst this traffic, sinking ships as quickly as they could reload their torpedo tubes.

The U-boat massacre was as effective as the destruction of a half-dozen major American war plants by saboteurs. In a typical night's work, a U-boat might sink two 6,000-ton freighters and a 3,000-ton tanker. On average, this would mean the loss of 42 tanks, eight six-inch howitzers, eighty-eight 25 lb. guns, forty two-pound guns, twenty-four armored cars, fifty Bren carriers, 5,200 tons of ammunition, 600 rifles, 425 tons of tank equipment, 2,000 tons of stores, and 1,000 tons of gasoline.

Donitz quickly realized he had struck gold and immediately dispatched additional boats to the "golden west," as the Germans nicknamed these rich new hunting grounds. The campaign was waged for a full six months. The maximum German effort was made in May 1942, when Donitz had about 30 boats operating between Halifax and Trinidad. The operations in the Caribbean were made possible when the first U-tankers *(Type X)* and supply U-boats *(Type XIV)* became operational during the early part of 1942. U-tankers had no offensive armament, but each carried about 600 tons of reserve fuel which was used to refuel the medium-sized U-boats at sea. One U-tanker could keep a dozen *Type VII* s fully fueled for a month. The use of the U-tankers therefore increased the range of the smaller boats by a factor of two, and made it possible to keep 50% of the U-boats at sea in fighting condition at all times.

In late April 1942, the Americans, pressed by the British, finally began organizing coastal convoys, first along the northeast coast and gradually working south, down the Florida coast into the Gulf of Mexico and the Caribbean. By August 1942, an interlocking convoy system had been established encompassing all shipping between Cuba and Nova Scotia, and the toll of U-boat victims trailed off sharply. Nevetheless, the U-boats' six month spree in the western Atlantic netted some 360 merchant ships totalling about 2,250,000 gross tons for which only eight U-boats were sacrificed. It was the greatest shipping massacre of the war.

The Climax: August 1942–May 1943

The rich vein of targets along the American seaboard dried up rapidly as soon as an efficient convoy system was instituted there in the summer of 1942. On July 19, Donitz issued orders which shifted the focus of the tonnage war back to the North Atlantic convoy routes. The U-boat fleet now totalled more than 330, of which almost half were available for operations.

In May 1942, a German study had been prepared which had noted the steady decline in British imports over the previous two years. The report had concluded that if 700,000 tons of Allied shipping could be sunk during each month of 1942, the Allied shipbuilding capacity would be negated and Britain would be doomed.

With this in mind, Donitz had formulated a new system for increasing sinkings in the Atlantic. U-boats putting to sea from both France and Germany would gather into a pack of a dozen or so boats on the eastern side of the North Atlantic. The pack would then form a patrol line which would move steadily westward combing the principal Allied convoy routes currently in use. If a westbound convoy was contacted, the pack would pursue it across the whole breadth of the Atlantic. The victim would be attacked for six or seven consecutive nights. Then, after being refueled from a U-tanker in the vicinity of Bermuda, the pack would form a new patrol line off Newfoundland. The U-boats would then sweep back across the Atlantic from west to east hunting for an eastbound convoy. At the end of this sweep, those U-boats still well stocked with fuel and torpedoes would form a new pack while those which were short of fuel or were damaged returned to the Bay of

Biscay bases. On the basis of this general scheme, a three and one-half month cycle of convoy battles now began in which good results alternated with bad, according to the weather and the strength of the convoy escorts which the U-boats encountered.

Despite the increasing number of escorts now becoming available and the technological advances which were steadily improving the effectiveness of the Allied anti-submarine forces, the U-boats continued to triumph in the majority of the convoy battles conducted in the second half of 1942. During the last quarter of the year, U-boats sank an average of 650,000 tons of shipping each month. When this loss was compounded by additional sinkings by German aircraft, mines, and surface raiders, the 700,000 ton quota which was to finish off the British was consistently being met. What the Germans had not counted on, however, was the tremendous capacity of the American shipbuilding industry. During 1943, the Americans built and launched more than 20 million tons of shipping, more than double the German estimate of the total Allied construction capacity. Thus, even the inflated claims reported by the U-boats (which led the Germans to estimate Allied shipping losses for 1942 at close to twelve million tons, when the actual amount was about half as much) were inadequate to actually produce a German victory in the tonnage war.

But the Germans had more immediate problems. These were chiefly due to the technical progress being made by the Allies in anti-submarine warfare. During the autumn of 1942, the Allies had begun using airborne radar to hinder the passage of U-boats through the Bay of Biscay. Between October and the end of 1942, the Germans had gained temporary relief from this type of detection by devising a radar detector which warned when a U-boat was being monitored by enemy radar. In February 1943, however, the Allies introduced a new short-wave radar which the German device could not detect. The Germans were unable to develop any countermeasure to the Allied short-wave radar until late 1944, by which time the conflict in the Atlantic had been decided in the Allies' favor.

By the start of 1943, the massive Allied effort in the area of Operational Research in anti-submarine warfare had begun paying dividends. During the first quarter of 1943, short-wave radar equipped aircraft, carrier-based aircraft, and surface escorts equipped with both radar and high frequency direction finding equipment as well as improved anti-submarine weapons such as the "hedghog" depth charge mortar, made a dramatic and simultaneous debut on the North Atlantic convoy routes. Moreover, during the same four month period (February-May 1943), the Allies substantially increased the number of both air and surface escorts available to convoys on the North Atlantic. Between February and May, the number of very long range *Liberator* anti-submarine aircraft available for North Atlantic patrol and escort work climbed from ten to more than sixty. The Allies' naval resources were also strengthened despite the fact that American escort forces had to be withdrawn immediately before the decisive clash due to the United States' commitment to the Pacific War. By the start of 1943, 96% of the North Atlantic responsibilities were jointly shouldered by the Royal Navy and the Royal Canadian Navy while the American commitment comprised only two coastguard cutters and a few Iceland-based destroyers. Nevertheless, by increasing the average size of the convoys enough vessels were conserved to allow the number of escorts per convoy to be increased from six to nine vessels. More importantly, additional warships conserved in the same manner were formed into five British convoy support groups, later joined by one American support group. These support groups had a sudden and decisive effect on the Battle of the Atlantic. Each support group was comprised of between five and seven destroyers and frigates. Three of the support groups were bolstered by the addition of one escort carrier apiece. Generally, a support group would accompany a convoy through the "Atlantic gap" area which could not be reached by aircraft based either in Iceland, Greenland, Newfoundland or Northern Ireland. If the support group included an escort carrier, it virtually closed the "gap" entirely, depriving the U-boats of their favorite hunting grounds. Support groups with escort carriers were extremely effective because a convoy escorted by such a group virtually bristled with submarine location equipment and anti-submarine weaponry.

The numerically strengthened and technologically improved anti-submarine forces rapidly overwhelmed the U-boats between the beginning of March and the end of May 1943. March is perhaps the worst month, weatherwise, in the North Atlantic. For the first nine days of the month in 1943, westerly gales, snow and hail squalls tossed the ocean continuously. At sea on March 5, were approximately 50 U-boats in a number of packs. The culminating struggle began on March 7, when Convoy SC-121, straggling badly from the weather, fell prey to the wolfpacks. Between March 7-10, she lost six ships from which 199 merchant sailors perished in the icy sea. The next two convoys, *SC-122* and *HX-229* fared even worse, losing 22 ships of 146,000 tons between March 8-18. Donitz was particularly pleased with this battle as he was able to concentrate a record of 44 U-boats from packs *Sturmer, Dranger* and *Raubgraf* against the two convoys, which represented about 80% of all the boats in the North Atlantic. Although during the first three weeks of March the U-boats sank 85 ships, sixty-eight percent of which had been in convoys, for the loss of only one submarine, it proved to be their last major period of success.

Soon after the introduction of the support groups in March 1943, Allied merchant sinkings began to decline while the toll of U-boat sinkings slowly began to mount. In March the U-boats destroyed 105 Allied ships of 590,000 gross tons. The following month their effect was halved.

May brought ultimate disaster for the U-boats. Whereas the preceding month's tonnage score had been only average, the U-boat losses for April 1943 had remained average also. Fifteen U-boats had been sunk in April, representing about 9% of the operational fleet. But in May, Donitz lost 41 U-boats, more than 25% of his operational strength. For each submarine the Germans lost in May, only 4,500 tons of Allied shipping was destroyed. One year earlier, the ratio had been 60,000 tons per U-boat lost. The May figures were intolerable. On May 24, Donitz withdrew all but a token number of U-boats from the North Atlantic convoy routes. He had always fought to keep the U-boats in that theater. Their withdrawal was tantamount to an admission of defeat.

On May 31, Donitz reported to Hitler. He described the situation in detail, noting the Allies' apparent technological edge. He then described the desperate search for counter-measures which German scientists were conducting. The *Naxos* short-wave radar detector was being tested. The *Zaunkonig* accoustic homing torpedo for use against escort ships was ready to be put into service. The *LuT* torpedo, which was to weave back and forth across a convoy's line of advance, would be available by the autumn. There was the *schnorkel* breathing apparatus that could be fitted onto presently operating U-boats to relieve them of the necessity of surfacing to recharge batteries. Finally, there was, on the drawing board, two versions of a revolutionary new type of U-boat. The planned *Type XXI* and *Type XXIII* U-boats were to have an underwater speed of 17.5 and 12.5 knots respectively. This would allow them to operate as "true" submarines.

Hitler was much impressed with the details of these "wonder weapons". In any event, he told Donitz that the U-boat war must be continued, if not to defeat Britain, then merely to tie down the maximum amount of enemy forces for the longest possible time. Thus, the U-boat remained at sea for two years after it was decisively beaten, if only as a delaying weapon. By the war's end, 785 German U-boats had been sunk, while the German underwater fleet had destroyed more than fourteen million tons of Allied shipping. From beginning to end it had been an unequal contest. For almost three years, the U-boat had dominated the struggle while Britain's fate had hung in the balance. Then, in the space of a few months, the battle had altered permanently in Britain's favor.

The Americans played a small role in the U-boat war. Appreciating the work of the American anti-submarine industry in preventing Britain's collapse between 1940-42, the triumph over the U-boats, which secured the Atlantic in 1943 and paved the way for the liberation of Europe in 1944, was a triumph of British and Canadian naval forces which bore the brunt of the fighting from beginning to end.

The Convoy System

Simply defined, a convoy is one or more merchant ships sailing under the protection of one or more warships. The practice of escorting unarmed merchant ships by warships is of very ancient standing. The English convoy system was begun in the thirteenth century to protect wine cargoes in transit from France. In the Anglo-Dutch and French wars of the seventeenth and eighteenth centuries, the warring powers customarily convoyed their merchant ships. During the Napoleonic Wars convoy bcame virtually obligatory for British ships simply because British insurance companies refused to insure an independent ship unless she was exceptionally fast and well armed. Thus the convoy has traditionally been accepted as the best means of protecting urgent maritime trade. This is because the convoy concentrates friendly naval forces at the very point where enemy raiders are forced to strike.

Despite this obvious fact, shipowners and certain naval "experts" have traditionally opposed the convoy system; the former finding it too inconvenient; the latter believing it too defensively oriented. Misguided by this opposition, during the First World War the British government withheld the introduction of the convoy system for the first three years of the war. The result was disaster. More than 90% of the U-boats' victims in that war were ships sunk while sailing independently. When the British finally regained their senses and adopted the convoy system in June 1917 the volume of U-boat victims declined precipitously. Remembering the painful lesson of World War I, the British lost little time in introducing the convoy system at the outbreak of the Second World War. During the autumn of 1939 mercantile convoy routes were established which connected the British Isles with sources of raw materials in every corner of the world. Each of these routes was allocated an alphabetical code which usually had a "self evident" significance. For example, "OG" was used to designate "outward-Gibralter" bound convoys. The addition of the third letter "F" or "S" was used to signify fast and slow convoys. Fast convoys consisted entirely of ships which could maintain a speed of at least nine knots. Slow convoys only managed a speed of about seven and one-half knots.

From port to port a fast convoy averaged ten to fourteen days in transit. The same voyage by a slow convoy required thirteen to nineteen days. The most vital convoys followed routes across the Atlantic between the United Kingdom and North America. The first of the famous "HX" (Halifax, Nova Scotia) convoys, around whose passage the Battle of the Atlantic was largely to revolve, sailed on September 16, 1939. By 1942, either a fast or a slow convoy would depart from Nova Scotia for Great Britain every four or five days and a convoy bound for North America would depart at similar intervals. As the war progressed and America realized her reputation as "the arsenal of democracy", the importance of the North Atlantic convoy routes steadily increased. Across these routes came the food, weapons, and equipment which sustained Britain. Later in the war American forces which participated in the *Torch* invasion of North Africa were convoyed across the

The Principal Convoy Battles [1940-1943]

Date	*Convoy Designation[s]*	*Ships in Convoy inc.Escorts*	*U-Boats Participating*	*U-Boats Sunk*	*Ships Sunk*	*Tonnage Sunk [G.R.T.]*
10/1940	SC-71 HX-79	79	12	0	32	154,661
9/1941	SC-42	70	19	2	18	73,211
7/1942	PQ-17	40	11	0	16	102,296
11/1942	SC-107	42	18	3	15	82,817
12/1942	ONS-154	45	19	1	15	74,461
3/1943	SC-121/ HX-228	119	37	2	16	79,872
3/1943	SC-122/ HX-229	89	44	1	22	146,596

NOTES: This table gives the details involved in the most successful anti-convoy operations undertaken by the German U-boats. During the entire war these were the only seven battles in which the U-boats sank more than 50,000 G.R.T. All of the battles occurred on the North Atlantic Convoy Routes except the battle of PQ-17 which was intercepted by German air and surface units as well as U-boats on the North Russia Run in July, 1942. The German operation to intercept PQ-17 was codenamed "Rosselsprung" (Knight's Gambit). The German capital ships *Tirpitz*, *Admiral Scheer*, and *Admiral Hipper* were withdrawn before contacting the convoy so as not to expose them to attack by British carrier-borne aircraft. Nevertheless, PQ-17 was mauled by the combination onslaught of German aircraft and U-boats. Despite its strong escort of six destroyers, PQ-17 lost 23 out of 36 merchant ships. The high losses were predominantly caused by the fact that the convoy was ordered to disperse because of the threat posed by German surface units. As a result, two-thirds of the convoy's cargo was sunk.

North Atlantic. The North Atlantic convoy routes were also used to ship armaments which eventually reached the Russian allies by way of Murmansk. And the maintenance of the North Atlantic convoy routes was absolutely essential for the build-up which preceded the invasion of Normandy in 1944.

The typical North Atlantic convoy consisted of 45 to 60 merchant ships steaming in nine to twelve columns. Whenever possible the ships would be evenly divided among the columns to maintain a uniform formation. A nine column, forty-five ship convoy had a frontage of about four nautical miles and a depth of about one and one-half miles, occupying about six square miles of surface area. When straggling due to bad weather or enemy attacks, the same convoy might spread over sixty square miles or more. Because the use of heavy ships was confined to escorting troop convoys, a merchant convoy's escorts were generally destroyers and corvettes.

During the passage the escorts formed the convoy's screen. Each unit of the screen was assigned a segment of an imaginary circle encompassing the convoy. By day, if the weather was clear, the escort would patrol this segment using its submarine detection equipment. At night, or in thick weather, the escort kept to a definite station in close proximity to the outer column of the convoy. In the early period of limited numbers of short-ranged escorts, pursuing a U-boat for more than one hour was forbidden. Escort doctrine emphasized that the escort's duty was to remain with the convoy. Later, as more escorts became available their doctrine became more offensive. The escorts were able to patrol a larger circle surrounding the convoy and thus keep submarines beyond effective torpedo range. Escorts were also able to begin working in pairs and eventually they developed a particularly effective anti-submarine tactic.

One escort would pursue a U-boat advising a follow-up escort of the submarine's actions. The U-boat commander would switch to "silent running" to elude his pursuer. When the U-boat's hydrophones assured the submarine commander that the danger had passed, he would order a resumption of the boat's full power unaware that these engine noises were now being detected by the follow-up escort. A depth charge attack by the second escort usually crippled the U-boat. The first escort could now return to aid in the destruction of the trapped prey.

At sea, the internal discipline of the convoy was the responsibility of the convoy commodore. In convoys in which the majority of the ships were British the convoy commodore was usually a retired flag officer of the Royal Navy. In predominantly American convoys the commodore was usually a United States Naval Reserve officer who had considerable merchant marine experience. Tactical command of the convoy was the responsibility of the escort commander. Using the various detection devices of the escort group, the escort commander had the authority to divert the convoy anywhere within a forty mile belt to avoid suspected U-boat concentrations.

In the Spring of 1943, the North Atlantic merchant convoys were finally afforded adequate protection and between February and May the U-boat threat was overcome. First, the strength of the escort groups was increased from an average of five vessels to seven escorts per convoy. In addition, support groups and escort carrier groups began to be assigned to provide additional protection to North Atlantic convoys. The support groups varied in strength between five and seven vessels specifically outfitted and trained for anti-submarine operations. Two British escort carriers *Biter* and *Archer* and the U.S. Navy's *Bogue*, were introduced during this period with a decisive effect against the U-boat operations. In effect, the escort carriers finally closed the Atlantic "air gap", that area of the ocean beyond the range of long-ranged shore-based aircraft. The coupling of the escort carrier to the convoy finally ended the U-boats' reign of terror for the Atlantic convoys. By the end of May 1943, Donitz was forced to withdraw his wolves from the North Atlantic convoy routes. The Battle of the Atlantic had been decided.

Die Rudeltaktik: The Wolfpack

Because of the ever increasing Allied shipbuilding capacity, Donitz' objective throughout the war was the quickest possible sinking of the greatest possible enemy tonnage. From the beginning, Donitz recognized that unless the U-boats could overcome the defenses of Allied merchant convoys the tonnage war would inevitably be lost. His concept of *Die Rudeltaktik*—the submarine "wolf pack" attack—was developed specifically as the means by which the U-boats could penetrate the anti-submarine screens of convoys.

The key to the problem of successfully attacking a convoy lay in the difference in speed between the merchant ship and the submerged U-boat. The average speed of a convoy, even in good weather, was somewhere between seven and nine knots. In comparison, the U-boat, until the *Schnorkel* was introduced in 1944, had an average submerged speed of only two to three knots. If the U-boat increased her submerged speed, her batteries would quickly become exhausted and she would be forced to surface to recharge them. Thus, the pre-*Schnorkel* U-boat resembled a slightly mobile mine, with its anti-ship effectiveness limited to the range of its torpedoes and the visibility of its periscope.

To attack a single, fast moving ship, the U-boat needed to be in a position ahead of the target when it was first sighted. Even then a sudden zigzag by the target ship might thwart any possibility for a successful attack. Similarly, to attack a comparatively slow-moving convoy, the submerged U-boat required a good sighting position from somewhere ahead of the convoy. Moreover, except in fine weather and bright moonlight, the visibility afforded by periscope was so poor it prohibited attacking submerged at night. Furthermore, if a U-boat fired her torpedoes while submerged, she could not reload and overtake a convoy for a second attack while remaining submerged.

Taken together, these facts led Donitz to abandon operations by single submerged boats and to adopt tactics in which groups of boats operated on the surface at relatively high speed, diving only when forced to do so. The principal advantage of these tactics lay in the fact that the U-boat's surface speed not only exceeded that of the merchant ship, but frequently topped that of the convoy escort vessels. Thus, the U-boat could operate in a "hit and run" manner, launching an attack and then fleeing on the surface before the surface escorts of the convoy could get close enough to damage the submarine with shellfire.

The second inescapable problem of defeating the convoy system was the problem of finding the convoys themselves. In the vast areas of the Atlantic, even the most unwieldy convoy is only a speck. Fortunately, Donitz was aided on this front by the excellent work of his operational intelligence staff. Although from time to time, whenever British naval codes were changed, the U-boat service was temporarily deprived of such information, for most of the first four years of the war, German cryptographers were supplying Donitz with specific information concerning departure and arrival schedules for Atlantic convoys, information on the escort strength of various convoys, rendezvous points for convoys and approximate courses of independently routed ships, and weather reports from all ocean areas. This information, of course, was invaluable in locating targets for U-boat concentrations.

Despite the advantage provided by this type of detailed intelligence, the number of "eyes" which could be trained along a certain convoy's projected course was crucial in the struggle to actually contact the target. As the U-boats were not equipped with radar, Donitz solved the problem by deploying a number of boats into pack formations which spread out along a line perpendicular to the convoy's course and searched in an organized cooperative fashion. The U-boats were sent out in groups, generally of six to nine boats, but sometimes as many as 20. Each pack deployed in a concave patrol line, with an interval of about ten miles between each boat. As the patrol line combed the Atlantic in a generally easterly or westerly direction, the individual boats would maintain radio silence, with the pack as a whole being directed by radio from Donitz' command post at Lorient.

When an individual submarine sighted a convoy it would radio its course and position to Donitz who would then radio orders, homing every member of the pack in on the projected course of the convoy. The U-boat which originally established contact would continue shadowing the convoy at the maximum distance from which it could observe the convoy's smoke or masts. By doing so, it could keep Donitz advised of any change in the convoy's course and this information would be relayed to the gathering pack members.

When a "quorum" of at least three U-boats was in contact with the convoy, the attack could begin. At this point Donitz would turn over control of the situation to the individual U-boat commanders. The pack, however, had little opportunity to cooperate tactically as the enemy's HF/DF—High Frequency Direction Finder, or "Huff-Duff"—equipment prohibited communications between the individual boats. Nonetheless, the multi-faceted attack would confuse and disrupt the escorts and improve each boat's chance of obtaining a good position from which to launch an attack. Under cover of darkness the U-boats would converge on the convoy on the surface to lessen the effectiveness of the enemy's asdic. The compact silhouette of the U-boat was a source of natural protection which was not shared by merchantmen. A U-boat which gained a favorable position would fire a "fan" or salvo of three or four torpedoes which diverged along several paths, increasing the chances of a hit. As a convoy, except when straggling, formed a compact target, a salvo might allow several hits on different ships in successive columns within the convoy. After its attack, the U-boat generally submerged to escape counterattack. Maintaining a course parallel to the convoy, the U-boat later resurfaced and maneuvered into position for a fresh attack. Of course, any ship which dropped out of the convoy and became a "straggler" was easily finished off in the absence of any guarding warship.

Unless the convoy managed to elude the pack by a radical change of course, the merchantmen might be hounded by the wolfpack for several successive nights. The action then might be broken off by Donitz after the majority of the boats had exhausted their torpedoes. Alternately, the convoy might escape its shadowers due to the interference of bad weather, not infrequent in the often stormy Atlantic. In any event, the attack was usually lifed when the convoy reached a point where continuous air cover could be provided.

Of course, the primary weakness of the wolfpack concept was the necessary radio communications between the shadowing U-boat and Donitz' headquarters in France. While these communications allowed the growing U-boat fleet to remain under a centralized control, the introduction of HF/DF equipment in Allied escort vessels rapidly undercut this advantage. As more HF/DF equipped escorts joined the convoys, the shadowing U-boat keeping Donitz informed could be quickly located and either forced to submerge or be destroyed. The Germans remained ignorant of this Allied capability and continually attributed U-boats lost in this manner to allied radar detection. Thus the genius of Donitz' tactics fell victim to Allied technological superiority.

It is worth noting, however, that Donitz had formulated *Die Rudeltaktik* expecting to deploy 300 U-boats against the convoys from the very beginning of the war. The failure of the U-boat offensive was a failure in numbers, not in tactics.

SUBSUNK: How the U-Boats were destroyed

Date	*a/c land*	*a/c ship*	*a/c & ship*	*bomb -ing*	*a/c mines*	*ship mines*	*subs*	*ships*	*other*	*total*
1939	0	0	0	0	0	3	1	5	0	9
1940	1	1	2	0	0	2	2	11	4	23
1941	3	0	2	0	0	0	1	24	5	35
1942	35.5	1	6	0	3	0	2	32.5	6	86
1-6/1943	45	2	8	0	1	0	2	29	8	95
7-12/1943	71	22	5	2	0	0	2	30	9	141
1-6/1944	22	10	8	5	3	0	2	37	11	98
7-12/1944	29.5	6.5	10	19	5	1	5	31	32	139
1-5/1945	39	1	2	36	4	3	3	46	17	151
Total:	*246*	*43.5*	*43*	*62*	*16*	*9*	*20*	*245.5*	*92*	*777*

Notes: a/c land: U-boats sunk by land based aircraft. *a/c ship:* those sunk by ship-based aircraft. *a/c & ship:* sunk by aircraft and ships cooperating. *Bombing:* those destroyed in dockyards and U-boat pens. *a/c mines:* those destroyed by mines dropped from aircraft. *ship mines:* those destroyed by mines laid by ships. *subs:* those sunk by Allied submarines. *ships:* those sunk by surface ships. *other:* includes those lost in unknown, accidental, scuttling, and Russian action.

514 of the U-boats were sunk by British Empire forces, 166 by U.S. forces, 7 by Russian forces, and 12 shared between the British and the Americans. Only about 75 operational boats were surrendered at the end of the war, although over 200 were scuttled, and several hundred more captured in various stages of completion.

Interesting trends can be seen from the data. The large "peak" in the land a/c category in late 1943 represents the Biscay offensive. Also shown is the ineffectiveness of aircraft in the first years of the war. Bombing only became effective in 1945, despite the great energies expended on it earlier. By 1942, the escort ships had hit their stride and their effectiveness remained relatively constant thereafter.

● ● ●

The Fall of France initiated a unique period in the course of the Second World War. For months afterwards, though the Luftwaffe contended with the RAF for mastery of the skies, and though the Kriegsmarine vied with the Royal Navy for command of the seas, nowhere were British and German troops in combat. Indeed, nearly four years would pass before large scale ground operations would be resumed in Northwestern Europe. Meanwhile, the focus of events shifted to the Mediterranean, the lifeline of the British Empire and Mussolini's *Mare Nostrum*.

PanzerArmee Afrika and the War in the Desert, June 1940–December 1942

By Albert A. Nofi

On 10 June 1940 the Second World War erupted into the Mediterranean as Benito Mussolini brought a reluctant Italy into the struggle on the side of Adolf Hitler. For five years the Middle Sea and the adjacent coasts would know the horrors of war as campaign followed campaign with brutal regularity, and as men died in their tens of thousands. But one campaign, at once the earliest and the smallest, though by far the longest, was unique—the struggle for the desert wastes of Libya and Egypt on the road to Suez and the east. This conflict, the last in history to which the term "chivalrous" may be applied, was characterized by brilliant strokes, tenacious fighting, and honorable comportment marred only by the very nature of war itself. And above it all stands the character and talents of one man, Erwin Rommel, leader of the *Afrika Korps.*

First Round: June 1940–February 1941

In spite of the fact that they had over 225,000 men in Libya, in June of 1940 the Italians were ill-prepared for war. Many of the units in the command of Marshal Rodolfo Graziani were under strength and short of equipment. Others had not yet completed their training. In view of this, the Italians undertook no offensive operations for the first three months of the war. This was fortunate for the British, under Gen Sir Archibald Wavell, had but 60,000 troops to cover the entire Middle East. Nor were the British units much better off in terms of training and equipment, since most first line materiel which had not been lost in France was being held in Britain pending the expected German invasion. But unlike the Italians, the British did not remain idle.

On the very first night of the war the Western Desert Force, an odd assortment of infantry and armored units under MG Sir Richard O'Connor, commenced raiding operations against isolated Italian frontier outposts. Meanwhile, Wavell scraped together what troops he could to support O'Connor. And Graziani collected troops and equipment in anticipation of a grand offensive into Egypt. By the end of August he was still not ready, but Mussoini finally managed to prod him into action. In early September the Italian *Tenth Army*, composed of about seven divisions and supported by a considerable air force and swarms of nearly useless light tanks, marched into Egypt. They halted after advancing less than sixty miles. Graziani's explanation was that he had to pause to permit his supplies to catch up. This was reasonable, since most Italian formations had little motor transport, and the movement of supplies was always difficult. So the *Tenth Army* established a series of fortified camps in an arc stretching 40 miles inland from Sidi Barrani, with additional camps some 20 miles in the rear. The assumption was that as soon as supplies would move up the troops would resume the offensive. But September became October and then November and Graziani showed no signs of activity. Meanwhile, the British continued their harrassing raids. If Graziani intended to resume the offensive he never got the chance. Later in November 1940 Wavell gave O'Connor the go-ahead to undertake a "five day raid" designed to disrupt Italian communications and preparations for a further advance.

O'Connor was given 7th Armored Division, 4th Indian Division, and an *ad hoc* infantry brigade called Selby Force. The Italians outnumbered O'Connor's forces by about four to one, but he expected to take advantage of surprise and his mobility to gain local superiority and isolate and destroy individual Italian formations before reinforcements could move up. He was aided by the fact that there was a gap of nearly 20 miles between two groups of camps in the Italian position. After establishing forward supply dumps near the area of operations, O'Connor brought his troops up in a series of well conducted night marches, using his light armored forces aggressively so as to prevent Italian reconnaissance from detecting his presence. Early on the morning of 9 December the Western Desert Force fired the opening rounds of the most spectacular offensive the desert was ever to witness.

Thrusting through the gap in the Italian front and attacking from behind, O'Connor managed to destroy three Italian fortified camps in a little over 24 hours, using his infantry in close assaults supported by a regiment of heavy tanks, while 7th Armored Division screened against possible Italian counterattacks. Although many Italian units resisted stoutly, the suddenness and audacity of O'Connor's movements created an irresistible momentum. In three days O'Connor captured nearly 40,000 men and mountains of supplies and equipment. He had never accepted the idea of a "five day raid" and now proposed to press on, with the intention of clearing the Italians out of Cyrenaica. Although Wavell soon deprived him of 4th Indian Division for an operation in Italian East Africa, O'Connor received permission to take Bardia and Tobruk and was given the weak but willing 6th Australian Division as a replacement.

Marshal Graziani, not always an idiot, pointed out to Mussolini that the Italian Army had sufficient strength to hold Tobruk, but not both Tobruk and Bardia. Mussolini overruled him and 40,000 men were ordered to hold Bardia at all costs. O'Connor invested the town on 16 December and a fierce battle raged. On 3 January 1941, the Australians finally entered the fortress. By 5 January the battle was over and O'Connor pressed on to Tobruk. Defended by an inadequate and demoralized garrison, Tobruk managed to hold out for two weeks. In eight weeks O'Connor had taken over 80,000 prisoners, destroyed seven divisions, and cleared the Italians out of Egypt and eastern Cyrenaica. Now, his objective was western Cyrenaica and perhaps Tripoli itself.

In an audacious move, O'Connor ordered 6th Australian Division to push along the coast while 7th Armored Division crossed the desert south of the Jebel

Achdar. Both formations encountered stiff resistance from smaller Italian formations, but there was no large scale, organized opposition. On 5 February the leading elements of 7th Armored Division reached the coast road near Beda Fomm, scant hours before the retreating Italians. The Battle of Beda Fomm (5–7 February) followed.

Beda Fomm was fought between small units on both sides. The British blocking force never amounted to more than a small brigade. The Italians, straggling in over a narrow road, disorganized and confused, never managed to launch a coordinated attack. If they had, it probably would have been successful. As it was, several times the piecemeal and uncoordinated efforts of some Italian formations almost broke the blockade and some small groups actually did succeed in escaping. But in the end the Italians had no fight left. Fully 25,000 men were taken, as well as a considerable amount of equipment. The offensive had succeeded beyond anyone's wildest expectations. In 61 days the Western Desert Force, which never comprised much more than two divisions, had advanced over 400 miles, destroyed ten divisions plus a great many independent units, taken 130,000 prisoners and mountains of supplies and equipment. In the process, O'Connor had greatly buoyed British spirits, already rising after the defeat of the Luftwaffe in the Battle of Britain.

How had O'Connor managed it? In precisely the way he anticipated doing it. He used his superior mobility to gain local superiority against the Italians and, with the possible exception of the fighting at Bardia, the British were superior in numbers in every engagement. Of course, their materiel superiority almost goes without saying. The Italians, with masses of leg infantry, were unable to cope with O'Connor's fast moving units. The more successful he was, the more demoralized the Italians became, making it still easier. Right to the end there was hard fighting, but O'Connor had an irresistible advantage over the Italians. He knew what he was doing and how he was going to do it. Not for nearly a year would the British have a general with the same sort of determination. The Italians were to get one very shortly, plus the means to accomplish his goals.

With the clearing of Cyrenaica, O'Connor pressed for an advance on Tripoli. There were barely five Italian divisions in Tripolitania and he felt confident that he could handle them easily. With Tripoli in British hands the way would be open to resume control of the Mediterranean, a commodity now in dispute with the Italian Navy. In addition, it would permit the Royal Air Force to bring the war to Italy. In retrospect O'Connor's assessment of the situation was probably correct, but military considerations are not the primary concern in warfare. The Clausewitzian dictum, "War is an extension of politics," was understood by Churchill. In October of 1940 Italy had invaded Greece. Although the Greeks put up a stubborn resistance and had even driven the Italians back, they called for assistance. Churchill realized that it had to be furnished. And O'Connor's Western Desert Force was the only source of combat ready troops. One new Australian infantry division and one new and understrength armored division would garrison Cyrenaica, while O'Connor's Australians would be sent to Greece with a contingent of New Zealanders and his armored division returned to Egypt for rest and refit. Information had reached Wavell's headquarters that a German contingent had arrived in Tripoli. It was expected that the Germans would not be able to launch an offensive until summer, and by that time the British would be ready. But, though in an orthodox sense, the German units in Tripolitania were not prepared for an offensive in the early spring of 1941, they had a highly unorthodox commander. And *General der infanterie* Erwin Rommel planned to go over to the attack as soon as possible.

Rommel, an experienced armored commander, had reached Africa as the result of a deal made between Hitler and Mussolini half-a-year earlier. In August of 1940 Hitler had agreed to eventually support the Italian offensive against Egypt with one or two mobile divisions. Of course, by February of 1941 it was no longer a question of supporting an offensive but of preventing the total defeat of the Italians in Africa. A considerable Luftwaffe contingent was sent to Sicily and Tripolitania, and a newly organized unit followed, with Rommel designated as commander. This was the *Deutsches Afrika Korps.*

Rommel's First Offensive: March–October 1941

Rommel's orders were fairly clear. He was supposed to concern himself primarily with the defense of Tripolitania and to lay the foundations for future operations. No one expected him to undertake any serious offensive moves, particularly since he had only one unit which could be called "reliable," the *5th Light Africa Division.* The rest of his forces were comprised of the Italian *Ariete Armored Division* and four low order Italian infantry divisions. No one had specifically ordered Rommel *not* to undertake any offensive moves either; the situation in Cyrenaica appealed to him. The British command, concerned with operations in Greece and Italian East Africa, had two divisions in Cyrenaica, both "green" and incomplete. The 2nd Armored Division, less one brigade, was about El Agheila, while the 9th Australian Division was in the vicinity of Benghazi. A motorized Indian infantry brigade completed the Allied forces in the province. Rommel saw his opportunity and began to plan for a major offensive, while conducting local tactical operations designed to improve his position. Technically, these were reconnaissances in force. But on 31 March Rommel's reconnaissance in force turned into a full blown offensive.

Coming on cautiously at first, Rommel soon discovered that Allied resistance crumbled easily and was soon pushing his available troops to the limit. While *5th Light* and *Ariete* formed two combined columns which passed eastwards south of the Jebel Achdar, the Italian *Brescia Infantry Division* pushed along the coast, shepherding the remnants of 2nd Armored Division and several Australian formations before it. On 6 April the Axis troops came up with a prize worth many brigades, when they captured the staff and commander of the British Cyrenaica Command and Gen O'Connor as well. Thus, to the confusion engendered by the suddenness and audacity of the Axis attack was added the loss of command-control. Although determined, Allied resistance in Cyrenaica was fragmentary and lacking overall direction. By 9 April it was virtually over, with Axis forces less than 100 miles west of Tobruk, attempting to cope with a shortage of supplies by using British materiel. On that date Wavell made a momentous decision.

Realizing that with his relative paucity of manpower he would be unable to meet Rommel in open battle, Wavell decided to fall back into Egypt after heavily garrisoning Tobruk. If the fortress could be held, valuable time would be gained for future operations, and even if the fortress fell, it might inflict such damage upon the Axis divisions as to bring them to an effective halt anyway. To insure that Tobruk remained in his hands he threw a division of Australians into it. Then he waited. He did not have to wait long.

On 11 April, Rommel invested the fortress and made his first assault. Poorly coordinated, without air support and very tired, the attackers faltered. Rommel decided to hold off for a few days to await the arrival of additional forces. Meanwhile, small Italian and German formations pressed on to the Egyptian frontier to secure the Axis flank from counterattack.

Now began the siege of Tobruk. From time to time the Axis would launch a determined attempt to storm the fortress. Each time they would be beaten off, with occasional limited gains being wiped out by spirited counterattacks. The sea at their backs, the defenders could always count on the Royal Navy to bring up reinforcements and supplies and equipment, and to evacuate the wounded. Thus, a proper siege never developed. Something resembling World War I did, with rows of trenches, harrassing bombardments, and trench raids, and an occasional bloody assault which led nowhere. And Tobruk *was* held. But if the situation around Tobruk brought to mind 1917, off to the east a different type of war occasionally erupted.

While some Axis forces had invested Tobruk in early April, other units had pressed eastwards towards the Egyptian frontier, eventually to form a sort of defensive line inland from Sollum and Halfaya Passes, with the fortress of Bardia in their rear. Initially the Axis "front" was merely a series of unconnected strongpoints, principally those at Halfaya and Sollum. Gradually, however, the position was extended and made more or less continuous, aided by very favorable terrain. Of course, as with all positions in the desert the southern flank hung in the air, there being nothing to rest it on. Only one line in the desert had good flank security on both ends, the Alamein line. Rommel's basic battle plan for any Allied offensive coming out of Egypt was fairly simple. He figured that Italian infantry, with some German support, would hold the defensive line, while German and Italian mobile troops would fight a battle of movement in the rear, should the enemy try to turn his flank. Should the opportunity present itself, the mobile forces would attempt a stroke at the enemy's lines of communication. The Allies launched two offensives against the Sollum-Halfaya line. Both times Rommel made use of his basic battle plan.

In mid-May 1941, under pressure to do something to compensate for the recent loss of Greece, the British had run a convoy through the Mediterranean. This brought 238 tanks of various types to the Western Desert Force. It was upon these vehicles that Wavell pinned his hopes for an early counteroffensive. His basic plan was to advance on a 20 mile front between Sollum and Sidi Omar, a small place a few miles behind and south of the main Axis lines. The 4th Indian Division, newly returned from victories in Italian East Africa, was to advance on the right, while 7th Armored Division was to attempt a turning movement around the Axis southern flank to prevent reinforcements from coming up. Unfortunately, one brigade of heavy infantry tanks was earmarked to advance with the infantry division. This divided Wavell's available tank force and necessitated extreme caution in the initial phases of the operation, so that the two elements of the armored division did

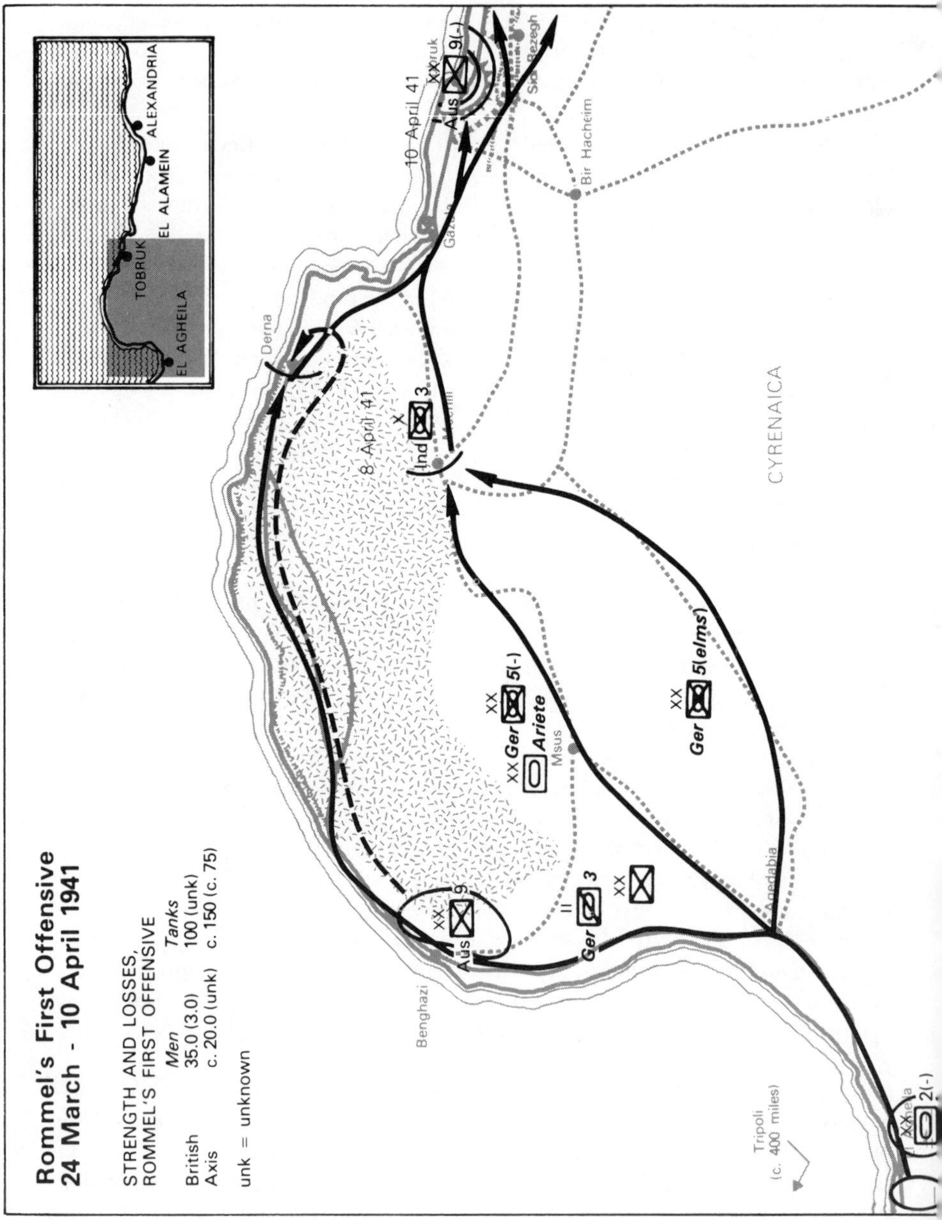

not become too greatly separated during the attack on the defenses, for Wavell intended that they join together again after the Sollum position had been overrun. He wanted a tank battle to develop and needed a full tank division. The operation, code-named *Battleax,* was scheduled to begin on 15 June. But Allied security was clumsy and Rommel got wind that something was afoot due to an unusual amount of radio traffic. Accordingly, he began moving his newly arrived *15th Panzer Di-*

vision up into close support of the Italo-German infantry holding the front. Then he alerted *5th Light Division* for possible movement on short notice to the Sollum line, while strengthening his defenses against a possible sortie from Tobruk. And he waited.

The British attack began well. Two Indian infantry brigades attacked the front of the Halfaya position while a British brigade, supported by the brigade of heavy tanks, turned the flank of the Sollum line and succeeded in capturing Capuzzo. Meanwhile 7th Armored Division pushed westwards to take up defensive positions in order to cover the infantry. At this point, the British plans began to go wrong. The flanking tank-infantry force failed to take Sollum, stopped by a determined defense and the use of some of Rommel's handful of 88mm anti-aircraft guns in an anti-tank role, the first time this valuable expedient had been used in Africa. In addition, the Indian infantry failed to make any headway at Halfaya. Meanwhile, Rommel collected his mobile formations and prepared for a counterstroke. He delivered it on 16 June.

While *5th Light Division* probed around the southern flank of 7th Armored Division, *15th Panzer Division's* lead elements fell on the British tank infantry forces near Sollum. Both of these operations developed into full scale attacks by the next day. The 7th Armored Division, threatened with total annihilation, retreated a few miles eastwards during the night, partially exposing 4th Indian Division. The division commander thereupon fell back in turn on his own authority. The net result was that by 18 June both sides were substantially back to where they started from. The only difference was that a final Indian infantry assault had cleared Halfaya Pass.

The roots of the British defeat in *Battleax* are not difficult to find. The entire operation was poorly conceived, with the burden of the fighting given over to the infantry and with the armor divided. Success would have depended on a quick seizure of the Halfaya-Sollum area and a swift junction of the infantry and armored elements. As things turned out, 7th Armored Division never operated as an intact formation. In addition, the British were handicapped by the fact that most of their higher ranking officers were infantry-minded and failed to understand the capabilities of tanks. This led to mishandling of armored formations. For example, the heavy tank brigade was ordered to leaguer *forward* of an infantry brigade rather than in the more customary place, behind the infantry. The result was that the brigade, without any infantry to cover it, was cut to pieces. Defeat had resulted not from a lack of will or courage, but from a failure to understand the new ways in warfare. But Churchill—an old cavalryman—failed to understand this and pinned the blame on Wavell, who, after all, had only been acting under instructions. In Wavell's place came Gen Sir Claude Auchinleck.

"The Auk's" first concern upon arriving in Egypt was to reorganize the desert army. This proceeded rapidly, aided by the fortuitous arrival of 300 cruiser and heavy infantry tanks, as well as considerable reinforcements and mountains of other supplies. Churchill pressed for an immediate resumption of the offensive. Auchinleck refused, demanding more time to properly organize and train his men. To replace Auchinleck so soon after he had been appointed was apt to raise embarrassing questions about Churchill himself, so the latter had no choice but to acquiesce.

Both sides began to prepare for a further battle by building up their forces, accumulating supplies and strengthening their positions. For the Axis this meant convincing Hitler and Mussolini of the need for certain types of equipment, then trying to get them across the Mediterranean in the face of the Royal Navy, and carrying the materiel forward from Tripoli or Benghazi over the *Via Balbia,* the coast road. Much equipment requested was never forwarded. Although the Italian Navy made strenuous efforts to protect shipping, much equipment loaded never reached ports in Africa. And finally, much of the equipment which did reach Africa was consumed *en route* due to the inefficiency of the Italo-German supply apparatus. Rommel, a brilliant tactician and fine strategician, was not a logistician by any stretch of the imagination. It was a serious flaw in his education, which led to constant disputes with hard working Italian and German staffs. Meanwhile, supplies were slow in coming and often inadequate to the need.

Auchinleck's problems were of a different sort. Although he suffered from some material shortages, his principal concerns were strategic. He was the senior British commander for the entire Middle Eastern Theater. In addition to operations in the desert he was also responsible for operations in East Africa, where some Italian units were still holding out. He also had to concern himself with events in Vichyite Syria, an increasigly restive Iraq, and a threatened Caucasia, for Auckinleck had assumed command in Cairo barely a week after Hitler's invasion of Russia and the news from Russia was not good. British staffs were haunted by the possibility of a German thrust over the Caucasus. Auchinleck was not interested in starting something in the desert unless he could be certain of victory. When the time came, Auchinleck intended to win, so a little waiting wouldn't hurt. He waited almost five months.

The Winter Campaign: November 1941–June 1942

With the end of *Battleax* the war in North Africa entered a quiet phase as both sides strove to build up their strength. Auchinleck's preparations soon began to outstrip Rommel's. As the commander of the only theater in which British ground forces were actively engaged against the enemy, Auchinleck had a distinct advantage when it came down to demanding men and material. Rommel's forces were engaged in what the Axis High Command considered to be a side show to the events unfolding in Russia, which Hitler had invaded in June of 1941. By November of 1941 Auchinleck felt that preparations would be sufficiently advanced as to permit the Eighth Army—the rebaptized Western Desert Force—to undertake an offensive. But not everything had gone Auchinleck's way. As commander of Eighth Army he had been forced to accept General Sir Alan Cunningham, fresh from a successful colonial campaign against the Italians in East Africa. Although likeable, fairly intelligent and sincere, Cunnigham had two serious handicaps: he knew virtually nothing about mechanized warfare and he had never commanded more than four brigades together in his life. Churchill charged Cunningham with the conduct of an operation involving six full divisions and six independent brigades, with nearly 500 tanks.

Auchinleck's decision to launch an offensive in November was not based purely on the condition of the Eighth Army. He was under considerable pressure from Churchill to do something impressive. In addition, it was becoming increasingly obvious that Rommel intended to make a major assault on Tobruk very shortly. Indeed, preparations for the attack had reached the point where the assault formations were beginning to move into their assembly areas.

Despite the difficulties of squeezing supplies from a pair of megalomaniac dictators, Rommel had still managed to accumulate enough fuel, equipment, and ammunition to permit him to contemplate offensive operations once more. The blow at Tobruk, to be undertaken by Italian infantry and German armor, was to be the tocsin call for a renewed general offensive in the desert. Actually, he felt strong enough to try conclusions with the Eighth Army itself without first settling the matter of Tobruk, but caution prevailed. As long as a hostile garrison existed in Tobruk the Axis command could never enjoy secure communications.

Cunningham's plan for the coming offensive, called "Crusader," was well conceived, a tribute to the efficiency of his staff and his own intelligence, plus the guidance given by Auchinleck. The bulk of his armor was grouped into XXX Corps, while his infantry and some armor went into XIII Corps. The basic idea was for the infantry corps to take on the Sollum-Halfaya defenses frontally, while the armor swept around to the south. Somewhere behind the Sollum line Cunningham expected a tank battle to develop and was confident of victory. During this action resistance on the Sollum line would be overwhelmed and the infantry corps would come up to support the armor. Meanwhile, the Tobruk garrison would prepare to make a sortie in support of the attacking forces.

The British armored brigades, three in number, jumped off at dawn on 18 November, supported by a considerable contingent of infantry. Bold conduct soon produced results and the brigades made notable gains, but gradually lost contact with each other. Meanwhile, Rommel threw in both of his German armored divisions and a series of sharp, but usually short, tank actions resulted. The British came out of these very well, suffering surprisingly small losses. But Rommel's assessment of the situation was that he had severely damaged the various British tank brigades. He therefore decided to bring 7th Armored Brigade to battle near Sidi Rezegh with the entire force of both his armored divisions. There, instead of a short, sharp fight, he found the entire weight of British armor confronting him. From 21 November to 24 November an incredibly confusing battle ranged southeast of Tobruk, in which small combat teams from both armies fought it out, often on two fronts. Meanwhile, the Tobruk garrison became active and began to push out of its encirclement with the intention of relieving the siege and aiding the main action. Although the British were apparently superior in numbers to the Germans, the action was something of an even match inasmuch as the Germans were the technical superiors of the British in the handling of armor in a mobile battle. Gradually, this technical superiority began to tell, and when additional German, and some Italian, armor joined the fight, the British numerical superiority was lost. British tank losses began to become serious and Cunningham even proposed breaking off the offensive and retreating to Egypt. But XIII Corps had made considerable gains on the Sollum-Halfaya front and was even advancing behind some of Rommel's armored formations, threatening their communications, while the Tobruk garrison was being very annoying in his rear. At this point he made a serious error. Rather than attempt to bring the battle to a successful conclusion where he was, Rommel decided to launch a sweeping blow against the rear area of the Eighth Army. He planned to raid into Egypt. The idea was for his armored divisions to hook in behind the XIII Corps and attack it from the rear while the Italian *XX Mobile Corps* formed a screen to the west in order to block a possible British retreat in that direction. But the command and communications structure of the Axis forces were not up to the task, particularly after three days of confused mobile fighting. Several formations, both German and Italian, failed to receive their orders. Others were just unable to undertake the movements prescribed. The attack got underway on 24 November with minimal forces. By 27 November it was over, having caused minimal injury to the Eighth Army. Indeed, the absence of so much Axis force on this adventure permitted British formations south of Tobruk to make such good progress that a junction with the Tobruk garrison was made on 27 November. Beyond that, the British had even managed to give their armored brigades a little rest, sending one home to Egypt and distibuting its tanks to the other two. Thus, Rommel's depleted panzer divisions were faced with a pair of fairly fit and reasonably rested formations.

Although Rommel managed to recover much of the ground lost during his "raid" he did so at the price of further depleting his armor, while the British even managed to receive a few shipments of new equipment.

On 4 December Rommel decided to give up the fight and ordered a withdrawal to the Gazala line, which had been put in readiness for just such an eventuality. This was accomplished by 12 December. In retreating he was forced to abandon considerable amounts of equipment and a full infantry division, the *Savona,* which had been trapped in Bardia. But in general the retreat went off well. The British, surprised that Rommel should fall back so suddenly, had some difficulty in following up in strength. Also, they were in the midst of a command change. Right in the middle of the most serious portion of the fighting around Sidi Rezegh, Cunningham had shown serious signs of battle fatigue. He was replaced shortly after by MG Neil M. Ritchie, one of Auchinleck's staff officers.

Although Rommel was willing to attempt a stand at Gazala, he felt that a retreat to the old El Agheila position might eventually be necessary. As a result, he made preparations for just such an eventuality and even began sending some Italian formations back in anticipation of just such a move. This was fortunate for the Axis. On 15 December a reinforced XIII Corps came up against the position with the intention of pinning it in front and launching a long flanking movement into its rear. Rommel immediately took steps to save what forces he still had and ordered a general withdrawal to El Agheila. Within two weeks the Axis forces were back where they had started in March. Rommel seemed beaten and neither Auchinleck nor Ritchie expected anything from him for some time to come. But Rommel was unpredictable, and the exigencies of war helped him turn the tables once again.

In early December 1941 the Japanese Empire had gone to war against the United States, the British Empire and the Commonwealth. In Russia, the Germans were still threatening the Caucasus, although the Red Army seemed to have halted them temporarily. And in the Mediterranean the balance of sea power had shifted in favor of the Axis after Italian frogmen sank two British battleships in Alexandria harbor on 19 December. The net result of these events was to divert vitally needed supplies, equipment, and reinforcements from the British forces in Egypt and

Libya, while facilitating the shipment of supplies and equipment to the Axis troops in Libya. The first relatively unscathed convoy to reach Libya in many months arrived on 5 January 1942. By 18 January Rommel was ordering a new offensive by the *PanzerArmee Afrika.* The audacity of this operation is exceeded only by O'Connor's 1940 operations and Rommel's own operations in the Summer of 1942.

Rommel had barely 160 tanks with him, half of which were unreliable Italian vehicles. His ten divisions amounted to no more than three full strength units in terms of combat power. He also had marginal control of the air. British forces in Cyrenaica were actually superior to his in numbers. But, as in March of 1941, they were scattered in penny packets as if on occupation duty during peace-time. Thus, on the El Agheila front there was but one brigade. Rommel, therefore, did an "O'Connor," making up for an inferiority in numbers by using momentum and concentrating sufficient strength where needed, rather than relying on overall superiority. It worked.

The *PanzerArmee* jumped off on 21 January in almost a perfect replay of the operations of the previous March. In the highly mobile action which followed, many British units simply disintegrated. Both sides suffered considerable losses, not that either had very much to lose. Exhaustion, coupled with lack of fuel and supplies, brought both armies to a halt on Rommel's old Gazala line. The *PanzerArmee Afrika* and Eighth Army both settled down to an energetic bout of rebuilding.

Rommel's Second Offensive: June–July 1942

For four months the British Eighth Army and the Axis *PanzerArmee Afrika* glared at each other across the Gazala line, while each made frantic preparations for a renewal of the battle at some indeterminate future date. Both were under considerable pressure to resume the fighting at the earliest possible moment, but both Rommel and Auchinleck were able to resist these pressures. Neither intended to resume the offensive with less than an optimum supply situation. Of course, Rommel was under considerably less pressure than Auchinleck. Having just successfully completed a victorious campaign, Rommel's credit was high in Rome and Berlin. His dictator superiors were willing to listen to his opinions respectfully. Auchinleck's principal problem was Churchill, who believed himself to be something of a military genius. Fortunately, Auchinleck was aided by all of the brass of the British high command who felt any premature offensive was apt to end in disaster.

Meanwhile, the supply situation for both sides improved considerably. The Axis troops benefitted from a close siege of Malta which was being pressed very aggressively by a sizeable German reinforcement to Italian air power in the Central Mediterranean, and by an extremely aggressive Italian light naval force. As Malta suffered nearly continuous aerial bombardment and close sea blockade, it was unable to interfere in the transportation of supplies to Libya. Thus, Rommel was able to accumulate a considerable store of supplies and equipment, and to build his formations up to strength again. The British were in an even better material condition. Although their supply lines stretched 'way around South Africa and into the Atlantic where the U-Boats roamed, the Allies were beginning to hold their own against the German Navy. In addition, the industrial might of the United States was firmly committed and President Roosevelt was rightly willing that American units in training forego modern equipmnent so long as British units in combat needed it. Churchill could ask for anything for his desert army and the U.S. would supply it. Africa was the only theater in which the Western Allies were engaged in land combat with the Nazi Empire, and that was where Allied fortunes would be decided.

By late May of 1942 it was becoming increasingly obvious to Rommel that Allied preparations for an offensive were beginning to outstrip his own. He therefore determined to launch an offensive before the Allies were too strong. Hitler gave him permission to launch a limited operation designed to throw the British back into Egypt. The schedule had to be tight, and the offensive limited, because other important operations were going on elsewhere and Axis resources were growing slender. Rommel needed the Luftwaffe contingent in Sicily to support his operation, but that force was charged with the blockade of Malta. To keep the Sicilian air force in the desert too long would relieve the pressure on the island fortress. That would have disastrous effects on Rommel's supply lines. In the event, he was supposed to return the dive bombers and fighter-bombers within a month.

While Rommel planned for his offensive, Auchinleck's preparations for defense proceeded apace. Ritchie, the actual commander in the field, was very inexperienced. He thought he could solve the problem of mobile warfare by establishing a chain of fortified camps. This was remarkably like Graziani's defensive arrangements in late 1940, but no one seems to have noticed. The British Gazala line comprised a series of "boxes" stretching inland for about 40 miles. Each box was a self-contained fortress connected to the others by minefields and barbed wire. Behind the line of boxes Ritchie kept additional infantry formations, some heavy tank brigades and his two armored divisions. His basic assumption—a perfectly valid one—was that Rommel would attempt to turn his exposed southern flank and strike at Tobruk. He planned to use his mobile forces to crush Rommel up against the line of boxes and destroy him there. The plan might have worked. But Ritchie kept his armor too far forward and charged with too many tasks. Armored brigades were supposed to screen Rommel's advance until the time came for a proper tank action. Then the scattered brigades were supposed to join together to form a powerful armored corps. The problem was that no one could be even moderately certain that the armored brigades would be capable of joining together after operating as light cavalry for some time.

Rommel's preparations also envisioned a turning movement, with the panzer divisions striking deep behind the British lines covered on either flank by additional mobile formations. Meanwhile, Italian troops would take the southernmost of the fortified boxes. He figured that he would be before Tobruk in four days.

The battle of Gazala (26 May–13 June 1942) was one of those battles in which nothing went according to plan. Both sides counted too much on the cooperation of the enemy, a fatal flaw in military planning. Rommel did turn the British flank, but the expected smashing blow by his panzers never came. This was fortunate for him, since he lost very heavily on the first days. But Ritchie also temporarily lost the use of one of his armored divisions on the very first day. Both sides did not exactly operate with sustained brilliance, but Ritchie proved overcautious at several critical junctures. Probably the most critical decision of the campaign was

Rommel's. On 29 May, seeing that he was getting nowhere fast, he called off the advance on Tobruk, and proceeded to concentrate his three German and two Italian mobile divisions. With their backs up against the central "box" of the Gazala line, they began to dig in.

This was remarkably audacious, for it effectively cut Rommel's mobile forces off from their supplies. They were actually surrounded by Allied troops. While beating off repeated Allied attacks, Rommel managed to overwhelm the British 150th Infantry Brigade Group box and re-establish his lines of communication. While his armored divisions held the "Cauldron," his motorized infantry divisions, one Italian and one German, took on the Bir Hacheim box, held by a brigade of Free French. Rommel's troops held the "Cauldron" for eight days (2–10 June) against everything that the British could throw against it. On 11 June, with Bir Hacheim taken, Rommel sortied from the "Cauldron" and pressed his mobile divisions towards the coast. Although Ritchie still had sufficient strength to crush the Italo-German drive, a series of staff foul-ups, minor decisions not taken, and the confusion of the situation caused the British to lose a two-day fight at a map reference point called "Knightsbridge" (12–13 June). But the action permitted most of two infantry divisions isolated in boxes on the Gazala line to escape. On 14 June the entire Eighth Army was in retreat towards Egypt, with 2nd South African Division holding the fortress of Tobruk. After pausing briefly to allow his supplies and infantry to come up, Rommel seized Tobruk, with nearly 35,000 prisoners and mountains of supplies, in 24 hours (20–21 June) and pressed on. This is the point at which he lost the war. He had been lent sufficient air power to permit his victorious action on condition that the Luftwaffe contingent be returned to Sicily in time for the Malta operation. With the spectre of the Pyramids beckoning him, he chose to ignore his instructions. The aircraft briefly lent to him in late May never made it back to Sicily. Malta was never taken, nor even subjected to renewed continuous air attack. As a result, Rommel's supply situation began to deterioate. But Egypt seemed to lie defenseless, and Rommel meant to have it.

Auchinleck had other ideas. While Rommel's troops were pressing eastwards, one reconnaissance battalion making a remarkable 158.7 kilometers in 24 hours on 26–27 June, Auchinleck relieved Ritchie and took personal command of the battered Eighth Army. Whereas Ritchie intended to wage a positional battle at Mersa Matruh, Auchinleck envisioned a running fight between Matruh and Alamein and made his dispositions accordingly and unorthodoxly. On 26 June the first Axis formations came up to the Matruh position. A confusing, chaotic running fight began. At one point the entire New Zealand Division was surrounded by barely a regiment of Germans, only to break out. After two days of this sort of confusion (26–28 June) Auchinleck began to fall back, reaching the Alamein line on 30 June. Here the remnants of six divisions, plus reinforcements from the garrisons of Egypt, were putting together a defensive line. The Alamein line had numberless advantages. It was, above all, the only line in all of Egypt and Libya which could not be turned. In addition, it was close to the British base at Alexandria, it was well watered, and well known to British officers who had speculated on its defensive merits even before the war. Here was where Auchinleck intended to make his stand.

The First Battle of El Alamein (1–7 July 1942) was remarkably confused. For two weeks, Rommel was on the offensive, trying to slip his depleted divisions behind the defending formations in an effort to turn the British out. British commanders, under Auchinleck's watchful eye, waged a mobile battle, using fortified boxes as bases rather than bastions. Axis units found themselves under continual counter attack whenever they probed. Finally, exhausted, Rommel began to settle down. Auchinleck's turn had come. For two weeks he threw in new units and old in an effort to crush Rommel on the field. But he too met with little success. Finally, both sides ran down into exhaustion. For the British, the battle had been a major victory. For Rommel, who had squeezed every ounce of energy and will out of his troops, both German and Italian, it was a major defeat. After Alamein, the tremendous power of the United Nations began to shift the balance irrevocably in the Eighth Army's favor. But meanwhile, the exhausted contenders went through another orgy of entrenchment and fortification.

The Alamein Line: August–November 1942

Auchinleck's victory at Alamein was probably the least understood victory of the war. Certainly it was the most poorly rewarded. The basic problem was that no one realized that it was a victory. Rommel had driven hundreds of miles closer to the Nile. Although he had been stopped, and stopped by his own methods in a mobile action, Churchill and the more conservative members of the British high command saw only the loss of territory. Auchinleck had often refused to follow instructions, particularly when his judgement told him Churchill didn't know what he was talking about. So "The Auk" had to go, and what better time to replace him than in the aftermath of a "defeat"? In his place came Gen Sir Harold Alexander, to command the Middle Eastern Theater, and LG Sir Bernard Law Montgomery, to command Eighth Army. Much to Churchill's surprise, the pair did precisely what Auchinleck had done: they refused to resume the offensive immediately, preferring to wait until they were certain of victory. Furthermore, both officers concluded that Auchinleck had been right all the time about the way to fight Rommel! They accepted his opinion that Rommel would attempt to renew his drive on Egypt in September, and adopted his defensive plan.

Meanwhile, both armies tried to rebuild. Again, this proved considerably easier for the British, with American resources now available in almost unlimited quantities, while the Axis suffered from their failure to take Malta. Fully 35% of the supplies embarked in Italian ports for Africa never arrived at their destination, much of it lost due to *Ultra* intercepts. Of the materiel which did arrive, virtually all arrived many hundreds of miles behind the front, usually at Tripoli or Benghazi. This necessitated a long overland journey which tended to consume precious fuel and increase ordinary breakage. In addition, for much of the trip the truck convoys came under the eyes of the Royal Air Force. The net result was that the Axis troops on the Alamein line were always short of ammunition, supplies and fuel. By mid-August Rommel realized that the Allied preparations were beginning to outstrip his own. It was time to act, even though he was ill and needed an extensive period of medical attention.

Rommel proposed an offensive for the end of August. The basic idea was to pass his armored and armored infantry divisions (of which he had six, half of which were Italian) through the weakly held southern end of the British front. These formations would advance some 30 miles to the east after clearing the British outposts and minefields, and then turn northwards towards the sea. The idea was to pin the Eighth Army against the coast and annihilate it. But while it sounded good it had several flaws. First of all, it required an enormous amount of fuel and that commodity was in short supply. Secondly, for the first time the turning movement had to be *through* a defended line, albeit a lightly defended one. Should the opposition prove greater than expected the entire operation would be a failure. Nevertheless, confident that he would win, Rommel set the night of 30–31 August as the time for his offensive.

The British, relying on Auchinleck's defensive preparations, were not about to make the same errors they had committed in the past. The southern end of their line was precisely where they expected Rommel to attack and they intended to conduct a fighting withdrawal with light armored forces which would draw Rommel's armor against Alam al-Halfa Ridge. There strong infantry and armored contingents would conduct a defensive combined arms battle.

Although the Axis attack got off on schedule it soon bogged down. Both German panzer divisions began to have problems with the lightly armored screening forces which the British had deployed in front of them. By 0909 progress had been so poor that they were over six hours late. Fuel consumption had been so great that Rommel had to order the attacking armor to turn northwards immediately, having made barely a third of the planned advance. This was precisely what the British deployment was best prepared to cope with. Rommel's hopes were destroyed in a two day battle on the western edge of Alam al Halfa Ridge. On 2 September he gave the order for a withdrawal, while Montgomery hesitated to try for a crushing blow. Although Montgomery finally threw in an infantry division in an attempt to cut off the retreating German armor, the move was too little and too late. By 4 September the main part of the action was over, although some heavy fighting continued for three more days. At the cost of less than 2,000 casualties the Eighth Army had delivered another defeat to Rommel. Now it would assume the offensive in its turn.

In many ways the famous [Second] Battle of El Alamein (23 October–4 November 1942) was anti-climactic. One Italian historian called it the "battle without hope." Rommel's last chance to win in North Africa was at Alam al-Halfa. His defensive action against Montgomery in October was a hopeless operation even before it began. By October, Allied materiel superiority was so great the British could, and did, lose tank for tank and gun for gun and man for man and still come away the victor. In addition, even if Rommel had somehow managed to halt Montgomery's drive, he would have been in even worse shape than before the offensive, for on 8 November *Operation Torch* deposited an enormous Allied army in Morocco and Algeria. In the end, the results would have been much the same.

Nor was Alamein a particularly interesting fight. Basically, it was 1917 all over again, with tanks for a touch of modernity.

Rommel's defensive preparations placed one German and five Italian infantry divisions in a heavily entrenched and mined defensive belt stretching from the sea to the fringes of the Qattara Depression. Behind this he deployed his mobile troops in three groups, with an Italian and German division in each. These were to be available for immediate action should the British succeed in breaking through the front. That was about all Rommel could do. A pre-emptive retreat would have resulted in the loss of virtually all of his infantry, which was largely non-motorized. In addition, the retreating columns would have been subjected to a brutal harrassment by Allied air and mobile ground forces. He had no choice but to stand his ground.

Montgomery's plan for the Alamein battle was medieval. Basically, he envisioned a powerful assault by four full infantry divisions against the northern sector of Rommel's line. Once the infantry achieved a breakthrough, an armored corps would pass through the gap. It was all very 1917, with armor substituting for the cavalry of one of Haig's "Big Pushes." It was also the sort of thing at which both Germans and Italians were well acquainted. Montgomery intended to fight a battle of attrition, which was the only kind he was certain to win.

The offensive began in the evening of 23 October with a heavy preliminary bombardment. Then the infantry went forward on a narrow front against the Italian *Trento Division* and elements of the German *164th Light Division.* But the front was too narrow and the *Trento,* with the aid of some German infantry, managed to handle the opposition rather well. The situation grew worse for the British—actually only one of the four assault divisions was British, the others were Australian, New Zealanders, and South African—the next morning. A narrow corridor had been driven into the Axis front. But the corridor held by the attacking formations was literally jammed with men and equipment and the Axis artillery had a field day. The situation continued for four days, with the Allied infantry making small gains at horrendous cost.

When the attack began Rommel was in Germany on sick leave, a circumstance not unknown to Montgomery. His replacement, LG George Stumme, suffered a fatal coronary on the very first day of the battle. Even as Rommel flew back to Africa, the officer temporarily in command, LG Wilhelm Ritter von Thoma, was captured—some say willingly. Thus, for a brief period the Italo-German *PanzerArmee Afrika* found itself without anyone at the helm. Although tired and ill, Rommel resumed command as soon as he arrived, throwing himself into the battle. Axis counter-attacks achieved little in the face of superior Allied firepower. Meanwhile the infantry battle continued and on 2 November a fresh British assault finally succeeded in breaking through the Axis defensive zone. But Montgomery's armored corps was unable to immediately exploit the "success." It had been partially committed to action during the most difficult portion of the infantry battle and needed to pause for reorganization. In addition, British communications were in horrible shape. The situation was such that Rommel was able to begin to retreat on 3 November and might well have gotten away. But at this juncture Hitler intervened, issuing a "stand fast" order. Rommel, obedient to his Nazi Master, complied. For 36 hours the Axis troops held their ground. Then Hitler rescinded the order and a retreat became possible. But by that time Montgomery had managed to sort out his troops and was ready to take up the pursuit. Rommel was forced to abandon over 35,000 Italian and German infantrymen who were without transport. In the face of a sluggish pursuit, the mobile core of the *PanzerArmee Afrika* fell back. The Battle of El Alamein was over.

The Great Retreat: November–December 1942

After El Alamein, Rommel found himself retreating along the coast road, the famous *Via Balbia,* with the equivalent of two divisions. It was all that he could save from the wreckage of a dozen divisions. But the survivors came out in good order, with their morale high, a willingness to fight if need be, and above all with a determination to survive. With this insignificant force, half German and half Italian, Rommel would display his genius as never before. Repeatedly he would take up a defensive position, daring Montgomery to come at him. Each time the British general would hesitate. At no time would the remnants of the *PanzerArmee Afrika* have been able to put up more than a token resistance if Montgomery had honestly pressed the issue. But Montgomery never fought a final action, preferring to attempt flank marches with the intention of trapping Rommel against the coast. Rommel was always one step ahead. The flanking columns usually found only an empty stretch of road when they did reach the coast. In an effort to explain why he was not pursuing the enemy more energetically, Montgomery once even blamed a heavy downpour, claiming it slowed his troops to a crawl, but if the downpour was heavy enough to slow down the British Army, it must have been heavy enough to slow down the Italo-German Army as well. It might almost be said that Rommel was conducting a retreat, rather than that Montgomery was conducting a pursuit. The Axis troops made brief stands at Fuka—where the last of the non-motorized Italian infantry was taken prisoner after a spirited, if short fight—Mersa Matruh, Sidi Barrani, and Solum-Halfaya, in Egypt. Rommel then decided that Cyrenaica could not be held under any circumstances. This was a well-reasoned assessment of the situation. By 9 November the combined Italo-German *PanzerArmee Afrika* totalled some 7,500 men, 21 tanks, and about 100 guns of all types. The only reinforcements available comprised a weak division of Italian infantry in western Cyrenaica, and that was without motorization. Facing this handful were a corps of two armored and one infantry division, cautiously attempting a turning movement. And things were getting worse.

On 8 November *Operation Torch* had begun, with the landing of a large Anglo-American force in Morocco and Algeria. Now, in addition to Montgomery's Eighth Army advancing from Egypt, Rommel was threatened by the Allied First Army advancing from Algeria. Indeed, some Allied units in Algeria were actually closer to Rommel's base at Tripoli than the entire *PanzerArmee Afrika.* It was time to abandon not merely Cyrenaica, but perhaps also Tripolitania and retreat into Tunisia, there to await evacuation.

The rest of the retreat was in many ways a repeat of the first few days. From time to time the Axis troops would make brief halts—twice of nearly three weeks in duration. As soon as the British managed to crank up sufficient force to attempt a turning movement Rommel would abandon his position and fall back again. Energetic use of mines, both real and dummy, served to hinder the movement of Allied supplies along the Via Balbia, thus gaining time. At the end of December the *PanzerArmee* was in Tripolitania, somewhat stronger but still outnumbered. By the end of January it was occupying the Mareth Line in Tunisia. Libya was completely in Allied hands on 4 February 1943. The campaign for the desert was over.

It had been a brilliant campaign at times, with bold leadership displayed by many of the participants. The campaign had reaffirmed the value of courageous leadership. It had pointed out the general superiority of mobile troops when opposed by non-mobile troops. And it had served to instruct the Allied armies in their trade in anticipation of the hard struggle which was yet to come for the liberation of Europe. For all too often overlooked was the purpose of it all. Rommel, for all his personal and professional virtues, ultimately served what was perhaps the vilest cause in human history, and the campaign in the desert was but one phase of a vast undertaking necessary to remove the cancer of Nazism from the earth.

The Desert Fox

Erwin Rommel (1891–1944) was of bourgeois Swabian Protestant background. At an early age, he entered the Imperial Army, was commissioned, and began garrison duty. His career in World War I was relatively undistinguished until the Caporetto Campaign of Oct-Nov 1917 when, as adjutant and acting battalion commander in the *AlpenKorps*, he conducted himself, and led his unit, so aggressively as to capture thousands of the enemy in a series of sweeping infantry penetrations. (He would tactlessly boast of this at times to his Italian colleagues in a later war.) Ending the war as a highly decorated company officer, he was among the talented handful selected to remain in the post-war *Reichswehr*, with its 4,000 officers. The next dozen years he spent in garrison, in his spare time reading and composing an account of his wartime activities entitled *Infantry Attacks!*

The rise of Adolf Hitler helped Rommel's career considerably, as the Fuhrer was impressed by the book. By the Polish Campaign of 1939, Rommel was commandant of Hitler's military household. Having already served as a Hitler Youth adviser, he pleased his master so well that he was given the newly raised *7th Panzer Division* for the French Campaign of 1940, an unusual command for an infantry officer. In France, Rommel's division earned the nickname "Ghost" as it sped rapidly across the countryside, outstripping most other German formations. At the conclusion of the campaign, Rommel participated in occupation activities. In late 1940, Hitler selected him to command the troops being sent to Africa.

After his remarkable career in the desert, Rommel briefly commanded German forces in Tunisia, despite increasingly difficult relations with his superiors. Later he commanded *Army Group B* in Northern Italy and was chiefly responsible for the rapidity of the German occupation of much of Italy in the late summer of 1943. Subsequently, he was transferred to France to expedite preparations for resisting the anticipated Allied invasion.

Rommel was seriously wounded by Allied aircraft shortly after the invasion began, at a time when he was involved in the "July Plot" to assassinate Hitler. (Rommel was to become Hitler's replacement in a "peace" government.) His popularity in Germany prevented Hitler from putting him on trial but, under threat of harm to his family, he committed suicide on 14 Oct 1944. Hitler gave him a magnificent funeral.

Rommel's stature as a commander has been somewhat tarnished with time. Nevertheless, he clearly ranks among the greater captains. An aggressive, sometimes foolhardy tactician, he was unsurpassed at desert warfare.

Like most officers of the *Reichswehr*, Rommel had no political ties before he encountered Hitler. Thereafter, he became personally attached to the Fuhrer, though despising most of the other Nazis. His disillusionment with Hitler appears to have begun around the time of Alamein and to have steadiy deepened thereafter. By mid-1944, he was at least marginally involved in the plot to assassinate Hitler, which cost him his life.

The Sea War and the Desert War

Without a struggle for control of the Mediterranean Sea the war in the desert would not have been possible. Ultimately, the decisive factor in the desert war was the sea war. Every bullet, every ounce of fuel, and every man in both armies came over the sea. For the Axis it represented the only line of supply. For the British, with an alternate life-line around Africa, the Mediterranean still represented an important line of supply. The net result was that if either side had been able to assert control over the Mediterranean, the land war would have become almost superfluous. But neither side was ever able to assert full control over the Mediterranean.

The principal problem was a lack of means. Although the Royal Navy was stretched thin as a result of the demands of a world war, it was still capable of putting sufficient power into the Mediterranean at need, to offset any advantages the Italian *Regia Marina* might gain. Conversely, the Axis could always offset any British advantages. Finally, both sides viewed the naval war as something less than important, due largely to the glamor surrounding the fighting in the desert.

Precisely because neither side could assert control, the Mediterranean boiled over with fire and steel for the duration of the campaign, and even later during the fighting for Tunisia. Both sides had sufficient power to dispute control. Repeatedly, one side would sortie. The other in turn would sortie and some kind of sea battle would develop. The key to these battles was not annihilation, although at least one, Cape Matapan (29 March 1941), was perhaps the neatest naval action of the Second World War. The basic idea was to accomplish one's mission at minimal loss to oneself and maximum loss to the enemy. The mission was usually the escort or interception of a convoy. The action generally broke off when the convoy in question had been successfully guided to port or turned back. There was no point in wasting precious ships in secondary operations. If one was lost, the balance of power might shift dangerously. There was no real way in which either side could strike a mortal blow at the other, although the Axis had a chance and bungled it.

In the very center of the Mediterranean lies the island of Malta. During World War II Malta was a British possession. Lying athwart the principal Axis supply lines to Africa, Malta proved the most serious thorn in the side of the Axis convoys. From Malta, British aircraft and naval forces could intercept convoys to Africa and wreak serious damage, while reconnaissance aircraft could keep track of Italian naval movements. Of course, Britsin paid a price for possession of Malta. The fortress-island suffered roughly two air raids daily for the duration of the Mediterranean struggle. In addition it suffered the privations of siege. Attempts to supply the island with special fast moving heavily escorted convoys often proved incredibly expensive, if not occasionally impossible, in the face of Axis air power and Italian light naval forces. But the price was paid, and willingly paid. For the service rendered by Malta was incalculable. During the most critical portion of the fighting in

North Africa, from July through December of 1942, aircraft and warships operating out of Malta claimed fully 35% of the supplies destined for Axis forces in the desert.

Repeatedly, both Italian and German naval experts recommended that the island be taken. But, Hitler, mindful of the destruction of airborne forces in the Crete Operation, demurred, supported by his Russian front generals. Finally, Mussolini was won over to the project and he convinced Hitler of its merits. Hitler transferred a German air corps to Sicily in anticipation of an assault. The result was that in the first six months of 1942 barely 6% of supplies loaded failed to reach the Axis forces in Africa due to the presence of powerful Axis air forces in Sicily. Then, in May, Rommel "borrowed" these air forces to facilitate a limited undertaking in Libya designed to clear the Gazala line, take Tobruk, and throw the British off balance for a while. But when this was accomplished, he pressed on. Air craft which might have restored the situation in the Central Mediterranean were lost on the road to Alamein. The assault on Malta, scheduled for mid-July 1942, was called off. The elite German and Italian paratroopers who were to spearhead the attack eventually turned up as infantry on the Alamein line. And, with the pressure off, Malta began to erode Axis convoys again.

Thus, in the final analysis, it was sea power which shaped the course of the fighting in the desert. And it is not stretching things overmuch to say that it was Malta which shaped the course of the struggle for the Mediterranean. In the end, the Allies understood the value of Malta and willingly paid every price to retain control. The Axis, essentially land-bound, failed to fully appreciate the importance of the island and frittered away their best chance of seizing it. It was a fortunate situation for the Allies.

MALTA AND NORTH AFRICA

Period	*Axis Supply Losses (%)*	*Landed (tons)*
Jan-Sep '40	0.0	148,817
Oct '40-Jan '41	3.9	197,792
Feb-Jun '41	6.6	447,815
Jul-Dec '41	26.8	356,294
Jan-Jun '42	6.2	441,878
Jul-Dec '42	35.5	337,409

The table sets forth the influence of Malta on the arrival of Axis supplies in North Africa. For each period losses are indicated as a percentage of materiel loaded which never arrived in African ports. The *Regia Marina* ran 1,210 convoys to Africa between June 1940 and December 1942. These loaded roughly 2,500,000 tons of supplies, of which roughly 1,930,000 tons actually arrived at their destination. The actual arrivals during each period are noted above. Roughly 14% of all materials loaded never arrived in Africa.

Desert Warfare

The desert is ideally suited to mechanized operations. Its vast distances, untroubled by significant terrain features, offer an almost perfect chessboard for the conduct of operations on almost any scale. Surprisingly, despite the fact that both the Italians and the British had been preparing for war in this region for many years, it was the Germans—specifically Rommel—who first developed a real understanding of this environment.

The British, and to a considerable extent the Italians, thought of the desert as just another place wherein to use their standard tactics: meticulous preparations, followed by artillery bombardment, followed by infantry attacks supported by heavy tanks, and the whole backed up by lighter, faster tanks both as reserve and pursuit formations. This was essentially right out of 1918, with the lighter tanks substituting for the cavalry.

British tankers thought of the tank as something of a surrogate horse, capable of taking the enemy in front just as the mounted arm had traditionally done. While such "cavalry charges" could work against relatively unsophisticated troops, rear-area establishments, and such targets as lightly escorted truck convoys, they were suicide against well handled, balanced combined arms forces.

Defensively, both the British and the Italians were also more or less stuck in 1918. Large forces were regularly immobilized in well-fortified positions backed up with extensive amounts of artillery and bolstered by vast minefields. In the desert, loss of mobility may be equated with defeat.

Rommel—like most great tankers, an infantryman—came to the desert uniquely qualified. To be sure, practically any German panzer general would have been considerably superior to his opponents, but Rommel was more than that. To the already innovative German concepts of mobile warfare, he added a number of notions uniquely his own. Perhaps the most important of these was that mobile warfare was "war of the sea on land." This concept, which Rommel pioneered during his successful dash across France with the *7th Panzer Division* in May of 1940, meant that mobile forces should fight on the move rather than merely using their mobility to get to a place where they would engage in essentially static combat.

In the desert, this idea was even more applicable than in France: consider the innumerable time-worn similes likening the desert to the sea. Linked with the practical fact that non-motorized forces—and motorized forces led by non-motorized minds—are virtually useless in the desert, this innovative doctrine had the effect of vastly multiplying the value of the forces under Rommel's command.

Rommel always led from the front, a practice far more common among German than Allied generals. While at times this put him out of touch with his headquarters, it frequently enabled him to respond immediately to significant changes in the tactical situation.

Another important element of Rommel's success was surprise: hitting the enemy where and when and how he least expected to be hit. In the desert, with its vast distances impossible to secure properly, surprise was not difficult to achieve if one thought in terms of mobile operations. Significantly, the Alamein line is one of the very few in the theater which permits little surprise based on mobility: it bears a stronger resemblance to the Western Front in 1918 than to the western deserts. Finally, like most great generals, Rommel understood the importance of combined arms operations.

Ultimately it was not the tanks which lay at the root of German tactical success in the desert: it was the intelligent use of tanks *in combination* with mobile infantry and artillery and anti-tank formations. Sending tanks in without support of the other arms was sending them to a fiery doom, but in a coordinated, well-timed surprise attack, success could be anticipated every time against British forces, provided the quantitative differences were not too great.

Offensively, one sent forward highly mobile reconnaissance formations, behind which came antitank troops supported by infantry, with vast amounts of artillery on call. Behind these forces, in fairly close support, came the main body of armor and mobile infantry. One absorbed the shock of the enemy's armored counterattacks with one's anti-tank forces, throwing in one's own tanks when his momentum was broken, with the primary intention of getting behind him. Having done so, one cut loose and ran wild across his lines of communication, supply, and retreat.

Once your own attack gained a sustained momentum, it was pressed at all costs—fueled by captured enemy supplies, if need be. Any large enemy formations left behind could be taken care of by less mobile infantry—in the desert this meant the bulk of the Italian forces—as one pressed to the limit of one's abilities. In the most extreme case, shortly after Gazala in June of 1942, reconnaissance elements of the *Afrika Korps* logged 158.7 kilometers in 24 hours, the greatest advance in recorded history.

Defensive tactics were not much different from offensive tactics. One liberally seasoned the front with minefields lightly held by infantry, holding back the mobile forces. As the enemy intentions became evident, one let him wear himself out against infantry, artillery, and anti-tank forces. Meanwhile, tanks and mobile infantry could search out the enemy's rear, inflicting the greatest materiel damage possible while severing his communication and supply lines.

An important element of German tactics in the desert was that offensive and defensive tactics should be used interchangeably: go from one to the other as the local tactical situation dictated, regardless of whether one was on the operational offensive or defensive. Overall, such an approach—so much more flexible than that of the British—would always inflict more damage on the enemy than was received. By suffering the least damage, one would emerge the victor. Or rather one would emerge the victor so long as the quantitative superiority of the enemy was not so overwhelming that he could lose far more men and materiel than you yourself had, and still have vast resources available to continue the fight—which is precisely what occurred.

On Fighting a War in the Desert

The conduct of war entails finding solutions to many problems not normally encountered in more peaceful pursuits and not directly related to the killing of your fellow man. Waging war in a desert presents even more interesting problems than the "ordinary" sort of warfare.

The most obvious problem encountered in desert fighting was, of course, the heat and absence of water. Casualties in North Africa from heat stroke were far greater than in other theaters of war. Lack of water was always a considerable problem, particularly inasmuch as many of the wells in the Western Desert supplied unstorable water. Surprisingly, water represents numerous storage problems. It may not just be bottled up and used at a later date. Certain types of wells will supply water which can last indefinitely. Others will supply water which will be undrinkable in three days. A great many places named on any map of North Africa are not actual places, but merely wells. Water, of course, is useful in combating heat stroke. Water also helps keep a mechanized army moving, but that's a problem which ties in with fuel supply. Besides, you can use non-potable water in your radiator.

If heat stroke was a major health problem, the desert theater at least presented few other health problems. To be sure everyone tended to be plagued by sand fleas. But no serious outbreaks of the traditional military diseases occurred on either side. This was due primarily to the essentially antiseptic nature of the desert. Curiously, exposure proved to be an interesting health problem in North Africa. After dark, particularly in the winter, the desert becomes very cold. Many troops came down with colds and such—a peculiar problem not anticipated by either side.

WATER CONSUMPTION:
Desert Conditions

Consumption	*Per Man/ Per Day*	*Remarks*
minimum	2-3 gals	limited periods only
normal	3-4	not cooking or washing
normal	6	cooking and washing
march or bivouac	5	
combat	2-6	
hospitalized	10	

The desert also presents difficult problems for the mechanic. Sand manages to work its way into everything. This increases the wear and tear on equipment of critical parts. Items which have to be heavily greased suffer particularly in this fashion. So the supply of spare parts was always a major problem, and a tank had some 8,000 parts made of 30,000 pieces.

The key problem for the logistician was in the land transshipment of the replacements and material. Rommel needed 60,000 tons of supply per month in 1942. In the last six months of 1942 an average of 56.209 tons of supplies were being unloaded in North Africa per month. But they had to be unloaded in places like Tobruk, over 300 miles behind the Alamein position; or Benghazi, nearly 600 miles in the rear; or even Tripoli, about 1500 miles off. From these ports literally every ounce of material had to be trucked across the length of Africa up to the front. Motor gasoline weighs 6.11 pounds to the gallon, in drums up to 7.41 pounds per gallon. A 2.5 ton tank truck consumes, in moving 160 kilometers, 20 gallons of gasoline, and 1.6 gallons of other petroleum products, without considering additional consumption to wear of the vehicle, desert climate, and combat conditions. Thus, to get 1000 gallons of gasoline from Tobruk to the Alamein position costs 120 gallons of gasoline and 9.6 gallons of other POLs. Then we must figure in an average of 10% for wastage and spillage. Our 1000 gallons now reads 768 and we have yet to send the tank trucks back, which will cost another 132 gallons! We have still to bring forward a single ounce of ammunition, spare parts, foodstuffs or other POLs, and only 636 gallons have reached the front! And we are operating from Tobruk, not Tripoli! Nor have we calculated in loss due to enemy action!

How did the British solve the problem? They took advantage of a railroad which extended from Alexandria to the vicinity of Alamein and extended it across the Libyan frontier. That Rommel did not activate this line when he captured nearly 300 miles of it in mid-1942 is indicative of his lack of ability as a logistician. Rail transport is more efficient than road; a standard gauge steam locomotive (2-8-0) consumes 55 pounds of coal per kilometer of train being pulled, or about 700 pounds per hour. It can transport, in that kilometer, almost half a million gallons—on paper. Even off paper the record is impressive. Furthermore, railroads are very difficult targets to knock out from the air and usually can be repaired overnight. Rommel's shortsightedness in this area—his chief of supply in early 1941 was a lowly major—may well have cost him the campaign.

To some extent all of these problems of desert war are similar to problems troops in other climates have to face, the principal difference being one of degree. Like the arctic or the jungle, the desert has its peculiar problems. But these are not nearly so obvious as those of the arctic or jungle. In many ways they are more like those encountered in mountains, but not so apparent as to seem to require more than minimal preparation. The result was that most armies paid little attention to the problems of mechanized desert warfare in the pre-war period.

• • •

Hitler had been concentrating forces in Tunisia ever since *Operation Torch*. These had held the advancing American, British, and French to limited gains. Rommel's arrival from the east with the remnants of the once-mighty *Panzer-Armee Afrika* initiated the short, but bitter Tunisian Campaign. Despite initial success, it was a campaign the Axis could not win in the face of overwhelming Allied air and sea power, not to mention their considerable ground forces. By 12 May 1943 it was over, some 240,000 Italian and German troops passing into captivity, a loss equal to that dealt Germany by the Russians at Stalingrad that winter. And now the Allies were poised to bring the war to Europe.

Sicily: The Race for Messina, 10 July–17 August 1943

By Albert A. Nofi

Sicily. Sun-baked, craggy heart of the Mediterranean, where, amid palm and vine and flower, history and legend have unfolded for tens of centuries, from before Alkibiades to after Garibaldi. In mid-1943 the southernmost bastion of an increasingly embattled *Festung Europa*— where vast Allied hosts undertook the first and greatest amphibious assault against Nazi-dominated Europe, and where greatly outnumbered Axis forces conducted one of the most brilliant rearguard actions of modern times.

Where Do We Go From Here?

The Sicilian Campaign was ultimately born of the need to do something at a period in the Second World War when Allied options were somewhat restricted. The North African Campaign, undertaken in November of 1942, had dragged on longer than anticipated. As a result, top-level Allied strategists meeting at Casablanca in January of 1943 could clearly see that the considerable manpower and shipping resources committed to that operation would not be available for other employment before the end of spring. Therefore, the Americans, led by President Franklin D. Roosevelt, Gen George C. Marshall, and Adm Ernest J. King, reluctantly had agreed that this left insufficient time for these forces to be reconcentrated in Britain for a cross-Channel invasion of Europe during the summer. The British, led by Prime Minister Winston Churchill and FM Sir Alan Brooke, were less displeased, not being fully convinced of the wisdom of the cross-Channel operation anyway.

The problem then became one of deciding what exactly to do. Various proposals were considered, such as seizing Corsica or Sardinia, and King even suggested that the United States shift its attention to the Pacific. None of these were viable alternatives. Sicily was clearly the best choice—the idea first having been advanced and then consistently championed by Churchill, who often saw strategic matters more clearly than his generals. A landing in Sicily, he argued, would have significant strategic benefits at minimal cost. Most importantly, taking the large, triangular island in the very middle of the Mediterranean would make Allied maritime communications far more secure and greatly reduce the cost of supporting operations in the Indian Ocean. A Sicilian venture might also serve to divert German attentions in some small way from Russia, where the drama of Stalingrad was reaching its final act. Also, it would, of course, further weaken Italy, a project close to Sir Winston's heart.

There was perhaps another, unspoken purpose in so limited and confined an objective as seizing Sicily. Frankly, British military leaders were not impressed by American prowess as displayed in North Africa. A limited undertaking with clearly defined goals would serve to give the aggressive, but ill-prepared, Americans a bit more seasoning.

Churchill's proposal was adopted. Gen Dwight D. Eisenhower, Allied Commander-in-Chief in the Mediterranean, was instructed to prepare for an invasion of Siciy in July, upon conclusion of the North African Campaign. His objectives were to secure Allied communications, relieve pressure on Russia, and further erode Italy's ability and will to continue the war. No decision was taken, however, on what to do *after* Sicily. The operation was to be a dead end, undertaken primarily because "something had to be done in the European theatre in 1943."

Plans and Preparations

Operation Husky was difficult to plan. In February of 1943, an Anglo-American staff began meeting in room 141 of the Hotel St. George in Algiers. Designated "Task Force 141," they quickly began to generate the mountains of paper necessary for any modern army to function. All such documents, however, had to shuttle back and forth among London, Cairo, and Algiers, since the various Allied headquarters were located in such widely dispersed places. A further complication arose from the fact that many of the officers—such as Patton and Montgomery—who would have to command in the invasion were actively involved in the ongoing Tunisian campaign, while others were in the continuing air and sea struggle for control of the Mediterranean. Thus, they were not in the position to invest significant amounts of their time.

The preliminary proposal for the invasion called for the British and American forces to conduct a series of landings over a period of four or five days, beginning on the southeastern coast near Cape Passaro and working around for a final assault on Palermo in the northwest, supported by massive naval and air resources. Once ashore, the armies would drive on Messina, attaining that objective in about two weeks. This was essentially an American plan: aggressive, complex, and far reaching. Most Britons had second thoughts very early. As Gen Sir Bernard Law Montgomery expressed it for them all, the operation was much too dispersed, spreading the troops over 300 miles of coastline. Should something go wrong, disaster could result. The British had seen too many disasters in the war. Ultimately, it was clear that the Allies could not lose. A cautious strategy could keep the costs down.

On 2 May, Montgomery presented his version of the invasion plan to Walter Bedell Smith, Eisenhower's Chief-of-Staff, in the men's room of the Hotel St. George. British forces would land on the southeast coast and advance upwards towards Messina along the coast road, while the Americans would land along the eastern side of the southern coast and advance so as to cover Monty's left. As one officer put it, the British would be the sword in the right hand of operational commander FM Sir Harold Alexander, and the Americans would be the shield on his left. After considerable discussion and bargaining, Montgomery's plan was adopted eleven days later. In fact, once suggested, it was inevitable that this be so. The bulk of the forces necessary for the operation were being provided by the British, particularly naval and air forces. Since they bore the weight, their lead had to be followed. Later in the war, with the Americans providing the men and material in overwhelming amounts, their decisions would be automatically implemented. Task Force 141 had a bare two months in which to plan.

An amphibious landing is the most complex and most dangerous of military adventures. In the spring of 1943, the Allies were remarkably short of experience. British efforts at Dakar, Madagascar and Dieppe had been unfortunate. The American operations at Guadalcanal the previous August and at Attu in May had met insignificant resistance during the actual landings. Allied experience from the North African operation in November was more extensive, but their enemy—the Vichy French—were reluctant at best and a political solution was reached within a day or so. Moreover, all of these operations had been conducted with improvised equipment, and frequently little of that. By spring of 1943, Allied industrial superiority was beginning to tell. Specialized vessels for amphibious operations were increasingly available, more aircraft were at hand, and airborne forces were available. All of these factors had to be taken into consideration in the development of the invasion plan.

Operation Husky was a classic amphibious operation. Preceded by an airborne landing near Syracuse, the British Eighth Army under Montgomery would land four infantry divisions, a separate brigade and several commandos on the southeastern coast, while the American Seventh Army under LG George S. Patton would follow-up its own airborne operation by putting ashore three infantry divisions and miscellaneous forces sufficient to comprise another. In immediate reserve would be the bulk of an American armored division. Back in Africa, a British and an American infantry division would be available, along with the bulk of an American airborne division.

The airborne troops—American parachutists and British gliderborne troops—were intended to keep the enemy off the beaches during the initial moments of the landing, and were to seize vital installations such as bridges and airfields. There was to be no preliminary naval bombardment, though the fleets were available to provide support on call.

The most serious omission in the planning was the failure to subordinate Allied air power to the landing. The RAF and the AAF both desired to fight independently; thus, neither committed reasonable numbers of aircraft to ground support or air cover over the beaches, claiming that by "strategic" bombing and long range fighter missions they could eliminate the enemy threat from the air. It was a weakness in the plans.

At the time, everyone was optimistic. The Allies were going to put nearly half a million men ashore with 14,000 vehicles, 600 tanks, and 1800 guns, all supported and protected by 2,600 ships and 3,600 aircraft. Eisenhower believed victory would be attained in about two weeks. The optimists, however, failed to reckon with the enemy.

The Axis

The defense of Sicily was predominantly an Italian responsibility. Gen Alfredo Guzzoni, commanding the Italian *Sixth Army,* was in overall charge of the defense. Under him were some 300,000 or so Italian and 30,000 German troops. Much of the Italian force consisted of overaged reservists in coast defense formations that lacked heavy equipment and any degree of mobility. Certain prime ports and naval bases—Messina, Catania, Augusta-Syracuse, Trapani, and Palermo—were well fortified from seaward attack, but lacked any landward defenses whatsoever. About 70,000 of the Italian troops were mobile after a fashion, comprising three "leg" infantry divisions, one motorized infantry division, and many miscellaneous formations, including some *Bersaglieri* battalions. There were also two good German divisions, the *Sizilien Panzergrenadier* (soon redesignated the *15th*) and the *Hermann Goring Panzer,* both recently rebuilt from cadres which had survived the Tunisian disaster.

Guzzoni's basic problem was how to defend an island rimmed by nearly 500 miles of practical landing beaches. In close cooperation with FM Alfred Kesselring, German Mediterranean commander, Guzzoni decided to scatter a number of small, mobile, combined arms combat teams just ashore of southern and eastern coasts. These forces—dubbed "mobile groups" and "tactical groups"—would support the coast defense troops by making immediate counterattacks as the Allied landings developed. They would gain time for the mobile divisions to come up and deliver major counterstrokes. While Guzzoni and Kesselring agreed as to the basic plan, they disagreed as to the details. Kesselring believed the Allies would land in the west. Guzzoni thought they would come in the south and southeast. In the end, they compromised. Two Italian divisions and the bulk of the panzergrenadiers would concentrate in the western end of Sicily. One Italian division would concentrate in the southeast with the *Hermann Goring,* and the *Livorno*— best of the available Italian forces—would be in the south-central part of the island.

None of the Axis commanders was optimistic about the possibility of holding Sicily. Aside from the fact that the Italian forces were poorly prepared, the island was too exposed to Allied air and naval activity. Indeed, Kesselring believed the Allies would land in Calabria simultaneously with their Sicilian venture, thereby bottling up everyone on the island. They did not plan to hold Sicily; they did plan a drawn-out rearguard action designed to inflict casualties and secure time.

Lodgement: 10–15 July 1943

The weather grew ugly as the convoys neared Sicily on the night of 9–10 July. The *mistral* blew up, whipping the seas into a frenzy and causing considerable discomfort among the troops. For a time it was feared that the invasion would have to be postponed, but it began to clear after midnight. Though the high winds wreaked havoc with the airborne operations, the troops being scattered widely and many falling into the sea, they had also convinced the defenders that a landing would be impossible that night.

The landings began at about 2:30 that morning. They were uniformly successful with a minimum of casualties—many caused by the heavy surf. The absence of a preliminary bombardment proved beneficial, for a large number of the defending troops were overrun, barely aware an invasion was under way. In the British sector, one coastal battery was taken with its crew asleep at the guns. Here and there, however, the defenders managed to get into action, notably on the American 3rd Division beaches at Licata on the Allied left, where a coastal battery caused considerable trouble. Nevertheless, by dawn the Allies had successfully landed the bulk of seven divisions, plus miscellaneous forces equal to yet another.

Enemy resistance began building in the morning. Italian and German aircraft began to roam the skies over the beaches, having local superiority by default of Allied air command. Several ships were hit, an American destroyer and minesweeper were lost, and an ammunition ship went up spectacularly. Men both ashore and afloat became trigger happy as they endured repeated, though relatively ineffective, attacks.

At about 1000, elements of the *Livorno Division* and *Mobile Group F* launched a combined arms attack against the American 26th Infantry Regiment and the Rangers and paratroopers in and near Gela. Naval gunfire and some tough house-to-house fighting beat them off within an hour; there was panic, however, among some elements on the beaches and a more serious attack might have proven disastrous. That such did not come was the fault of the inexperienced commander of the *Hermann Goring*, who wasted five precious hours getting his division in hand. When he finally attacked, at about 1500, his troops were easily repulsed, though not before battering an American battalion. Under a hail of naval gunfire, the relatively green Luftwaffe ground troops broke and ran.

The counterattack had been the most serious threat to the security of the Allied beaches on 10 July. For everywhere else, the day had gone well. The British 5th Division, on the Allied right, had managed to link up with a detachment of their gliderborne troops holding a vital bridge near Syracuse and took that port from the rear by 2100; the German troops assigned to the landward defense fled north in panic. As night fell, all other Allied objectives had been attained, and in some cases exceeded.

On 11 July, the Axis forces managed a far more serious effort. A coordinated Italo-German attack was made on Gela. Four battalions of the Italian *33rd* and *34th Regiments* struck from the northwest while two tank battalions and one of panzergrenadiers from *Hermann Goring* attacked from the north and east in two combined arms task forces. Under pressure the Americans fell back, unable to cope with Panzer IV's and Tiger Tanks. Destroyer gunfire helped some, but by 0930 the Germans were on the plain but four miles from Gela and the Italians in the foothills not a mile off.

In Gela itself Patton had landed. Describing the situation in his usual colorful fashion, he caused an ensign from a naval fire control party to volunteer his services. Light cruiser gunfire soon began falling among the enemy troops and tanks. The drive on Gela slowed, the Italians unable to move under a hail of 6-inch shells, the Germans just barely able. By 1100, the panzers were within 500 yards of the beach, but 1st Division's artillery was now ashore. Lined up along the dunes, the guns poured a deadly direct fire into the advancing armor, as the navy again added a healthy contribution. By noon it was over, the enemy streaming away. It was the stoutest effort to break the invasion the enemy would make.

Over the next few days the Allies consolidated their position, slowly moving inland. Meanwhile, Axis airpower had virtually free rein over the beaches. On the evening of 11 July, this caused an unfortunate "incident" when a flight of C-47 aircraft carrying reinforcements for the paratroopers at the front was shot up by tired, trigger-happy seamen. Allied air continued to be conspicuous by its absence.

On 12 July, a strong attack by elements of *15th Panzergrenadier* and the *Livorno* were beaten off by the 1st Division and 2nd Armored. The tally of prisoners began to rise, mostly Italian reservists but also some Germans. There was considerable skirmishing along the front, though nothing serious. On the night of 13 July, a British airborne attempt on the coast—behind the far left of the Axis lines—met disaster at the hands of "friendly" anti-aircraft.

Still the Allied front advanced, despite stiffening resistance and continued Axis air attack, which was particularly serious in the British sector after the first day or so. By 15 July, the Allies controlled about a fifth of the island, the entire southeastern corner. Supply remained difficult as this area possessed only small ports, but the beaches were still operating. Many airfields had been taken and considerable air power was now locally at hand. The Allies had a secure foothold and a base for the future.

Allied Offensive: 15–23 July 1943

Surprisingly, the Allies had no particular plans for operations in Sicily after securing their beachhead, beyond the vague notion that Montgomery's Eighth Army would drive northward along the east coast, covered by Patton's Seventh to its left. By 15 July, it was apparent that such an undertaking was going to be difficult.

As the British entered the Catania Plain—a considerable expanse stretching some 20 miles southward of Mount Etna—they began to encounter stiff resistance from the *Hermann Goring Division*, by now reinforced with airdropped elements of the *1st Parachute Division*.

On 12 July, Montgomery, without resort to higher headquarters beforehand, ordered XXX Corps—51st and Canadian Divisions—to make a "left hook" around Etna to the west. This arbitrary action, approved after the fact by Alexander, deprived Patton of one of the principal axes which he had been assigned. It also infuriated him. To mollify him, Alexander ordered him to clear western Sicily, an operation which he had already begun in the form of a "reconnaissance in force."

As Montgomery slowly battered his way across the Catania Plain, Patton cut loose, creating a special Provisional Corps—3rd, 82nd Airborne, and 2nd Armored Divisions—to undertake the task. Against negligible resistance this corps swept through western Sicily in an arc curving up from the south coast. Some outfits, such as 3rd Division, covered upwards of 25 miles a day on foot. The going was easy, and morale soared. On 22 July, Palermo fell, deliriously happy citizens greeting equally delirious troops.

Meanwhile, in the center, Patton's II Corps—45th and 1st Divisions—drove without authorization right across Sicily for the north coast and reached it on 23 July, though failing to pocket any substantial forces. It had been a spectacular drive, but its material benefits were modest. The withdrawal of the German and Italian mobile forces had been well in hand when Patton began his movement, so the enemy's ability to resist was not seriously weakened by his operation. Gaining Palermo was useful since it was a major port, but supply considerations were not serious. Most important was the boost in morale.

On the east coast, Montgomery's attempt to clear the Catania Plain had been moderately successful. By 23 July, the Eighth Army had secured about half the area, but at considerable cost. Casualties in XIII Corps—5th and 50th Divisions—had been particularly severe. Further, the enemy strength was actually increasing. Guzzoni, now more or less sharing command with the German Hans Hube of *XIV Panzer Korps,* received the *29th Panzergrenadier Division.* Efforts were being made to strengthen the four Italian mobile divisions, which had suffered some casualties and considerable desertion, by intermingling small German units with them. Though Axis plans called for the evacuation of Sicily in the interests of conserving manpower, they intended to make the Allies pay dearly for the property.

Holding Action: 23 July -10 August 1943

By 23 July, the basic pattern of operations in Sicily was becoming apparent: the Axis would hold as much as possible for as long as possible. The Allies, with seven divisions in the line and over four more in support, were confronted by three full German divisions, the bulk of the infantry of a fourth, and four Italian divisions of fair to indifferent quality.

From right to left, the Allies deployed the British 50th, 5th and 51st along the Dittaino River, just south of Etna's outer slopes, with their 78th, newly arrived, moving into the line on the left to maintain liaison with the Canadian 1st Division, Montgomery's left-hand unit. To the left of the Canadians, Patton had his 1st and 45th Divisions, with the 9th and 3rd ready to enter the line, and the 82nd Airborne and 2nd Armored in the rear.

Facing this host the Axis had the reinforced *Hermann Goring* below Etna, with about two-thirds of their *1st Parachute Division* to its west, where it maintained contact with the *Panzergrenadier* and the *Livorno,* intermingled to a great extent. Further west were the *Assietta* with additional elements of the *15th Panzergrenadiers.* On the coast was the *Aosta* rapidly being reinforced by advance elements of the *29th Panzergrenadiers.* The *Napoli* was in the rear. It took several days for this line to be consolidated, during which time the Allies made slow progress. Meanwhile, far more important events were transpiring on the political front.

On 19 July, Mussolini, his imperial ambitions rapidly crashing down around his ears, had gone to Feltre, in northern Italy, to meet his partner Hitler. His intention was to beg for more men and guns and aircraft. *Der Fuhrer* was not in the mood to listen and launched one of his increasingly frequent tantrums. To make matters worse, even as they spoke Allied bombers descended upon the railroad marshalling yards in Rome, the Eternal City itself. Material damage was slight. The shock was immense. The true implications of Mussolini's warmongering policies of two decades were finally and fully brought home to all but the blindest.

On 20 July, King Vittorio Emmanuele III told Mussolini, "We can not go on much longer." On 26 July, the Fascist Grand Council met. In a meeting carefully engineered by the King and several monarchists, Mussolini suddenly found himself deposed. In a trice he was whisked away in an ambulance to "protective custody," and old FM Pietro Badoglio installed as Prime Minister, proclaiming that the "war goes on" whilst beginning secret armistice overtures to the Allies. Negotiations, however, take time, and the war did go on.

By 2 August, the Allies had made some limited advances all along the front in Sicily, most notably on the American side, where the 3rd Division relieved the 45th and the 9th began to enter the line. A major new drive was planned with Alexander's 15th Army Group coordinating both Patton and Montgomery again, rather than letting each have his head. The Eighth Army would strike at Etna in front in a holding action, while attempting to turn it on the left with the Canadians and 78th Division. The American 1st and 9th would advance in the center and the 3rd along the coast. The attack jumped off on 3 August and made slow, painful progress in terrain wholly unsuited to any but infantry combat. The toughest fighting took place in the 1st Division sector, at the village of Troina.

Troina lies amid a considerable group of rugged hills rising to some 1,000 meters. It was defended by two combat groups of the *15th Panzergrenadiers*. For six days the 1st Division battered itself against the tough German resistance. Each time it was beaten off. Reinforcements in the form of the French 4th Tabor of Goums—a Moroccan battalion reputedly capable of remarkable things in mountains—proved of little help. The 39th Infantry Regiment of the 9th Division was thrown in. Some gains were made. The Germans held on tenaciously, counterattacking two dozen separate times during the engagement. Only on 6 August did elements of the 1st penetrate the village, and then only because the Germans chose to withdraw. As the 1st had battered itself against Troina, the 9th, to its left, had driven back the Italo-German troops to its front and threatened to cut the *15th Panzergrenadiers* off from the rear.

Things on the coast were not going well either. The 3rd Division found it slow going, confronted with terrain greatly favorable to the defense and some tough German infantry supported by German and Italian light artillery—just the thing needed for the rugged, craggy countryside. On 8 August, an effort was made to bypass some of the enemy's positions. A rifle battalion was lifted in landing craft behind the enemy lines nine miles to San Fratello. The Germans, however, were already pulling out, leaving only a few stragglers to be gathered up by the advancing Americans.

Over in the British sector progress had been equally difficult, but gradually the Catania Plain had been completely cleared. Though Axis troops still held the massive bulk of Etna, the 50th and 51st Divisions had secured the eastern slope along the coast and the 78th was threatening to pocket the entire volcano as it pressed around it from the west. The German high command—by now the Italians were virtually ignored—decided it was time to go. Even Hitler agreed that an evacuation was the optimal move, in order to "save valuable human resources."

Rearguard: 10–17 August 1943

From 10 August, the primary objective on the Axis forces in Sicily was their safe evacuation to Calabria, the "toe" of the mainland of Italy. Actually, some units began to be pulled out as early as 3 August, when the seriously battered *Napoli* started crossing the turbulent, two-mile wide Straits of Messina, to be followed by the badly cut up *Livorno.* Thus, by 10 August, Axis forces in Sicily had been reduced considerably. Moreover, the remaining Italian formations had been largely incorporated into the German units. Along the east coast *Hermann Goring,* incorporating elements of the *1st Parachute Division,* held the bulk of Etna against the increasingly successful encroachments of the Eighth Army. In the center, *15th Panzergrenadier* and the *Aosta Division* held the right flank of Patton's Seventh Army firmly in place. On the northern coast the *29th Panzergrenadier* and the *Assietta Division* held Patton's left, the 3rd Division, to minimal gains.

Although the Allied high command began to suspect that the Axis would attempt a massive evacuation starting about 3 August, they did not apparently pass the word down to Patton and Montgomery. Both pressed their attacks energetically, the friendly rivalry between them becoming deadly serious for the troops who had to undertake the "race to Messina." As the Axis front narrowed, the going got tougher.

Overly impressed by the potential success of his 8 August "end run," Patton essayed another by the same unit—the reinforced 2nd Battalion of the 30th Infantry Regiment—early on 11 August, putting it ashore in the rear of the *71st Panzergrenadier Regiment* at Brolo. The landing was badly managed. The Germans, already pulling back, reacted swiftly and virtually isolated the outfit somewhat inland of the beaches. Allied air strikes called in to support the troops did little damage to the enemy and literally wiped out the battalion's supporting artillery. Fortunately, after a very bad 29 hours, the bulk of the regiment came up along the coast in relief.

In Montgomery's sector, meanwhile, the *Hermann Goring* finally gave up its grip on Etna, though still holding the British 50th and 51st Divisions to limited gains along the coast. However, the *15th Panzergrenadier* lost the northern slopes to the combined might of the British 78th, the Canadian, and the American 9th Divisions on 13 August. This unhinged the northern flank of the German line. The *15th Panzergrenadiers* and the *Aosta* pulled back toward the northern coast, to gain the security of the *29th Panzergrenadier* and *Assietta* prior to heading for Messina and evacuation. Patrols of the 1st and 9th Divisions began probing towards the rear of the Axis troops along the coast, who fell back to the security of the first of three planned phase lines for the final stages of the withdrawal. The front now extended just south of Taormina on the east coast to just east of Falcone on the north.

On the night of 15–16 August, both Patton and Montgomery essayed "end runs"—the former for the third time, the latter trying something new for a change. Patton put the 157th Regimental Combat Team and a battalion of paratroopers ashore about a mile behind the enemy front, using all the panoply of an amphibious landing with considerable naval support. Montgomery threw elements of Number 40 Commando and the 4th Armored Brigade carelessly ashore near Scaletta. Both operations proved failures. The Axis, by now overwhelmingly German, had pulled back to their second and third phase lines, save for some extremely active rear guards and stragglers. Late on the night of 16–17 August, the last Axis troops pulled out of Sicily, having managed to completely break contact with the Allies.

The first Allied troops to enter Messina were elements of the American 7th Infantry Regiment on the morning of 17 August. The British came up about three hours later. Patton had won his race with Montgomery, but the real prize had eluded both men: the fine divisions which the Germans had committed to the defense of the island had gotten clean away.

The Evacuation: 10–17 August 1943

The basic Axis defensive plan for Sicily always envisioned an eventual evacuation to the mainland of Italy. By early August the Allied position was sufficiently strong as to cause the Axis commanders to begin thinking seriously about pulling out. Indeed, some Italian forces—such as the badly battered *Napoli Division*—had begun to ship out as early as 3 August. On 8 August, Hube ordered the German troops to pull out beginning on the 10th. On 9 August, Guzzoni received orders to commence a complete evacuation of the Italian forces.

The withdrawal was well planned, with schedules provided to prevent panic-stricken flight to the rear. Troops were allocated routes of march to the ports. Careful attention was taken to see that they were fed. The wounded were taken out first, then the least vital able-bodied men, then the combat troops.

Enormous anti-aircraft forces were deployed on both sides of the Straits, upwards of 500 pieces in all being reported—including some 150 of the highly effective German 88mm and Italian 90mm guns. Scores of barrage balloons were lofted to further bolster the defenses, and Axis fighters were concentrated in southern Italian airfields, while German and Italian light combat vessels, mostly motor torpedo boats, were committed to surface defense.

The Italian and German operations were conducted simultaneously, but separately. Each side used its own vessels and departed from different ports, save that both used the faciities near the Messina port complex cooperatively. The Italians made use of two large train ferries, several small steamers, and four large motor rafts. The Germans used 13 of their Siebel motor rafts, each capable of lifting 1,000 men, a number of small motorships, and 16 motor torpedo boats. Amazingly, despite overwhelming Allied air and naval superiority in the Central Mediterranean, the evacuation was a total success.

Allied air forces were singularly ineffective in halting or even seriously impeding the evacuation effort. Despite an average of some 250 sorties per night, casualties were minimal—six German and one Italian motor rafts and light vessels sunk and seven or eight others badly damaged. Too many of the sorties (about 40%) were undertaken with heavy bombers. Virtually all were undertaken against the ports and landing sites, rather than against the vessels at sea. Civilian casualties in the bombed ports were probably higher than those among the evacuees. If the performance of the Allied air forces was poor, that of their navies was execrable.

In the face of total Allied naval superiority, virtually nothing was done to interfere in the evacuations by surface attack. The American Task Force 88, covering the northern cost of Sicily, was not even officially informed by Allied Command of the fact of the evacuation. Adm Andrew Cunningham, Allied naval commander in the Mediterranean, refused pointedly to commit forces to the Straits, thereby displaying in full measure precisely the degree of timidity which he frequently accused the Italians of. Nevertheless, some British light forces based on Augusta did intervene repeatedly, on local initiative. Their success was virtually nil. Too few in number to effectively force the well defended Straits and once having an unfortunate encounter with an Italian light cruiser, they managed only one victory, knocking out an Italian motor raft on the night of 11 August.

The Axis withdrawal from Sicily was one of the most brilliant rear-guard operations of the Second World War, surpassed only by Dunkirk. Altogether over 100,000 men were pulled out, including many thousands of wounded and several thousand Allied prisoners. The Italians brought out some 62,000 men, 227 vehicles, and 41 pieces of artillery, along with 12 mules. The Germans evacuated about 40,000 men, 9,600 vehicles, 47 tanks, 94 pieces of artillery, over 2,000 tons of ammunition and fuel, and some 15,000 tons of miscellaneous supplies. All these men and equipment would be desperately needed later for the defense of Italy.

Perhaps Samuel Eliot Morison's judgement on this operation in his *Sicily-Salerno-Anzio* is the most incisive comment possible, "The Allied generals imagined that they were driving the enemy back in a series of brilliant offensives. Actually the Axis was conducting a series of rear-guard actions to cover an orderly evacuation of Sicily, which was carried out with complete success."

Afterward

Sicily was vitally important in the development of the Allied grand offensive against Germany. The occupation of Sicily cleared the Mediterranean of Axis sea power, thereby permitting the re-routing of convoys for the Middle East and India from the Cape of Good Hope route, thus realizing a considerable savings in critically short shipping. The venture had also dealt a mortal blow to Italy, having brought about the downfall of Mussolini and his replacement by a government anxious to conclude an armistice at the earliest possible moment.

The campaign had pointed up serious flaws in the Allied command structure, many of which had caused men to die unnecessarily. In future operations greater care was taken to insure the safety of airborne forces. An attempt, not altogether successful, was made to curb the grandiose ambitions of Allied air commanders. The development of effective air-ground support teams was taken in hand. Considerable experience was gained in the use of naval gunfire to support operations ashore. Also, the American Army in particular gained vitally needed combat experience. All of these paid dividends later, notably at Normandy.

Sicily also clarified Allied strategy in the Mediterranean. Any surrender of Italy had to be predicated upon the presence of Allied forces on the mainland to help prevent the Germans from taking over the country. Thus, an Italian campaign became inevitable as soon as the first Allied troops landed in Sicily.

In objective terms the Germans "won" the battle for Sicily. Their brilliantly conducted rear-guard operation turned a planned two-week conquest of the island into a drawn out, month-long soldier's battle in which they gave far better than they received. Discounting Italian casualties, the Allies lost 66% *more* men than the Germans did—some 20,000 to 12,000. On top of it all, the Germans had also managed to evacuate all the manpower and most of the equipment of more than three top quality divisions. Ultimately, however, the Germans were driven out of Sicily, and the walls of *Festung Europa* were breached. It was, as Winston Churchill said, "the end of the beginning."

Armies of the Sicilian Campaign

Armies vary greatly in structure, composition, and technique. More importantly, they vary in capabilities. As creatures of the societies which field them, armies inevitably reflect the strengths and weaknesses of their societies. Major elements of five armies clashed in Sicily, and some proved more capable than others.

The Americans. The American Army ought to have been the finest in the world, as a representative of the most powerful political and industrial democracy in history. however, though capable of considerable serious, sustained effort, it was flawed and far weaker than it ought to have been. A major problem was attitude. Americans had already begun to see war as a management problem rather than as a clash of will. This might have worked out, but in practice "management" was more frequently mismanagement. For example, the best quality manpower went into the least critical jobs, those in the rear, leaving less well-qualified men for the combat arms.

It was also an overspecialized army, with far too many men holding special titles and ranks, and a superabundance of officers, most of whom were non-combatants. Operationally, the army tended to rely upon "industrial warfare"—massive expenditures of ammunition and gasoline—rather than upon sound tactics and well-trained manpower. While generally this resulted in far fewer casualties, it also put the American soldier at a considerable disadvantage when fighting in situations where he lacked maneuvering room or adequate artillery and air support. Such proved to be the case in Sicily, where the rugged nature of the country militated against sweeping movements and the use of great volumes of fire.

The preparation of the individual soldier was neglected in several other ways. Despite paying lip-service to individual initiative, the army stressed "team-work." At the same time, it ignored the enormous potential benefits of developing cohesive combat units through promotion of *esprit de corps;* an American infantryman ultimately was part of a pool who was temporarily assigned to a particular outfit. That the men did not all fall apart in combat is remarkable; as it was, the US had a higher proportion of psychological casualties than any other army. Of course, American units could and did do well on numerous occasions.

The British. The British Army was the product of a strongly stratified society. Officers and enlisted men came from totally different backgrounds. However, *noblesse oblige* was well understood. Though officers were members of a privileged class, they paid for it in blood, having far higher casualties than in the American Army. Ties between officers and men were generally good. The time-honored territorial recruitment policy of the British Army fostered the creation of tough, cohesive combat units; men served with others from their home areas, frequently under officers recruited from the local gentry. There had, of course, been serious tactical and operational problems early in the war. But by mid-1943, the British Army was at its peak, having unlearned all the wrong lessons at the hands of the Germans.

To be sure, there was often a lack of aggressiveness and sustained brilliance in the planning of operations, but this was tied to an increasingly desperate manpower shortage.

The Canadians. The Canadian Army—along with its Australian and New Zealand brothers—was among the finest armies in the world. In many ways, the Canadians combined the better features of both the American and British without their flaws. Lavish regard for the well-being of the men, dedicated officers, and attention to technological superiority were all present, along with a commendable aggressiveness and considerable flexibility.

The Germans. The German Army was undoubtedly the best in the world on a unit-for-unit basis: well-trained, fairly well-equipped, and remarkably democratic in its structure. Virtually anyone who could demonstrate leadership ability—regardless of class or "intelligence"—was officer material. Cadres were kept lean, if only because it was better to do without a person in a particular slot than to put an inefficient one in it. Officers were required to be solicitous of their men—even to remembering their birthdays—and administration was deliberately on a personal basis: business machines did not sort through thousands of cards to find an eligible officer; the unit commander looked around for himself. This process was perhaps managerially inefficient, but promoted strong ties of confidence and loyalty.

Of course, the Germans were masters of combat. *Kampkraft*— "fighting skill"—was the only measure of a man's fitness. War was understood as a clash of will conducted with maximum violence. By mid-1943, the army had passed its peak, but was still superior to all comers. In Sicily, certainly, the Allies encountered only the best: the tough panzergrenadiers of the regular army and the cream of the Luftwaffe ground forces, the parachutists and the *Hermann Goring.* All these divisions were veterans, or at least contained sizable veteran cadres, and were composed of the finest available manpower. To be sure, the Luftwaffe units had occasional administrative difficulties and their higher leadership was often poorly qualified to lead a division in combat, but in Sicily this meant little since it was essentially an infantry rearguard action anyway. One of the tragedies of the 20th Century remains the fact that the finest mass army in history was an instrument of evil.

The Italians. The Italian Army was in bad shape. Never properly prepared for war, its experiences over the last three years had done little to improve it. Almost anything that could be wrong with an army was. Equipment was poor, ammunition in short supply, training unrealistic, officer recruitment largely social, and treatment of enlisted men execrable. There was little will to fight, though some units, with strong traditions and specialized missions—such as the *bersaglieri*— were up to anything. In Sicily most of the troops were overaged reservists in coastal and local defense units. These melted away quickly. Of the regular forces, only one division was properly equipped even by the rather impoverished Italian standards. The manpower itself was basically sound, as demonstrated by the good account given when under German control.

Getting Ashore: The Problems of Amphibious Warfare

An amphibious operation essentially consists of three phases:

1. Getting to the beach,
2. Getting on the beach,
3. Getting off the beach.

Each aspect has its own special problems which experience has shown requires special equipment and tactics.

Getting to the Beach. Traditional methods of transporting men and cargo are unsuited to amphibious requirements. In normal manpower movements, most of the equipment can be stowed and the troops usually debark over the gangway at a port. In amphibious operations, however, the troops must have all their equipment with them; it is most often usually divided into what they can carry and what will be carried behind. In addition, they must leave the ship some distance from shore—primarily over the side via cargo nets and into small landing craft. The principal vessel designed for this sort of operation is the Attack Transport (APA), usually a converted transport or passenger vessel. In addition, certain specialized vessels exist to deposit men directly ashore, such as Landing Ships Infantry (LSI) and Landing Craft Infantry (LCI); both are sea-going, after a fashion, and are capable of lifting fairly large numbers of men in relative comfort and depositing them on or near a beach that is poorly supplied with docking facilities.

More important than the manpower difficulties, however, are the cargo problems. In normal—"administrative"—cargo movements, the heaviest stuff goes down into the bowels of the ship. In amphibious operations, and indeed any movements requiring the troops to go into action almost immediately, something called "combat loading" must be resorted to, using ships specially equipped to handle it—AKA's (Attack Cargo Ships). Simply put, combat loading means that what you need first gets loaded uppermost, and with a minimum of packaging. This also means you increase your shipping requirements by approximately 50% in terms of measurement tons. The capacity of ships to carry cargo is calculated in "measurement tons" of 40 cubic feet. The actual amount of cargo by weight which can be carried in this space varies greatly with the type of material, but a rough average is two tons of general cargo. This means that a ship rated at 4,000 tons has a "lift" capacity of 16,000,000 cubic feet, or roughly 8,000 tons by weight. The shipping requirements for the American infantry and armored division fully equipped with supplies and fuel for 30 days and seven "units of fire"—full days' ammo rations for all weapons—would be:

Tons of Lift Required for Movement

	Administrative	*Amphibious*
Infantry Div	45,000	67,500
Armored Div	89,200	133,800

This capacity was approximately the lift required for the divisions committed to *Operation Husky.* Considering that there were roughly eight divisions, including one armored, in the initial landings and reserves afloat and that British outfits were larger than American ones, the total demand for shipping ran roughly 750,000 tons—somewhat more than the capacity of 75 Liberty ships. The actual ocean-going shipping committed to Sicily was considerably more since much of it was in the form of relatively low capacity landing ships.

Getting on the Beach. Having arrived off the beaches to be invaded—ignoring the difficulties of coordinating numerous convoys (19 for the US units alone) during the buildup period and the concentration period, as well as the complexities of providing escorts—the real difficulties now begin. The difficulties are essentially in the form of traffic management. The accompanying diagram gives a general idea of the way these things were done in mid-1943. As time went on, of course, amphibious operations became far more sophisticated. Needless to say, each particular operation was a special case. However, there were always general similarities in such operations.

The diagram represents an eight-battalion landing on a front of approximately six miles, which is roughly the scale of the initial landings of the 1st Division at Gela in Sicily. Special light craft and buoys marked the boundaries of the various areas shown. Each area had a specifically designated function. The Naval Gunfire Support Areas were reserved for the heavy ships—battleships, cruisers, and destroyers—which were to plaster the beaches before and during the landings. Lighter gunfire support vessels, including rocket firing LCI's, would have designated areas within the Boat Rendezvous Areas.

The Transport Area is where the APA's and AKA's muster to lower their landing boats, load them, and send them off to the Boat Rendezvous Areas, all under the watchful eye of the Command Ship and possible subordinate command vessels as well. The LCI and LST (Landing Ship Tank)

Areas are where vessels of these ilks congregate, ready to bring in the follow-up waves after the landing boats—LCVP's (Landing Craft Vehicle and Personnel) in American and LCA's (Landing Craft Attack) in British service—have gotten the initial waves ashore. Further back would be additional troops and equipment; aircraft carrying LST's for gunfire observation, an expedient first tried in Sicily; salvage and repair ships; and additional naval vessels to provide anti-submarine and anti-aircraft screens.

Getting off the Beach. Presuming everything goes well—and *no* amphibious operation failed after 1942—the troops have secured a toehold and begun moving inland as quickly as possible. An enormous buildup of men and material now begins. Generally, this leads to a considerable glut of munitions, supplies, equipment, and whatnot on the beach. Special shore parties from the navy and beach engineer units from the army now take control of sorting and distributing these materials. In Sicily the American Beach and Shore Regiments proved less than efficient, though the Navy Shore Parties and British beach battalions proved more than capable.

As ports become available, engineers, including the famed Navy Construction Battalions or "Sea-Bees," start clearing away wreckage and mak-

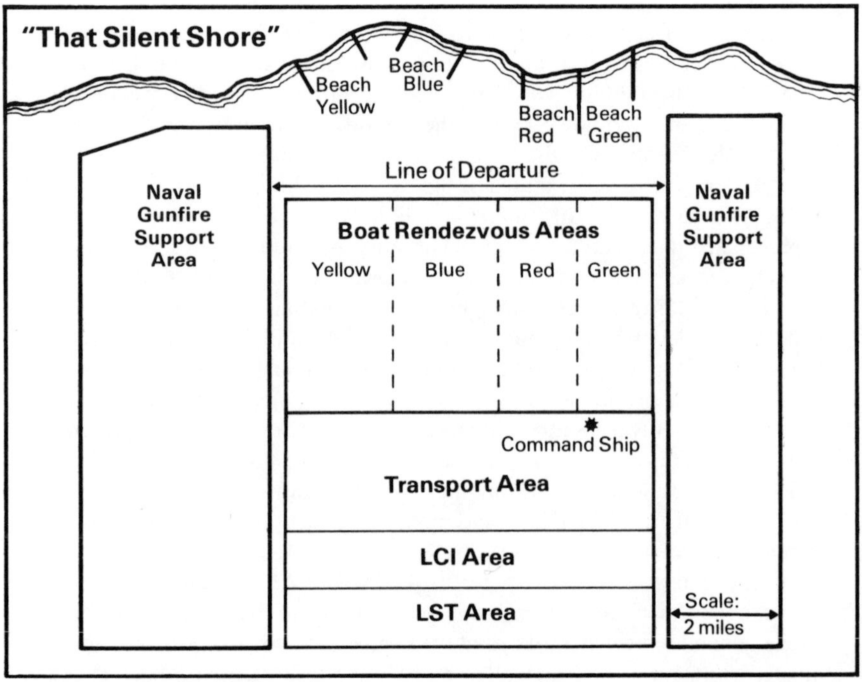

ing them ready to receive cargo. Usually these troops also manage to improve the capacity of the port by a considerable measure.

All of this sounds efficient. Nevertheless, there is much that can go wrong. In Sicily, for example, LST's found that they were unable to get in close enough to beach properly. Some engineers devised a pontoon off-loading system. It worked and was used elsewhere in similar circumstances. Normally, a recently invaded beach "looks like a junkyard." Once the build-up is well in hand, the troops can begin serious operations. In general, supply by way of the beaches continues for some days or even weeks after the invasion, often necessitating continuation of essentially the same operation as first brought the troops ashore. Once enough ports are available, however, the beach is shut down and policed up.

Shipping had to be collected from all over. Allied advanced planning had neglected the production of landing vessels and APA's and AKA's early in the war and the situation was only beginning to be resolved in mid-1943. The Allied powers operated a sort of worldwide pool of shipping, with heated arguments between Britain and America, Army and Navy, as to who should get what and when and how soon. This debate applied even to heavy warships. To release two battleships for Sicily, two American ships were sent to patrol the North and Norwegian Seas. Not included in the figures above are DUKW's and LVT's, essentially motor vehicles suitable for land or water operations. Scores of these were first employed in Sicily and proved enormously useful, but their numbers are uncertain.

Assault Shipping for the Invasion of Sicily

	American	*British*	*Total*
Headquarters Ships	2	3	5
Attack Transports (APA)	20	37	57
Attack Cargo Ships (AKA)	7	0	7
LST's	76	72	148
LSI(L)'s	90	145	235
LCT's	100	138	238
LCM's	154	241	395
LCVP/LCA's	324	272	596
Total	**773**	**908**	**1,681**

Key: LST: Landing Ship Tank; **LSI(L):** Landing Ship Infantry (Large); **LCT:** Landing Craft Tank; **LCM:** Landing Craft Medium; **LCVP:** Landing Craft Vehicle and Personnel; **LCA:** Landing Craft Attack; **LVT:** Landing Vehicle Tracked.

• • •

The fall of Sicily confirmed the Badoglio government's intentions to quit the war. In delicate negotiations with the Allies, Italy undertook to surrender upon the landing of Allied forces. Aware of what was in the offing, Germany poured troops into its reluctant Ally. On 9 September an Anglo-American landing occurred at Salerno on the west coast of Italy. Despite intensive German efforts to break the invasion on the beaches, the troops clung to the coast. Naples fell by the beginning of October and the Allies pressed northwards. But Hitler was not willing that they should go too far. The Allied advance soon bogged down in front of the famed Abbey at Monte Cassino, which formed the linch-pin of what Hitler dubbed the *Gustav Line.* Months of sanguinary fighting ensued as the Allies tried repeatedly to capture the Abbey. Desperate measures were employed. The historic Abbey was bombed into ruins, many priceless art treasures were lost in an ill-conceived effort to evict German defenders who were not, in fact, present. In January of 1944 a landing was made behind the Gustav Line at Anzio, only to be rapidly bottled up. Finally, in May of 1944 the Allies cracked the Gustav Line. Rome fell to the advancing Allies on 5 June. The balance of the war in Italy was anti-climactic. Although hard fighting continued over the next eleven months, with the Allies gradually inching their way northwards, events in Italy had become of secondary importance even before the fall of the Eternal City. The focus of the war had shifted to northwestern Europe again, where preparations were already in hand for the final confrontation with Germany. Indeed, the Allies had been striking at the heart of Germany for almost four years, from the air.

The advent of air power added a new and terrifying dimension to war. As enunciated by its proponents, Trenchard in Britain, Mitchell in America, and above all Douhet in Italy, air power could hold hostage entire populations hitherto secure far behind the fighting fronts. No nation would be safe with its cities exposed to bombardment by vast fleets of heavy bombers. And the threat of total destruction would obviate the need for any other type of armed force.

Terror bombing tactics were attempted several times in the 1930s. But, as used by Japan against China, Italy against Ethiopia, or by the Nationalists in the Spanish Civil War, they proved less than decisive, though frightening enough. Proponents of air power scoffed at objections raised to their theories, on the grounds that the aircraft used were too few to be decisive, their payloads too small to have a proper effect. The glamor of air power added weight to their arguments. And then the Second World War broke out. The German Luftwaffe was the first to employ terror bombing. Poland suffered heavy aerial attack in the opening weeks of the war. But the decision was reached on the ground, where the panzers, aided by dive bombers, overcame all resistance. Then came their offensive in the West, and terror bombing appeared to have worked. Rotterdam was subject to a massive bombardment on the morning of 14 May 1940. The effects were devastating. Rumor, fanned by German propaganda, had it that 30,000 had died. The Netherlands capitulated. That the actual death toll was upwards of 800 went unnoticed as the Luftwaffe contemplated its next objective, England. Despite dropping over 36,000 tons of bombs on English cities, resulting in great loss of life and damage to industrial and housing and historic sites, the Luftwaffe failed to break Britain's will. As the war developed into a stalemate between a defiant Britain and an otherwise triumphant Germany, the Royal Air Force unleashed the mightiest air offensive of the war, against Germany itself. In the prophetic words of Winston Churchill, "We shall bomb Germany by day as well as by night, in ever increasing measure, casting upon them month by month a heavier discharge of bombs, and making the German people taste and gulp each month a sharper dose of the miseries they have showered upon mankind."

Although the British began the air war against Germany, the Americans came to play an enormous role within months of their entry into the war. The two powers had somewhat different approaches to strategic bombardment, the British going in for area attacks under cover of darkness and the Americans specializing in high level precision day light raids, the net effect on Germany was devastating.

The air battle over Germany cost some 80,000 Allied airmen their lives. An estimated 300,000 Germans, largely civilians, also perished, mostly in the great fire raids on Dresden and Hamburg. Almost every German city was subjected to heavy bombardment damage, each bearing great scars of rubble-strewn wasteland. Almost 13,000,000 Germans were made homeless, some 20% of the population. The German armed forces had suffered as well. The army, navy, and air force were forced to curtail operations due to an increasing fuel shortage engendered by the bombings. Rapid movements of men and materiel became increasingly more difficult as a result of the disruption of the German rail net. And enormous numbers of men and equipment vitally needed on the fighting fronts had to be diverted to the defense of Germany's urban and industrial centers against the ever growing Allied air domination.

But the war could not be won in the air alone. To achieve final victory, Allied armies had to be landed on the shores of Europe to engage and break the enemy in the field.

Overlord: The Normandy Invasion
6–26 June 1944

By Albert A. Nofi

Nothing in military history quite compares with the Allied assault on *Festung Europa* on 6 June 1944. Operations have occurred involving greater numbers. Many campaigns have been far more hotly fought. Far greater casualty lists have been incurred. But never has there been an operation of such scale involving greater risk or with greater consequence.

The Problem

The Normandy Invasion was made inevitable by certain events between 10 May 1940 and 7 December 1941. The German conquest of France in May and June of 1940 successfully ejected Britain from the Continent. Their subsequent failure to break British resistance in the Battle of Britain in August and September meant that, though triumphant virtually everywhere, Germany could not win the war. So Hitler sought less direct ways of reaching a decision, which led to the invasion of Russia on 22 June 1941, and yet another war which he found he could not win. Meanwhile, on the other side of the world, the United States, the ultimate power, was becoming increasingly concerned about and involved in the great struggle. Then, on 7 December 1941, the United States was suddenly dragged into the conflict by the precipitous action of Japan, Hitler's ally. It was this act which marks the beginning of *Operation Overlord.*

Planning

Even before Pearl Harbor, American strategists had addressed themselves to the problem of how to defeat Germany. Their conclusion was that the best—perhaps only—way to obtain a decisive result would be to undertake a massive amphibious landing somewhere in Western Europe in order to bring the main strength of the German armies to battle and destroy them with the superior human and materiel resources of the Free World. When America entered the war this became the primary American military objective. However, attaining that objective would require time. America had barely begun to mobilize in 1941. British resources were already stretched almost to breaking. Nevertheless, some American planners saw such an invasion possible in late 1942 or early 1943. The British, with memories of 1914–1918 butcher's bills and over two years of hard experience in the new struggle behind them, demurred. Far better to let the Germans exhaust themselves against the Russians, whilst the Allies engaged in a "peripheral" strategy, snipping off exposed outlying bastions of *Festung Europe*, such as North Africa and Sicily and Greece, and raining destruction on Germany's industry and populace through the "Combined Bomber Offensive." When these had sapped German strength sufficiently, an undertaking against western Europe might be launched, with the foe already reeling in defeat.

The differences between the British and American concepts led inevitably to disputes. Nevertheless, although the Americans thought the British way was indecisive, they also had to face the logistical realities. Manpower and materiel would take time to accumulate. Meanwhile, such forces as were already available had to be used. So a peripheral strategy was adopted in 1942 and extended into 1943, while a slow build-up began in Britain. During this period Allied leaders hammered out basic strategy in conferences at Quebec and Casablanca and Cairo and Teheran. At this last, in late 1943, the decision was made to launch an invasion sometime in 1944.

A joint planning staff had been created in England under MG Sir Frederick Morgan in March of 1943. This had already undertaken some of the preliminary planning necessary for the invasion. In January of 1944 Gen Dwight D. Eisenhower was named Supreme Commander. With nearly two years experience in commanding inter-Allied forces behind him, Eisenhower was uniquely qualified for the job. Morgan's staff, initially about 500 officers and 600 enlisted men, rapidly expanded to nearly 1200 officers and over 3700 enlisted men. Integration of personnel was carried out to a remarkable degree. Eisenhower's immediate Deputy Commander was Air Chief Marshal Sir Arthur Tedder. Each branch of the headquarters had a commander of one nationality and a deputy of the other, thus insuring minimal friction as the planning proceeded.

The specific problems of the invasion had already been partially addressed by Morgan's original planning staff. A choice of invasion site had been made, the coast of Normandy between the mouth of the Seine and Cherbourg. It was not the optimal invasion site, which lay just across the Straits of Dover around Calais. But it offered many advantages. Normandy was within range of fighter aircraft operating from British fields, and only a short sea voyage from ports in southern Britain. German defenses, while considerable, were less formidable than at the Pas de Calais. Moreover, it could be effectively isolated from the rest of the continent by Allied air power, for the Seine and Loire bridges could be taken out in the weeks and days before the invasion. *Operation Overlord,* initially the designation for the invasion itself, soon became the code-word for the overall Allied plan of operations in France. The Normandy landings were dubbed *Operation Neptune.* In addition, a second invasion was planned to occur simultaneously in the South of France, though *Operation Anvil-Dragoon* was, in the event, postponed ten weeks due to a shortage of assault shipping.

Very early in the final planning stages Gen Sir Bernard Law Montgomery, who would actually command the troops going ashore, raised objections to the scope of the initial landings. At his urging the invasion front was expanded from three divisions landing on a 25-mile front to five divisions on a 60-mile front. While this would complicate initial shipping requirements, the expanded front would facilitate the capture of Cherbourg, the only major port in the area, which was a necessity for further operations.

While all this planning was going on, the forces were being accumulated. Battle-hardened American and British divisions were pulled out of the Italian Front. The rate of reinforcement from the United States was stepped up. The naval commander-in-chief, Sir Bertram Ramsey, oversaw the concentration of over 5500 shipping and landing vessels, naval escorts and fire support ships. And the air commander-in-chief, Air Chief Marshal Sir T. L. Leigh-Mallory, unleashed his air fleets.

First came an air offensive against the German Luftwaffe. American heavy bombers of the Eighth Air Force struck at the aircraft factories which supported the Luftwaffe, drawing its fighter strength into action against powerful squadrons of escorts. At heavy cost, the offensive broke the back of Germany's fighter forces. Then the Allied air began taking on German communications lines throughout western Europe, destroying bridges and locomotives and railroad marshalling yards. Finally, in the weeks before the invasion itself, they began to concentrate on the coast defenses.

While all of this was going on, Allied intelligence played a difficult game. The Germans knew invasion was inevitable. Such massive preparations as were necessary made it almost impossible to prevent the enemy from finding out. Of course, if German attention could be divided and diverted from the actual objective to others, the invasion would be protected. A complex series of "cover plans" was evolved, dubbed *Bodyguard.* LG George S. Patton, whom the Germans believed was to lead the invasion, was given a fictitious command, the "First United States Army Group," composed of a few thousand troops maintaining dummy installations in eastern Britain, from whence an invasion of the Pas de Calais was most practical. Other deceptions indicated landings in other areas, even in Normandy itself, lest the lack of information suggest to some wily German analyst that the invasion was to come there.

On the Far Shore

Despite Hitler's rhetoric about the Atlantic Wall, German preparations for meeting an invasion had been lax until January of 1944. At that time FM Erwin Rommel, the famed "Desert Fox", was named commander of *Army Group B*, the command directly responsible for the western coast of Europe. Rommel threw himself into preparations for the invasion, travelling hundreds of miles, surveying virtually the entire coast in person, visiting every division under his command. Hard driving, Rommel sacked officers who failed to cooperate fully. He planned a virtually impregnable system of defense. There would be a barrier of over 220,000,000 mines stretching along the beaches of France and the Low Countries, supported by extensive obstructions in the water and on the beaches, and bolstered by reinforced concrete strongpoints above the beaches. Inland, he would plant anti-glider obstacles, heavy posts sunk into the ground with mines attached. The work was already in progress and accelerating, but materiel was difficult to obtain. Although he trebled the number of mines planted on the coast, from some 1,500,000 to over 4,500,000, he was hard pressed to obtain more. Over a million artillery shells held in French naval arsenals were released to him for conversion into mines only at the end of May. Concrete and reinforcing steel were in short supply. What was available often went where it was least needed, at the already heavily fortified Pas de Calais. Though Rommel was in command of the Atlantic Wall, he was not free from outside interference: above him were old FM Gerd von Rundstedt, head of *O/B West,* and Hitler himself.

Both Rundstedt and Hitler believed the invasion would come at the Pas de Calais, a matter which Rommel doubted. With several other higher officers, Rommel believed the threat at Normandy was strong. In any conflict with Hitler, he was bound to lose, so the Pas de Calais generally had priority for materiel. In similar fashion, Rommel's task was made more difficult by a dispute over tactics.

Rommel believed that the invasion must be crushed on the beaches. To this end, he urged that the ten panzer and panzergrenadier divisions available be concentrated well forward, able to strike at the landings as soon as they began. His experience with Allied air power in Africa led him to believe that holding the panzers back would only subject them to devastating air attack as they endeavored to move up, thus rendering them useless for the critical battle. Rundstedt disagreed. He believed that the Allies should be let ashore and then smashed with a mobile counterattack by the concentrated might of the panzers. An appeal to Hitler only made matters worse. Der Fuhrer supported neither. Instead, he allocated some of the panzers to Rommel's direct command and reserved others for Rundstedt, but then prohibited either from committing them to combat without his approval. Thus it remained on the eve of the invasion, as 1,500,000 German troops anxiously awaited the inevitable Allied assault.

Concentration, 1–5 June

Men began boarding ship at the beginning of June. At the same time paratroopers were concentrated at airfields. Everyone was put under guard to insure against leaks. All aircraft were repainted in a special "invasion" scheme, featuring three broad stripes on each wing. Midget submarines of the Royal Navy put to sea so as to arrive off the beaches in time to serve as guides for the landing craft. Security, already tight was tightened still more. Travel was virtually prohibited and even the immunity of the diplomatic pouch was suspended. Coded messages were sent out putting the French Resistance on the alert. The press was briefed, and then locked up with the troops.

Allied air forces stepped up their attacks on the Loire and Seine bridges and along the entire length of the Atlantic Wall. Special attention was paid to German radar, with virtually all installations in the Normandy area destroyed, but just enough left untouched at the Pas de Calais so as to permit detection of a mock-invasion fleet ready to put to sea. Minesweepers began clearing channels through friendly minefields, while minelayers planted new barriers to seal off the Channel from German submarines and surface craft. Meanwhile, the meteorologists contemplated their charts and tables.

The invasion had been set for 5 June. Unfortunately, on 3 June the weather-

[continued on page 119]

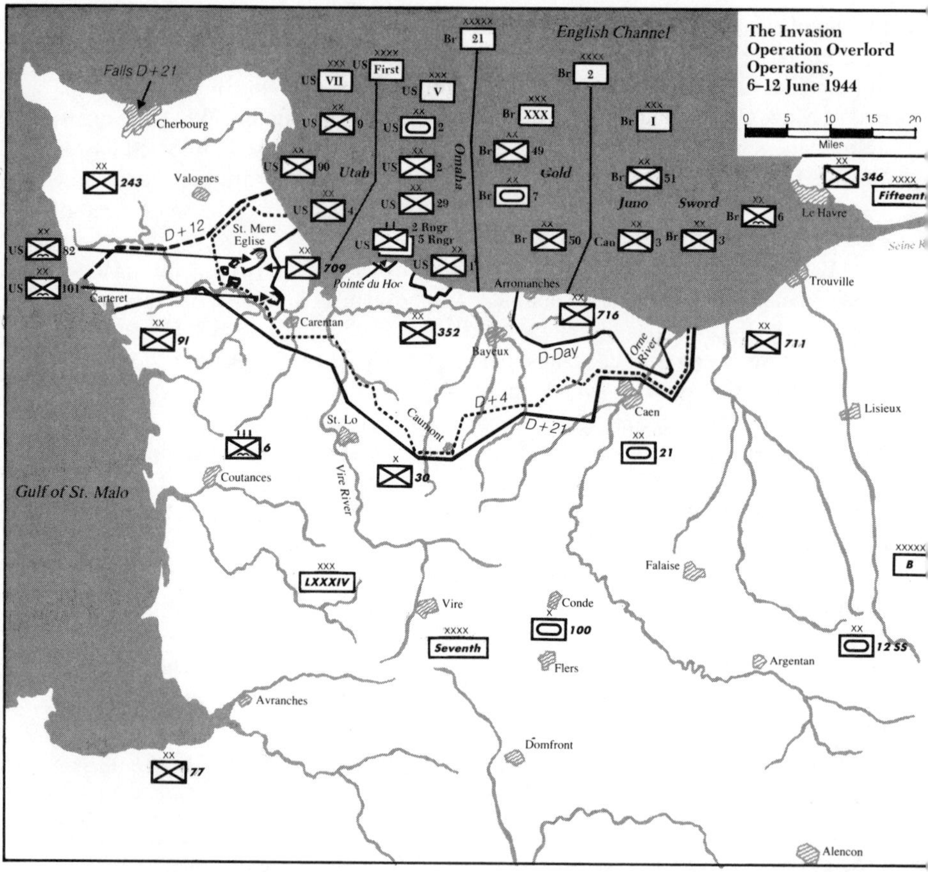

The general location of the principal defending units on D-Day has been indicated on this map, along with the first wave Allied landing forces and divisions available for landing over the immediate few days after the assault. In addition the general outline of the front has been shown for the evening of D-Day, D + 4, D + 12, and D + 21, the day on which Cherbourg fell to the American VII Corps. Between D + 12 and D + 21 the main front shifted not at all, the principal Allied effort being the reduction of Cherbourg. By D + 21 the Allies had ashore 21 full divisions plus miscellaneous forces equal to about four or five others, while the Germans had only managed to concentrate 18, with miscellaneous forces equal to about another, all of which were very battered. On D + 21 (27 June), however, the Germans were reinforced by four SS panzer divisions—*1st, 2nd, 9th,* and *10th*— which did much to stabilize the situation. By D + 50 the Allies had only marginally expanded their bridgehead. Then they undertook a massive breakout, *Operation Cobra.*

[continued from page 117]

men predicted unfavorable conditions. Eisenhower postponed the operation one day. On the night of 4 June, with the weather predictions for the 6th better, though not optimal, a major conference was held at Eisenhower's headquarters. Montgomery, who would have to command the actual forces on the ground, believed the invasion must go ahead. The Supreme Commander weighed all the factors. A postponement now meant a delay until the 8th, for ships would have to refuel. The dangers of a leak grew greater with every hour. Quietly he spoke, "Okay. We'll go." The next day he penned a brief communique to be issued in the event of failure, concluding "If any blame or failure attaches to the attempt it is mine alone", and then went off to bid his paratroopers good luck.

The massive invasion fleet, greatest armada in history, put to sea. From a dozen ports the troopships sailed for the middle of the English Channel, where they mustered at a map grid labelled *Piccadilly Circus,* and were formed into five massive convoys for the approach to the beaches. The warships, from great battleships to tiny patrol craft, guarded and guided them and made ready for their own role in bombarding the beaches. Overhead, Allied heavy bombers lumbered by to drop thousands of tons of explosives on the beach defenses in the final critical moments. At airfields in central England over 18,000 British and American airborne troops boarded aircraft and gliders and took wing for France. The powerful drone of thousands of engines overhead spread the word to those few in England who do not yet realize that the "mighty endeavor" was at hand.

Nightdrop

The first men to land were the pathfinders. Their mission was to mark the way for the troop-carrying aircraft and gliders using flares and torches. Most lost their own way in the dark. Few drop zones were properly marked. The airdrops, the British 6th Airborne Division on left, and the American 82nd and 101st Airborne Divisions on the right, were badly scattered, the divisions unable to concentrate and operate effectively. Men came down dozens of miles from their objectives. The losses were enormous. Nevertheless, the drops were a perverse success. The mission of the airborne was to cover the flanks of the invasion beaches and secure passages through marshes and flooded ground and across the rivers which lay behind them. The widely scattered troops promoted confusion and chaos in the German rear area, their efforts facilitated by the dropping of numerous dummy paratroopers all along the coast. German radio and telephone lines were soon jammed with calls reporting that an airborne invasion had begun from so many different locations that decisive action was impossible. As the parachutists and glidermen began to sort themselves out, they formed small combat groups and took on targets of opportunity when unable to attack their proper objectives.

"Away all Boats!"

Even as the airborne troops fell from the skies in the predawn hours, the great armada began to arrive off the beaches. Overhead, countless light bombers and fighter bombers gave the defenses a final pounding. As the skies lightened, the Germans manning the coast defenses awoke to the realization that this is no ordinary air raid, but rather the preliminaries of a full scale invasion. Acting with commendable speed, their batteries began to fire, seeking targets among the minesweepers clearing the coastal waters.

The Allied warships began to open fire as the German batteries revealed themselves. The noise increased as the troops, many tired, frightened, and seasick, began to climb into their landing craft. As the slow, dangerous process proceeded, the naval gunfire never ceased and wave after wave of bombers struck at the enemy.

Even before dawn the Germans had begun to realize that something special was afoot. Rommel's headquarters—he was on leave at the time—appealed to Rundstedt to release some panzers. He agreed, but kicked the request upstairs to Supreme Headquarters for confirmation. Headquarters refused; Hitler was asleep and no one wished to disturb him. Haggling continued through the night. Finally, at 1000, Der Fuhrer's permission was obtained and the panzers began to move. The delay resulted in their movement being exposed to Allied air power and they suffered greatly.

Gold, Juno, Sword

The British and Canadians on the Allied left were assigned three small beaches, Gold, Juno, and Sword. Their mission was to drive inland, establishing contact with the 6th Airborne Division holding the Orne River crossings, and take Caen, while establishing contact with the Americans at Omaha on their right.

The British and Canadian beaches were narrow. Gold and Juno were suitable for a single division-sized landing at best. Sword, a brigade-sized one. They were also not within mutual supporting distance of each other. Further complicating matters, the offshore waters in their vicinity were somewhat treacherous, with many rocky shoals. The beaches themselves, however, were ideal: flat, hard sand with few natural obstacles. The defending unit, the thinly spread *716th Infantry Division,* was a low-order outfit composed of overage German troops with a sprinkling of so-called "Ost" battalions, Russian deserters and Prisoners-of-War. It had little mobility and much of its equipment was fixed in permanent positions. The result was that the landings went well. The troops came ashore in good order. Consolidation of the beaches began immediately and by noon the three toeholds had been linked into a broader beachhead. Then things began to get difficult.

The *21st Panzer Division* came up, full of fight though already battered by Allied air power. The division smashed into the Canadian front, forcing them back almost to the water's edge between Sword and Juno. At that critical juncture, naval gunfire was called in. The *21st Panzer* was slowly blown to pieces. Then the third brigade of the 6th Airborne Division landed, its dropzones fortuitously situated so that it commenced an immediate counterattack. The Germans fell back. By evening, the beachhead was secure. But the *21st Panzer* had gained time for the Germans. Caen, the primary British objective for D-Day was not taken.

Utah Beach

Utah Beach was over on the Allied far right. Not originally an objective, it was added to facilitate the capture of Cherbourg. Assigned to the U.S. 4th Infantry Division, Utah Beach was highly unattractive to Allied planners, being just at the base of the Cotentin Peninsula, at the head of which stands Cherbourg. The whole base of the peninsula was low-flying, flat land—mostly marshes or land that had been flooded purposefully by the Germans. Most unattractive of all was the fact that there was a two-mile wide strip of inundated land *directly* behind Utah Beach, extending for over eight miles up the east coast of the peninsula. Only very narrow causeways and trails provided a means of exiting from the beach itself, and it was thought that very few Germans could hold up many times more than their number of troops at these points. The inundation also divides Utah from Omaha, making a juncture very difficult. As such, it was feared that the Germans might have the ability to defeat each beachhead in detail.

To counter some of these arguments, it was decided to drop two airborne divisions immediately behind Utah Beach—one to secure the causeways off the beach and one to secure bridges over a belt of flooded land further inland. The beachhead assault unit—the 4th Infantry Division—was to join with these paratroopers as soon as possible on D-Day.

Responsibility for Utah was given to VII Corps, under the command of MG J. Lawton "Lightning Joe" Collins. His mission was to secure a lodgement, drive across the peninsula to the town of Carteret, establish a defensive line facing south across the Cotentin, and finally to capture Cherbourg.

The Germans were taken somewhat aback by the Allied assault in this area on June 6. Most German staff officers thought the place practically unassaultable—for much the same reasons that many Allied planners had disliked the area. The *709th Infantry Division* had responsibility for this sector. This unit was second-rate and over-stretched; it covered the Cotentin coast from Cherbourg to the Vire. Only one battalion covered the Allied landing area, with an unenthusiastic *Ost* battalion in reserve near St. Mere Eglise. Strongpoints on Utah Beach were few. However, the Germans in the Cotentin had something that they did not have in the Omaha sector: strong, first-rate reserves. Within striking distance of the beach on June 6 was the *91st Infantry Division* and the elite *6th Parachute Regiment* (one of the few droptrained parachute units in the Wehrmacht at this time). In addition, *Seventh Army* and *LXXXIV Corps* artillery units were in strength in the area behind Utah. Not only were these batteries capable of firing on the Allied fleet, but each one was a strongpoint in itself, surrounded by barbed wire and occupied by over 100 Germans.

As it turned out, the Allied invasion of Utah Beach was highly successful. The parachute drop was confused and scattered, but it similarly confused the Germans. Although the designated beach was missed (the actual beach was over a mile to the south), everything went fairly according to plan. The stage was set for the drive on Cherbourg.

Bloody Omaha

The American portion of *Operation Overlord* was spearheaded by the landing at Omaha Beach carried out by V Corps, under the command of MG Leonard T. Gerow. V Corps' mission was to obtain a lodgement between the tiny port of Port-en-Bessin and the Vire River. As soon as possible after D-Day, V Corps was to push to St. Lo and Caumont in order to cripple German communications and cohesion in Normandy. Allocated to the assault was the 1st Infantry Division ("Big Red One") and 29th Infantry Division, supported by two ranger battalions and a special engineer brigade.

Omaha Beach was completely unlike any other assault beach in Normandy. Its 7000 yards of crescent curves and unusual assortment of bluffs, cliffs, and "draws" were immediately recognizable from the sea. It was by far the most defensible beach chosen for D-Day, in fact, many planners thought it improbable that a major landing could take place there. The high ground in this area commanded all approaches to the beach from the sea and tidal flats. In addition, any advance made by American troops from the beach would be limited to the narrow passages between the bluffs formed by rivers and streams which had long-since dried up. Advances directly up the steep bluffs were extremely difficult, if not impossible. To make matters worse, the Germans realized that the American assault would be channeled in this manner and had arranged their strongpoints so that they could command all approaches.

Compounding the American invasion headaches on Omaha was the Allied intelligence failure to identify a full-strength, first-rate German infantry division guarding the beach. This division, the *352nd,* was an experienced unit with extensive service on the Russian front. It was thought to be no nearer the beaches than St. Lo and Caumont, 20 miles inland.

H-Hour at Omaha Beach was 0630 hours. In the half-hour prior to this touchdown, this strip of sand was the target for one of the most intensive and potentially destructive bombardments ever witnessed. From 0600 to 0625, 480 B-24's saturated the German defenses with 2½ million pounds of bombs (using instantaneous fuses so as not to crater the sand). At the same time, eight destroyers, three cruisers, and two battleships fired at specific targets in the draws. When all this fire lifted and the first wave was well on its way to shore, 9 LCT(R) rocket launching vessels fired 9000 4.5" rockets on to the beach in a saturation bombardment.

As soon as the first waves hit the beach, plans began to go awry. It was obvious that the bombardment had not worked the wonders everyone had thought it would. German resistance was stiff and energetic. The situation grew ugly. The assault bogged down. Companies were quickly reduced to half-strength. Most officers went down dead or wounded within minutes of hitting the beach. But, even as the deadly fire inflicted greater and greater casualties on the troops, individuals began to take the initiative. BG Norman D. Cota, 29th Infantry Division Deputy Commander, lead a scratch force in an attack up a gully. At about 0900 his men gained the bluffs above the beach. Other such provisional combat teams were formed and began moving up off the beach.

Naval gunfire support ships edged in as close as they could to substitute for artillery pieces swamped in their landing craft by the running seas. Air power added its contribution. Slowly, painfully, the movement off the beach took place. By dark a defensible perimeter had been established some thousands of yards inland. The epic of Omaha was over.

Consolidation, 7-12 June

As night fell on D-Day, the Allied foothold in Normandy was precarious. The three principal sectors were not linked, supplies and reinforcements had not been landed as rapidly as planned, and, most importantly, the Germans were beginning to build up their own forces. A serious effort had to be made to enlarge and strengthen the lodgment before the enemy became too powerful. Most particularly, the situation at Omaha was very dangerous. Not only was the beachhead small, but it lay in the center of the Allied position. Should Omaha be destroyed, the entire landing would be in jeopardy.

On 7 and 8 June, as the Allies poured men and materiel into the beachheads, serious fighting occurred all along the front. Fortunately the Germans were still weak, notably so in the Omaha area. As the British experienced pressure from *21st* and *12th SS Panzer Divisions,* Omaha was subjected only to the attentions of the battered *352nd Infantry Division* and the second-rate *30th Mobile Brigade.* On 9 June, with eleven Allied divisions ashore, Omaha and the British beaches were linked. The next day Carentan fell and a juncture was made with Utah, thereby establishing a continuous front.

Over the next three days the Allies built up their strength considerably, adding two armored and three infantry divisions. By this time they were actually numerically superior to the 17 German divisions confronting them and could begin considering large scale offensive operations, the Americans to take Cherbourg and the British, Caen.

The Caumont Gap, 12-18 June

By the night of 11 June the American V Corps, MG Leonard Gerow commanding, was advancing on the city of St. Lo. This was a major road and rail junction controlling routes into the Cotentin Peninsula. Its fall would represent a major Allied victory, effectively isolating Cherbourg. The defenders were the *352nd Infantry Division* and the *3rd Parachute Division.* Most of the German armor, *12th SS* and *21st Panzer Divisions,* was off holding the British away from Caen. Unbeknownst to the Allies, there was a great, yawning gap in the German lines between these first-rate divisions. Held up by the heavy bocage and German delaying teams, the Americans did not see their opportunity until it was almost too late. The Caumont Gap represented a chance to break open the whole Normandy front before the campaign had gotten properly underway. Guarding this gap on the morning of June 12 were two German reconnaissance battalions.

The American offensive that opened on this day was not truly aggressive. The 2nd Division attack toward Hill 192 (about 2 miles east of St. Lo) failed disastrously, costing 600 casualties over two days. The 29th Division attacked along the line of the Elle River, achieving little progress, even though heavily supported by tanks and artillery. The 1st Division (which faced the Caumont Gap) advanced with moderate speed but not aggressively. Caumont fell on June 13, but the advance of all three divisions stopped in their tracks (mostly due to heavy casualties and lack of supply) at the end of this day. The German line was saved by the timely arrival of the *2nd Panzer Division* in the Caumont Gap.

General Bradley called off this half-cocked offensive on the morning of June 14. Primarily, he was concerned with his exposed left flank at Caumont for the

British were still being held away from Caen by *Panzer Lehr.* He was similarly concerned with the "blinding" of American intelligence by the bocage country. If the British were being bloodily repulsed by a firm defense, Bradley thought it logical to assume that the Germans were in similar force to his own front.

The Caumont battle represented the American initiation to the Normandy hedgecrows. The bocage was a factor that the Allies had not really considered in the Overlord planning. However, as Caumont showed, it was a lesson that had to be learned out of necessity. Success in this campaign would demand nothing less.

The Fall of Cherbourg, 18-29 June

The major problem facing the Allies once they were ashore was supplying the bridgehead with all necessary material to support a sustained drive across France. Although great faith was placed in the artificial "Mulberry" harbors, it was recognized that a port must be taken within the first few weeks of the invasion in order for this supply problem to be solved. The only major French port within striking distance of a Normandy beach was Cherbourg, which was about 18 miles northwest of Utah Beach. As the American VII Corps drove across the Cotentin Peninsula (which they cut at Carteret on June 18), it became clear that the American intention was to drive north toward this city and not to the south toward Carentan.

The plans for the attack on Cherbourg were drawn up by MG Collins of VII Corps, along with his divisional commanders. It was clear to all concerned that the Germans had virtually disintegrated on this front. Many divisions had been split up by the American drive across the Cotentin, such that a portion remained south of the U.S. lines and a portion to the north. The American attack involved the 4th, 9th, and 79th Infantry Divisions, 4th Cavalry Group, and strong corps artillery and armor (both tank and tank destroyer) support.

The attack on Cherbourg opened on the morning of June 19, with the 9th Division on the west, 79th in the center, and 4th on the eastern flank. German opposition was slight, except for a tough fight in the vicinity of the cities of Montebourg and Valognes. The battle progressed rapidly, giving most American commanders the impression that Cherbourg would fall within two or three days. However, U.S. forces had not yet come in contact with the strong Cherbourg defense perimeter (which had given General Erwin Rommel some problems in 1940 when he took the city), along with its numerous second-line troops (naval and training personnel, artillery, etc.). By June 21, the Americans were fighting in the outside defense perimeter supported by Allied naval forces off Cape Levy. For over seven days the fighting raged within the Cherbourg perimeter until the Germans' surrender on June 27.

The Americans had won their first major victory in the Normandy campaign. The stage was now set for the smash-out from the Normandy hedgerows.

Operation Epsom, 22–29 June

On 18 June, General Montgomery summarized the two weeks of fighting on the European continent for his troops. He concluded that the Allies were in France to stay, were maintaining the initiative, and were swallowing up Rommel's last mobile reserves. "We must now capture Caen and Cherbourg as the first step in the full development of our plans," was his final directive. The German defense of Caen had so solidified with incoming reinforcements that progress for the British Second Army, commanded by LG Sir Miles Dempsey, was quite slow. Accordingly, Montgomery ordered this army to launch a pincer assault on Orne, and the right along the line of the Odon River (really nothing more than a stream).

"Operation Epsom" was the name given to the attack along the Odon. Epsom was to involve both the XXX and VIII Corps. The attack was carefully planned. Each division was to attack along an extremely narrow and compact front. The ground was favorable for the attack along the line of departure, although heavy bocage sprung up a few kilometers south of the main line of German resistance. The Germans were truly prepared for this assault. Helped immensely by the delay provided by the Channel storm, the Germans were well dug-in and well organized in infantry-anti-tank teams throughout the front. Some of their best divisions were deployed here, such as *Panzer Lehr, 12th SS Panzer,* and *21st Panzer.*

Epsom's objective was to strike across the Odon in order to cut the critical road and rail lines south of Caen. The initial attack on June 25 was very bloody and the advance much slower than Dempsey had anticipated. German *Army Group B* reported "a complete defensive success," although it was a success won only by "employing its last reserves." Over the next few days, the continuous British assaults created a salient in the German lines. This salient was more than five miles deep, but dangerously narrow—never more than two miles across at its widest point. By the 29th, the Germans seemed to have gained the initiative and were counter-attacking with strong combined arms teams from *9th* and *10th SS Panzer Divisions.* The fighting became very confused as counter-attack followed attack along the entire front. Eventually, the massive British corps artillery and highly-efficient anti-tank guns completely shattered any hopes of a German breakthrough, although hopes for the Epsom offensive were dashed as well.

Afterward

The fall of Cherbourg may be taken as marking the conclusion of the Normandy invasion. Henceforth, the operations in Normandy could proceed in a more orderly fashion, with the great port as their principal logistical base, although supply over the beaches continued for some weeks more. The invasion had not been a complete success. Neither had it been a disastrous failure. Indeed, although territorial gains had been somewhat less than according to plan, casualties had also been low. Save for Omaha, the landings had gone well. The consolidation phase had also proceeded nicely, though one could always wish for more. The Germans had never managed to collect themselves for a single massive counterstroke, which was also helpful. The failure to take Caen was unfortunate, but it did force the Germans to concentrate an unusual proportion of their forces in that sector. This helped shape the future course of the campaign, for inevitably any Allied breakout from the beachhead would have to occur at the other end of the front. Over the next month both sides strove to build up their forces.It was a race that the Allies could not lose, even in the face of massive logistical difficulties. And when the breakout came, it was irresistible.

Forces at Hand: D-Day

Major Combat Formations	*Divisions*			*Brigades and Regiments*			*Equated Divisions*
	Inf	*Arm*	*A/B*	*Inf*	*Arm*	*A/B*	
Belgian				1			.3
British	10	3	2	7	7		19.6
Canada	2	1			1		3.3
Czech				1			.3
French		1					1.0
Netherlands				1			.3
Polish		1				1	1.3
United States	14	5	2		8		23.6
TOTAL	**26**	**11**	**4**	**9**	**16**	**1**	**49.6**
German	47	10	3	1		1	60.6

The Allies had a total of 41 divisions and 26 separate brigades available in England, about 80% of which were committed to *Overlord.* In addition, there were three American and five French infantry divisions, two French armored divisions, the equivalent of one Anglo-American airborne division, and five French separate infantry regiments in the Mediterranean Theater available for operations against Southern France. The Americans and British had managed to convince the Germans that they had about 90 divisions on hand in Britain through various deception operations such as *Fortitude,* which created the fictitious "First U.S. Army Group" under Patton. Worldwide, the German estimate of American strength was about 20 divisions too high (22% over the actual figure) and that of Britain fully 22 divisions overstrength (70% over the mark). Note that the eight American units listed under Armored Brigades and Regiments were actually armored cavalry groups.

Allied information about the German strength was remarkably accurate, save for a failure to identify the *352nd Infantry Division* at Omaha until it was too late to do anything, which was partially responsible for the disastrous situation which developed on that beach. Of the German formations, only 13 of the infantry divisions were actually capable of field operations, the balance being so-called "static" outfits, largely without transport and with much of their heavy equipment in fixed fortifications. At this time Germany possessed about 285 divisions of all types, only 60 of which were under *O/B West,* or about 21%. A total of 164 (57.5%) were deployed against Russia. Note that figures for armored divisions include one panzergrenadier outfit and that German parachute units listed under Airborne were by and large *not* jump qualified, but were merely an elite sort of infantry.

Material Resources

Manpower	*Allies*	*Germans*	*Ratio*
TOTAL	**2,876,000**	**1,500,000**	**191.7%**
Ground Combatants	1,000,000	700,000	142.9
Replacement Pool	120,000	20,000	600.0
Replacement Rate	50,000	6,000	916.6
Equipment			
Heavy/Medium Tanks	5,500	1,400	392.9
Light Tanks/Other AFV	2,000	800	250.0
Artillery Pieces	4,800	3,200	150.0

Allied figures include the forces committed to the invasion of Southern France. Total manpower includes all forces, such as supply and air personnel, in addition to ground troops. Replacement Pool comprised those personnel at hand on D-Day to make up losses in combat units. The Allied pool, although considerably larger than the German one, was actually too small: by D+20 casualties had reduced the pool to about 60,000. Replacement Rate is the number of men made available each month for use as replacements. About 90% of the Allied rate was American, the balance British. Ratio is Allied strength expressed as a percent of German strength.

Casualties: D-Day

Operation	*Allied*
Airborne	2500
Gold-Juno-Sword	3000
Utah	500
Omaha	2500
TOTAL	**9500**

German casualties on D-Day are not known with any degree of certainty, estimates varying from 4,000 to about 10,000. Actually, the losses incurred by the Allies, some 5.8% of the total force landed, but perhaps 13.6% of the initial assaulting infantrymen, were considerably lower than anticipated. Normal planning parameters suggested that upwards of 18.7% of a force attacking a fortified zone frontally would become casualties on the first day, 70% within the first 12 days. Given that at Normandy there was the added complication of an amphibious assault, many Allied planners believed upwards of a third the invasion force would become casualties, about 50,000 men on D-Day alone. That this did not occur was due partially to the meticulous Allied preparations and partially to the failure of German preparations and troops to be as good as expected.

The Allied Build-up: D-Day to D + 21

June	*Units committed*
6	Br 6th A/B Dn; 3rd, 50th Inf Div; 8th, 27th Arm Bde; 1st, 4th Cdo Bde; 101st, 102nd, 104th Beach HQ; Cdn 3rd Inf Dn; 2nd Arm Bde; U.S. 82nd, 101st A/B Dn; 1st, 4th, 29th Inf Dns; 3rd, 6th Arm Cav Grps; 1st, 5th, 6th Engr Bdes; 359th Inf Rgt; 2nd, 5th Rngr Bns [156,000 men, 4800 vehicles ashore]
7	Br 4th Arm Bde
8	U.S. 2nd, 90th Inf Dns
9	
10	Br 7th Arm Dn; U.S. 2nd Arm Dn
11	Br 51st Inf Dn [c. 370,000 men, 50,000 vehicles ashore]
12	Br 49th Inf Dn; U.S. 9th Inf Dn
13	Br 11th Arm Dn, 3rd Arm Bde
14	Br 15th Inf Dn; U.S. 79th Inf Dn
15	U.S. 4th Arm Cav Grp
16	U.S. 30th Dn [c. 555,000 men, 83,500 vehicles ashore]
17	
18	
19	
20	
21	U.S. 83rd Inf Dn
22	U.S. 3rd Arm Dn
23	
24	Br 43rd Inf Dn
25	
26	
27	Br 53rd, 59th Inf Dns [c. 750,000 men, 120,000 vehicles ashore]

The rate of the Allied build-up was remarkable, considering that the men and equipment had to come in over the beaches. In fact, the Allied build-up exceeded the German one. By 4 July, D + 29, roughly 1,000,000 Allied soldiers were ashore. Of the approximately 3,700,000 American troops committed in northwestern Europe from D-Day to the surrender of Germany, 1,600,000 (c. 43%) came across the beaches at Normandy or through the Mulberry port in the British sector.

The German Build-up: D-Day to D+21

June	*Units committed*
6	*243rd, 352nd, 716th Inf Dns* on the beaches; *21st Pz Dn; 91st, 243rd Inf Dns; 30th Mobile, 100th Pz Bdes; 6th Para Rgt.* by nightfall
7	*12th SS Pz Dn; 346th, 711th Inf Dns*
8	*3rd Pz Jgr Bde*
9	*Pz Lehr Dn*
10	*2nd, 3rd Para Dns; 77th Inf Dn*
11	*17th SS PzGrn Dn; 265th, 353rd Inf Dn*
12	
13	
14	
15	
16	*275th Inf Dn*
17	*266th Inf Dn*
18	
19	
20	
21	
22	
23	
24	
25	
26	
27	*1st, 2nd, 9th, 10th SS Pzr Dns*

The German build-up was severely hampered by a number of factors. Rundstedt and Hitler's belief that the Normandy invasion was essentially a diversion for a massive descent in the Pas de Calais region made them reluctant to commit forces from the *Fifteenth Army* guarding that sector for several weeks. In addition, Allied attacks on communications facilities severely impaired the German ability to move formations, which depended heavily on rail transport. Allied air power also prevented movement in daylight, for the long columns of motorized formations—a panzer division could take up 100 miles of road space—made tempting targets for the omnipresent fighter bombers. Finally, the activities of the French Resistance fighters ambushed units on the road, causing at least one division of SS to "retaliate" by the butchery of an entire French village.

To the Beach

The maritime aspects of *Overlord* were supervised by Admiral Sir Bertram Ramsey. Altogether over 5500 vessels and some 266,000 seamen took part in D-Day operations. Hundreds of vessels more played a role in operations subsequent to D-Day as well. The statistics alone are impressive.

Naval operations, of course, began several days before the actual invasion, as minesweepers began clearing channels through minefields while minelayers planted fresh fields designed to protect the flanks of the invasion armada from German surface and underwater craft. Many vessels were required merely to "police" the area, seeing to it that transports and landing vessels kept to their assigned sea lanes, marking rendezvous points, designating landing craft lines of departure and beach boundaries, and acting as rescue craft for sunk or damaged shipping. Then there were the warships, from battleships to anti-submarine trawlers; all had fire support or escort missions, which also required special command arrangements and communications facilities. On more than one occasion during the campaign heavy naval gunfire played a decisive role.

Landing Ship and Landing Craft Commitments

Type	*ETF*	*WTF*	*Total*
Headquarters	3	1	4
LSI/AKA	36	19	55
LST	130	106	236
LSD	3	3	6
LCA/LCVP	408	283	691
Guide Vessels	11	15	26
LCI	155	93	248
LCT	487	350	837
LCAA	18	11	29
LC Gun	16	9	25
LC Support	83	38	121
LC Rocket	22	14	36
LC Smoke/Survey	100	53	154
Miscellaneous			1656
TOTAL	**1434**	**996**	**4124**

One of the more unusual aspects of the naval preparations were the "Mulberry" harbors. Since the Normandy coast lacked immediately available port facilities save for Cherbourg, two complete portable harbors were constructed in pieces in England and towed across the Channel for emplacement on the French coast in the first days of the invasion. Mulberries were composed of several parts. Beginning on D-Day itself old warships and merchantmen were sunk just off-shore to provide a breakwater. Several vessels seriously damaged during the invasion were actually added to this barrier. Bolstering the breakwater were "Bombardoons," concrete and canvas caissons 200 feet long, which provided some docking facilities for larger ships, and "Phoenixes," 6,000 ton concrete caissons which formed the principal part of the artificial harbors. Inside these harbors were various types of docks at which ships could unload, the cargo passing over floating pontoon roadways—"whales"—to the beach. The Mulberries were completed by D + 10 and proved immensely useful, but the one in the American sector was badly battered by an unseasonably severe gale on 21 June and had to be abandoned. The British Mulberry continued to operate until the beachhead was closed in September, by which time sufficient port facilities had been captured as to make it redundant.

Not included in this table are some 294 merchant vessels of various sorts standing off the beaches. Also excluded are the DD-tanks, M4 Shermans fitted with detachable canvas "bloomers" and twin propellors to permit them to operate amphibiously: large numbers of these sank before reaching the beaches. Note that "Miscellaneous" includes many small landing craft, ships' boats, and the like used to act as couriers, carry wounded back to hospital ships, and communicate from ship to ship and from various sections of the beach to various other sections. It also includes vessels laying a flexible gasoline "pipeline under the ocean" (PLUTO) from England to Normandy. **Abbreviations** *L* stands for landing, any vessel equipped to land or facilitate the landing of troops over a beach; *S,* ship, capable of transoceanic voyages; *C,* craft, a vessel of limited sea-keeping capabilities; *I,* infantry carrier; *T,* tank carrier; *D,* dock, containing a small dock in a rear well capable of loading troops into smaller craft; *A,* for assault, and *VP,* for vehicle and personnel, were the British and American landing craft which are most familiar from film and photo, capable of carrying a platoon of men or a tank; *AA,* anti-aircraft equipped; *Support,* munitions resupply, medical equipment, etc.;) *Gun,* equipped with one or more small artillery pieces; *Rocket,* capable of laying down a heavy barrage of rocket fire; *Smoke/Survey,* equipped to lay smokescreens and make artillery observations. *ETF,* Eastern Task Force, for the British Beaches, and *WTF,* Western Task Force, for the American beaches.

Airpower: A Summary

Combat Aircraft at Hand, 6 June 1944

	Fighters	*Bombers*	*Total*
R.A.F.	2172	624	2796
U.S.A.A.F.	1311	1922	3233
ALLIED TOTAL	**3483**	**2546**	**5029**
Luftwaffe	420	400	820

Note that Allied totals exclude about 2,000 additional fighters and about 1,000 additional bombers on other assignments in the British Isles. Czech, Polish, French, Dutch, and Norwegian squadrons have been included in the R.A.F. totals, along with other Commonwealth forces.

Sorties: D-Day	*Allies*	*German*
	c. 10,000	2

A sortie is a single aircraft operating a single mission, thus if one aircraft engages in two separate missions in a single day, landing in between to refuel and remunition, it is counted as two sorties. On D-Day Allied aircraft averaged two missions each. Most heavy bombers had spent the last few weeks taking out vital communications installations all over France, escorted by the fighters. At the very last minute the bombardment began to concentrate in the vicinity of Normandy, and then on D-Day itself the bombers plastered the beach defenses and immediate rear areas even as the landing craft were approaching shore. All this put considerable strain on aircrew. Thereafter the pace of sorties slowed considerably, to about 5000 per day. The Germans had only two FW-190 fighters available for immediate employment. They made one sortie each, remarkably coming away unscathed despite total Allied air supermacy. Thereafter the Germans managed to build up to an average of about 250 sorties per day, still considerably inferior to Allied capabilities.

Airborne Operations	*Transports*	*Gliders*	*Men*
R.A.F.	462	972	5300
U.S.A.A.F.	1166	1619	13000
TOTAL	**1628**	**2591**	**18300**

Certain Allied planners had predicted that the airborne aspects of Normandy might result in upwards of 80% casualties. Others had predicted overwhelming success. Neither was correct. Casualties actually ran about 15% among the troops, considerably less among the transport aircraft.

Cobra: Patton's Offensive in France, Summer 1944

By John Prados

By the middle of July 1944 a million Anglo-Allied troops were ashore in France attempting to breakout from the Normandy beachhead and sweep across Europe. No more than 650,000 German soldiers opposed them, desperately straining to prevent just such a breakout. The battle area, Normandy, was a greatly varied region. In front of the British Second Army, on the Allied left, it was a region of small farms and semi-urban zones, while the American First Army, on the right, had to cope with difficult hedgerow country, with numerous fields cut by thick, impenetrable hedges. As the Germans had concentrated the greater part of their forces in front of the flat, open country facing the British, the Americans conceived a massive offensive designed to crush the Germans to their front and swing wide the doors to France and all of Europe. This plan, *Operation Cobra,* was the product of inter-allied strategy, of a month of tactical frustration in Normandy, of technological innovations, and of a breakthrough in ways to apply firepower. *Cobra* was developed by Gen Omar Bradley, American First Army Commander, and was to be executed by one of the most brilliant American officers of the war, LG George S. Patton.

Origins of *Cobra*

The Allied plan for a breakout from the Normandy peninsula was the outcome of long months of study and staff work that began some time before the first Allied soldier landed in France. The assembled generals were formally briefed on the plan by British commander Gen Bernard Law Montgomery on 15 May 1944. At that time it was estimated that the Allied forces could reach their jump-off positions for this offensive by D + 17, seventeen days after the invasion. In the event, the predictions proved to be over-optimistic. Caen, the major British D-Day objective, for example, did not fall until 9 July (D + 33). The impact of the initial failure to attain objectives is difficult to assess. There was a race to build up forces in Normandy through June, and this the Allies clearly won, since by mid-July there were 34 Allied divisions on the continent, against 20 German divisions in Normandy. At all times the Germans lacked the capability to throw the invasion into the sea; their buildup was hampered by Allied air interdiction and by Hitler's belief in the possibility of a second invasion. The Allies lost one of their artificial harbors in a storm in late June, but then Lawton Collins' VII Corps captured Cherbourg on 29 June.

While the Allies did not reach their planned phase-lines, this failure seems to have changed their basic plans for the breakout startline rather than altering the basic ground strategy. In a directive the day Cherbourg fell, Montgomery ordered Bradley to "pivot," and directed First Army to prepare "a strong right wing in a wide sweep south of the bocage/hedgerow country." The British were to support this effort by attriting the Germans in their front, by preventing the shift of German reserves, and by threatening a breakout toward the Seine River.

At First Army, the grand sweep of Montgomery's vision of the proper strategic approach was absent from the offensive planning of Bradley's staff. As Bradley relates it, the idea of massive air bombardment first occurred to him as a means of wiping out some unsuspecting German division. Hooking such a bombardment into a concurrent advance was a logical progression of the concept, especially in view of the British demonstration of the concept in action at Caen from 7–9 July. At any rate, the plan for the offensive originated on 10 or 11 July, and by the 13th was official.

First Army planned conservatively.

Rather than the "wide sweep" envisioned by Monty, Bradley foresaw only an indeterminate future. He refused to provide for specific exploitation objectives for the forces beyond the limited one of encircling the German divisions between Coutances and the west coast of Normandy. In addition to providing for limited objectives, Bradley allotted huge forces for the attack. A continuous bombardment by several thousand aircraft would only accent the attack. It was to be followed by the advance of three infantry divisions to open a hole through which two armored divisions and another of infantry could pass. A further five divisions were available as circumstances warranted, and the activation of Third Army, with Patton commanding, was impending. The only concrete aims Bradley had provided for this exploitation force, however, were the base of the Cotentin peninsula, to outflank the German defenses, and Brest, a distant but much-needed port at the tip of the Brittany peninsula. Bradley evidently felt that the situation should be played as it unfolded, and therefore refused to designate phase-lines beyond the immediate objectives, thus avoiding the danger of the planning outrunning the progress.

One immediate difficulty was that there did not yet exist a solid jumping-off line for the offensive. Bradley reasoned that he must fight his way south of the Cotentin swamps so that his reserves could exploit onto ground with a reasonable road net. This entailed the capture of the town of St. Lo, which had been the object of much combat since D-Day. The fighting along the American front to this time had been quite fierce. It had taken five days—until 8 July—for the Americans to take one village, La Haye du Puits, from the *353rd Division*. Yet this division consisted at the time of only four depleted rifle battalions and two artillery battalions. Similarly, Bradley called off one corps commander's attacks after the attacking divisions gained only 12,000 yards in ten days of constant assault. St. Lo was not reached until 18 July. That day, elements of the 115th Infantry of the 29th Division penetrated the town. The conquest of St. Lo cost the Americans some 10,000 casualties, but the result was to give Bradley his desired jump-off position for *Cobra*—

the St. Lo-Perriers road, which Bradley felt was a convenient, prominent and vital landmark for bombers to distinguish the Allied positions from the German front line when the planes came in to drop their ordnance.

At this point, there was a total of 14 infantry, six armored and two airborne divisions in the American force structure, either in England or on the Cotentin and four additional divisions were expected in August. Fifteen of these divisions had actually been deployed on the front by Bradley, and 12 divisions (four armor and eight infantry) were involved in *Cobra*.

In the breakthrough sector, Bradley concentrated three infantry divisions (9th, 4th, and 30th) of Collins' VII Corps on a 4.5 mile front, with 1st Infantry, and the 2nd and 3rd Armored Divisions in reserve. The available artillery support worked out to 83 guns per kilometer of front, comparable to levels prevalent on the Russian Front in 1942. However, a bombardment zone of 7,000 yards by 2,500 yards was to be pounded for three hours by every aircraft the Allies could muster. This sector of the German front covered Marigny and St. Gilles, important road junctions from which the exploitation forces could move south.

The Americans would also profit from a technical innovation. Hitherto the defense had benefited from the difficulty of deploying forces in the hedgerow country. Tanks particularly were restricted to the roads. Various devices were concocted to solve the hedgerow problem. By 5 July, the British 79th Armored Division was demonstrating a "hedgecutter" device. Later, XIX Corps came up with a "salad fork," and V Corps had a "brush cutter" and a "green-dozer." All were outdone by a New York sergeant, Curtis G. Culin Jr., of the 2nd Division's 102nd Cavalry Squadron, who perfected a hedgecutter with tusk-like prongs that would dig the nose of a tank down into a hedgerow, where it could develop the traction necessary to carry away the vegetation. Bradley ordered a crash program to equip tanks with the device, and the result was soon being called a "rhinoceros." Thus, during *Cobra* the American armor would have increased tactical mobility.

The initiation of *Cobra* was originally scheduled for 20 July. Bad weather forced postponement to 24 July, and then again one further day. On the 24th, however, some of the aircraft had not received the cancellation order and went on to bomb the designated targets, while some short bombing caused casualties among the Americans. The Germans were thus afforded some tactical warning. But most Americans had high hopes for *Cobra*. Bradley had told an air force officer that "the attack [is] designed to break out of the Cotentin and complete the liberation of France," and to Collins he said, "if this thing goes as it should we ought to be in Avranches in a week." Perhaps the most pessimistic was Patton, who wrote on 23 July that *Cobra* "is really a very timid operation, but Bradley and Hodges consider themselves regular devils for having thought of it. At least it is the best operation that has been planned so far." Eisenhower merely stated laconically that by D + 50 the Allies had reached approximately the line planned for D + 5. But *Cobra* would indeed change all that.

The Horses Are at Caen

In the rhyme about the egg-person, the king's horses and men were absent when Humpty sustained his fall. Subsequently, they were unable to salvage the situation upon their arrival. The same thing happened to the Germans in Normandy in July 1944. There, the panzer and mobile units with the greatest defensive capabilities were facing the British front when *Cobra* kicked off. The reasons why are of some interest and deserve comment. Responsibility for this mishap must be apportioned among Adolf Hitler, FM Erwin Rommel, and FM Hans Gunter von Kluge.

Hitler was instrumental in over-extending the German army. For six weeks after the invasion he insisted on the hypothesis of a second Allied landing, thus holding down the rate of German buildup in Normandy. At the same time, through early July when the limited German defensive capability had become apparent, he refused to consider a withdrawal from Normandy. Further, the losses of the Western front units were not replaced. Between 25 June and 24 July, *Seventh Army* and *Panzer Group West* reported losses of 74,000 men, yet replacements totalled only 10,078 (excluding about an equal number sent by the Luftwaffe to the *II Parachute Corps* and called "useless" by its commander). Only 17 replacement tanks reached the front between the invasion and mid-July. This attrition of the front in Normandy was the basis of a critically weak frontal defense there.

Under Hitler, the famed "Desert Fox," FM Erwin Rommel, was in top command in Normandy, in charge of *Army Group B* that controlled *Seventh* and *Fifteenth Armies* along with *Panzer Group West.* Rommel warned Hitler of the weakness of Normandy. At Berchtesgaden on 29 June, Rommel recommended that *Seventh Army* (*Panzer Group West* not yet deployed) conduct a fighting withdrawal to the line of the Seine River and Paris. His weekly report for 2 July explicitly anticipated an American attack in the St. Lo-Coutances sector, and the theme of weakness before the Americans continued. In Rommel's last report, that of 15 July, he stated that "within a measurable time the enemy will succeed in breaking through our thinly held front, especially that of the *Seventh Army,* and in thrusting deep into France." Two days later while driving, Rommel's car was attacked by an American fighter-bomber, and the marshal became a casualty, to be invalided back to Germany.

Rommel's role was not wholly beneficient on this occasion. It is true that he had warned his superiors of the situation in the West and that he specifically expected attacks in the Americans' sector, but at the same time Rommel was the architect of the deployment that placed the preponderance of German armor opposite the British. He had any number of opportunities to remove some of the panzers from around Caen and move them to the American sector, or to send his reinforcing divisions there. Neither happened. In late June there was but one German mobile division on that line. Two more were added before the eve of *Cobra,* but during this same period Caen was reinforced by four panzer divisions and two heavy tank battalions. Similarly, of eight new infantry divisions arriving in Normandy during this period, six went to Caen and only two to the Cotentin sector where the Americans would launch *Cobra.* The Rommel policy amounted to a quasi-systematic starvation of the American sector, lowering strength there while simultaneously warning of an American offensive.

The command echelon immediately above Rommel was *Commander-in-chief West (OB West)* under FM Hans Gunther von Kluge. Kluge, initially very optimistic about stopping the Allies in Normandy, had arrived from Russia on 3 July to take over *OB West* from von Rundstedt. Even at *OB West* there was concern over the American sector: their assessment in the first week of July believed the US troops freed by the fall of Cherbourg, Collins' VII Corps, would be used to put renewed pressure on the German *LXXIV Corps*. Yet like Rommel, Kluge concentrated his attention on the British sector, an attention even more focused after Kluge assumed command of *Army Group B*, in addition to his other duties, when Rommel was wounded.

In his covering letter to Rommel's 15 July report, Kluge discussed the Caen sector at some length. He too pointed to the overall implications of the loss rates:

> Nevertheless, despite all our fervent efforts, the moment is approaching when this sorely tried front will be broken. Once the enemy has penetrated into the open country, organized operations will no longer be possible to control owing to our troops' lack of mobility. As the responsible commander on this front, I regard it as my duty to draw to your attention, my Fuhrer, to the consequences which will ensue.

Kluge continued to funnel the lion's share of new German capability to the Caen sector. In fact, the day before *Cobra* one of the two strongest panzer divisions in Normandy was replaced in the line facing the Americans at Caumont and sent to Caen. No doubt the weight of forces around Caen played its part in the defeat of Montgomery's *Goodwood* operation, but the German positions along the St. Lo-Periers road were critically weak as a result.

On the eve of *Cobra*, 14 German divisions were positioned against the British. Half of these were panzer divisions, and they were accompanied by three Nebelwerfer brigades and four Tiger tank battalions. Opposite the Americans were only five divisions and a dozen assorted *kampfgruppe* and regiments. Only three of these divisions were mobile: *Panzer Lehr*, *2nd SS Panzer* and *17th SS Panzer Grenadier*, and all of them were far below strength: *Panzer Lehr* had about 50 tanks while *2nd SS Panzer* had 57. The front was so weak that Gen Paul Hausser, *Seventh Army* commander, had organized the defenses around blocking key road junctions rather than maintaining any cohesive front line, for little more could be done with the 17,000 troops available. In fact, Hausser delayed compliance with Kluge's order to withdraw *Panzer Lehr* and *2nd SS* to form reserves pending the expected arrival in August of the *363rd Division*. In the end, the only reserves behind the front were two tank companies of *2nd SS*, plus the *275th Infantry* (under *Seventh Army*) and the *353rd Infantry* (under *LXXXIV Corps*) *Divisions*. At the time the sector was attacked, *Panzer Lehr* with its attached units, numbered no more than 3,200 men.

The *Cobra* Breakthrough

The abortive bombing of 24 July cost *Panzer Lehr* some 350 men and about 10 tanks or assault guns. Discussing the situation that night with Hausser, Kluge remarked "without any doubt there's something new in all this air activity. We have got to expect a heavy enemy offensive." Next morning at 0900 the first of the American bombers struck home with the first of 4,150 tons of bombs. MG Fritz Bayerlein, commander of *Panzer Lehr*, lost all contact with his forward posts after about an hour of the two hour and twenty-five minute bombardment. Three of his battalion command posts were wiped out, and the attached *13th* and *5th Parachute Regiments* were completely disrupted. It is estimated that 1,000 men were lost to the bombardment alone. On the night of 25 July, the remnants of Bayerlein's division amounted to 14 tanks. At 0125 of the 26th, Bayerlein reporter: "after 49 days of incessant fighting, my division is now destroyed. The enemy is advancing unimpeded for St. Gilles."

Not surprisingly after such a bombardment, the American advance was not entirely unimpeded, but it was not German defenses that held up the assault groups. Rather, Collins' VII Corps experienced great difficulty in negotiating the cratered country created by the bombing. In fact, the deepest advance on *Cobra's* first day was by the 47th Infantry Regt. of 9th Division, which made only about 2,200 yards. The commitment of Collins' exploitative force, 1st Infantry with 2nd and 3rd Armored Divisions, had to be postponed for a day. Only the fact that there *was,* in effect, no German defenses prevented this development from exercising a great effect on the evolution of the *Cobra* battle.

Where was the German defense? *Panzer Lehr* was so disorganized by the air bombardment that Bayerlein reported that, after regrouping, it could only retreat. The reserves, *275th* and *353rd Infantry Divisions,* were both weakened by regiments detached to the front (one of them in the *Cobra* bombardment area), were quickly involved in the fighting, and were of only local importance as a result. The Germans could only resist with divisions brought up from the rear. This was quite unfortunate, given that the Germans had relieved *2nd Panzer Division* with an infantry division on 22 July in an area on the flank of the American axis of advance; the *2nd* was relatively strong with 100 tanks, but Kluge sent it down to Caen. It was then ordered back to the Cotentin from Caen, along with *116th Panzer* which also had substantial strength. Kluge also relieved the commander of *LXXXIV Corps.* None of the German units arrived along the front before 28 July, when leading elements of *2nd Panzer* approached the battle zone.

As it happened this was too late: 26–27 July were the decisive days. Collins committed VII Corps armor on the 26th. At the same time, Middleton with VIII Corps maintained steady pressure on the Normandy coastal sector, preventing the withdrawal of the German units in that front. Four combat commands of US armor fanned out behind the German line, seizing road junctions and the roads south. CCA of 2nd Armored Division made six miles that day. Both CCA and CCB of the 2nd made over seven miles on 27 July. The German *2nd SS Panzer* and *17th SS Panzer Grenadier* were able to keep the US 3rd Armored from capturing Coutances on 28 July, but instead that coastal road junction fell to Combat Command B of 4th Armored. Trapped in a pocket were three German infantry divisions along with the two SS divisions. The mobile SS units escaped to rejoin *Panzer Lehr,* while 8,000 prisoners from the infantry units went to American collecting points.

By 28 July, Bradley sensed that the door had been pushed open, and he ordered George S. Patton, whose Third Army was scheduled to become operational at 1200 on 1 August to "supervise" the advance of Middleton's VIII Corps.Both of Middleton's armored divisions (4th and 6th) made over eight miles that day. Only at that point did the advance of the Germans' *2nd* and *116th Panzers* force a frontal battle, on 29 July. The Germans substantially held their positions on the northern hinge of the front, by then at Tessy-sur-Vire, while little in the way of defense op-

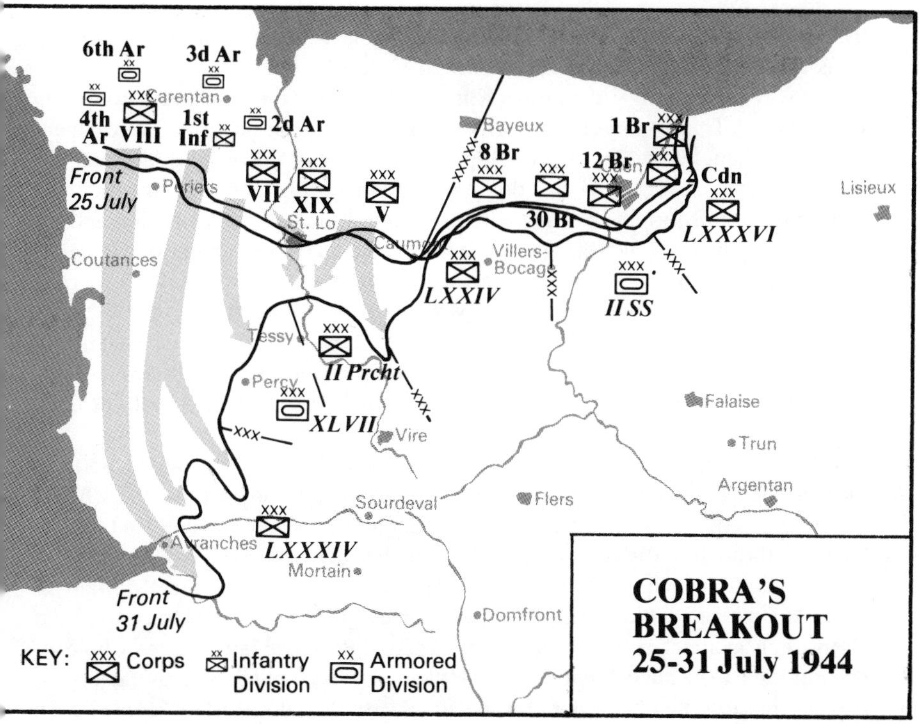

COBRA'S BREAKOUT 25-31 July 1944

posed Middleton's armor. Combat Command B of the 4th Armored advanced 18 miles on 30 July to capture Avranches, at the base of the Normandy peninsula. Patton then had an open road corridor to a position behind the German front, and he occupied himself by pushing seven divisions over a single bridge in record time. *Cobra* had broken out when CCA/4 Armored took the bridge over the Selune at Pontaubault on 31 July.

All the King's Horses

At 0100 of 31 July, von Kluge received a call from the chief of staff of *Army Group B,* LG Hans Speidel, informing him that the left flank of *Seventh Army* had collapsed. Kluge in turn reported to Hitler's headquarters, OKW, that it was known that the Americans were in Avranches but that otherwise the situation was completely unclear. The Fuhrer had already been told on the 27th by Kluge that the front had "burst," this was the result. At OKW, Hitler morosely remarked to Jodl that "it is totally impossible under the circumstances to wage a pitched battle in France. We cannot do that. We can still manage to regroup our forces, but even then only to a limited extent." Change could only come from control of the air, but Hitler insisted on keeping the fighters in Germany. But from the notion that the German army could not maneuver, Hitler drew the conclusion that only by holding present positions and counterattacking could resistance be offered. Hitler concluded that "we must therefore imbue everybody in *Army Group* [sic] *West* with the absolute necessity of conducting this struggle with the utmost fanaticism." Thus was born the German counterattack at Mortain.

It was apparent to Hitler and to Kluge that although the Allies had broken out with Patton's Third Army, reinforcements and supplies for that force were dependent upon a single road bridge crossing the See River at Avranches. Although the Americans had enlarged the corridor leading to that bridge, by moving east to the road junction of Mortain, it might still be possible to recapture Avranches and cut Patton off at the neck of Normandy. This at least was Hitler's intention.

Hitler formed a small nucleus staff within OKW to take personal control over the attack toward Avranches, and set Mortain as the initial objective. He elaborated a plan requiring the use of elements of four panzer divisions, and sent this to Kluge on 2 August. The plan was marked "not to be altered," and Kluge was instructed "not to pay any attention to the American breakout, which [will] be dealt with later."

Here once again, Kluge's preoccupation with the Caen sector showed through. The British had begun their *Operation Bluecoat* on 30 July, and while it had not proved any more successful than Montgomery's other assaults in terms of breaking through, it did demonstrate the British proclivity for repeated attacks on the German front. Kluge, noting this, protested Hitler's orders for the Mortain attack: "apart from withdrawing the essential defensive armored divisions from Caen, such an attack, if not immediately successful, would lay open the whole attacking force to be cut off in the west." Hitler acknowledged these arguments on 4 August, but repeated his orders for the attack. By the 6th, Mortain loomed even larger at OKW. Then, Hitler added forces—60 Panther tanks from Paris and 80 Mark IV's plus the reconnaissance battalion of *11th Panzer Division*. Accommodating these units in the attack plans then necessitated a 24-hour postponement, and the attack was rescheduled for the night of 7–8 August. Hausser's *Seventh Army* order of the day put the problem in a very stark light.

> The Fuhrer has ordered the execution of a breakthrough to the coast in order to create the basis for the decisive operation against the Allied invasion front. . . . On the successful execution of the operation the Fuhrer has ordered depends the decision of the war in the West and with it perhaps the decision in the war itself.

But Hitler's horses could not even be concentrated effectively, owing to Allied offensive pressure and the limited assembly areas assigned to the *Seventh Army*. Hausser kept *116th Panzer* deployed defensively, and then the division commander never sent off the tank battalion with which he was supposed to support the attack. The *1st SS Panzer*, pulled out of the front at Caen, was slow on the march. The Panthers from Paris had not arrived by H-hour. Altogether only three divisions out of six crossed the start-line on time, and only one of these, *2nd Panzer*, was anywhere near full strength.

Nonetheless, the German atack made some headway against the US 4th and 30th Divisions and CCB of 3rd Armor. The *2nd Panzer* was in Mortain town by 0315 of 7 August with a loss of only three tanks. But the day dawned bright and clear, and with it came the American fighter-bombers. Heavy air attacks at Mortain, the artillery fire of First Army, and American possession of the high ground to the north which dominated Mortain forced *2nd Panzer* to dig in rather than press the attack. The next afternoon, Kluge cancelled the second phase upon receiving news of a Canadian offensive south of Caen. By 9 August, *2nd Panzer* was back where it had jumped off, with the loss of 30 tanks and 800 men. The horses could not put the front back together again.

The Falaise Gap

On the afternoon of 7 August, Kluge reported the attack to be halted with the loss of over half the tanks. Hitler was incensed. The Panzers had jumped off with only 120–190 tanks instead of the 400–500 planned. On 8 August, he objected that the attack was launched too early in too little strength, and he demanded a new attack on the 11th, after all possible forces had been concentrated in strength, promising the aid of the Luftwaffe fighter reserve. In the meantime both the Luftwaffe, with bombers, and the Navy, with frogmen, made repeated attempts to destroy the bridge at Avranches. The Americans had been loose behind the lines for a week now, and Patton's tanks were all over the Brittany peninsula and outside Brest, and beginning to move toward encircling the German army now hanging on a limb. For the first time, Kluge warned OKW on 10 August that the army was in danger of being encircled. Hitler attributed all to the failure at Mortain, as his 14 August signal shows: "the present situation in the rear of the army group is the result of the failure of the attack at Avranches."

By the time of the German attack, Bradley had moved a total of 12 American divisions through Avranches. Several of these were in Brittany, specifically Middleton's VIII Corps, but Patton had a fresh corps—MG Wade Haislip's XV Corps—freely deployable and the possible targets ranged from Paris north and west. There is no doubt that the most attractive possible target was the German army itself—still in Normandy as the Americans moved through France. On 8 August, even as Hitler insisted upon a second offensive with several corps in line and an ample frontage, Bradley and Monty were making the decision to move for a junction of their armies in the German rear. The British Commonwealth forces would move for Falaise—the objective of the Canadian attack that day—while the US could capture Argentan, a town about 13 miles south of that. The striking edge of the encirclement was to be Patton's Third Army, using XV Corps for its instrument.

Haislip's XV Corps consisted of five divisions up front. These were the 79th, 80th and 90th Infantry Divisions and the 2nd French and 5th Armored Divisions. These forces had reached assembled positions by 9 August, and for the attack Patton resorted to the device of simply assigning each successive parallel road into the German rear to another division. This would have the effect, when the movement was completed, of placing strong US forces astride each of the possible routes the Germans might use to withdraw. The British, meanwhile, would seal the other shoulder of the encirclement once they could reach Falaise. The only hole in the planning was the gap between the towns of Falaise and Argentan, but the Allies argued the possibilities of confusion between forces meeting up in this area, and consequently decided to halt their respective army groups at the two towns. Instead, the Allies felt that the "gap," as it became known, could be sealed by air bombardment and artillery fire to prevent the escape of the trapped Germans. With the plans set, the Allied forces forged ahead.

On the German side, Hitler continued to insist upon a renewed attack around Mortain once all elements had reached their positions. This was to be commanded by *Panzer Group Eberbach* (*nee West*) with two panzer corps included in the units from Caen which were to be relieved for this purpose. Eberbach did not feel that he

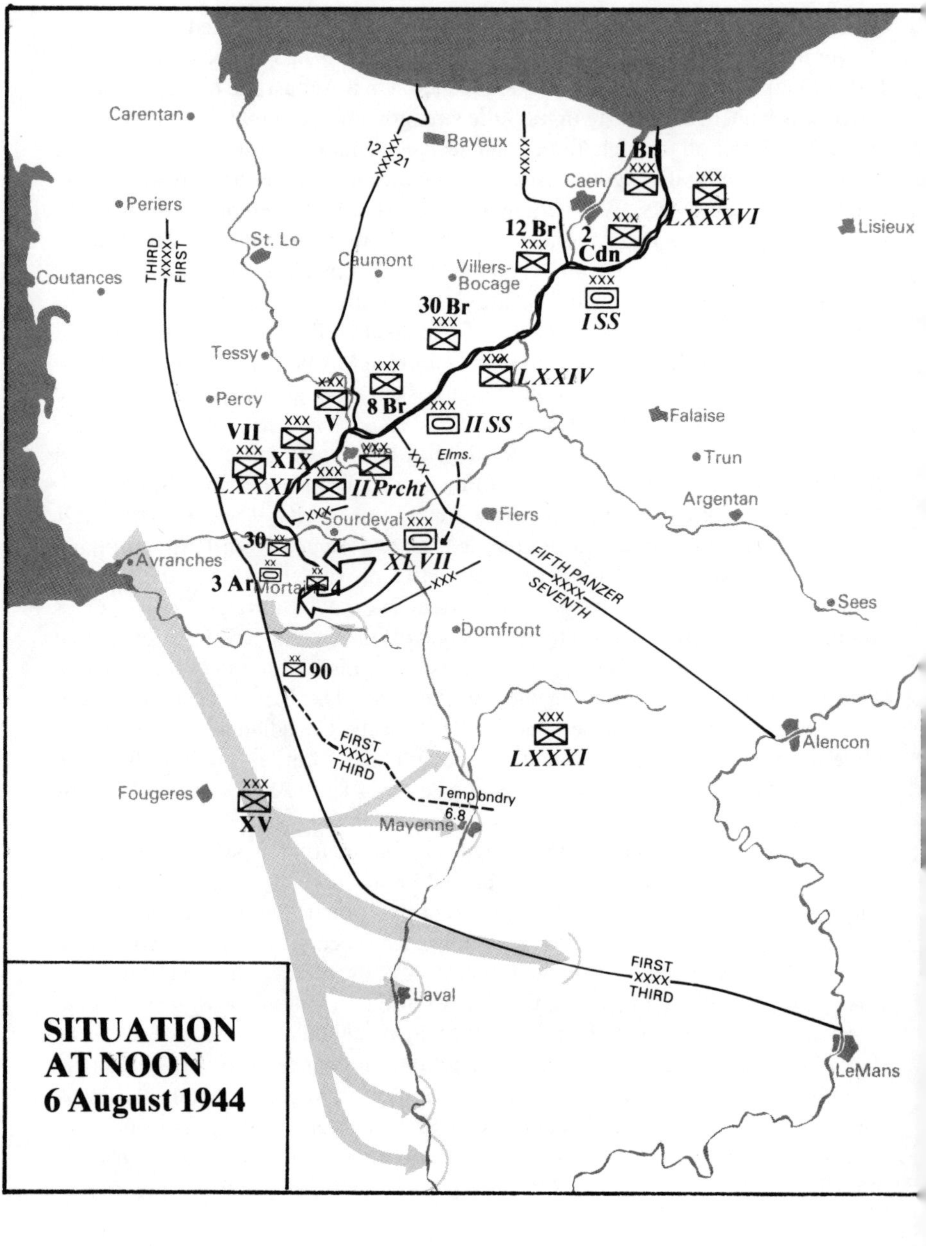

SITUATION AT NOON 6 August 1944

could complete his concentration by 11 August, the scheduled date, and held out for the 20th. With such a date, *Army Group B* lost the race to attack, for the approach of the divisions of XV Corps increasingly enveloped the Germans' southern flank. With this development, Eberbach felt he could not attack west against Avranches without first clearing his flank by an attack southwest to establish a front against Patton's XV Corps.

Eberbach accordingly planned an attack with Hitler's acquiescence to assemble at Carrouges and then move off. The force would comprise *1st SS, 2nd* and *116 Panzer Divisions* along with elements of *9th Panzer,* two *werfer* brigades and a heavy artillery battalion. It was to be further reinforced by *10th SS Panzer Division* as an exploitation force. *Panzer Group Eberbach's* attack never got off the ground. Instead, the assembling divisions were engaged by XV Corps units: the 2nd French and 5th Armored Divisions. In fact, the German divisions were badly beaten in the fighting. Eberbach estimated that, by 13 August, *1st SS Panzer* had no more than 30 tanks. The erstwhile 100-tank divisions, *2nd* and *116th Panzer,* had shrunk to 25 and 15 tanks respectively. And *9th Panzer DIvision* had almost ceased to exist as a unit.

Reflecting this state of affairs, Kluge on 12 August changed the axis of advance for the planned *Panzer Group Eberbach* attack. It was now to be directly to the west: i.e., right into the Falaise Gap. Gone was the notion of a renewed advance toward Avranches, since if the panzer group was to have any success at all it would be impossible to use the positions gained as jump-off positions for an Avranches attack—the distances involved were impractical. With a panzer group that amounted to a weak panzer division entertaining thoughts other than withdrawal from an exposed position would have been seriously questionable. The Germans had taken 31,000 casualties from the beginning of the *Cobra* attack until 7 August, and another 11,000 from 7–14 August. Kluge disappeared near the front all afternoon the next day, and Hitler believed to the end that Kluge had tried to arrange a surrender to the Allies. Hitler was to say a fortnight later that 15 August was the worst day of his life.

Even Hitler, however, who prided himself on holding his "nerves" in the midst of disaster, was led by events to conclude that withdrawal was necessary to save the German army. On the afternoon of the 15th Jodl at OKW ws told that the situation west of Argentan was worsening by the hour. Hitler reluctantly authorized a withdrawal to reorganize the defense short of the Seine, along the Dives River.

Bradley halted Patton just short of Argentan on 13 August. The next day, Patton sent the 80th Division to reinforce the two divisions in place, 2nd French and 90th. On the 14th, Patton ordered Haislip to move some forces east, toward the Seine, because Bradley intended to stay put at Argentan and not turn the "gap" into a pocket. The XV Corps commander therefore sent his 5th Armored and 79th Infantry Divisions off to the east. The American disposition near Argentan thus lost two divisions and 15 artillery battalions. Suddenly, on 16 August, Monty phoned Bradley to suggest that the Allies should indeed close the gap, at Trun between Falaise and Argentan. The Germans began their withdrawal that same night.

The Allied delay in making a decision to close the gap between their army groups is of critical importance in understanding the German escape from the

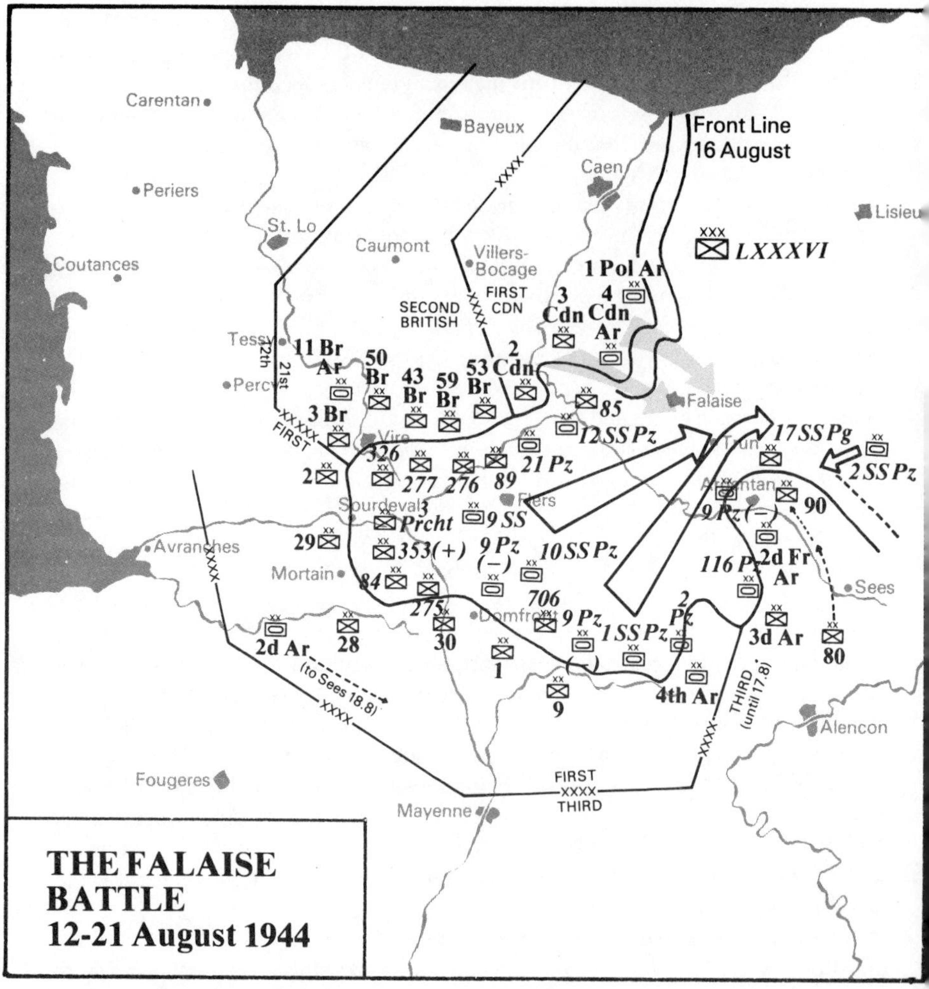

THE FALAISE BATTLE 12-21 August 1944

Falaise situation. With the delay causing departure of two XV Corps divisions, there was simply a preponderance of German forces converging on Trun—long columns of trucks and combat vehicles from every side road, in several cases so jammed that US airstrikes were able to target over 1,000 vehicles at once.

With the glut of Germans in the countryside, the reduced XV Corps had considerably lessened chances of reaching Trun itself to seal the German escape route. Further, *12th SS Panzer* and other elements opposing the British did a superb job of holding up the Canadian advance to delay the fall of Falaise to Montgomery. Hausser of *Seventh Army* and Meindl of the parachute troops personally led some of the battle groups of troops holding open the escape corridor and then thrusting through to safety. Finally, the Germans were aided on 20–21 August by the offensive action of *2nd SS Panzer Division* from outside the developing Falaise pocket. Thus, in the end about two-thirds of the German army escaped, although it could do little to save its equipment. The German army in the west was then in poor condition to fight any sort of battle. Paris had fallen to the Allies by 25 August.

Conclusions

Whatever Hitler might do about reorganizing the defense closer to the German frontier, *Cobra* and the Falaise battle had ended the Germans' immediate possibilities in the West. Casualty estimates for the last stage of the battle place German losses at 10,000 with an additional 40,000 prisoners. This brought overall German losses in Normandy to 210,000 prisoners and 230,000 casualties, and the remaining units had little strength. On 21 August, for instance, *Panzer Group Eberbach,* with six of the seven panzer divisions that had been inside the pocket had a combined strength of 2,000 men, 62 tanks and 26 guns. Over 1000 trucks and 436 AFV's were lost or abandoned in the Falaise pocket. Certainly a major disaster.

The overall reasons are apparent enough, and were put to Hitler at the time by Kluge in his suicide note of 18 August. The front as a whole was too weak, wrote Kluge, citing Rommel's earlier appreciations in support. Although it was true the counterattack had failed, it was apparent in advance that the panzer forces were too weak to prevail, and even if they did the notion of rolling up the Allied Normandy lodgment area was beyond the plausible.

More specific conclusions are possible about the initial *Cobra* period of operations and the later Mortain-Falaise action. In *Cobra,* Kluge was to be faulted for his concentration upon Caen, particularly as this led him to send away from the American flank one of his two most powerful panzer units. The *Seventh Army* commander, General Paul Hausser, was also at fault for leaving the little armor he did have in the line rather than in reserve. Hausser's defense is that the Americans were so powerful that infantry alone without tank support could not hold defenses against them.

In the Mortain-Falaise action, divergent conceptions at Hitler's headquarters and at Kluge's lay at the heart of much German difficulty. In this case, Hitler's ability to hold his "nerve" had the incidental result of imposing an excessively rigid attack plan on a frontal command that had few resources but was under much pressure. Even so, *Seventh Army* was not able to execute the plan in a coordinated fashion in spite of a day's delay. Kluge and Hausser played some role here. Finally, Hitler's preoccupation with a second attack fatally delayed the beginning of the German withdrawal to Falaise.

On the Allied side there is much to commend in this period of mid-July to mid-August. Bradley should be given high marks for the XV Corps' encircling operation, which amounted to an improvisation by a command long committed to a limited campaign in Brittany. Perhaps some would like to have seen Patton's Third Army activated sooner, but Bradley's explanation of his need to control the tactical development of the battle until the breakout was obtained is a compelling one. Montgomery conducted his operations creditably well, although one might wish for more imagination and tactical finesse in Monty's operations and plans. Both Bradley and Monty were well served by their airpower and intelligence capabilities. And some will always insist that Patton saved the day.

Caen: Action on Montgomery's Sector

The latest British attack on Caen was just grinding to a halt when Bradley began considering *Cobra*. By 9 July Montgomery had taken half the city. His three divisions, 3rd and 59th British and 3rd Canadian, had not been able to advance on the east bank of the Orne River, however, and had not been able to substantially enlarge the Normandy bridgehead or to break out of it. The 7-9 July advance thus had only an indifferent outcome.

Montgomery already had another advance in the works, an operation with massive air support just like *Cobra*, called *Goodwood*. The timing of *Cobra* was originally contingent upon *Goodwood*, as the British would attack two days ahead and it was hoped, fully engage the German reserves. The British attacked on 18 July with a large force; next to Caen were the 2nd and 3rd Canadian Divisions and the 3rd British. Massed in a small assembly area across the Orne were three armored divisions: the 7th, 11th, and the Guards. These jumped off behind some 2,100 aircraft.

Montgomery and his army commander, Gen. Miles Dempsey of the Second British Army, it is said, were prepared to accept losses for the success of the *Goodwood* attack—some 200-300 tanks during the operation in fact. It turned out that British intelligence underestimated the depth of the German front as well as the amount of reserves that the Germans would be able to commit, missing elements of *2nd Panzer Division* and *1st* and *9th SS Panzers*. At a crucial moment for the attack, a Panther battalion from the *1st SS Panzer Division* came up on the disengaged side of an armored brigade and occupied a critical hill line. The British 11th Armored Division alone lost 126 tanks on 18 July, of a total of 270 tanks knocked out that day. Montgomery lost a further 200 tanks before the *Goodwood* fighting ended.

Goodwood was regarded as a failure by Gen. Dwight D. Eisenhower's Supreme Allied Headquarters because it failed both to break out and to reach its tactical objectives. *Goodwood* did clear out Caen and a strip of land around it, at the cost of 500 of Second British Army's 2,600 tanks. But perhaps the most important result of *Goodwood* went unseen at the time—the repeated British offensives confirmed Kluge in the need to keep the bulk of the German armor opposing them. This, of course, contributed to the weakness of the German front in Bradley's sector when the Americans unleashed *Cobra*.

Concern over movements of German mobile troops increased once *Cobra* began. On 28 July, Montgomery ordered Dempsey to move armor from the Orne to the Caumont area with the object of attacking on 30 July using VIII and XXX Corps. The idea was to prevent German units withdrawn along the Caen front from successfully intervening in the US sector. Operation *Bluecoat* massed the same armored divisions as had *Goodwood*, along with the 15th, 43rd, and 50th Infantry Divisions. *Bluecoat* did tie up elements of *21st Panzer*, and associated air strikes inflicted severe damage on the *9th SS Panzer* which was then in transit behind the German front.

The need for some forces to quickly rebuild a front before the Americans led to the dispatch of two panzer divisions from Caen on 26 July, the close-to-strength *2nd* and *116th.* Hitler's resolve to counterattack toward Avranches then took the horses away from Caen. Some units such as *21st Panzer* remained engaged on the front, along with over a hundred 88mm and 75mm anti-tank guns. But by early August the Germans' only mobile reserve along the British front was Kurt "Panzer" Mayer's *12th SS Panzer Division,* with 50 tanks.

For his part, Montgomery activated a new army, Canadian First under Gen H.D.G. Crerar. This force occupied the area across the Orne from 1 August. Monty soon decided that the fresh army should spearhead the British breakout and drive to encircle the Germans, this operation to be known as *Totalize.* For his first operation, Crerar planned to use the Canadian 2nd and 51st Divisions as an assault force along with the Canadian 4th and Polish 1st Armored Divisions as an exploitation force. In a very complex attack plan, Crerar's troops were to attack behind a thousand RAF planes that were to unload more than 5000 tons of bombs over the German lines. The Canadians would also have the support of 720 artillery pieces.

The German defenses in this sector turned out to be manned by their *89th* and *272nd Infantry Divisions* with stiffening from the *12th SS Panzer.* The Germans were well dug-in in good positions, with fifty 88mm guns and another 60 tanks or assault guns dug-in in the defensive zone. *Totalize* jumped off against these positions the day after the Germans' Mortain attack, 8 August.

It happened that "Panzer" Meyer was driving up the Falaise-Caen road just after the RAF bombing ended, and he came across groups of German infantry streaming back in panic. Meyer challenged the stragglers and got them to re-occupy the high-ground positions they had abandoned, and he reinforced these with some panzers. Then Meyer ordered two *kampfgruppen* of *12th SS Panzer* to counterattack the heads of Crerar's Canadian columns. The result was that Canadian First Army gained only three miles during its first day of attack. That night Kluge feared that a breakthrough had occurred south of Caen, but by the next afternoon Kluge considered that the situation had been restored.

For his part, Monty had by now agreed with Bradley and Eisenhower that an attempt should be made to encircle the German armies. In addition, he must have felt that Crerar's attack had so much weakened Canadian First Army it would be unable to seize and hold Falaise. Crerar felt that penetrating the German anti-tank gun screens was an expensive proposition and searched for new ways to negate the German defenses. The German positions in Quesnay Woods and on Potigny Ridge were particularly troublesome. An attempt was made to outflank these by moving the Canadian 2nd Division, but this maneuver failed against strong defenses. A new concept then emerged.

Crerar decided he would mask the Quesnay-Potigny position by using a heavy airstrike. Then Canadian 2nd Infantry and 4th Armored Divisions, with their 2nd Armored Brigade, would force the Laison River under cover of a smokescreen and using steamroller tactics—solid phalanxes of tanks and carriers 250 yards square. This assault went in on 13 August and was successful. By nightfall the lead elements of Canadian 2nd Division were only three miles from Falaise.

That night, however, the Germans scored a new coup. A Canadian scout car fell into German hands with notes detailing Crerar's entire plan of attack. Armed with this information, the Germans were able to concentrate their forces to meet the Canadians. Thus, throughout 15 August the remnants of *12th SS,* which amounted to 500 infantrymen, 15 tanks and twelve 88mm guns, were able to hold the Canadian advance at the last ridge north of Falaise. Meyer still held this position on 16 August, when troops of the Canadian 2nd broke into Falaise from the west. Even then, Germans in Falaise were able to hold that town another day, and 60 grenadiers from Meyer's division controlled the town's Ecole Superieure until 19 August.

As a result of the tough resistance of *12th SS Panzer Division,* the Canadian advance was held up for several crucial days. This obviated the Allied orders, late though they were issued, to close the neck of the position by effecting a junction between the Canadians and Haislip's US XV Corps. Consequently, Falaise remained a gap and was never turned into a pocket. The Germans were even able to redeploy one of the divisions inside the neck, *2nd SS Panzer,* to the outside where it could counterattack more effectively to aid troops escaping from the Allied armies. So ended the Falaise battle for the British.

One must acknowledge that British claims to success in exhausting the German army in Normandy lie close to the mark, but the real question to be posed is whether this was in fact the proper strategy to select. At the time of *Goodwood,* for instance, Dempsey's British Second Army alone had five times as many tanks as the entire German Army in the West. The disparity in airpower was at least as great, and Montgomery's entire capability could be concentrated against selected sectors of the German front. To adopt an attrition strategy in the face of such factors amounted in part to giving the Germans a bonus chance to attrite the British superiority—they themselves had relatively less to lose.

British performance at the combat level was quite good, however. They made relatively few mistakes, although such errors at crucial moments played a role in the failure of *Goodwood* and of some of the June attacks. The British infantry also proved to be the measure of its opponent, and it is unfortunate that so many of its attacks were set-piece affairs before the defenses of Caen. Indeed, there is no doubt that Montgomery would have shown altogether better in the campaign as a whole had Caen fallen on D-Day as originally planned.

Airpower in *Cobra* and Beyond

Airpower proved to be of great importance in the Normandy fighting, both the presence of it and the lack of it. For the Allies, airpower provided a key to unlock the German defensive front along with a vital means for isolating the battlefield. The Germans, for their part, constantly wished they had enough aircraft to disrupt these Allied operations.

By 1944 the Luftwaffe was no longer the instrument it had been earlier in the war—a fact which provided a good deal of aid and comfort to the Allies in Normandy. At the overall level it was true that German aircraft production was up (4,545 single-engine fighters, for example, were delivered in the second quarter of 1944), but even this did not make good the wastage, such as the 5,527 fighters lost in the three months ending in June. By the end of June, total Luftwaffe fighter strength amounted to 1,435 aircraft, but only about 450 of these (at 65% serviceability) were deployed in the West. The fuel situation was equally dismal. The Luftwaffe depended upon synthetics for 95% of its requirements at a time when production in this category was radically cut by Allied strategic bombing. Synthetic fuel production in June, 53,000 tons, did not match the 124,000 tons of consumption.

Under the Luftwaffe, the *Third Air Fleet* was responsible for the West. This force comprised perhaps 750 planes of which the majority were fighters (15 *gruppen*). The force had been reduced by eight *gruppen* that had been withdrawn to Germany for reorganization and then retained there. There was no contest between this force and the Allies' 17,000 planes. German fighter efforts thus concentrated on defensive air cover missions over important rail and road junctions behind the front, as well as patrols over the Germans' operating airfields. The bombing effort had long worked mainly at night to mine the waters through which the Allies moved their supply ships to Normandy. This did not mean that the Luftwaffe was totally ineffectual, however. At the height of the St. Lo battles, on the night of 17–18 July, 100 bomber sorties were flown against Allied troop concentrations, and another 120 bomber sorties were targeted similarly on 24–25 July just before the *Cobra* jump-off. The height of activity was the campaign against the bridge at Avranches, in the course of which 277 sorties were flown between 7–11 August. On at least one occasion, the US Third Army headquarters was strafed by German fighter-bombers. But on 11 August the fuel situation finally forced the Luftwaffe to seriously curtail its operations.

Fuel considerations and scarce aircraft in the field played little part, by contrast, in the Allies' air efforts over Normandy. Rather, the crucial constraint on Allied aerial operations was weather. They possessed enough troop carrier aircraft to provide simultaneous lift for three airborne divisions or 2,000 tons of supplies, enough heavy bombers to conduct a strategic air offensive over Germany, and enough tactical aircraft to place a full-scale tactical air force at the disposal of both the British and the Americans.

The most conventional of the Allied air efforts was that devoted to tactical air support by the IX Tactical Air Force of MG Elwood R. Quesada. IX

TAC, as it was called, provided all fighter cover and fighter-bomber strike aircraft for the ground forces. A typical day for this air force would find 20% of its sorties allocated to offensive fighter activity, 10% on German Communications in the band from 50–70 miles behind the front, 40% as strike sorties in direct support of Bradley's First Army, and then 30% similarly targeted in Montgomery's British sector.

Quesada's force possessed substantial capability, so much that it was possible to accord constant air support to very low ground combat echelons. For example, a US armored division might have two or three columns simultaneously on the move and *each* of them would have a standing patrol of 3–4 P-47s overhead on half-hour shifts. The columns would identify themselves with fluorescent panels and normally would have forward air controllers with the lead elements who were in continuous contact with the aircraft. Larger air strikes could be called in on several hours notice.

The major air innovation of the campaign was the use of heavy bombers in a tactical bombing role distinct from their normal use strategically. In effect, Allied officers would plot bomb drop zones of given sizes and pummel them with the planes of the VIII Air Force and the British Bomber Command. Kluge wrote tellingly on 22 July of the use of strategic bombers in this fashion:

> Whole armored formations, allotted to the counterattack, were caught in bomb carpets of the greatest intensity, so that they could be extricated from the torn-up ground only by prolonged effort and in some cases only by dragging them out. The result was that they arrived too late. The psychological effect of such a mass of bombs coming down with all the power of elemental nature upon the fighting troops, especially the infantry, is a factor which has to be given particularly serious consideration. It is immaterial whether such a bomb-carpet catches good troops or bad, they are more or less annihilated. If this occurs frequently, then the power of endurance of the forces is put to the highest test, indeed it becomes dormant and dies.

Reading Kluge, one has the impression that the carpet-bombing tactics were immensely successful. However, carpet bombing was not an unmixed blessing, as a study of the actual instances will show.

The first use of carpet-bombing tactics came on 9 April 1944 on the Italian Front, when Fifth Air Force made an attempt to neutralize the German positions at Monte Cassino. That time, 800 bombers, 503 of them B-17 or B-24 heavy bombers, released their loads on a front 3,000 yards wide. Some short bombing caused casualties among Moroccan troops assigned to the attack following up the bombardment, and the attack failed.

Bradley writes that the Cassino experience for a long time led him to avoid the use of carpet-bombing in American planning, but Montgomery regarded them as additional firepower and used carpet-bombing in a first Caen attack on 7 July. This time, 467 Lancasters and Halifaxes of Bomber Command laid 2,560 tons on a zone 4,500 yards by 1,500 yards fronting Caen's northern outskirts. The German division most hit lost only 800 men, the attack followed the bombing by six hours, and the leading British elements were stopped the next afternoon by the craters left from the carpet-bombing. Only half of Caen fell, and the Germans reformed their front.

In Operation *Goodwood* of 18 July, Bomber Command again committed planes—2,100 bombers again along the Caen front. Again the attack made some ground but was basically a failure, and again the British encountered some difficulties that were collateral effects of the bombing.

Bradley made his decision to use carpet-bombing in *Cobra* on the basis of the British experience at Caen from 7–9 July. But while the British had maintained a distance of 6,000 yards between the forward units and the bomb-drop line, Bradley refused an Air Force request for a safety zone only 3,000 yards wide. Bradley assumed the bombers would come in along the roadmark of the St. Lo-Perriers road for accuracy, and did not wish to make such large withdrawals. The compromise safety zone was less than half the VIII Air Force request: 1,200 yards for tactical aircraft and 1,450 yards for the B-17s and B-24s. In the actual attack, VIII Air Force did not fly in along Bradley's road, and Bradley claimed that had he known this was the flight plan in advance, he would not have allowed the air attack.

The target zone roughly corresponded to the frontage of the *Panzer Lehr Division,* and amounted to 7,000 yards by 25,000 yards. In the bombardment, 4,150 tons of bombs rained from 1,500 B-17s and B-24s, 380 medium bombers, and 550 fighter-bombers.

The American bombers were effective, but collateral effects of their activities were effective as well. The most advanced American battalion had not made its way through the bombing zone by the end of the first day of the attack. The US command had also to remove two infantry battalions from the assault after these were so badly beaten up in the bombing that they were combat ineffective. Casualties attributable to the bombing were not only extant but numerous. Even in the abortive attack of 24 July, when some bombers received instructions too late to cancel their missions, there had been losses. Then 25 were killed and 131 wounded in the 30th Division.

A balanced assessment must take into account both the results of the *Cobra* carpet-bombing and their collateral effects. The bombing certainly destroyed *Panzer Lehr's* defense except for isolated groups who could offer only sporadic resistance. On the other hand, the Americans took serious losses and were unable to negotiate the bombed zone. It is evident that the German line could have been reformed, *had there been German reserves available in adequate strength.* The lack of reserves had nothing to do with the bombing and indicates that success in *Cobra* came from conventional preponderance of force rather than novel applications of strategic airpower. It is instructive that the United States Army avoided the use of carpet-bombing in its operations plans through the remainder of World War II.

Military Intelligence and the Normandy Campaign

The Allied military intelligence operation was one of the most successful elements of their war effort during the Normandy period. By contrast, the Germans were the victims of what was probably the most successful deception action of the entire war. This was *Operation Bodyguard,* which was designed to make the Germans believe in the possibility of a second invasion of Europe.

Bodyguard was conceived as a measure to help get the troops ashore in Normandy by leading the Germans to concentrate most of their attention, and defensive preparations, elsewhere. It was an extremely complex effort involving a fictitious army group, "rubber divisions" composed of inflatable mockups of equipment along with divisional radio transmitters, and a good number of personnel. German photo recon planes were carefully allowed to look at the "rubber divisions" but were shot down if they strayed close to the real ones. Hitler was deceived by *Bodyguard.* Basically, the Germans were led to believe that the Allies had twice as many divisions as there were, with commensurately greater capabilities for invasion. Hitler, for one, therefore continued to believe that the Allies intended to land at the Pas de Calais, even after D-Day. This was of real importance in the Normandy fighting, for there were 18 German divisions on the Channel coast which were kept there and would have been of great use in Normandy, enabling the Germans to match or exceed the Allied rate of build-up during June.

Cobra had unfortunate consequences for the First Army Group, the fictitious organization set up by *Bodyguard* to conduct the "second invasion." The group commander, LG Leslie J. McNair, was on the American forward lines to observe the carpet-bombing. McNair was killed by one of the "short" bombs, leading to a crisis for *Bodyguard.* Luckily in that operation the Allies broke out of Normandy, ending the need for a successful deception.

Part of the reason the Germans were taken in is that the Allies had good coverage of what the Germans were saying to each other, Allied intelligence organizations had cracked the German code machines and were monitoring OKW teleprinter traffic with the front, a source of intelligence known as *Ultra.* Thus the Allies were informed of all Hitler's orders, of Kluge's reports, and of German arrangements for the reinforcement of Normandy—information crucially important to *Cobra.*

For example, the Allies were speedily informed when, on 31 July, Kluge countermanded Hausser's order to *Seventh Army* for a retreat. It was the first indication that the German command was in fact off balance. Subsequently the Allies kept track of differences between Hitler and Kluge in the planning of the Mortain attack.

Both Bradley and Eisenhower conceded that they were aware in advance of the German intention to counterattack at Mortain: in fact they held a conference the day *before* the German attack to make sure that all preparations had been made to defeat it. They were also concerned that a too-powerful defense would show the Germans that their plans were known in advance. Bradley issued orders for main defense lines in the hills north of Mortain specifically so that the Germans could penetrate the forward outpost line, a success that could allay their suspicions. The effect of the intelligence effort at Mortain is reflected in the early appreciation of the size of the German attack force: by 1200 on 7 August the word was out that this force possessed five rifle battalions, four artillery battalions, and only 2-3 panzer battalions.

Allied intelligence was not omniscient, however. At least two significant failures occurred during the period from mid-July to mid-August 1944. In *Operation Goodwood,* the British underestimated the strength and availability of *1st* and *12th SS Panzer Divisions* which constituted the German reserves. The *Goodwood* attack stumbled precisely upon the line at which these units engaged the advancing British Second Army. Another intelligence report played a role in the American failure to advance north with XV Corps from Argentan early in the Falaise Gap fighting. In this case, the report was that by 15 August the Germans had already withdrawn the bulk of their *Seventh Army* forces in the pocket (actually the withdrawal did not begin until the next night). Thus the Americans were led to believe that there was not much worth fighting for inside the pocket.

On balance one must conclude that Allied military intelligence served them to great advantage tactically, while the successful deception amounted to a strategic military factor of real weight. The "failures" mentioned above do not alter this judgement: *Goodwood* was of only local importance while the Falaise report merely contributed to preventing a big victory from being even bigger. That there was a victory, however big it was, was partially a result of the Allies' excellent military intelligence.

A Word on Organization

German Organization

The Germans were unfortunate in having a plethora of unit organizational schemes, all of which were in use at the same time. These are some of the principal ones. Armored divisions were actually employed as task forces, built around the regimental headquarters. Non-divisional artillery was organized into battalions of 12 to 18 guns, which were organized into "corps" of five battalions or, if the artillery was composed of *nebelwerfer,* into brigades of six battalions or so. Non-divisional assault gun and tank battalions (which were sometimes called brigades) contained between 10 and 50 vehicles. The parachute divisions were really just elite infantry, having little or no jump training. All of the infantry in the mechanized infantry divisions and half of it in the armored divisions used trucks rather than half-tracks, the latter being in short supply.

American Organization

The American Army had a "heavy" armored division, comprising two three-battalion armored regiments and a three-battalion mechanized infantry regiment. It had over 16,000 men, with few infantry and less artillery, but about 30 percent more AFV. American divisions were rather flexible. The infantry division had the anti-tank, tank, and artillery battalions which were usually, but not always, attached. The anti-aircraft battalion of the armored division was also attached. Other American units of note were the armored cavalry regiments, which had three reconnaissance squadrons, with about 70 light tanks, 70 half-tracks, and 2,700 men. Non-divisional artillery was organized into 12-gun battalions, which were controlled in batches of two or more Artillery Groups. Operationally, the Combat Commands in the armored division were used to form task forces from the pool of combat battalions attached to the division. Likewise, the airborne divisions were also task force oriented, with varying numbers and types of regiments being attached.

British Organization

British formations were somewhat similar to American or German ones in general. However, rather than having organic regiments, British divisions were composed of Brigades, each consisting of a number of battalions belonging to different parent regiments—British regiments having been made institutional ages ago. Terminology in cavalry and armor retained use of the word "regiment" for what in American or German usage was really a battalion. Otherwise there was little difference between British and other units.

Other Allies

The Poles generally adopted a British style of organization, using brigades and battalions. The French went in for the American pattern, if only because the U.S. was the prime supplier of equipment and political support. Several other Allied powers—Dutch, Belgians, and Czechs—contributed small forces to the campaign in France, usually organized on the British pattern.

• • •

Operation Cobra virtually destroyed the German Army in France. Allied forces leaped forward. On the left, Montgomery drove the British and Canadians along the coast. In the center Bradley's Americans pressed eastwards, with Patton in the lead. And from the South of France came strong French and American forces which had landed in mid-August. The objective was the Rhine and Germany itself. But the advance assumed the character of a race. Montgomery and Patton, most flamboyant of the Allied commanders, and the most egotistical, each sought the glory of being the first into Germany.

Highway to the Reich: *Operation Market-Garden,* 27–26 September 1944

By Phil Kosnett and Stephen B. Patrick

By September of 1944, the Allies had driven far from Normandy. All France, except a few beleaguered seaports, was in Allied hands, Belgium liberated. Four armies—French First, U.S. First, Third, Seventh—were approaching the German border. British Second and Canadian First Armies were heading north into the Netherlands. The Germans were reeling. Enormous casualties in men and armor had been taken in Normandy, at Falaise-Argentan, and in the great retreat to the German border. Germany seemed on the verge of collapse.

Yet the Allied advance was stopped in its tracks. First, those few untaken seaports were badly needed by the Allies. Short of ports, trucks, and transport aircraft, the Allied logistical network was faltering. Fuel and food were not reaching the front, and a shortage of replacements was weakening the Allied armies even more. Second, the Germans had reached the Westwall, their barrier of forts and natural obstacles reaching from Switzerland to Holland. And in Holland, the marshes and rivers proved excellent barriers to the Allied armor which had swept across the plains of France. The Allies needed a new plan to crack the German line before the Germans rebuilt their army. That plan was called *Market-Garden*.

Genesis: Montgomery Takes a Chance

The seed of *Operation Market-Garden* was planted by FM Sir Bernard Law Montgomery on 3 September 1944. At that time the British XXX Corps, part of the British Second Army of Montgomery's 21st Army Group, was driving towards the Meuse-Escaut Canal in northern Belgium. Montgomery suggested facilitating this advance by means of an airdrop into the German rear near Arnhem in the southern Netherlands. *Operation Comet,* as it was quickly dubbed, would drop the British 1st Airborne Division and the Polish Parachute Brigade on 6 or 7 September. The two outfits would then be in a position to attack forces confronting XXX Corps from the rear. The operation was cancelled when poor weather delayed the airdrop and German resistance slowed XXX Corps' drive.

On 10 September Montgomery presented Gen Dwight D. Eisenhower, Supreme Allied Commander, with a plan for an expanded *Operation Comet,* which he called *Operation Market.* In addition to dropping the British and Polish parachutists at Arnhem, this plan envisioned dropping the American 82nd and 101st Airborne Divisions along the road between Eindhoven and Arnhem. All of these units would proceed to capture the numerous bridges over the many rivers and canals which criss-cross the region. Due to a shortage of air transport, all of the airborne troops could not be dropped simultaneously, so *Operation Market* would have to take place over a three-day period. Meanwhile, XXX Corps, spearheaded by Guards Armored Division, would crack the German lines before Eindhoven and race northwards across the bridges secured by the airborne forces to effect a crossing of the Rhine at the Arnhem bridge, controlled by the British and Polish parachutists. This accomplished, the entire British Second Army would pass up the corridor through Arnhem, turn southeastwards into Germany, and drive on the Ruhr. At one stroke, the Westwall and the Rhine barriers would be broken, and Montgomery's forces would debouch onto the excellent tank country of the North German Plain, on the road to Berlin. Eisenhower considered the proposal briefly and then approved it, designating it *Operation Market-Garden.*

In its execution *Market-Garden* proved a disastrous failure, resulting in the destruction of a fine airborne division and dashing Allied hopes for a quick conclusion to the war. As one British officer put it, contemplating the numerous bridges which had to be seized and crossed, "I think we're going a bridge too far."

Market-Garden: The Surprise that Failed

On paper *Operation Market-Garden* was quite simple. The American 101st Airborne Division would land between the Willems and Wilhelmina Canals. With the help of the heavily armored British XXX Corps it would seize Eindhoven to the south of the Wilhelmina, while other elements took Veghel, north of the Willems Canal, thereby securing some 15 miles of highway, thus facilitating XXX Corps advance. Meanwhile the American 82nd Airborne Division would land between the Waal and Maas, securing Grave on the Maas, various crossings on the Waal-Maas Canal, and the city of Nijmegen on the Waal, securing another dozen miles of highway, though with a gap of some 15 miles between the 101st at Veghel and the 82nd at Grave. The final act, and theoretically the easiest, was a drop by the British 1st Airborne Division north of the Neder Rijn, near Arnhem, for the purpose of securing the Rhine bridge. This accomplished it was to hold until relieved by XXX Corps. Montgomery calculated that the entire operation would be over by D + 2.

The opposing German forces were, nominally, the badly depleted *First Parachute Army,* holding the sector directly in front of the proposed advance. Its commander, Gen Kurt Student, was nobody's fool, however, and he was expected to do well with what he had. Pinned against the Scheldte estuary were the remnants of the *Fifteenth Army.* They were considered effectively out of the picture. However, two factors occurred which were, for reasons still not clear today, not taken into consideration. The *Fifteenth* made a bold attempt to evaculate across the Schedlt , and the British made no serious effort to cut off their withdrawal. Once they got out, they withdrew north and west of Eindhoven to rest and refit. In addition, at about the same time, the German *II SS Panzer Corps* was pulled out of the Eifel and sent to the Arnhem to refit. This put the *9th* and *10th SS Panzer Divisions* in the Arnhem area. Both operations, conducted in the early days of September, were carried out rather openly. Yet neither was accounted for in the intelligence summaries upon which the planned operation was based. Finally, the headquarters of *Army Group* was also moved into the Arnhem area, which proved beneficial in giving the Germans badly needed, immediate command control once the attack was launched. It should also be noted that the Germans were able to capture, intact, the full plans for the whole *Market-Garden* quite early in the operation. While there is evidence that FM Walter Model, *Army Group B* commander, was always somewhat doubtful that he had the whole story in his hands, it enabled critical reaction time to be cut short.

Terrain was to pose a significant factor in these operations. Aside from the water barriers, which were accounted for in the planning, once north of the Waal, the direct road for Arnhem ran over a raised dike. While the road itself was a good road, more than sufficient for the purpose of carrying the armored drive, the ground around it was untrafficable. It was marshy and incapable of sustaining maneuvers by tanks. In one of the most curious lapses in intelligence, Montgomery ignored the offers of assistance from the Dutch military and civilian leaders who had been manning the Dutch government in exile since 1940. The failure to obtain detailed information on local terrain from people who lived there and were obviously friendly to the Allied cause was simply inexcusable.

The landings were all made on September 17, 1944. The southernmost landing, of the 101st, went well initially. The northern objectives of Veghel and the crossings over the Aa River and Willems Canal were secured quite rapidly. But because of delay experienced by the armored corps, the 101st would have no help in taking Eindhoven. The bridge over the Wilhelmina Canal, which was to carry the main drive, was blown by the Germans as the paratroopers approached. The canal was crossed, but without a bridge, that fact was of little value. As a result, construction of a new bridge was begun and the balance of the attack shifted west to try to take the canal bridge at Best. Here the faulty intelligence began to prove a problem. Instead of being undefended, Best was held by elements of the *Fifteenth Army*. The heaviest losses sustained by the 101st in the operation were sustained in the fighting around Best, and the Germans destroyed the bridge there, anyway.

Although the initial landings were achieved with surprise, the Germans brought in more anti-aircraft guns and these cut badly into drops of supplies during the succeeding days. However, on D+2, the 326th Glider Regiment was able to land and add two badly needed battalions to the 101st.

Because of the ongoing battle for Best, the 101st's resources were being drained, and their ability to hold on to their fifteen mile stretch of highway was now being strained. But on the afternoon of the 19th, the tanks of the armored corps finally broke through and this, plus the 327th, broke German resistance at Best. At that point, it appeared that the 101st had accomplished its mission. However, following the XXX Corps were the other elements of the British Second Army, VIII and XII Corps. These were assigned the task of widening the narrow corridor and assuming the mission of holding it against German counter-attacks. They were considerably delayed, and as of the 22nd, D+5, they were only five miles beyond the original front line. Therefore, the 101st had to bear the brunt of keeping the highway secure.

Model, commanding the German forces, weas aware of how thin the corridor was, and he was determined to try to cut it. He mounted a major counter-attack with the goal of retaking Veghel and the bridge located there. The 101st beat back this attack, but they were unable to hold off the Germans completely. The Germans managed to cut the corridor at Uden. This proved critical as the 101st simply lacked the strength to repoen the highway, and the British were forced to divert a tank brigade from their efforts to cross at Nijmegen in order to assist the 101st. For a day, the Germans blocked the highway and cut off completely the flow of supplies to the more northerly Allied forces. In an operation such as *Market-Garden,* this was a serious setback.

Further north, the 82nd had harder going. They had initially made their main drop zone in the Groesbeek Heights, since securing them would screen the American operations against a German attack coming out of the Reichswald. However, in this sector, the German anti-aircraft fire was more violent and many incidents were reported where the Americans actually landed on the German positions in order to avoid having to maneuver on the ground to knock them out.

The first phase of the landings, as conceived by the 82nd, was to secure crossings over the Waal-Maas Canal and the Grave bridge. This was accomplished before nightfall on the 17th. But Nijmegen had not been an initial objective. Rather, it was designated to be taken "on order" when the other objectives were secured. The failure to move on Nijmegen upon landing was a costly one. The problem was further complicated by the fact that the 508th Airborne Rgt., given the mission of taking the bridge, made the error of taking the most direct route to the bridge, which meant that it went right through the city. The bridge was so located that a maneuver to the east of the city would have brought them close to the bridge approaches without having to enter the built-up areas. By the time the Americans reached the bridge, the Germans had established strong defensive positions on the southern approaches and were reinforcing.

As time passed, the Germans began to bring more pressure on the Grave-Nijmegen highway. They committed troops from out of the Reichswald, which, though not of very good quality, were committed in such numbers that the Americans were forced to fall back on Groesbeek Heights to preserve their original drop zones for future reinforcements and resupply. This, in turn, forced the Americans to divert forces from the bridge attack to defend the Heights.

By the 19th, an estimated 500 SS troops held the southern approaches. As the tanks of the armored corps arrived, plans were laid for a rapid assault on the bridge, hoping that the sight of the tanks would surprise the Germans and allow the Allied force to drive them out of their positions. However, the attack failed.

With the armored corps now drawing up on Nijmegen, the failure to take the bridge was causing the advance to drop further behind the time table. The 82nd's commander, MG James Gavin, formulated one of the most daring plans of the whole operation. He decided to try a daylight amphibious assault on the north side of the river. The boats available were almost literally cockleshells. In fact, the whole operation was an exercise in raw courage, since the Germans quickly got the range and dumped everything they could into the forces crossing the river. Undoubtedly, an organization with less *esprit* than an airborne unit would not have gotten across; it was that hazardous an operation. But they did cross and, once on the other side, were able to come up on the German positions from the rear. The bridge fell on the 20th of September, and the tanks were able to continue their slow progress north.

Events had not gone well during the opening phases of *Market-Garden*. However, the worst was yet to come. For it was at Arnhem that failures began to accumulate into disaster. The British 1st Airborne Division had landed in good order, though at some distance from its objective, since the drop zone was to the northwest of the city, while the bridge was on the southeast. In part, the fault for this must lie with the division commander, MG Robert Urquart. He was not a trained paratrooper, though his credentials as an infantry commander were good. He was chosen because they felt that the main operation would be a conventional infantry operation. In that respect, the British were correct. But when the RAF said that it was impractical to land closer to their objective, Urquart was in no position to refute this. Moreover, the decision was also made to land only two of the division's three brigades on the first day, because to land the third would require a second trip and surprise would be lost by then. So, the division with the longest to hold was sent in with the weakest force and was required to cover the most ground in order to seize its objectives.

The British moved out promptly upon landing. One parachute battalion moved rapidly through the city of Arnhem, before the Germans could react, seizing the northern approaches to the bridge, as well as the north end itself. But when they tried to move across, they were met with fierce German fire.

Difficulties soon became apparent. Virtually upon landing their radios began to fail, so that, in short order, almost no information was getting in or out. The 1st did not know of the difficulties being encountered by XXX Corps, and the people outside of Arnhem had no idea of the growing disaster in Arnhem. To top it off, rapid German reaction soon cut off the battalion at the bridge from the main body, and the "front" was so fluid that the division commander was cut off from all contact for a day and a half, forced to hide in a house behind the German positions.

The *9th* and *10th SS Panzer Divisions,* already in the area, were able to deploy rapidly and bring a much greater force to bear than the 1st had with it. An airborne division of World War II was basically light infantry. The only heavy support they could bring in was what could be landed in gliders, which wasn't much. In all other respects, they were armed about the same as a conventional infantry division, but had fewer men. This made them no match, on a one-for-one basis, with a mechanized division, particularly one which had its heavy weapons at hand. While the tanks, as such, were not that great an advantage for the Germans, their presence did ensure that the bridge would not fall to the British as they assisted in repelling British attempts to storm over the bridge. On the other hand, the tanks could not force their way onto the north side of the bridge and the vehicles knocked out trying to do so hindered their advance when they finally succeeded in crushing the British elements on the north side.

The valor of the 1st in defending themselves can never be questioned, but *esprit* and individual courage cannot replace expended ammunition and casualties taken. Gradually the Germans constricted the main body against the Rhine, eliminating any chance for them to reinforce the battalion holding the bridge. Likewise, they pressed in on that battalion both from the north, and, ultimately, from the south. By the 21st, D+4, all the men at the bridge had either been killed or captured, with almost no exceptions. On the same day, the Polish Parachute Brigade landed at Driel, on the south side. This landing was to reinforce the hold which the British expected to have on both sides of the bridge. Instead, the Poles landed in heavy flak and were faced with the task of trying to force a crossing of the Neder Rijn to reinforce the remainder of the 1st, now fairly well pinned against the river. They were unsuccessful. The same day, the lead elements of the armored corps started to cross the Nijmegen Bridge, and the following day the Household Cavalry and 4th Dorsets made contact. The 4th attempted on its own to cross to the north side, but it, too, was unsuccessful. It soon became apparent that even if a crossing were forced, the situation was too far gone to be salvaged unless a bridge were available to take the main body over. Lacking the bridge, as they did, the only alternative was to try to withdraw the 1st to the south bank. So, on the 26th of September, the remainder of the 1st Airborne was evacuated.

The final element of the operation was the *Garden* phase. Had it been able to keep to the timetable Montgomery had assigned, and reached Arnhem by D+2, the whole story would have been different. As it turned out, event after event conspired to delay *Garden*.

The XXX Corps was composed of the Guards Armored, 43rd, and 50th Divisions. The initial assault began at 1415 hours on the 17th, right on schedule. It promptly ran into fierce resistance. The Germans had simply taken cover during the artillery and ground support air attacks, and emerged to meet the advancing corps. By nightfall, the corps had only gone seven miles and was still six miles from Eindhoven, an objective they had expected to reach in only a few hours. The 18th went better and they were able to pass through the 101st's positions and link up with the 82nd. However, as already noted, the German counter-attack against the 101st forced the British to return a brigade back down the road to reopen it. Again the corps stalled at Nijmegen and was not able to cross until the 21st. At this point, the failure to consult with the Dutch on the local terrain came home to haunt them. The Guards Armored Division was sent right up the dike highway toward Arnhem. Six miles south of Arnhem a single German self-propelled gun executed the classic ambush, knocking out the lead vehicles. Unable to deploy off the road, the entire attack came to a complete halt and the British were forced to waste precious time looking for other routes to the west. One column, the 43rd Division, tried for the next most direct route, running through Driel, while the second column, with the household Cavalry and 4th Dorsets, swung wider to outflank any German resistance on the more direct routes. They made contact with the 1st on the 22nd. By that time the bridge was completely in German hands and any chance of forcing it with tanks was lost because the tanks had been stopped on the Nijmegen-Arnhem highway.

In one view, *Market-Garden* was more successful than not. It had taken two of its three objectives and put a salient *almost* 50 miles deep into the German positions. But Market-Garden was to be the first phase of Montgomery's longed-for drive into the heart of Germany, and by failing to take Arnhem, the whole plan was impossible to accomplish.

Montgomery, as always, complained that the real cause of the plan's failure was the lack of sufficient support. He did not have the forces he felt necessary to do the job. It might be pointed out that if he had stretched himself thinner, his failure would have been that much greater. Given the forces available, he did not take the prudent commander's step of revising his goals to accord with the means at hand.

Still, there were other factors which brought the plan closer to fruition in planning than in execution. The intelligence situation, as Montgomery believed it to be, perhaps justified his belief that the Germans could not effectively bring forces to bear on Arnhem before relief arrived. How he conceived the D + 2 date for the arrival of the tanks is not clear. Where he thought the *Fifteenth Army* had gone after they evacuated over the Scheldte is equally unclear. Certainly, even if the *II SS Panzer Corps* had not relocated, those forces would have been available to throw against the attack, though perhaps they would not have been successful.

The real core of the problem seems to lie in the fact that the plan violated the military maxim of simplicity. While each phase was relatively simple, the operation was a pyramid. Not only did he have to have each individual phase work out successfully, but there was no room for error, since any failure in the 101st sector would be compounded in delay further up the line, as in fact occurred. An operation has to be planned to allow for error. Montgomery was guilty of the same shortcoming that Hitler was to make in the Ardennes. An operation which hinges on everything going as planned is almost foredoomed to failure. The properly planned operation allows for things going wrong and the time needed to improvise expedient plans to correct the problem. Had the Nijmegen Bridge been secured by the time the XXX Corps reached the 82nd's sector, the tanks would probably have been over the road to Arnhem on the 19th. Even allowing for the error in going up the Nijmegen-Arnhem Road, this would have put them at the bridge approaches on the 20th, rather than the 22nd. And that two-day delay was sufficient to permit the Germans to wipe out the battalion holding the north end of the bridge and constrict the remainder of the division so badly that reinforcement would have been pointless. Because of the failure of *Market-Garden,* another six months were to pass before another Allied soldier crossed the Rhine, except as a POW.

Skill and Valor

Market-Garden was a desperate battle, and in desperate battles the best and worst of soldiers' qualities come to the fore. The American, Polish, and British paratroopers were the elite troops of a tough and experienced army; they may very well have been the finest soldiers in Europe. The British XXX Corps troops were among the best in the British Army, and the blame for their failures belongs far more to their leaders than to the men. As for the Germans, there were scared, untrained, inexperienced, underarmed teenagers as well as the remnants of the iron army which had conquered a continent. The German Army wasn't dead, but it was clearly inferior to its opponents, who were proving it from the Ukraine to the North Sea.

There is no question that the Allied paras at Arnhem were better than the Germans they fought. That they lost was a matter of hardware. The paras fought Tiger tanks with grenades and a few poor PIAT's, and the ammo ran out quickly. The paras shot down hundreds of raw troops, and more hundreds arrived by road and rail. All the British could do was scan the sky for the supply planes which usually missed, and look southward toward the tank column that it seemed would never arrive. Given their position it is simply amazing that they did as well as they did. They were outnumbered, outgunned, and seemingly without hope of rescue. Their guts and their talent and their desperation, and perhaps most importantly their *esprit de corps*, held them together where almost any army would have surrendered. There is a point at which these factors disintegrate in the face of overwhelming superiority. At Arnhem and Oosterbeek that point was reached and the British 1st Airborne Division died, however heroically.

One very sad part of the operation was the bad feeling created between the airborne and XXX Corps. Fights were common, and the Americans joked bitterly that Patton and Third Army wouldn't have "betrayed" the paras as Second Army had. Of course, this is debatable. But one thing is certain: despite their valor, skill, and sacrifice, the Allies suffered a terrible defeat, and the glowing words in the history books are nothing to the men who died.

The Objectives: Fourteen Bridges—One Road

The southernmost water obstacle to *Market-Garden* was the Wilhelmina Canal four kilometers north of Eindhoven. Only thirty meters wide where the highway crossed it at Zon, the Canal could be bridged by engineers, if need be, in a few hours. The main crossing at Zon was to be seized by units of the 101st on D-Day. Like all bridges on the route, it had been wired for detonation. Another crossing at Best, four kilometers westward, was assigned a low priority. *Result:* The Zon bridge was blown up on D-Day, the Best bridge on D plus 1. British engineers bridged the canal on the morning of D plus 2.

The Zuid Willems Canal at Veghel, twelve kilometers north of Zon, was twenty-five meters wide. A highway bridge and a railroad bridge there were to be taken by the 101st on D-Day. *Result:* Both bridges were captured on schedule.

Thirty kilometers north of Veghel, the Maas River presented a formidable obstacle 250 meters wide where the highway bridge stood at Grave. The bridge had to be seized on D-Day to keep the two northern airborne divisions from being isolated. One battalion of the 82nd was assigned. *Result:* The bridge was seized on schedule.

The Maas-Waal Canal, 65 meters wide, stretched between the two rivers eight kilometers northeast of Grave. Five bridges spanned it. Any one would be sufficient to carry the Garden drive; the 82nd hoped to take them all. *Result:* One bridge fell to the Allies on D-Day, one on D plus 1; the others were blown up by the Germans on D-Day.

The Waal was 280 meters wide at Nijmegen, where a highway bridge and a railroad bridge crossed. The 82nd planned to take both "on order," or low priority. The approaches in the city were heavily defended, making a direct assault fruitless. *Result:* Both bridges were taken on D plus 3 after an amphibious assault by a battalion of the 82nd across the frighteningly wide river; the battalion outflanked the defenders and took the bridges from the rear in conjunction with a frontal assault.

Finally, the Lower Rhine (Neder Rijn), fifteen kilometers to the north. The highway bridge over it at Arnhem was *the* focus of the entire operation. It was to be taken by the 1st Airborne on D-Day, along with a railroad bridge and pontoon bridge a few kilometers to the west. The capture of the rest of the corridor would be a pyrrhic victory without the capture of a bridge across the Rhine here. *Result:* The railroad bridge was blown up on D-Day. The pontoon bridge was found to have been previously dismantled. A parachute battalion captured the highway bridge on D-Day, but the Germans retook it on D plus 4.

Besides taking and holding the bridges, the airborne needed to hold open the highway corridor. The 101st was responsible for the stretch between Eindhoven and a position slightly north of Veghel, a distance of about sixteen kilometers. The protection of the bridges and the highway from both easterly and westerly attack would require a double line of twenty kilometers, normally far too long a frontage for nine battalions. However, the marshes and the Zuid Willems Canal would slow any German thrust from the east; it was thought no threat from that quarter could be expected before the arrival of three glider battalions on D plus 2. The nine parachute battalions could repulse any thrust from the west, or at least delay it until linkup with the *Garden* forces.

The 82nd was responsible for the area between Grave and Nijmegen, roughly the same frontage. Once again, terrain (marshes to the west, the Groesbeck Heights to the east) would aid the nine parachute battalions in repulsing the Germans. A bridgehead over the Waal was to be held, it was thought, with only a small force and little difficulty.

The *1st* Airborne's objective was somewhat different in that it had no highway to guard. It was to protect the bridges and maintain a bridgehead on the north bank of the Neder Rijn. Because it had a shorter frontage to guard, only six battalions of the division were to be landed on D-Day.

Two stretches of road were left unguarded. The area between Veghel and Grave lacked water obstacles and the British thought it could be quickly traversed. The road was not to be guarded until the arrival of British infantry divisions, which would take over the airborne divisions' frontages as well. Further north, the area between Nijmegen and Arnhem was left unguarded. The Allies believed the Germans could only reach the highway there via Arnhem or Nijmegen, which the Allies would already have captured. Besides, it was a very marshy section where the highway ran on top of a dike. The Allies had thought about landing troops there to seize the Arnhem bridge from the south, then dismissed the notion because of the soggy ground. Curiously, the Polish Parachute Brigade was assigned to drop there on D plus 2 anyway.

One important point in the Allies' planning was that they knew the airborne lacked the firepower to hold-out for long in the face of organized German resistance. Quick linkup with the *Garden* forces was essential. If the airborne troops were not rescued in a very few days, the Germans could wipe them out. It was a gamble, and perfect timing was crucial.

Paradrops and Glider Landings

By September of 1944, the Allies had considerable experience in airborne operations. *Market* would be the second multi-division drop of the war, and much had been learned from the confused and costly corps drop at Normandy. The tactical doctrine was well established, the equipment battle tested.

The standard transport aircraft was the American C-47, which also served as a civilian airliner (the DC-3). It was mechanically reliable and cheap; it's such a sturdy aircraft that many are still in use today. About twenty-five fully equipped paratroops could be carried at a maximum speed of 400 kph. Flying low to the ground, a C-47 could drop its "stick" of paratroops and bank away in a very few minutes; 650 meters was standard drop altitude. When the paradrops were made during the day on ground marked by pathfinders (scouts) and easily visible landmarks like rivers, drop accuracy was excellent. When the drops were made at night under adverse wind conditions as at Normandy, paratroops were scattered over fifty kilometers.

The obvious limitation of parachute drops is the inability of heavy equipment to land that way; parachutes in World War II could not support a light vehicle or heavy gun. The 75mm howitzer was the heaviest paradropable Allied artillery piece and had to be dropped in seven pieces. The answer to the weight limitation was the glider. Gliders were also used to carry infantry, as a squad landing together, unburdened by chute and straps, could get into action much quicker than paratroops. The corresponding danger was that when a glider was shot down or it cracked up in landing, every man aboard could die.

Three types of glider were used in *Market.* The Waco, used by the Americans, carried thirteen fully-equipped men and two pilots. It was towed by a C-47 at 200 kph and was constructed of plywood. While it could not carry artillery, it was a simple and sturdy vehicle, light enough that two could be towed by one C-47, though this was not done at *Market* for safety reasons. Length was 49 ft.; Span, 83 ft. The Horsa, a heavier British glider used also by US artillerymen, could carry 29 men or a jeep, or a 75mm howitzer. It occasionally disintegrated in flight, but its high carrying capacity made it useful. Length was 67 ft., Span, 88 ft. Finally, the Hamilcar was a massive glider with a carrying capacity of 17,500 lbs. A strain to the bomber pulling it, the Hamilcar was used to carry supplies, jeeps two at a time, and 6-pounder antitank guns.

A major consideration for the location of the landing zones was the terrain. Much of the area was too marshy for gliders to land on without cracking up; at Normandy many men died when they landed in flooded marshland. This deterred the Allies from landing gliders at the south end of the Arnhem bridge on D-Day. At the same time, the slow-moving C-47 transports and glider tugs were very vulnerable to flak and landing zones had to be chosen where anti-aircraft positions could be suppressed by ground attack aircraft. The 101st's zones were on firm ground near St. Oedenrode (halfway between Zon and Beghel) and just east of Veghel. Flak fire there was very light.

The 82nd's main zone was on top of the Groesbeek Heights, a defensible plateau. The 504th landed astride the Grave bridge, flak was light and the troops near their objectives.

The situation for the First Airborne was not as simply solved. Unlike the other divisions' bridges, First Airborne's were in a major urban area. Flak could not be suppressed as easily there as in the open areas of the American zones, and Intelligence suspected a high concentration of guns. Therefore the British drop zone was moved from Arnhem to Wolfheze, twelve kilometers to the northwest. This was a serious violation of a basic tenet of airborne doctrine: *Land at objective.*

An airborne drop began hours before the arrival of the main force, when squad-sized pathfinder teams were dropped to mark the drop zones with panels and smoke; they would find the zones by landmarks, and hide until the approach of the main force. If they weren't killed by the ground attack planes, which seldom happened, they would release the smoke. If it was an American drop, the landing force would consist entirely of paratroops. If British, gliders would land in the initial wave as well. American doctrine demanded secure landing zones before committing gliders; they were considered too vulnerable to flak. Once the paratroops cleared any flak positions, the gliders would land.

Drop Schedules

101st AIRBORNE

D-Day: 501, 502, 506 Parachute Infantry Regiments, 326 Airborne Engineer Battalion, 81 Airborne AA Battalion, Division Recon Platoon.

D plus 2: 327 Glider Infantry Regiment, 1 Battalion/401 Glider Regiment, 321, 907 Glider Field Artillery Battalions, 377 Parachute F.A. Battalion.

82nd AIRBORNE

D-Day: 504, 505, 508 P.I.R.s, 307 Abn. Eng. Bn. (-Co.A), Bty. A/80 Abn. AA Bn., 376 Para. F.A. Bn., Div. Recon Plt.

D plus 1: Bty. B/80 Abn. AA Bn., 456 Para. F.A. Bn., 319, 320 Glider F.A. Bns.

D plus 6 (delayed from D plus 2): 325 G.I.R., 2 Bn./401 G.I.R., Bty. C-F 80 Abn. AA Bn., Co. A/307 Abn. Eng. Bn.

1st AIRBORNE

D-Day: 1 Parachute Infantry Brigade, 1 Airlanding Brigade, 1 Light Artillery Regiment (50%), 1 Light AA Bty, 1 Airlanding Recce Squadron, 204 Antitank Bty, 1, 4 Parachute Engr. Sqns.

D plus 1: 4 P.I.B., 1 L.A.R. (50%)

D plus 4 (delayed from D plus 2): 1, 2 Bns/Polish Parachute Brigade

D plus 6: 3 Bn/P.P.B. landed by airplane

Decisive Indecision

Garden was the ground drive to link up with the *Market* airborne forces. *Garden* was to eventually involve *most* of the British Second Army. At the outset it involved barely sixty tanks.

Garden began at 1415 hours on 17 September. Guards Armoured Division attacked out of the Neerpelt Bridgehead over the Meuse-Escant Canal and headed towards Eindhoven, which was supposed to be reached in only a few hours. The first *Garden* troops reached Eindhoven on the morning of 18 September. This was the first in a series of setbacks which would doom *Market-Garden*.

Garden Timetable

Objective Reached	*Time Planned*	*Actual*
Valkenwaard	1515, 17th	1800, 17th
Eindhoven	1715, 17th	1200, 18th
Veghel	2400, 17th	0700, 19th
Grave	1200, 18th	0830, 19th
Nijmegen	1800, 18th	1530, 19th
Arnhem	1500, 19th	•

The initial assault group for *Garden* was the Grenadier Guards Group of Guards Armored Division, a force of about sixty tanks and two infantry battalions; 350 guns and dozens of fighter-bombers participated in the initial "softening up" bombardment. This was a lot of firepower, all concentrated upon the road and an area about two kilometers in radius from the first German roadblock. The planners said this would blow any defenders out of the way, and Grenadier Guards could just roll up the road. It didn't work out that way. The bombardment had little effect, and bunker-to-bunker fighting was necessary to open the road. Small roadblocks and individual anti-tank guns sighted on the highway between Neerpelt and Eindhoven slowed the advance to a crawl.

As the Guards moved northward, Division Intelligence interrogated the prisoners and got some rude shocks. Troops from *Fifteenth Army* infantry regiments were found; *Fifteen Army* was supposed to be bottled up in the Breskens Pocket, 250 kilometers to the west opposite the Canadians. Worse, troops from *9th SS Panzer Dvision,* about twenty tanks and supporting infantry, were found to be supporting the line.

According to information available to the Guards, this division was supposed to be further south fighting the Americans. British Second Army Intelligence knew better, but had neglected to inform the division. These additional troops slowed the Allied advance.

In hindsight, it is easy to see where the British armor made its first mistake. By attacking on a narrow, one-tank front, instead of advancing on a wide front, the British allowed the Germans to concentrate their forces opposite the spearhead on the highway. Guards Armored could have overwhelmed the six weak battalions between Neerpelt and Eindhoven, if only Guards Armored could have deployed opposite them. As it was, the Germans had the time to get troops into Eindhoven, another hard-fought battle. And the armor had yet to reach the first bridge!

Once Eindhoven was cleared, the Guards were able to advance at a fair clip to Nijmegen. Behind them came 43 (Wessex) and 50 (Northumberland) Infantry Divisions, the remainder of XXX Corps. About 9000 combat engineers and bridging troops accompanied the Corps. They had much to do, due to the loss of the key bridges over the Wilhelmina Canal. Following XXX Corps, XII Corps and VIII Corps infantry divisions were to move up the highway to take over 101st's zone as well as guard the Veghel-Grave road. Because of a massive traffic jam south of Neerpelt, these divisions would not arrive for more than a week. So 101st had to extend its front north of Veghel and XXX Corps infantry had to drop off around Grave. So great was the traffic jam that even XXX Corp's rearmost units, 8th Armored Brigade and the Dutch 'Princess Irene' Brigade, were unable to drive north. Supplies and engineer equipment were delayed. When the German *107th Panzer Brigade* counterattacked and cut the road at Veghel on the 22nd, the XII and VIII Corps were around Zon, having been still further delayed by a German infantry force which had infitrated to a position near Valkenswaard. A brigade of Guards had to be pulled back from Nijmegen to help the 'Screaming Eagles,' short on armor-piercing weapons, to counterattack.

Once the Guards reached Nijmegen they found their path blocked again. British engineers aided the 2/505th Battalion of the 82nd in a bloody, valiant, and successful amphibious assault on the 20th to take the Nijmegen bridges from the rear. As the rest of the 505th and the Grenadier Guards and Irish Guards attacked frontally the Germans collapsed. Somehow, the bridge stayed up.

Now there was a clear path to Arnhem. With hours of daylight and not a German in sight, and the British still holding on at Arnhem bridge, Guards Armored stopped for the night "to await supplies and infantry support." To the American paratroopers, the British had "stopped for tea."

That was perhaps the most decisive decision of the campaign; Guards Armored would attack in strength the next day, but by then the Germans had retaken Arnhem bridge and put a strong armored blocking force between the Waal and Neder Rijn at Elst. Guards and 43rd (Wessex) would link up with the Poles and the British Airborne on the 22nd, D plus 5, but any chance to re-establish a strong bridgehead over the Neder Rijn had been lost. Earlier the same thing had happened at Valkenwaard when the Guards bedded down for the night instead of driving up to Eindhoven. These two incidents illustrate an accusation often leveled at *Garden*— that the ground troops just weren't in a hurry. The XXX Corps troops fought well, took casualties—but in the long run didn't do their job.

Tactical Air Support

The role of tactical air support (that given by fighters and fighter-bombers) during an Allied airborne operation was basically fourfold. Phases One and Two were carried out in sequence before the landing. Phases Three and Four were carried out simultaneously with the troop operations on the ground.

Phase One: Carrier Escort. As the glider trains and paratroop transports passed through enemy airspace to reach the drop zones, it was necessary to ensure that no enemy aircraft or anti-aircraft fire interfered with the passage of the troops. Because the transports were slow, unmaneuverable, and unarmored, and the columns densely packed, any enemy penetration could have disastrous effects.

The standard Allied practice was to divide the escorting fighters into three layers. The top layer would fly above the transports, the second layer with the transports, and the bottom layer close to the ground. The first two layers formed a screen against enemy fighter infiltration. The bottom layer was detailed to attack any anti-aircraft batteries along the route. The fighter screen was directed by ground-based radar while the fighter-bombers relied on direct observation to find and destroy the batteries.

Phase Two: Drop Zone Suppression. Immediately before the gliders and paratroops landed, fighter-bombers carried out an extensive bombardment of the drop zones. Anti-aircraft batteries, field fortifications, large woods and buildings would be bombed, strafed and rocketed to clear the way. Fire would be kept up until only minutes before the paratroops and gliders went in. Prior aerial photography would provide target fire plans,

Phase Three: Close Support. The use of fighter-bombers as aerial artillery to assist ground forces was accepted doctrine in World War II. By 1944, the standard Allied practice was to assign squadrons to circle behind the front on-call, in so-called "cab ranks." When the ground forces radioed coordinates for a strike, the fighter squadrons would attack and return to base for rearming, while others assumed their cab rank stations. The key here was communication. Only with extensive pre-planned radio codes and coordinate designation could ground support be counted on.

Phase Four: Interdiction. Aircraft would fan out around the front or airhead to attack any enemy forces or supplies moving toward it, delaying the enemy counterattack, weakening the enemy forces already in combat, and permitting the Allied troops more time to expand and coordinate their gains before being faced by heavy enemy forces. The main thrust of the interdiction would be against roads and rail. Other planes would attack targets of opportunity such as town garrisons and river traffic; any movement toward the airhead would be attacked.

Operation Market: The tactical air support failed miserably. The first phase, carrier escort, was a success. The thousand P-51s and Spitfires protecting the transport streams were met by no more than fifty Luftwaffe fighters, which never came within sight of the transports. Six hundred P-51s, P-47s,

P-38s, Tempests, Typhoons, and Spitfires were responsible for flak suppression. While many flak batteries avoided destruction by holding their fire (and thereby hiding) until after the fighter-bombers had passed, and then firing on the transports, losses were light. Only about forty transport planes of four thousand were downed by flak, many only after their paratroops or gliders had been released. Most of the drop zones were lightly defended, and again the fighter-bombers carried out their tasks efficiently.

It is at this point that the air support for Market went downhill. After the troops were safely delivered, the fighters departed to assist the *Garden* ground forces in their struggle northward. No cab ranks were assigned to the airborne divisions. Even if, as the airborne divisions ran into trouble, support aircraft returned to help them it would have done no good. Communications simply did not exist. Plans had been laid out only sketchily. First Airborne Division had only a single fighter-frequency radio, which was knocked out on D-plus-2. The American divisions were a little better off. Still, the lack of cab rank planning meant that any request for ground support had to go from the infantry unit requesting it to the powerful radio at division headquarters to the British Second Army to the airfields in Britain. Obviously by the time the planes arrived it would be too late for them to do much except bomb whatever targets of opportunity presented themselves. The fighter-bombers were assisting the *Garden* forces, who had more artillery than they could deploy stacked along the road.

It has been argued that if the fighters had been assigned to *Market* they would have done little good, as many of the planes were socked-in through most of the battle. Perhaps, but nobody expected that to happen during the planning stage. The lack of ground support assured that the airborne would have to rely on their infantry and limited artillery firepower until linkup with the *Garden* forces. If interdiction slowed German response it might not have been so bad.

There was no interdiction. There was no plan *at all* for any organized attempt to keep German reinforcements from reaching the airheads. The marshy soil and few good roads meant that bottlenecks could have been created. Allied fighter-bombers could have had a field day attacking the German columns. Fighters on carrier escort which violated orders and attacked ground columns destroyed nearly two hundred motor vehicles and ten trains between 17 and 26 September. This was done by a few dozen planes attacking at random. The lack of interdiction assured that the Germans could concentrate their armor and artillery at the airheads promptly.

Market-Garden was in many respects a poorly-planned operation. The misuse of tactical air support is a good example of this. Of course, it is unfair to say that a proper utilization of air support would have saved *Market-Garden.* There were too many errors elsewhere for this to be decisive. But it was this kind of shoddy planning which permeated *Market-Garden,* and the allies paid the price for it.

The Great Mistakes

Market-Garden was probably more influenced by bad management and errors of judgement than is normal for a battle, even a lost battle. The mistakes were made on both sides. But the sum of these sins of omission and commission spelled victory for Germany. Here now, is a summary of some of the more notable mistakes of the *Market-Garden* operation.

Market Troop Allocations. The Allied planners, faced with a shortage of transport aircraft, could land only eight regiments plus support (recon, engineer, and artillery) units on D-Day. The units chosen were the six American paratroop regiments, one brigade each of British parachute and airlanding troops, and part of the artillery for the 82nd and 1st. This meant that the British, with the greatest distance between drop zone and objective, farthest from reinforcement, closest to the enemy reserves, would land with the weakest initial force. This problem could easily have been solved by dropping only two regiments of the 101st on D-Day—even if this would have turned out to be an insufficient force for the 101st's mission, the *Garden* link-up on D-Day would have allowed quick reinforcement for the Americans.

The 1st Moves in Slowly. With the airlanding brigade guarding the drop zone for the next day's lift, only three battalions were initially available for the push into Arnhem. Instead of rushing immediately toward the bridge, the brigade advanced cautiously, taking time to accept gifts from cheering crowds of civilians. One battalion snuck into the bridge area at dusk; the others, along with reinforcements from the airlanding brigade, were pinned down in costly street fighting. Dropping at a distance from Arnhem's heavy flak defenses was acceptable, moving in slowly was not, and allowed the Germans time to recover from their total surprise.

The Failure at Nijmegen. The crossings over the Waal were as vital as any bridge in the corridor. By designating them low priority "on order" objectives the Allies sacrificed their advantage of surprise and delayed an assault until the Germans were fully prepared.

The Lack of Tactical Air Support. By not providing for close communication between the airborne forces and the air forces, command deprived the *Market* troops of enormous firepower, firepower the light infantry needed badly. As it was, with little artillery and usually little ammunition, the airborne, especially the British, were forced to rely on infantry to fight armor which fighter-bombers could easily have destroyed.

Garden's Narrow Front. Because the *Garden* forces advanced on a one-tank front, they were unable to outflank German resistance easily and were repeatedly stopped by single guns on roads flanked by marsh impassable to tanks, preventing a detour. Not until September 22, D plus 5, did the British attempt a three-pronged drive on Arnhem. Even then the main drive by the Guards over a dike-top road was easily blocked.

The Failure of Intelligence. The short period of planning for *Market-Garden* made it inevitable that errors would be made, but not ones as inexcusable as those that were made by British intelligence. Dutch underground spies had informed the British of the presence of *II SS Panzer Corps* in Arnhem early in September; the British had ignored the report. The British believed the German *Fifteenth Army* trapped in the Breskens Pocket, but at least 65,000 men escaped by water in *broad daylight,* in the sight of Allied fighter-bombers which did not intervene! Even more incredibly, the *Market-Garden* planners did not take this into account. Many *Fifteenth Army* troops fought against the 101st during the battle for the corridor. In their planning many important terrain features were overlooked by the British. A good road over flat, firm terrain east of the dike-top road would have allowed a much quicker, less bloody passage to Arnhem from Nijmegen. A ferry over the Neder Rijn at Driel was overlooked. Usable either to reinforce or evacuate, the ferry was not noticed until it had been destroyed. The Huissen ferry east of Arnhem was used by the Germans to transport an armored blocking force which stopped the British drive cold. Dutch soldiers in England could have provided the British with a detailed terrain analysis—had they been asked. When they volunteered the information, they were ignored.

Grabner and the Arnhem Bridge. Capt Paul Grabner, in command of *9th SS Panzer Recon Battalion,* was ordered on D-Day to patrol south from Arnhem to Nijmegen, dropping off a company to guard the Arnhem highway bridge. He followed his patrol route and reached Nijmegen, dropped off a few vehicles to stiffen the infantry there, and started back for Arnhem. Unfortunately, he had neglected to drop off the company at the Arnhem bridge. Minutes after he had crossed the bridge on the first leg of the trip, a British parachute battalion arrived and set up a perimeter on the north end. Grabner's error meant that the Germans would have to fight for four days to get back the key bridge. (Grabner, incidentally, died in the first attack on the bridge.)

Model and the Nijmegen Bridge. Field Marshal Model was the German army group commander. Early in the battle his subordinates proposed that the troops holding Nijmegen be withdrawn north of the Waal and the bridge blown to prevent a crossing. Model refused, saying that the Allies would never cross the Waal and the Nijmegen bridge would be needed to support the German counterattack. The Allies did cross the Waal, and when the Germans did finally try to detonate the bridge charges it was too late—the electric cables had been cut.

Model and the Glider. An officer, acting against orders, carried a complete set of *Market-Garden* plans into battle. His glider crashed and the plans were delivered to Model on D plus 2. Model thought the plan a decoy, as it seemed to him too fantastic to be true (admittedly a reasonable assumption). Even after it was obvious that at least the early stage of the battle corresponded with the plan he had, he ignored the document totally.

Market in Perspective: The Airborne in Europe

Market was by far the most ambitious airborne operation of the war, but there were others before and after which influenced the development of airborne doctrine and methods.

Before World War II paratroops has been used only sparingly, mostly by the Soviets, who did not expand their use during the war. Soviet paras dropped disastrously during the Winter War, and were used as commandos and in recon missions only. The Germans began their use of paratroops and airportable troops in Denmark and Norway in April of 1940, when tiny detachments were used to seize airfields, bridges, and crossroads. The Allies didn't grasp the importance of the airborne due to the small size of the operation. For the Germans, it was a successful experiment.

The German airborne woke up the world the next month during the invasion of the low countries. A few hundred sappers dropped and glided onto the Belgian fortress of Ebaen Emael, destroying it and unhinging the entire Belgian line. Five parachute battalions and three glider/airportable regiments struck the Netherlands. They took bridges, destroyed communications, shot up supply dumps, and paralyzed the Dutch Army. German infantry practically walked into Holland. *Now* the British realized the value of airborne, and both they and the Americans slowly began to organize airborne units.

The Germans used their airborne unsuccessfully to cut the British line of retreat across the Corinth Canal in Greece in April, 1941. The next month the entire German airborne force hit Crete. This was the first true airborne *assault,* facing prepared front-line troops in fairly strong positions. The airborne took one of three airfields attacked, securing reinforcement and thereby the island, but airborne casualties were close to 50%. Hitler declared that the surprise was gone and decreed the end of major airborne operations. Thereafter operations were few. A descent on Malta in collaboration with Italian airborne and amphibious forces was planned in 1942 but never executed. A series of unopposed drops in Tunisia in late 1942 helped secure port and airbase facilities for Germany. The following summer an airdrop was used to reinforce friendly forces in Sicily. In November of 1943 a battalion dropped in support of amphibious units during the capture of the Aegean island of Leros from an isolated Anglo-Italian garrison. And one battalion executed a combat drop during the Battle of the Bulge in December of 1944. For the most part, however, parachute forces were an elite infantry arm of the Luftwaffe, helping both to consume surplus personnel and to beef up Goring's political muscle.

The Allies learned a different lesson from Crete. The airportable idea, depending so much on the capture of airfields, was minimized. The foolishness of sending lightly equipped airborne against front-line positions was obvious now. Allied doctrine followed the lesson of Holland: Vertical Envelopment.

Major Airborne Operations of World War II

Operations	*Date*	*Forces*	*Strength (%Loss)*
Netherlands	10 May 40	*7th FD, 22nd LD*	16.0 (20%)
Crete	20 May 41	*VIII FK, XI FK*	15.0 (45%)
Sicily	10 Jul 43	US 82nd Div; Br 1st Bde	6.0 (25%)
Normandy	6 Jun 44	US 82nd, 101st; Br 6th Divs	20.0 (15%)
Southern France	15 Aug 44	US 1st TF; Br 2nd Bde	8.0 (10%)
Netherlands	17 Sept 44	US 82nd, 101st; Br 1st Divs; Pol Bde	35.0 (33%)
Rhine	24 Mar 45	US 17th; Br 6th Div	20.0 (c.8%)

This table includes all airdrops of over 6,000 men into combat, counting parachutists, glider-borne, and airlanded troops only. Abbreviations: *FD*= *Fleiger-division*, "Flying Division"; *LD*= *Luftlandeddivision*, "air-landing division"; *FK*= *Fleigerkorps*, "Flying Corps"; *TF*= Airborne Task Force, an ad hoc formation organized for *Dragoon*. Note that most German units actually designated parachute—*fallschirmjager*— were actually elite infantry with little or no jump training.

The British made the first of many paracommando raids in 1941, and battalions dropped in North Africa in late 1942. The first combat drop was Sicily. A regiment each of American gliders and British paratroops made the first large-scale night drop of the war to take key objectives for the amphibious forces. The inexperienced pilots dropped men in the ocean and mainland Italy. The glider trains wandered over the invasion fleet and were decimated. Battalion objectives were taken by platoons. The Axis troops were confused, at least, for there was no way to tell where the real attack was coming from. It was a bloody disaster. Smaller drops at Salerno achieved little.

The next big drop was part of the D-Day Normandy invasion. Three divisions landed, again a night drop. The pilots were better, but the wind was worse, and men landed in Cherbourg and Le Havre. Again, the Germans hesitated to commit themselves anywhere. Some units landed together and *ersatz* units banded together, and the key river crossings and crossroads were secured to form a hard crust on the flanks of the beachheads. While the operation was a success, the casualties were needlessly high. Many heavily laden men drowned in the swamps and the Channel. In August there was a major drop in Southern France. It landed in daylight, together and effectively. By *Market* the Allies had learned a lot. No more night drops; improved pathfinder methods to maximize drop cohesion; more heavy weapons. *Market* was the best organized drop to date, a perfect example of vertical envelopment used to seize key objectives. The failure came when the troops were forced to fight strong ground units without adequate support and relief.

After *Market* the Allies were very cautious with their airborne. *Operation Varsity,* coinciding with Montgomery's Rhine crossing, was conducted in daylight, within range of artillery west of the river, and was in fact begun *after* the river crossing. It was not at all necessary to the success of the crossing, but Montgomery demanded it in a typical fit of conservatism. *Varsity* was-letter perfect, and it marked the first meaningful use of glider-borne tanks. It was an impressive operation, but it was wasteful.

Market is often decried by critics of the airborne concept, who claim that the elite men and resources did not return the expense. With the increase in effectiveness of air defenses it could be the last great airborne attack in history. And whatever the critics say, it is a fact that if *Market* had succeeded it would have drastically altered the course of the drive into Germany, and it would have indeed been worth it.

Allied Casualties

Operation Market Units	*Killed*	*Missing*	*Wounded*	*Total*
82nd Airborne Div	215	427	790	1432
101st Airborne Div	315	547	1248	2110
1st Airborne Div	286	6041	135	6462
Polish Parachute Bde	47	173	158	378
XVIII Airborne Corps HQ	4	8	–	12
RAF Transport Crews	31	217	17	265
USAAF Transport Crews	31	155	66	252
British Glider Pilots	59	636	35	730
US Glider Pilots	12	65	34	98
***Market* Total**	**1001**	**8332**	**2520**	**11853**
Operation Garden Units				
XXX Corps				1480
XII Corps VIII Corps				3874
***Garden* Total**				**5354**
Grand Total				**17207**

Even as Montgomery essayed *Operation Market Garden,* Patton, in the Allied center, pressed on into Lorraine seeking victory and glory in his own way. But, as Montgomery was finding, German resistance was stiffening again.

Patton's Third Army: The Lorraine Campaign,

19 September–1 December 1944

By Joseph Balkoski

Prominently displaying the three white stars of a lieutenant-general on its hood, an olive-drab U.S. Army jeep sped noisily through the muddy, deserted streets of the French city of Metz. It was a chilly November day, and the low, grey overcast seemed only to heighten the somber view of shell-torn shops and houses lining the streets. In the jeep were three American soldiers, each in a long green trenchcoat and steel helmet. The senior was 58-year-old LG George S. Patton, his well-known ivory-handled Colt .45's conspicuously displayed at his sides. In the rear sat MG Hugh J. Gaffey, Patton's chief-of-staff and a former armored division commander. The driver was Master Sergeant William George Meeks, Patton's black orderly throughout the war.

As the jeep wound its way through the labyrinth of streets, signs of the recent German presence were still clearly visible. Under a prominent sign reading *"Sepp Dietrich Kaserne"* soldiers of the U.S. 5th Infantry Division loitered, watching German POW's being herded into groups for transportation to nearby camps, each with his hands held high above his head.

"Stop the jeep, George," said Patton to Meeks. "Hugh, I suppose I'm going to have to give these guys a pep talk."

The jeep came to a halt and Patton stood up. He maintained his impressive, martial pose for some time as a crowd of joyous, although tired-looking GI's gathered around him. Finally, he began to speak.

"Our success was primarily due to continued offensive, day and night, relentless and unceasing, and to that fact that we used maneuver. We held the enemy by the nose and kicked him in the pants. It is needless to point out to men like you the pre-eminent value of disciplined valor. You have demonstrated your courage, and have, I am sure, realized the safety which results from courageous actions. In my dealings with you, I have been guilty on too many occasions, perhaps, of criticizing and loud talking. I am sorry for this and wish to assure you that when I criticize and censure, I am wholly impersonal. You know that I have never asked one of you to go where I feared to tread. I have been criticized for this, but there are many General Pattons and there is only one Third Army. I can be expended, but the Third Army *must* and *will* be victorious.

"I am very proud of you. Your country is proud of you. You are magnificent fighting men. Your deeds in the battle for Metz will fill the pages of history for a thousand years."

Patton concluded, sat down. His eyes were filling up with tears. As he ordered Meeks to get the jeep moving again, the sea of GI's parted with a thundering ovation. The three men disappeared, only to repeat similar scenes throughout the Third Army front line.

Metz, the thorn in George Patton's side since September 1944, had finally fallen. The fight for this historic fortess city and other key areas of Lorraine proved to be the Third Army's most difficult and vicious battle of the entire war. In previous weeks, "Lucky Forward"—the Third Army—had registered its daily advance in terms of miles. In November 1944, however, progress was measured in yards—each one gained at costly sacrifice. In Third Army circles, the cheery optimism that had promised an end to the war by Christmas had vanished.

Breakout and Pursuit

The U.S. Third Army was born on 28 July 1944, amid the drama of *Operation Cobra* in the Normandy hedgerows. In a matter of days, Patton's force of nine divisions had made a decisive penetration of the German lines. "As a result of the breakthrough of the enemy armored spearheads," said German *Army Group B* commander Gunther von Kluge, "the whole Western Front has been ripped wide open." Von Kluge's words proved eminently accurate. Within one week, Brest, Lorient, and St. Nazaire were invested by Patton's forces; within two weeks, the German Army in Normandy was virtually destroyed in the Falaise Pocket. By 19 August, the Third Army was driving almost unopposed toward the Seine and beyond in the area south of Paris. "We have been going so fast," wrote Patton, "that our chief difficulty consists in our inability to emulate Ariadne and keep our spiderweb behind us. Our supply people, however, have really done marvels, and we always have sufficient of everything. . . . The weather has been just as good as it was for the Germans in 1940, and also for them in Poland in 1939."

The end of August saw the Third Army penetrating even further eastward, seizing bridgeheads across the Meuse River and reconnoitering the west bank of the Moselle. Optimistically, Patton wrote, "We have at this time, the greatest chance to win the war ever presented. If they will let me move on with three corps on the line of Metz-Nancy-Epinal, we can be in Germany in ten days. It can be done with three armored and six infantry divisions. It is such a sure thing that I fear these blind moles don't see it."

However, numerous difficulties were arising for the advancing Allied armies, the most frustrating being logistics. Quite simply, the Allies, particularly Patton, had outrun their supply lines. Logistical planners had envisioned a more orderly campaign. As a result, the plentiful supplies stockpiled in Normandy could not be transported to the fighting armies fast enough to maintain a mobile campaign. Patton's supply line stretched 400 miles from Verdun to Cherbourg. The trucks and trailers of the "Red Ball Express" were supplying Third Army with only 2,000 tons of supplies per day, some of which had to be rerouted to Paris to provide for its civilians. "At the present time," said Patton on 28 August, "our chief difficulty is not the Germans, but gasoline. If they would give me enough gas, I could go anywhere I want."

Stagnation on the Moselle

By early September 1944, a great debate was arising among Allied strategic planners over the merits and disadvantages of Eisenhower's "broad front" advance across France. British 21st Army Group commander, Sir Bernard Law Montgomery, pointed out the logistical nightmare which the Allies were currently facing, forcefully stating his case for a concerted drive toward the industrial German Ruhr. Of course, his force's assault would require virtually all available supply, leaving Patton's Third Army almost bone dry.

Upon pondering the problem, Eisenhower finally decided that in order to clear the Scheldt Estuary, Antwerp, and the V-rocket launching sites, Montgomery and 21st Army Group would get priority in supply for the time being. "For a very considerable time," Eisenhower wrote, "I was of the belief that we could carry out the operation of the northeast simultaneously with a thrust eastward, but later I have concluded that due to the tremendous importance of the objectives in the northeast, we must first concentrate on that movement."

Patton was disgusted. His army was, for all intents and purposes, stopped in its tracks. "Eisenhower kept talking of the future great battle of Germany," Patton wrote after meeting with the Supreme Commander. "We assured him that the Germans have nothing left to fight with if we push on now. If we wait, there *will* be a great battle of Germany. . . . God deliver us from our friends. We can handle the enemy."

During this delay, the Germans undertook the formidable task of preparing their defenses. On 3 September, *Army Group B* could only muster 100 tanks, while in one area, eight battalions of infantry defended a front of 120 kilometers! However, on 5 September, the respected old veteran, FM Gerd von Rundstedt, returned to the Western Front as German commander-in-chief West. Two days before, Hitler had personally ordered a concentration of armor opposite Patton on the Moselle. In this area, the German *First Army* was strengthened considerably in mid-September in expectation of a U.S. Third Army push into the industrial Saarland, a sensitive nerve in Hitler's frontier defenses. "Both as regards quality and diversity," an Allied intelligence report stated, "the enemy force opposing us shows the effects of the recent measures in Germany to step up the national effort. Paratroops and pilots, policemen and sailors, boys of 16 and men with ulcers—all of these have been through the corps cage in the last few days."

As for Patton, the offensive was still the catchword, supply or no supply. "I am doing my damndest to get going again, but it is hard," he wrote to his wife. "Once people stop, they get cautious and the enemy gets set." In protest over the supply situation, Patton, together with 12th army group commander, LG Omar Bradley, offered to resign on 15 September. However, both men eventually backed down. Instead, Patton chose a more devious method of avoiding SHAEF: "I must get so involved in operations that they can't stop me," he wrote. "I told Bradley not to call me until after dark on 19 September. He agreed." Meanwhile, Patton would advance by what he called the "rock-soup" method. ("A tramp once went to a house and asked for some water to make rock-soup. The lady was interested and gave him the water, in which he placed two stones. He then asked if he might have some potatoes and carrots to put in the soup to flavor it a little, and finally ended up with some meat. In other words, in order to attack, we must first pretend to reconnoiter and then reinforce the reconnaissance and then finally attack. It is a very sad method of making war.")

In middle and late September, Patton's three available corps assaulted the Moselle line with limited resources against increasing German resistance. Nevertheless, the attacks were moderately successful, although painfully slow. In the south, XV Corps, MG Wade Haislip, penetrated the Moselle and captured the Alsatian city of Epinal. In Patton's central sector, XII Corps, MG Manton S. Eddy, established a Moselle bridgehead after bitter fighting in the Pont-a-Mousson area. The critical rail center of Nancy fell to Eddy on 15 September. In the north, XX Corps, MG Walton Walker, faced the difficult Metz defenses, but managed to sidestep them to the south with the 5th Infantry Division—establishing bridgeheads over the Moselle in two separate places.

On 18 September, Hitler ordered a series of limited counterattacks against these bridgeheads, after it was noted that "*Fifth Panzer Army* shows a marked tendency to limit itself to defensive action." After these counterattacks proved abortive, Hitler sacked Gen Johannes Blaskowitz, commander of *Army Group G,* and replaced him with one of his favorites, LG Hermann Balck. Balck was truly a worthy rival to Patton. Employing a very similar style of personal aggressiveness (he had been wounded six times), Balck's dynamic leadership of armored formations advanced his career meteorically in Russia. However, Rundstedt and other high-ranking German officers in the West looked upon Balck with disfavor, probably because he was an ardent Nazi and a favorite of Hitler's. He also had no Western Front experience—he had been in Russia almost continually since 1941.

Upon assuming his position, Balck willingly submitted his army group to Hitler's personal strategic guidelines. The Fuhrer had no intention whatsoever of acceding to Rundstedt's plan of withdrawal to the West Wall; instead, Hitler ordered his force to defend where they stood, particularly along the line of the Moselle. Envisioning Patton's drive as the major Allied effort, Hitler ordered Balck to center his defense on the Metz-Thionville fortifications, while building up secondary defensive lines to the rear. In addition, the West Wall in this area was to be reinforced considerably.

Metz has always been an historic city in military terms. Although a vital location in many European campaigns for centuries, it had not fallen to direct assault since 1552. In the Franco-Prussian War, it was captured after a 54-day siege on October 1870. In the First World War, it had been heavily fortified by the Germans, but after 1918, the fortifications were allowed to deteriorate after the city passed back into French hands. Militarily, the forts surrounding Metz were antiquated by 1944, but the psychological benefits of the fortified position to the retreating German troops allowed Balck to develop his defense around this position.

Due to the weak forces and poor equipment at his disposal, Balck immediately opted for the tactic of mobile or "elastic" defense on the *Army Group G* front. Imitating the late First World War German trench defense schemes, Balck planned to keep his front lines almost denuded of troops. As a result, the terrific initial American artillery barrage and air bombardments would be hitting virtually nothing of importance. If an armored or infantry assault followed up, the forward German positions would be easily overrun. However, the attack would soon meet the main bodies of German infantry in secondary defensive lines, almost untouched by the air strikes and bombardment. Taking this tactic one step further, Balck told Rundstedt that he intended to counterattack any American breakthrough "on the spot" with mobile formations left behind the front line just for this purpose.

In order to slow down the initial American penetrations through the weak front line of his mobile defense, Balck employed field fortifications in Lorraine that came as close to First World War battlefield conditions as anything the Americans had yet seen in France. In particular, he was lavish in his employment of minefields. Afterwards, Balck wrote, "From army group level, I directed the layout of minefields. The minefields consisted of a few real mines and lots of dummy ones. Once you've forced the enemy to work his way slowly into a minefield, you know exactly where his point of main effort is. Then you can envelop him with your mobile reserves. With that tactic, I had great success against the Russians in Galicia, as well as against the Americans on the Western Front."

In addition to his forward defense line, Balck also had several fortified positions to fall back on should retirement become necessary. AMong these was the West Wall (or "Siegfried Line" as it was known to the Allies), the French Maginot Line, the Orscholz "Switch" Line (an extension of the West Wall between the Moselle and the Saar near Thionville), and the "West-Stellung" (a new fortified line near Sarrebourg ordered specifically by Balck in late September). All in all, Balck had extensive, although not truly formidable defenses at his disposal.

At the beginning of October, Patton continued his mini-offensive by attempting to test Balck's defenses. "For about ten days," he wrote, "we had been contemplating trying out the defensive qualities of the German forts covering Metz west of the Moselle. The 5th Division believed that Driant, one of those forts, could be taken with a battalion. On the third of October, they put their plan into execution. "After an initial penetration of the fort by tanks and infantry, the fighting stagnated into bloody, confused actions with absolutely no room for maneuver. By 9 October, the Americans had suffered 500 casualties and had not taken a single fort. A withdrawal was called for. "If we could get the supplies we need and with three good days of weather, we could take it," Patton said. "In fact, I am not going to let these soldiers get killed until we have things on our side."

Throughout the frustrating months of September and October, Patton continued to contemplate the "big picture" for his beloved Third Army. With a supply buildup and permission from SHAEF, he envisioned another lightning offensive that would penetrate the German front line defenses, push on through the West Wall "like crap through a tin horn," and roll right up to the Rhine and beyond—all in a matter of weeks. "The sooner we start this, the better, as the enemy continues to dig in and mine ahead of us," he said for all to hear, particularly Eisenhower.

On 2 November, Patton finally received welcome news. Eisenhower had decided to resume the offensive, and this time a *double* pronged assault both north and south of the Ardennes was provided for. Patton's Third Army was to be the southern thrust. Bradley ordered the attack "any time on or after the 8th, when you get a forecast of one good day's weather." "I will jump off on the 8th, bombers or no," Patton replied enthusiastically. In his diary, he wrote, "I feel 40 years younger."

Considering his experience at Fort Driant in October, Patton's new offensive envisioned an encirclement of Metz from the north and south by XX Corps, while XII Corps made a penetration of the German lines east of Nancy. Third Army order read:

> "TOP SECRET
> HQ 3rd U.S. Army
> 3 November 1944
> Subject: Operational Directive
> To: Commanding Generals XII, XX Corps.
>
> "Third U.S. Army will:
> "1. Envelop Metz defensive works from north and south to destroy enemy forces withdrawing from the Metz area.
> "2. Advance northeast within zones to seize Mainz, Frankfurt, Darmstadt area.
> "3. Be prepared for further offensive action to the northeast.
> "Time of attack: To be announced.
>
> By command of Lt. Gen Patton"

On 1 November, Patton's Third Army was approximately 225,000 men strong. It consisted of two corps (the XV had been taken away from him on 29 September), comprising six infantry and three armored divisions. At corps and army level, Patton had 19 tank and tank destroyer battalions, three cavalry groups, 38 field artillery battalions (including nine over 155mm), 22 anti-aircraft battalions, 33 general service, combat, and bridging engineer formations, and one ranger battalion. In addition, he had the promised use of the First Army's 83rd Infantry Division, lining the Moselle on Third Army's north flank near Luxembourg. Gasoline, rations, ammunition, and bridging equipment were in plentiful supply, with optimistic logistical planners promising to maintain the flow. Almost every unit in Third Army was at or near assigned strength.

In complete contrast to Patton's plentiful provisions, Balck was forced to make do with meager resources. "If replacements are not forthcoming," Balck reported, "the time will arrive when there is no longer any front to defend. The front is already strained to the breaking point, and one wonders how the few tired men can ever repair the situation." After inspecting his southern front, he added,"I have never commanded such jumbled up and badly equipped troops." Balck had two armies under his control: the *First* and the *Nineteenth.* In Lorraine, the *First Army* front corresponded almost exactly with that of the Third U.S. Army. *First Army* possessed three corps—from north to south, they were the *LXXXII,* the *XIII SS,* and the *LXXXIX.* On 1 November, *First Army* was 86,622 men strong, with approximately 100 tanks. It possessed nine divisions, including one panzergrenadier, one panzer, and seven volksgrenadier divisions, although none of these formations were at full strength. In addition, Balck had numerous independent machinegun, fortress, security, flak, and engineer battalions at his disposal, most of which were placed under the protection of the concrete Metz forts. Five battalions of reserve artillery in the *401st Volks Artillery Corps* were also provided by Hitler in the beginning of November, but Balck was extremely low on artillery ammunition.

The Battle for Metz

On 4 November 1944, the Third Army staff gathered for its daily briefing. However, unlike other meetings, there was a tense air of expectation among the officers on this day. At center stage, Patton was assuming his typical martial poses in front of an enormous situation map. He began to speak.

"Gentlemen, Third Army has been given the great honor of leading the new offensive in the west. Our D-day, as you know, is any time from tomorrow until the 8th, depending on the weather. Despite the difficulties we face, and notwithstanding my considerable talents as a bull artist, I can assure you that we will succeed in breaking through the Siegfried Line, penetrate into the heart of Germany, and win the war. I want hard-hitting and unremitting effort pressing our plan of operations. And always keep in mind that the Rhine is our objective. As a result of my intimate relations with God," he concluded, "I am in a position to express complete assurance that we will have the good weather we need for a lucky jump-off."

Despite Patton's special relationship with the Almighty, it rained almost continuously throughout the first week in November, postponing the attack until 8 November. Patton became fidgety, itching for the fight—he had an attack of shortness of breath on 5 November, but recovered by the next day. The rain was still so bad on the eve of the assault that Eddy and the commander of 6th Armored Division went to visit Patton to ask that the operation be postponed yet again.

"The attack will go on, rain or no rain," Patton insisted, "and I'm sure it will succeed."

After additional protests, Patton slammed his fist on the table. "I think you better recommend the men you would like appointed as your successors." The two generals meekly left. The attack took place as planned.

On 8 November at 0515 hours, about 500 American artillery pieces opened up their preliminary barrage on the nearby German lines. The rain had stopped. In the pre-dawn darkness, the gun flashes gave the horizon an eerie appearance, and each firing resounded for miles with a sharp crack like a door slamming noisily in an empty house. At 0800, Bradley rang up Patton.

"I am attacking, Brad," said Patton. "Can't you hear our guns?"

"What?! You're attacking without air support?" Bradley inquired. "Hang on Georgie, Ike is here and wants to speak with you."

"Georgie? This is Ike—your Supreme Commander, you know. I'm thrilled, boy! I expect a hell of a lot from you, so carry the ball all the way!"

"Thanks, General," Patton exclaimed. "We will, sir, we sure will!"

XII Corps Assault

Patton launched the five divisions of XII Corps in the attack as soon as the American bombardment lifted at 0600 hours. Manning the front line of this corps were

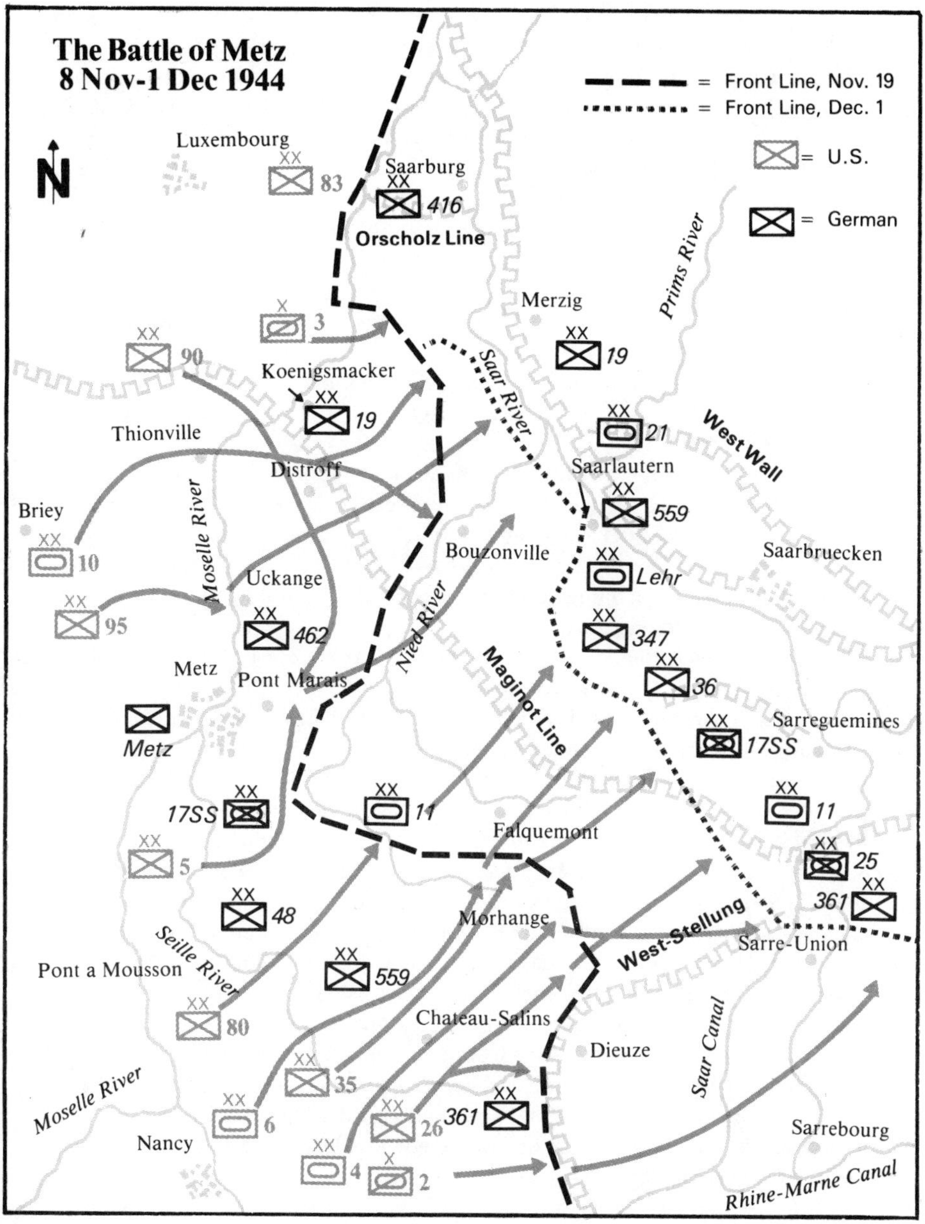

The Battle of Metz
8 Nov-1 Dec 1944

three infantry divisions, the 80th, 35th, and the green 26th. These were deployed south of Metz in a line roughly paralleling the Seille River. In reserve, ready to punch through any gap made by the infantry, were the 4th and 6th Armored Divisions, generally rated the best American divisions in France. Confronting the attacking Americans were the weak *48th, 361st,* and *559th Volksgrenadier Division,* with the depleted *11th Panzer Division* in reserve.

The general goal of the three American assault divisions was to bridge the Seille (a difficult task because the flooding river was triple its normal width) and to provide maneuver room for the waiting armored divisions. As the attack opened, the 26th Division achieved surprise, seizing some Seille bridges intact and clearing some bridgeheads deep enough to permit employment of the 4th Armored. Similarly, the 35th Division made quick initial progress past the Seille, permitting the employment of a combat command of the 4th Armored, but soon ran into punishing infantry engagements in the thick, dark forests near Chateau-Salins.

Typically, well dug-in German infantry would confront advancing GI's, who would then call on massive artillery concentrations to force their opponents from their positions. The 80th Division faced the most imposing terrain in the XII Corps zone: the huge Delme ridge, which ran like a twisted finger along the east bank of the Seille, and which commanded all the Seille crossing sites. Like her sister divisions, the 80th was initially successful enough to permit employment of the 6th Armored into the fighting.

However, after the first few days of the offensive, the German defense tightened considerably. Casualties on both sides were heavy, and the fighting was intense. After a week, both the 80th and the 6th Armored had forced the German line to sag, but it did not break. "I wish things would move a little faster in this Army, because I fear that at the moment, the French and the Seventh Army are stealing the show," Patton noted wistfully.

It is clear that Balck's mobile defense methods were paying dividends for *First Army*. Despite the massive American artillery and air superiority, American formations consistently ran headlong into infantry slugfests against determined German resistance. Although the Germans were being pushed back steadily day-by-day, there was no breakthrough resembling the one Patton had achieved in *Operation Cobra*. The 35th Division, for example, advanced twelve miles in eight days of assault, suffering severe disorganization and moderate casualties as a result. Of course, the surprisingly bitter cold (it snowed on the second day of the offensive) and the ubiquitous mud were almost as much of a hindrance to the Americans as the enemy. Trenchfoot alone reduced some American formations below 50%. This, like all non-battle casualties, was particularly galling to Patton. "To win the war, we must conquer trenchfoot," he insisted to reporters.

Nevertheless, Patton had reason to be optimistic over the results of the XIII Corps assault. The left wing of the German *First Army* was bending back almost double, and the roads connecting Metz with the outside world were slowly being cut off. Moreover, the Saar and the West Wall were drawing ever closer, and it was hoped that the buckling German line would not be able to stand much more punishment in the ensuing days.

XX Corps Assault

While XII Corps was launching its offensive on 8 November, the units of Maj. Gen. Walker's XX Corps lay inactive along the Moselle between Metz and Thionville. Walker's corps had the responsibility for the capture of Metz, although on this occasion, Patton planned to conduct adroit maneuvering rather than frontal assault to capture the fortress. After sitting tight on the 8th, the four divisions of XX

Corps were to be launched in the attack on the morning of the 9th, employing a more subtle and deceptive plan of attack than their sister corps to the south. Manning the front line of XX Corps were three infantry divisions: the 90th (along the Moselle near Thionville), 95th (directly shielding Metz), and the veteran 5th (just south of Metz). In addition, 10th Armored Division lay in reserve near Briey. On the German front line opposite Walker were three divisions of fairly high caliber, *17th SS*, *462nd*, and *19th Volksgrenadier*, plus a large number of independent fortress, machinegun, and security battalions in Metz itself.

The American scheme was to mask Metz with the 95th Division, applying diversionary attacks on the Moselle north of the Metz forts at Uckange in order to draw German attention to this area. Meanwhile, the 90th Division would make the major XX Corps effort by crossing the Moselle in the Thionvile-Koenigsmacker area, driving south along the Axis of the Maginot Line to cut the roads east of Metz. The 5th Division would also bypass the fixed fortifications of Metz, attacking northward to meet the 90th and complete the encirclement of the city. Like the armored divisions of XII Corps, 10th Armored was to pass through the lines of the 90th east of the Moselle and attack toward the Saar near Merzig, gaining a bridgehead over this river if possible.

C Company, 1st Battalion, 377th Infantry opened up the 95th Division's diversionary attack on 9 November, ferrying across the swollen Moselle at Uckange with little difficulty. The Germans were hardly fooled, however, as they sat and waited for the American assault to the north, near Thionville. At 0300 hours, the men of the 358th and 359th Regiments, 90th Division, shoved off into the bitterly cold, raging waters of the Moselle in their fragile assault boats. After a day's action, the entire division was across the river. In the days that followed there was heavy fighting around the old French forts near Thionville, as the 90th turned south. A counterattack by a mobile *kampfgruppe* of the *25th Panzergrenadier Division* on 15th November was repulsed at Distroff as the Americans pressed closer to Metz.

On 17 November, Balck realized that this attack was stretching his north flank to its limit. On this day, he issued orders for a general *First Army* withdrawal to the east, effectively leaving the Metz garrison to wither on the vine. As a result, the 90th Division advanced with impunity over the next two days, making contact with troops of the 5th Division at Pont Marais at 1030, 19 November. Metz was cut off from the outside world. Patton was so impressed with the 90th that he termed their attack "one of the epic river crossings in history."

At the time of the 90th Division assault, the 5th Division was attacking simultaneously out of a small bridgehead over the Moselle south of Metz. Helped by a massive air attack by 1,229 B-17's and B-24's from the Eighth Air Force, the 5th launched its attack across the Seille—swollen to 200 yards wide in this sector—on 9 November. After seven days of hard fighting, one regiment, the 11th, closed in on Metz directly from the south through the Frescaty airfield, after a bitter fight with the German *48th Machine Gun Battalion*. Another regiment, the 10th, drove up the eastern outskirts to surround the city. The third regiment, the 2nd, pushed up the valley of the Nied Francaise River to meet patrols of the 90th Division from the north on 19 November.

The German commander of "Festung Metz," Heinrich Kittel, vainly tried to organize his second-class troops for the defense of the surrounded city. By 17 November, however, the American vise was so tight that Kittel lost all telephone and wire communications with his outlying fortresses. In desperation, Kittel joined his troops on the front lines, where he was badly wounded and later captured on 21 November. Despite some booby-trapping (the U.S. 377th Infantry suffered 57 casualties on 18 November when a building exploded) and some house-to-house fighting, the Germans in Metz were surrendering in droves. Resistance in the city ended officially at 1435, 22 November, although some isolated forts continued to hold out longer (Fort Jeanne d'Arc did not surrender until 13 December). The direct objective of Third Army's offensive had been won. In a nearby field hospital, Patton visited the wounded. "Tomorrow, the headlines will read, 'Patton Took Metz,'" he said, "which *you* know is a damned lie. You and your buddies are the ones who actually took Metz!"

Drive Towards the Saar

The first phase of the offensive was over. The reactions of both Patton and Balck were mixed. "I had hoped to win this battle by 11 November, as it was my birthday and my lucky day in West Africa," Patton said. "However, I did not win it." As for Balck, he later stated, "I was able to keep the whole defense togther and seriously slow down Patton."

Third Army's next objective was to attack toward the Saar River and the West Wall with both XII and XX Corps, but Patton's men were tired. "The impetus of the attack is naturally slackening due to the fatigue of the men," Patton wrote. "I am trying to arrange to get at least one infantry division in each corps out of the line for a rest, but I doubt whether we can do it."

On the German side, *OB West's* reaction to the American offensive was swift. Reinforcements, including the elite *Panzer Lehr, 21st Panzer,* and *36th Volksgrenadier Divisions,* were arriving in large numbers. In addition, each step *First Army* retreated eastward shortened its line and brought it closer to the fortified positions of the Maginot and Orscholz Lines, as well as the West Wall.

On 18 November, the U.S. 26th Division, supported by tanks of the all-black 761st Tank Battalion, re-opened the XII Corps assault by attacking in the vicinity of Dieuze and the Etang de Lindre. A penetration was soon made which enabled the tanks of the 4th Armored Division to pass through the 26th Division lines. Each armored combat command split into two "task force" columns (each composed of two mechanized infantry companies and one tank company, or vice versa) in order to put maximum pressure all along the German line. Meanwhile, on the 26th's left, the 6th Armored attacked toward the Saar Canal.

On 23 November, "Task Force Churchill" of the 4th Armored crossed the Saar north of Sarrebourg against weakening German resistance. Meanwhile, 6th Armored penetrated the Maginot Line near Sarreguemines. The whole right flank of XII Corps swung the axis of its advance northwards, as the left flank divisions, 80th and 35th, also attacked the German defenses in the Maginot Line. By 2 December, although no decisive breakthrough had been made, the German line was retreating faster than it had since August. Unfortunately, American casualties were very high. For example, out of a total strength of about 16,000 men on 8

November, the 26th Division took 3,428 battle and 2,898 non-battle casualties in November—a loss rate of 40%. In addition, 89% of the casualties were in the infantry.

As soon as Metz had fallen, General Walker reoriented his available forces of XX Corps for a drive northeastward toward the Saar between Saarburg and Saarlautern. In this vicinity, the "Saar Moselle Triangle," the Saar was wide and easily defensible—the West Wall paralleled its east bank all the way south to Saarbruecken. For this reason, Patton planned on calling on the First Army's 83rd Division, currently lining the Moselle near its confluence with the Saar, to attack across the Triangle in the shortest direct route between the American position and the Siegfried Line. But in mid-November, Patton received a bitter blow during a conversation with Bradley.

"Incidentally, Georgie," Bradley remarked, "I don't like the way Walker is planning to handle the 83rd Division. I made it explicitly clear that you can have operational control only to a limited extent. As a matter of fact, I don't think you should have the 83rd at all."

Later that night, Patton wrote in his diary, "This is one of the few times in the history of war when one-tenth of an attacking general's force was removed *after* the battle had been joined. I hope history records Bradley's moral cowardice. I am sure that it is a terrible mistake."

Nevertheless, XX Corps's attack proceeded. Held up for five frustrating days by the flooding Moselle, 10th Armored, in its first action, crossed the Nied River at Bouzonville on 19 November. (In a little over two days, the 1306th Engineer General Service Regiment had built the longest American Bailey bridge of the war over the Moselle for the 10th Armored, all while under fire.) The division then turned north and encountered the German *416th Division* in the formidable Orscholz Line, employing dismounted infantry and engineers to systematically eliminate each German pillbox. However, lacking valuable infantry replacements, 10th Armored found the task of reducing a fortified line too difficult for an armored division, and gave up its attempt by 27 November.

Meanwhile, Walker reorganized the 90th and 95th Divisions in a concerted drive to destroy the enemy west of the Saar. As November drew to a close, the Germans fought skillful and tenacious delaying actions while retiring in good order toward the West Wall. During this retreat, the Germans usually did not maintain a definitive defensive line. Instead, detachments of a few dozen troops were left to defend in hamlets and crossroads while demolition teams blew bridges and created roadblocks. By 30 November, most of *LXXXII Corps* had retired successfully across the Saar. However, on 3 December, the U.S. 95th Division pulled off a *coup de main* at Saarlautern that was to foreshadow the seizure of the Remagen Bridge three months later. In a daring and skillful maneuver, Company B, 379th Infantry, ferried undetected across the 125-foot-wide river at 0545 hours. They then dashed over one mile of open ground at the run to seize the eastern side of the bridge, cutting all German demolition wires furiously. Meanwhile, Company L attacked from the western side to secure the bridge. Immediately, the Americans heavily reinforced this critical bridgehead over the Saar. Rundstedt later reported that "the Fuhrer was enraged" when he heard the news.

The beginning of December saw "Lucky Forward" closed up to the Saar-Blies River line everywhere except in the Saar-Moselle Triangle. Despite the exhaustion of his troops and the abysmal weather, Patton was determined to press ever forward. "We are attacking the Siegfried Line," he wrote. "I know that there are many generals with my reputation who would not have dared to do so because 'they are more afraid of losing a battle than anxious to win one.' I do not believe that any of these lines are impregnable. If we get through, we will materially shorten the war—there is no *if* about getting through; I am sure we will!"

Any hope of reaching the Rhine was now slim, but for Patton, bleeding the Germans white was satisfactory for the time being. "I want to kill as many Germans as possible between here and the Rhine, so that we won't be annoyed by the sons-of-bitches after we cross the river," he concluded.

The first week of December saw XII Corps attacking ponderously northward toward Sarreguemines, while XX Corps expanded its current bridgehead at Saarlautern. Additionally, the 90th Division crossed the Saar to create a new bridgehead near Merzig. All along the front, the Germans contested every inch of ground. In particular, XX Corps was engaged against the most heavily fortified sector of the West Wall on the Western Front.

The End of the Lorraine Campaign

In retrospect, who won the Lorraine campaign? In 25 decisive days, Third Army had virtually cleared the area of enemy troops, captured Metz, and advanced an average of 35–40 miles to the east. In doing so, it suffered 22,773 battle and 15,737 non-battle casualties, a rather high casualty rate of 17% for the army as a whole. Yet during the same period, it is certain that the Germans suffered a much higher rate of loss—in fact, they had more men taken prisoner than the total American losses in November.

Certainly, Patton was frustrated by the failure to break through in Lorraine. His pre-offensive promises not only included penetrating the West Wall, but reaching the Rhine as well, neither of which he achieved. On the other hand, the already tenacious German defensive methods were made doubly efficient by the atrocious weather and the resulting condition of the ground that Third Army faced. Moreover, the highly-vaunted American Air Force was unable to apply its massive power to its full extent in November. "Damn the weather," was all Patton could write in his diary on 3 December. "I have never seen or imagined such a hell hole of a country. There is about four inches of liquid mud over everything and it rains all the time, not hard but steadily."

The Germans were also able to employ both natural and man-made defensive strongpoints to slow down Patton. As a result of all these factors, the fighting in Lorraine was, for the most part, an infantryman's slugfest. The Americans were able to apply effective low-level tactics and massive artillery firepower to punish the Germans severely.

On the other hand, the German *First Army,* although mostly composed of second-class troops, never broke completely and was able to make every inch of ground gained by Third Army very costly.

The opening weeks of December found Patton preparing for a renewal of his drive on Germany, with a rested, resupplied Third Army. But it was not to be. On the afternoon of 16 December, Patton received a call from Bradley at his HQ in Nancy. The Germans had made an attack in the Ardennes, and the U.S. First Army needed help badly.

"George, get the 10th Armored on the road to Luxembourg," Bradley declared firmly.

"But that's no major threat up there," Patton retorted. "Hell, it's probably nothing more than a spoiling attack to throw us off balance down here and make us stop this offensive."

"I hate like hell to do it, Georgie, but I've got to have that division. Even if it's only a spoiling attack as you say, Middleton must have help. I've got to hang up, Georgie. I can't discuss this matter on the phone."

In this fashion, Third Army's offensive suddenly came to an end. Within a week, one division after another would be pulled out of Lorraine for the long trek north to the Ardennes. Soon, Third Army would launch a new, more difficult, and more dramatic assault in an entirely different direction—a campaign that would bring it everlasting fame and Patton his much-coveted glory.

Order of Battle: 8 November 1944

U.S. THIRD ARMY
Lt. Gen. George S. Patton, Jr.

XX Corps
Maj. Gen. Walton Walker

95th Division: 377th, 378th, 379th Regiments

90th Division: 357th, 358th, 359th Regiments

5th Division: 2nd, 10th, 11th Regiments

10th Armored Division: Combat Commands A, B, R

Corps Troops: 3rd Cavalry Group (Task Force Polk), 712th, 735th, 738th Tank Battalions, 609th, 705th, 773rd, 818th self-propelled Tank Destroyer Battalions, 614th, 774th, 802nd, 807th towed Tank Destroyer Battalions, 5th self-propelled Field Artillery Group, 40th, 193rd, 195th, 203rd, 204th Field Artillery Groups

XII Corps
Maj. Gen. Manton Eddy

26th Division: 101st, 104th, 328th Regiments

35th Division: 134th, 137th, 320th Regiments

80th Division: 317th, 318th, 319th Regiments

4th Armored Division: Combat Commands A, B, R

6th Armored Division: Combat Commands A, B, R

Corps Troops: 2nd, 106th Cavalry Groups, 702nd, 737th, 761st Tank Battalions, 602nd, 603rd, 654th, 704th self-propelled Tank Destroyer Battalions, 610th, 691st, 808th towed Tank Destroyer Battalions, 177th, 182nd, 183rd, 404th, 410th Field Artillery Groups

GERMAN FIRST ARMY

General der Panzertruppen Otto von Knobelsdorff

XIII SS Corps
Generalleutnant der Waffen SS Hermann Priess

559th Division: 1125th, 1126th, 1127th Regiments

48th Division: 126th, 127th, 128th Regiments

17th SS Panzergrenadier Division: 37th, 38th Regiments

11th Panzer Division: 110th, 111th Regiments

Lehr Panzer Division: 901st, 902nd Regiments

25th Panzergrenadier Division: 35th, 119th Regiments

36th Division: 87th, 118th, 165th Regiments

347th Division: 860th, 861st Regiments

Corps Troops: *1431st Fortress Battalion; 43rd Machinegun Battalion; 111th Flak Battalion; 401st Volks Artillery Corps*

LXXXII Corps
General der Infanterie Walter Hoernlein

416th Division: 712th, 713th, 774th Regiments

19th Division: 59th, 73rd, 74th Regiments

462nd Division: 1215th, 1216th, 1217th Regiments

21st Panzer Division: 125th, 192nd Regiments

Corps Troops: *1010th Security Regiment; 22nd, 25th Fortress Regiments; 44th, 45th, 48th, 53rd Machinegun Battalions; 43rd Fortress Battalion; 55th Engineer Battalion; 811th Flak Battalion; 243rd Assault Gun Brigade; 404th Volks Artillery Corps; 485th, 486th Anti-tank Battalions*

LXXXIX Corps
General der Infanterie Gustav Hoehne

361st Division: 951st, 952nd, 953rd Regiments

553rd Division: 1119th, 1120th Regiments

Artillery in Lorraine

The weapon the individual German soldier feared the most in the American arsenal was artillery. Most German observers jealously praised the American artilleryman's efficient firing techniques, specifically their excellent observation and communications systems. In addition, the American artillery pieces themselves were technologically superior to German models. However, what made the American artillery so devastating to the Germans was its employment in mass. Each American infantry division possessed four battalions of artillery, each of twelve guns. The U.S. armored division had three battalions of self-propelled artillery, each of eighteen guns. In addition, Patton possessed 38 independent battalions of corps level artillery on 8 November 1944, ranging in size from 105mm to 240mm.

A major army-level offensive required a complex artillery fire plan. According to typical American practices, a hypothetical line approximately 5,000 yards ahead of the "Main Line of Resistance" (MLR) was drawn up. Corps artillery battalions were given responsibility for all targets beyond this line and divisional artillery for all targets in front. A single gun in each battery or battalion would "register" by firing a few preliminary rounds against its prospective target, insuring accuracy when the battle began.

Before the actual attack was launched, the artillery would initiate its preparatory barrage. In the case of XII Corps on 8 November, this bombardment lasted three and one-half hours, firing 21,933 rounds. Depending on what the "priority" target was, this barrage would periodically lift and switch to new targets. XX Corps artillery fired one-half of its salvos against German artillery positions on 8 November. Other targets included enemy command posts and centers of communications, road junctions, and enemy routes of approach to the front line. When the barrage as a whole was lifted, all batteries were responsible for responding to the calls of their forward observers to crush enemy strongpoints that were holding up the ground attack.

If tactical surprise was desired in an assault, artillery would barrage for only a few minutes—and then only *after* H-hour. However, due to the extensive nature of the field fortifications in front of the German positions in Lorraine, tactical surprise was deemed secondary to clearing a safe avenue of attack for the infantry and armor.

The unusual nature of the terrain and the weather in Lorraine forced the Americans to employ most of their armored fighting vehicles and anti-tank guns as miniature, mobile artillery. For most of November, tanks could not operate off roads. As a result, in a typical engagement, tanks would rest immobile behind the front lines to act as direct and indirect support for the infantry. In November, the anti-tank guns and tank destroyers of XX Corps fired only 2,422 rounds of direct (observed) fire as opposed to 24,741 rounds of indirect (unobserved) fire. Moreover, due to the dearth of German aircraft in Lorraine, American anti-aircraft battalions were also employed as artillery. Due to their short range, these 90mm guns would be deployed close behind the American front lines to saturate German positions with rapid fire prior to an assault.

Because of the plentiful supply of ammunition that had been built-up for Third Army's offensive, American artillerymen were able to expend rounds in huge numbers. In October, Patton had limited his artillerymen to seven rounds per day, per gun, a figure which was to be more than quadrupled in November. On the average, a single American corps expended almost as much artillery ammunition in one day as *all* of German *Army Group G,* approximately 20,000 rounds per day.

U.S. XX Corps Artillery Statistics, 9–22 November 1944

Gun Type	*Number Available*	*Avg. Rounds Expended/Day*
105	191	4,563
155 (How)	93	1,061
155 (Gun)	22	330
4.5"	12	294
8" (How)	24	93
8" (Gun)	4	4
240	12	6
TOTAL	**358**	**9,308**

Total rounds expended: 138,073
Avg. rounds per day per gun: 29

The West Wall

"What is the basis for your belief that you will go through the Siegfried Line quickly?" asked a war correspondent of Patton at a news conference on 7 September 1944.

"My natural optimism," replied Patton. "My personal opinion is that I don't give a god damn where the German is; I will lick him. As soon as a man gets in a concrete line, he immediately says to himself, 'The other man must be damn good or I wouldn't have to get behind this concrete.'"

During the campaign in France, there was great confusion among the leaders of both sides as to the relative merits of the vaunted West Wall ("Siegfried Line"). Many Allied leaders, particularly Patton, were convinced that the West Wall was overrated and outdated. In fact, in mid-September, the 5th Armored Division had penetrated the West Wall defensive line in the Schnee Eifel without even knowing it! On the other hand, the West Wall defenses in the area of Aachen were clearly formidable, and many Third Army planners, heeding the warning of French officers, were convinced that the West Wall in Lorraine was equally strong.

On the German side, confusion also reigned. Balck and other Eastern Front veterans had to ask *OB West* for a definition of exactly what and where the West Wall was. Since 1940, many of the West Wall bunkers had been converted into store rooms for war materials. When the Allies approached the German frontier, there was terrific commotion at OKW due to the fact that the keys to these bunkers could not be found!

The West Wall was actually begun in 1936 as an answer to the French Maginot Line. Unlike the Maginot Line, the West Wall did not bear the stamp of a giant fortress. Instead, the German works—which ran from north of Aachen to the Swiss border—were really complex networks of very small fortifications and obstacles, deployed where the ground was most suitable for the attack.

However, the West Wall had deteriorated sharply in the years since the fall of France. Many of the actual defensive works had been neglected and were in poor shape. To make matters worse, most protective equipment, such as barbed wire, mines, and stationary artillery, had been removed for use on the Atlantic Wall. The apertures on the pillboxes could not fit the bigger, higher caliber guns that were required in 1944. Most casemates could not even fit the MG42 1942 model machinegun, which did not exist at the time of the construction of the Wall.

Of course, when Hitler realized that the West Wall would be necessary in the defense of Germany's frontiers, it was already too late to do anything about its terrible state of disrepair. It was already the end of August 1944 when "people's" labor battalions were rushed to the West Wall to begin its rehabilitation. By the time the Allies first encountered this line in October, these construction crews had hardly had time to accomplish a thing.

In Lorraine, the West Wall was relatively strong, for it ran directly along the east bank of the Saar River. Thus, the attacking Third Army would not only have to deal with a major river crossing operation, but with the fortifications as well. In addition, the West Wall was supported by two additional fortified lines in Lorraine: the Orscholz Line (which ran across the base of the "Saar Moselle Triangle" near Merzig) and the "West Stellung" (a rather weak line, consisting mostly of minefields, running from the Saar Canal southwest to the Rhine-Marne Canal). To make matters worse for Patton, the Germans were able to employ some of the underground fortresses and artillery positions of the Maginot Line to good effect during this campaign.

During the battles to penetrate the German fortified positions in Lorraine, Third Army headquarters had tens of thousands of the following leaflet printed, to be dropped behind German lines during the fighting:

"To the German soldiers in pillboxes, machinegun nests, and other fortified positions: This is not a propaganda leaflet. This sheet contains instructions on the surrender of your position as prescribed by the American Army. It gives you a chance to save your life. When our attack starts, your pillbox will become a death trap for you. You have only two possibilities: to perish in your positions and be buried or burned alive, or to surrender your fortification in an orderly manner to American troops. You will decide the course to take: a horrible death or a secure and better future. If you decide for security and life, the instructions on the back will be of great help to you. Our troops will accept your surrender if it is carried out in accordance with instructions. Should, however, a white flag be hoisted from the pillbox without the occupants following all the instructions prescribed, the whole contingent will be ruthlessly wiped out."

Patton and Antwerp

The fighting around the Belgian deep-water port of Antwerp prior to the November offensive greatly influenced Patton's operations, as well as those of other American armies on the Western Front. This campaign was undertaken by Field Marshal Sir Bernard Law Montgomery, commander of the 21st Army Group and Patton's arch-rival. Antwerp possessed the best and biggest port facilities in the European theater of operations. As a result, it was considered a vital prize by Eisenhower and SHAEF. "Not only was Antwerp the greatest port in Europe," Eisenhower wrote, "but its location, well forward towards the borders of Germany, would reduce our rail and truck haulage to the point where supply should no longer be a limiting factor in the prosecution of the campaign."

After the breakout of the Allied armies from Normandy, Antwerp was seized quickly and handily by Montgomery's forces. On 4 September 1944, the British 11th Armored Division, finding the road open, dashed into the city. Aside from a stiff fight near the docks, Antwerp fell with almost no losses. Much to the Allies' surprise, the port facilities were almost intact. However, the port was still totally useless to Eisenhower, for the Germans were not driven out of the area of the Scheldt Estuary which controlled the water approaches to Antwerp. As a result, no Allied vessel could safely negotiate the 60-mile inland waterway journey from the North Sea to this great port. Nevertheless, even Patton admired the speed of the British operations in the Low Countries. "The perfectly phenomenal advance of the 21st Army Group under Field Marshal Montgomery has just completely buggered the whole German show," Patton said. "I think it is a magnificent show, and as a result, it would seem to me that the German plan of defense is completely dissipated. The advance of the Guards Division and the other divisions up there has been something magnificent."

Despite this lavish praise, Patton would be seething in the next few weeks, as Eisenhower placed priority of supply with Montgomery in order to open up the ports of Calais, Boulogne, and hopefully Antwerp itself. As a result, Patton—who had already reached the line of the Moselle—was stopped in his tracks.

However, in the next few weeks, Montgomery made a puzzling strategic move. The operations in the direct vicinity of Antwerp and the Scheldt—seized so daringly in September—were ignored for the time being in favor of a risky operation designed to make a sudden penetration into the German Ruhr, *Operation Market-Garden.* Most of Montgomery's resources were diverted to this operation, while in Antwerp the Germans concentrated on

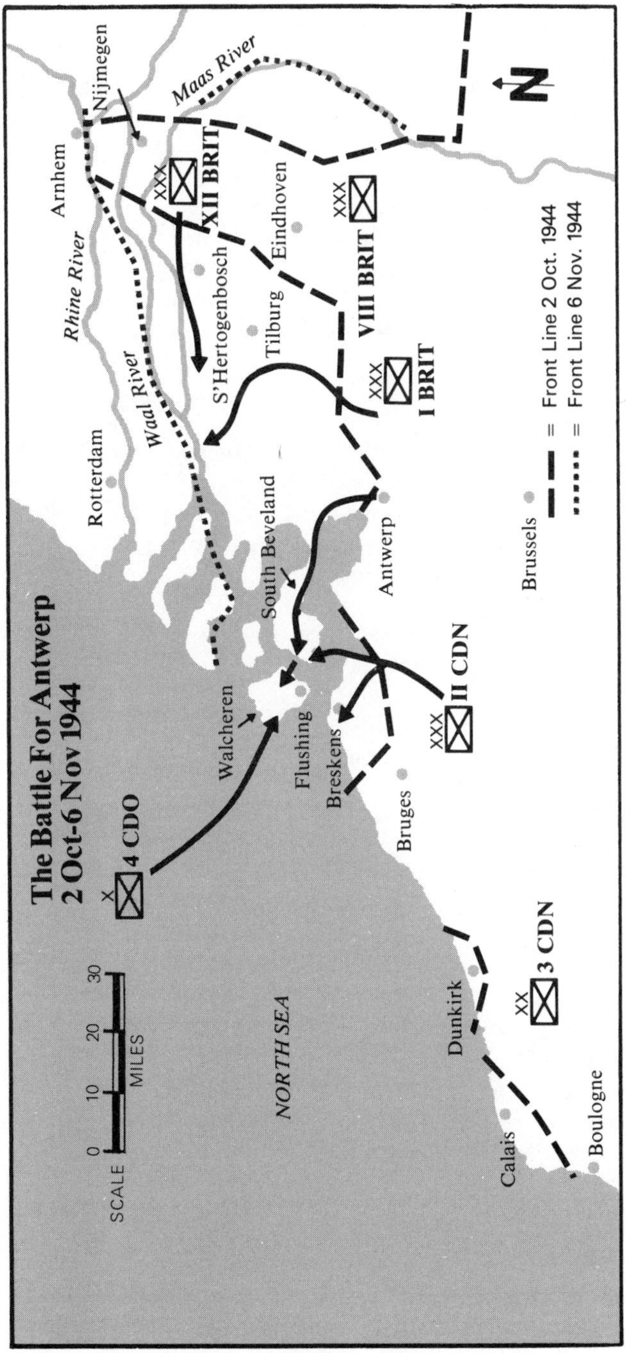
The Battle For Antwerp
2 Oct-6 Nov 1944
SCALE
0
10
20
30
MILES
NORTH SEA
X
4 CDO
Walcheren
Flushing
Breskens
Bruges
XXX
II CDN
South Beveland
Antwerp
Brussels
Rotterdam
Waal River
Rhine River
Arnhem
Nijmegen
Maas River
XXX
XII BRIT
S'Hertogenbosch
Tilburg
Eindhoven
XXX
VIII BRIT
XXX
I BRIT
N
= Front Line 2 Oct. 1944
= Front Line 6 Nov. 1944
Calais
Boulogne
Dunkirk
XX
3 CDN

building up a strong defense in the suburbs of the city as well as throughout the Scheldt Estuary.

When *Market-Garden* failed to achieve its objectives, SHAEF and Montgomery were in a dilemma. In early October, the Field Marshal himself wrote, "I realized that I should not be able to carry out my plans as quickly as I had hoped." Nevertheless, Eisenhower still accorded Montgomery priority in terms of supply in order to clear up the Scheldt.

"Unless we have Antwerp producing by the middle of November," Eisenhower wrote on 9 October, "our entire operations will come to a standstill. I must emphasize that, of all our operations, I consider Antwerp of first importance."

Patton was disgusted. "Monty does what he pleases and Ike says 'yes, sir,'" Patton wrote bitterly. "Monty wants all supplies sent to him and the First U.S. Army and me to hold . . . . To hell with Monty."

The Scheldt Estuary turned out to be a very tough nut for the British and Canadians to crack. Most of the area fought over by 21st Army Group was "polder"—land reclaimed from the sea. It was perfectly flat, totally open, interrupted by thousands of inland waterways and canals, and threatened with possible flooding by the destruction of its numerous surrounding dikes. In addition, off-road movement by vehicles was virtually out of the question.

Montgomery's plan provided for a three-pronged offensive against each of the three land masses controlled by the Germans which commanded the Scheldt Estuary: the "Breskens Pocket," the island of Walcheren and the isthmus of South Beveland. Launched on 2 October 1944, the attacks met with only limited initial success. Due to the defensive nature of the countryside, advances were exceedingly slow. It took two weeks to advance ten miles directly to the north of Antwerp, and three weeks to clear the 20-mile Leopold Canal defense perimeter in the Breskens Pocket. In early November, Walcheren was seized by an amphibious operation. Despite heavy losses, Montgomery was able to write to Eisenhower on 3 November, "I have to report to you that the approaches to Antwerp and the Scheldt Estuary are now completely free from enemy resistance. The full and free use of the port of Antwerp is now entirely a naval matter."

The necessity to undertake extensive minesweeping operations delayed the arrival of the first Allied ships in the port of Antwerp until 28 November. In the words of Eisenhower, "The capture of the Antwerp aproaches will have the utmost significance for us." But it had come too late to be of assistance to Patton's Third Army drive into Germany.

Aftermath: Patton to the Rhine

After Patton's remarkable December-January counterattack in the Ardennes—"the biggest and the best operation the Third Army has accomplished, not excluding the battle for France"—Patton turned his eyes back to his original September objective: the Rhine. "I will be first on the Rhine," Patton boasted on 13 February 1945. However, on this occasion, Third Army would have to share the glory with its compatriots to the north, for Patton's arch-nemesis—"higher authority"—had formulated a grandiose scheme for a late February offensive all along the Western Front.

At the beginning of February 1945, the Western Front stretched for over 450 miles from the Swiss border to the Scheldt Estuary. All along the front, there was not one serious Allied penetration of German territory—and the major barrier of the Rhine stil remained to be encountered. Eisenhower's plan for the impending battle of the Rhineland relied on a concerted, "broad front" offensive, designed to clear the west bank of the Rhine completely before attempting to cross it in force.

Employing six Allied armies, the assault was to be undertaken in four phases. First, Montgomery's 21st Army Group was to undertake *Operation Veritable,* launched from the Nijmegen corridor gained during the *Market-Garden* airborne operation. Veritable's objective was to breakthrough the heavily forested and fortified Reichswald area, clearing the west bank of the Rhine as far south as Dusseldorf—and hopefully trapping substantial German forces before they could escape over the Rhine.

Operation Grenade was the second phase of the Allied offensive. Launched by LG William Simpson's Ninth Army, Grenade was to operate in direct conjunction with Veritable, with which it was supposed to link up on the Rhine. However, Simpson faced the arduous task of an assault across the wildly swollen Roer River—the Germans had purposefully burst its dams, and its flooding would not subside until the end of February.

The third phase of Eisenhower's plan was labeled *Operation Lumberjack.* This operation was to be undertaken by Bradley's 12th Army Group, of which Patton's Third Army provided one-half the attack force. The other army, LG Courtney Hodges's First, was to drive for the Rhine at Cologne. Patton was to proceed northeastward along the Moselle valley in the direction of Coblenz.

The last phase of the Rhineland campaign was to be an assault by LG Alexander Patch's Seventh Army. Codenamed *Operation Undertone,* this part of the offensive was simply intended to protect Patton's southern flank as it drove on the Rhine.

Despite the desperate situation in which the Germans found themselves along the Western Front, Rundstedt, commander of *OB West,* could promise the Allies a hard-fought battle west of the Rhine. Although the elderly general favored a gradual, orderly withdrawal of German forces behind the barrier of the Rhine, this strategy was not to be employed. "I want him to hang on to the West Wall as long as is humanly possible," Hitler said to his staff. "Withdrawal would only mean moving the catastrophe from one place to another." Faced with this "stand-fast" order, Rundstedt threw most of his meager resources into the front lines in an "all or nothing" defense. Meanwhile, the Germans attempted to fortify their positions, and left all of the Rhine bridges standing.

To Patton, the Germans were "great people, but fools." "I am wondering how long this unnecessary killing will have to go on?" he asked a captured German general.

"The ordinary fighting man and the professional soldier have long seen the unnecessary continuance of fighting and recognize this," the general replied. "But the honor to which they are bound as soldiers makes them continue to fight, especially the professional soldier. As long as the country is at war, they are honor-bound to fight."

"Well, it seems foolish to continue to fight," was all Patton could reply.

On 8 February, British XXX Corps of First Canadian Army opened the offensive. Despite the largest artillery bombardment ever witnessed on the Western Front, the progress was exceedingly slow. The ubiquitous mud, the powerful German defenses, and reinforcements from the south all blunted Montgomery's punch. However, the vicious *Veritable* fighting was not in vain. Not only were the Germans suffering losses just as heavily as the British, but they were also obligated to virtually denude other fronts opposite the Americans in order to contain XXX Corps. On 3 March, the British linked up with a Ninth Army pincer from the south, pocketing a large number of Germans at Geldern. Within one week, German resistance west of the Rhine opposite Montgomery was wiped out, as British and Canadian forces closed to the Rhine near Wesel.

On the Ninth Army front, *Operation Grenade* had to be postponed until 22 February due to the flooded Roer. However, when the attack did come, the Germans were unprepared and very weak. Within ten days, Simpson's forces were on the Rhine adjacent to First Canadian Army.

Delaying his First and Third Army attacks to coincide with Simpson's, Bradley's *Operation Lumberjack* got off to a dramatic start. After bashing through the West Wall near Aachen, Hodges's First Army met weak resis-

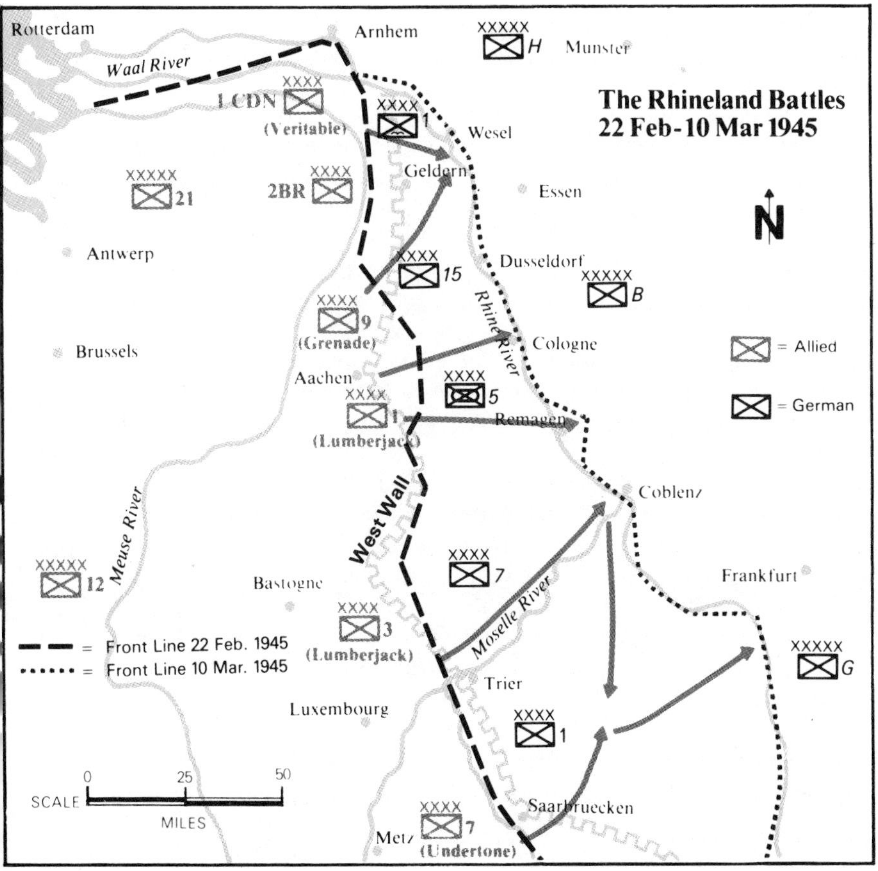

tance as it attacked eastward toward the Rhine. On 5 March, Cologne fell. On 7 March, the 9th Armored Division—which Hitler had claimed was "destroyed" in the Ardennes—snatched the Ludendorff railroad bridge over the Rhine at Remagen. As this bridgehead was spontaneously reinforced, the whole strategic picture on the Western Front had suddenly changed.

Third Army's role in *Lumberjack* took Patton out of the spotlight for the time being. While Simpson and Montgomery were attacking in the north, Patton's forces were conducting tedious and costly operations to penetrate the West Wall in the Ardennes-Eifel, while clearing the infamous "Saar-

Moselle Traingle" further to the south in Lorraine. "We were quite happy about the Remagen bridgehead," Patton said, "but we were just a little bit envious."

By 1 March, Patton's forces had just about bled white all the Germans opposite them. Gradually, resistance was evaporating until suddenly it disappeared altogether. By 10 March, Patton was on the Rhine at Coblenz—many of his units having driven an amazing 65 miles in a day and a half.

Hodges's and Patton's rapid successes led to a modification of the *Undertone* operation. Instead of simply supporting Patton's right flank, Patch's Seventh Army was to alter the axis of its advance to the north and northeast. Meanwhile, Patton would hold his northernmost corps stagnant on the Rhine while attacking south and southeast with his two southernmost corps, XII and XX, in order to meet Patch's columns in the Palatinate. It was hoped that a great deal of the German Seventh Army would be pocketed by this *Cannae* -like maneuver.

The *Undertone* modification proved to be remarkably successful. By 21 March 1945, Patton and Patch had surrounded approximately 20,000 German troops east of Trier, while closing to Rhine south of Coblenz and the Moselle almost unopposed. "I believe this operation is one of the outstanding operations in the history of war," Patton said. "We have put on a great show, but I think we will eclipse it when we get across the Rhine."

In retrospect, the combined Allied assaults in the Rhineland battles of February and March 1945 can be considered one of the worst defeats ever inflicted on Germany in the Second World War. Well over 300,000 men were lost to Germany in those two months alone. After the Rhine's west bank had been cleared, disorganization and psychological collapse among German units were rampant. Most importantly, no effective formations remained to defend the formidable Rhine barrier. In effect, the war in the west was over.

To Patton, no greater tribute to Third Army's exploits was delivered than that of a German officer captured on the Rhine. "The greatest threat was the whereabouts of the feared U.S. Third Army. General Patton was always the main topic of military discussion. Where is he? When will he attack? Where? How? With what? Those are the questions which raced through the head of every German general since the famous German counter-offensive last December. General Patton is the most feared general on all fronts. The successes of the U.S. Third Army are still overshadowing all other events of the war, including the campaigns in Russia. The tactics of General Patton are daring and unpredictable. He is the most modern general and the best commander of armored and infantry troops combined."

● ● ●

The stiffening German resistance which Montgomery had encountered in the Netherlands and Patton in Lorraine dashed Allied hopes that the war would be over by Christmas. Nevertheless, the onset of Winter found Allied forces well forward, with some elements in Germany itself. It could only be a matter of time.

The Ardennes Offensive: An Analysis of the Battle of the Bulge, December 1944

By Stephen B. Patrick

As Christmas of 1944 approached it looked as though Hitler's "Thousand Year Reich" was finished. In the East vast armies of Russians were pressing in towards the heartland of Germany, while in the West powerful American, British, and French armies had reached the frontiers of the Reich itself after a lightning campaign from Normandy all across France. Massive Allied air fleets were daily pounding the cities of Germany into rubble. Industrial production was faltering. Manpower was growing increasingly scarce. But Germany still had some fight left. In a remarkable come-back, the *Wehrmacht* launched its largest offensive in 18 months in an effort to smash the Allied forces threatening Germany from the West. The result is known to History as the Battle of the Bulge.

The Situation

The Allies had pushed Germany back at a frantic pace after breaking out at St. Lo. As 1944 came to an end, the Allies were seven months ahead of their time table. Eisenhower had overruled Montgomery's suggestion that they send a narrow probe racing into the German heartland for a quick victory. As a result, the Allies had advanced on a broad front and were now roughly on Germany's pre-1940 boundary. Three strong army groups were involved. Montgomery, on the north, had 21st Army Group, composed of British and Canadian forces. In the center was 12th Army Group under Bradley. It included, on its southern flank, the mercurial Patton with his Third Army. Recently joined up on the south was the 6th Army Group. It had advanced up from Marseilles under Devers.

The cost of the drive across France had been considerable. The American forces alone used up 10% of their AFV strength (500 tanks not counting those in independent battalions) and .4% of their artillery strength (100 pieces) plus eight million rounds of mortar and artillery ammunition per month. In September, they were using twenty thousand tons of supplies, six million gallons of gasoline and two thousand tons of artillery ammunition a day. All of this came down a long supply pipeline from Cherbourg to the front. Antwerp had been taken but was not available for supply operations until 28 November 1944, when the first convoy was able to sail into the port. The famous Red Ball Express truck convoys were one desperate means of keeping the pipeline open. But by autumn, the Allies had run out of steam. They had simply outstripped their supply lines. The 7th Armored Division, for example, was stalled six days in front of Metz before it had enough gas to resume its attack.

As a result, Eisenhower decided to ease the pressure in the center. On Bradley's right, Third Army was to push into the Saarland, Germany's coal region. In the north, Montgomery was to move on the Ruhrgebiet, the industrial heart of Germany. In the middle there was no objective of comparable importance. Therefore the left of 12th Army Group adopted a defensive posture. The front scarcely moved in that sector after September of 1944. The troops were spread thinly through the "quiet" wooded sector and became rather lax in conducting their essentially defensive task. The thinnest portion of the front was in the American VIII Corps area, which covered 120 kilometers with but four divisions, mostly battle-weary or "green" outfits. The relative inactivity on this front resulted in a casual attitude. At night American units often pulled out of their field positions into warm, comfortable quarters, allowing German patrols virtual free rein to roam about.

Hitler Plans an Offensive

Although his capacity for self-delusion was fast becoming monumental, when he wanted to Hitler could still grasp the basic facts of a situation with remarkable clarity and precision. It was clear that, unless he took some action soon, the Reich would gradually be crushed between the Russians and the Western Allies. And to Hitler it seemed that it was the Western Allies who represented the more dangerous threat to Germany, despite the fact that the bulk of the Wehrmacht was in the East. At first glance, this may seem curious. The truly battle-tested German units (or what remained of them after Stalingrad, Kursk and the Soviet advances of 1944) were in the East. The West, before D-Day, had been where divisions were sent for rest, reorganization and training. Germany's green troops were in the West.

There were a number of reasons why Hitler chose the West, all based on his preconceived notions. He put no stock in the revived French Army of De Gaulle. They had been beaten once by Germany and, as Hitler saw it, the French were weak links in the Allied chain. He also believed that England never really had its heart in the war, and given the right moment, would make a separate peace. He felt that England would rather fight with Germany against the common Bolshevik foe, rather than fight against Germany to their mutual loss. He believed that the Anglo-American alliance was fundamentally weak, holding that if Germany won, only England, and not the United States, would really lose. If Germany lost, only the United States would win—England would be too badly bled to profit by victory. Hitler conceived that a major defeat in the West would set these allies fighting among themselves, at least verbally. The next step would be American withdrawal or the British seeking a separate peace. Finally, he hoped, the British would wage war against the United States.

These were the reasons Hitler fixed on the West. He knew that the monolithic Soviet Union would afford no similar chance for internal division. He also knew that a purely military result was now beyond his reach. Any victory would have to be achieved with a militarily precipitated political conclusion.

The germ of the offensive began to take form in Hitler's mind as early as July 1944, even as the Allied lodgement in Normandy was proving ineradicable. It was reworked and recast several times and finally announced at a staff meeting on 25 September. At that time Hitler tacitly conceded the temporary loss of France, to be recovered in operations following upon the successful offensive to be launched from the West Wall.

An armored, blitzkrieg attack would be launched in the Ardennes, against the lengthening Allied flank. The spearhead units would be the *Fifth Panzer Army* of Gen Hasso von Manteuffel and the newly-formed *Sixth Panzer Army* of SS Gen Josef "Sepp" Dietrich, flanked on either side by the *Fifteenth* and *Seventh Armies* composed largely of infantry. The panzers would smash through the Allied lines and hook northwards to take Antwerp while the infantry armies covered their flanks. The first objective would be the Meuse River, which was scheduled to be crossed on the second day of the offensive. With this attained, fresh panzer units would be thrown in for the drive on Antwerp, supported by additional infantry. Antwerp would fall within a few days, isolating some 20 to 30 Allied divisions in the 21st Army Group, and totally reversing the tide of victory.

Hitler's plan was based on several assumptions. He expected that the Allied reaction to the onset of the offensive would be slow and piecemeal. He believed that they would initially be reluctant to break off their drives on the Roer and Saar areas and their operations in Lorraine. This would result in a period of indecision,

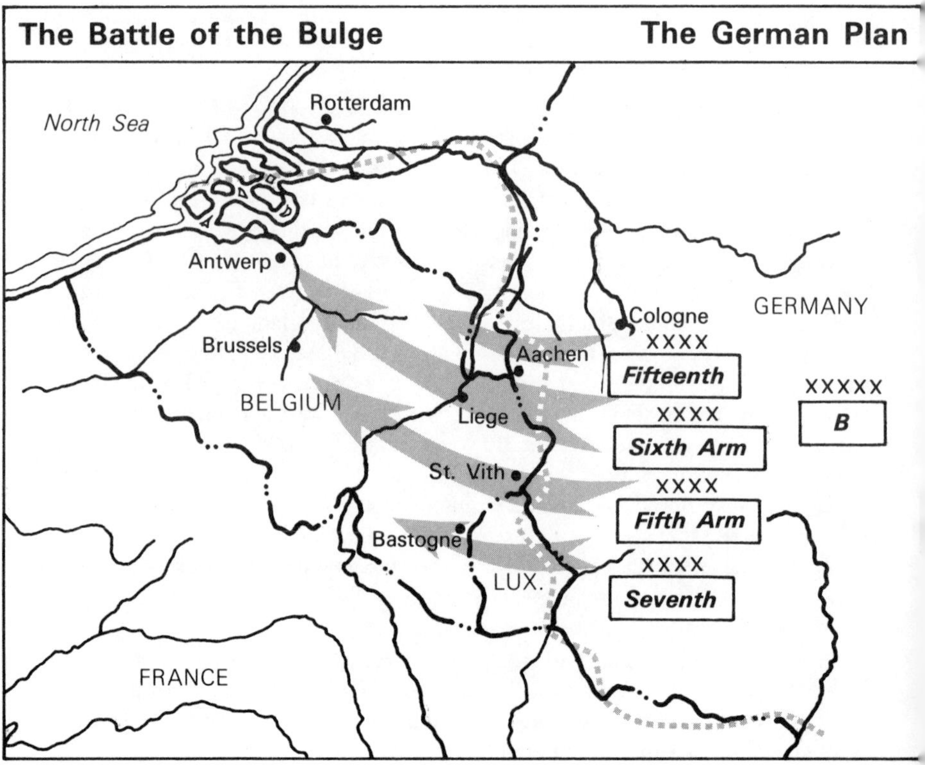

possibly with any changes in plans having to be approved in London and Washington, which would further delay a prompt reaction. Finally, he assumed that the weather would be bad, thereby keeping Allied air power out of action for some time. Maximum security would be exercised, so that very few officers would be informed of the proposed operation until the latest possible moment, thereby reducing the chances of an intelligence leak. Even the code-name of the operation was essentially defensive in tone so as to further disguise what was afoot. Hitler dubbed his offensive, *Wacht-am-Rhein*— "Watch on the Rhine." So tight was security that old FM Gerd von Rundstedt, who was western theater commander and would be in overall charge of the offensive, was not even informed of what was afoot until late October.

The Build-Up

Gen Alfred Jodl, Chief of Operations of the Wehrmacht, was responsible for developing the fine details of the plan. The army was ordered to concentrate additional forces to supplement those pulled out of the line, notably two SS panzer corps with five panzer divisions. Among the formations committed to the offensive were many of the newly raised *volksgrenadier* divisions, of which 20 could be available by 20 December. The German forces initially had two missions, deception and concentration.

Front-line formations were effective in concealing the extent of activity behind the lines. The very tight security also helped. Since all communications concerning the attack went by secured land lines, Allied radio interception and decoding operations—the famed "Ultra" Secret—were useless. Eventually, of course, the Allies did begin to piece together the extent of the build-up. But they were uncertain as to precisely what it boded.

Meanwhile the work of concentrating men and materiel went forward. Five panzer divisions, eleven infantry divisions, and two parachute divisions, plus miscellaneous formations would go in with the first wave. In reserve would be five more panzer divisions, two panzergrenadier divisions, five infantry divisions, and several special panzer brigades. A parachute battalion would even make a combat drop—the first in over a year. Initial planning called for the offensive to be launched sometime between 20 and 30 November, by which time the weather could be expected to be sufficiently bad as to keep Allied air power grounded. Planning delays, shortages of equipment, and unusually good weather resulted in several reschedulings until the final date was selected, Saturday, 16 December 1944.

Jodl and his staff had developed an extremely detailed plan. The attack was to have two prongs. The northern prong would attack from north of Aachen; the southern, through the Ardennes. The *Sixth Panzer Army* was to attack from between Monschau and Prum, cross the Meuse at Liege, then, using the Albert Canal from Maastricht on to protect its right flank, turn northwestwards toward Antwerp. To the left was *Fifth Panzer Army*. It attacked from between Prum and Bitburg. It was to bypass Bastogne, turn northwest and cross the Meuse near Namur, bypass Brussels and attack Antwerp. The plan emphasized that the panzer armies were not to stop for anything. They were to bypass strongly held positions and anything that did not fall on the first attack. They were to refuse any targets which distacted them from their objectives.

On 21 October Hitler put in one of his own little operational ideas. He met with Otto Skorzeny. Skorzeny was the "fair-haired boy" of the moment, having rescued Mussolini from captivity and more recently succeeded in capturing the Hungarian government, thereby preventing Hungary from leaving the war, both deeds in rather spectacular fashion. Hitler now put him in command of a *soi-disant* combat unit, the *150th Panzer Brigade.* In fact it had no armor at all, but was the core of *Operation Grief.* The troops were largely English-speaking. Their equipment and uniforms would be British and American in origins and their mission was to pass through Allied lines and sieze the Meuse bridges before the Allies could retreat across or demolish them.

Runstedt, meanwhile, learned of the planned offensive on 24 October, and then only incidentally, since Hitler briefed his chief-of-staff. This was not as heinous as it might first appear. FM Walter Model's *Army Group B* was the actual controlling headquarters for the offensive and Hitler had been dealing with Model for some time. Model had initially proposed some changes in the plan. He suggested that *Fifth Panzer Army* was, due to terrain considerations, better able to lead the main effort than *Sixth Panzer Army.* Hitler vetoed this. Dietrich, commanding *Sixth Panzer Army,* was a Nazi veteran from the pre-1933 days, and Hitler wanted him to have the honor of leading the offensive. Moreover, he did not trust the army overmuch since several of its leading figures had tried to assassinate him in July. Several other officers considered Hitler's plans less than optimal. Manteuffel proposed a less ambitious operation designed merely to cut up the American First Army. But Hitler would have none of this, and overruled any deviation from his plans.

Meanwhile the accumulation of resources continued. Eventually some 4.6 million gallons of gasoline were made available, over 900 tanks, and some 350,000 men in over thirty divisions. The cream of current arms production was supplied the troops, with a concomitant starvation of other fronts. And by 16 December, the army was as ready as it could be given Germany's increasingly strained circumstances.

Terrain

The one immutable factor with which both sides had to contend was terrain. In many respects it was the most crucial factor in the campaign. The objective, Antwerp, lay on a plain. All the land beyond the Meuse is flat and rather open. From the Meuse to the German border, it is another matter. The first obstacle the Germans had to cross was water—the Our-Saur River network. To the west of them lay the Ardennes.

Germany had twice caught France off-guard by attacking through the Ardennes, in 1914 and in 1940. In each case, however, they had used the Ardennes as a passage for their troops. The decisive battles had been fought west of the forest. Now, in 1944, they proposed to achieve a decision *in* the Ardennes.

The Ardennes are generally described as a forest. This is deceptive. Only about a third of the Ardennes is actually heavily forested. The forests, however, "work" in concert with rugged terrain. In the north lay the Hohe Venn, a dense, elevated marshland, only 25 kilometers from the Meuse. In the center the principal features are the Losheim Gap and the Schnee Eifel. The Losheim Gap provides the best tank country in the Ardennes, being largely open, rolling ground. The Schnee Eifel, just to its south, however, is an elevated, almost self-contained area with very good defensive qualities as it was both rugged and well-wooded. In the south lay the Ardennes proper. Although a fair road-net existed in the area, it offered little advantage to the attacker. The land was very hilly, some peaks reaching 2500 feet. The hills and plateaus were cut by numerous gullies, small rivers, and many ravines. The whole area was well forested. This made for very winding roads. As the general flow of the streams was south-to-north, the roads also had many culverts and bridges, and there was little possibility of using the many valleys for cross-country travel. With any amount of snow fall, movement in the Ardennes is quickly reduced to that possible on the roads, which, on top of everything else, were generally narrow. The entire region greatly favors the defense, for very small bodies of troops can readily block most of the practicable roads.

Beyond the Ardennes is the Meuse, the initial German objective. The river constitutes a considerable obstacle. It has steep banks and a swift current, both of which make fording difficult and bridge-building a major task. Beyond the Meuse, *Fifth Panzer Army* would also have to negotiate the Sambre, only a bit less of an obstacle. But once the spearheads cleared that, it would be relatively easy going all the way to Antwerp.

The Bulge

The Battle of the Bulge ran its course in only ten days, from the onset of the German attack on 16 December to the withdrawal of the spearhead units still short of the Meuse on 26 December. To be sure the Allied front was not fully restored until some weeks more, but Germany's chance for victory was by then long passed. It had passed in the first few days. The course of the battle may be readily studied in the accompanying maps. In brief, the initial German attack was not nearly as devastating as expected, the Allied command responded with far more alacrity than Hitler had believed possible, resistance had been considerably more tenacious than anticipated, and Patton's rapid shift of front and motor-march was beyond anything in the German experience.

The fascination which the battle holds goes beyond the simple facts of victor and vanquished. It has the charcter of grand theater—Hitler's flair for the dramatic certainly didn't fail him here. An almost Homeric epic of individual courage in the face of overwhelming odds, of men against machines, and all the horrors of war. In a sense the German attack was bound to fail, yet that only makes it all the more interesting.

Everyone has a reason why it failed. Almost all of them are right. Mechanically, the handwriting was on the wall almost from the start. Terrain helped the north shoulder to hold fast. The south shoulder held for a combination of reasons, among which were the lack of punch in the German *Seventh Army*, as well as a certain lack of decisiveness in exploiting such chances as did exist.

More crucial was the failure in the center. The Americans were spread so thin

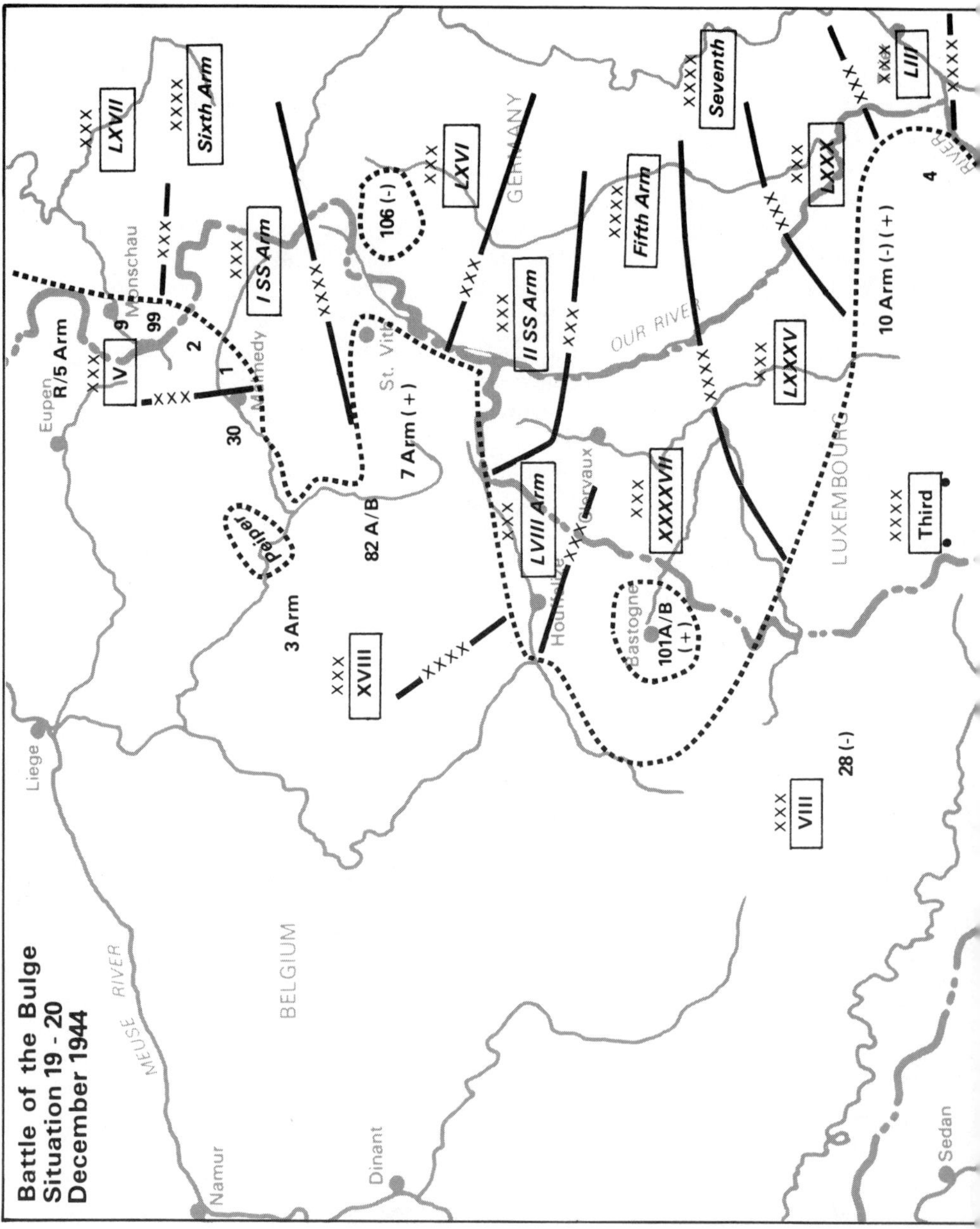

that battalions faced whole divisions. Yet, instead of collapsing in chaos, the American forces fell back. They took losses, severe ones without a doubt, but they refused to disintegrate. The result was that a bulge developed but no breakthrough. Breakthrough was essential to Hitler's plans. He had to be able to roll freely to the Meuse. Instead, the Germans ended up fighting for each foot of ground and this cost them time they did not have.

A second cause was the speed with which the Allies reacted once it was clear what was afoot. Hitler had been convinced that the Allies could not respond in time: that they would dither in consternation for so long they could not then react in time. Had Hitler been more realistic on that point, he should have anticipated exactly the reaction he got. Bradley promptly moved his reserves up. Eisenhower made two swift decisions, both of which Hitler felt he could not make on his own. First, he called off Patton's offensive and had Patton wheel his army to attack the German left flank. Patton reacted with the zeal of a cavalry commander (which he had been) coming to the rescue (which he was doing). Again, that sort of reaction was typical of Patton and could easily have been foreseen. Second, with Bradley's control disrupted, certain units in the north of 12th Army Group were cut off. Eisenhower promptly put these units under Montgomery's command so that they could be part of a coordinated defense rather than left to fight alone. Hitler could not believe that a co-ordinated Anglo-American response would be possible.

The net effect was that with incredible speed the Allies put as much as they could spare into stemming the attack. The overall superior strength of the Allies meant that the best Hitler could hope for in the Ardennes was local superiority. He had this on 16 December. But, to get it, he had so thinned the rest of his lines that when the Allies, in their turn, thinned their lines, there was no German force available to exploit these sectors. Thus, while in the first few days there were three U.S. Infantry divisions trying to hold off twenty German divisions, seven of which were armor, by 26 December the Allies had 29 divisions, eight of which were armor, facing 26 German divisions, eight of which were armor. The balance, in sheer numbers, had shifted to the Allies in the space of ten days. When the quality of the units is compared, the imbalance is even greater.

Still another cause was the terrain. The Germans, or at least Hitler, believed his propaganda from 1940 about attacking in the Ardennes with an armored "Blitz" despite prior tradition that it could not be done. No matter what size force marched through the Ardennes, it was another matter to fight through it. It was not tank terrain, but the Germans were using tank units to spearhead their drive through the woods. German armor did little besides consume gas and get in the way. Moreover, the terrain favored aggressive defenders. Even on the first day, the Americans were counter-attacking in small units. A platoon counter-attack isn't much to behold; particularly against an infantry regiment. But when the platton is holding a narrow passage, it can stop the regiment as long as there are people left in the platoon. In the Ardennes Thermopylae was repeated many times.

This blends in with another cause for failure. The battle was an infantry battle. No one on the German side seemed to realize this in their planning. Their concern was the armor and the elite *Waffen-SS* in their fast-moving motorized columns. It was the American infantryman who stopped the Germans and the lack of decent German infantry that permitted the attack to die. The *Volksgrenadier* units were simply no match for the Americans. Of course, this is due to no great insight from an American point of view. The U.S. did not have infantry units there with the clever intent of forestalling such an attack. The armor was needed elsewhere and the units that were there happened to be infantry. But Hitler knew, or should have known, what he would be coming up against. Much is made of the failure of American intelligence to predict the attack. The greater failure is that of German intelligence in not recognizing that the terrain and enemy would present such an obstacle as to require modification of the plan. There is an indication that von Manteuffel thought the scope of the plan too great but no one voiced the opinion that the Germans would never get out of the Ardennes in time.

A final cause, just as wrapped up in the others as each one before, was a failure to adhere to Hitler's own guidance. He was certainly correct that they could not

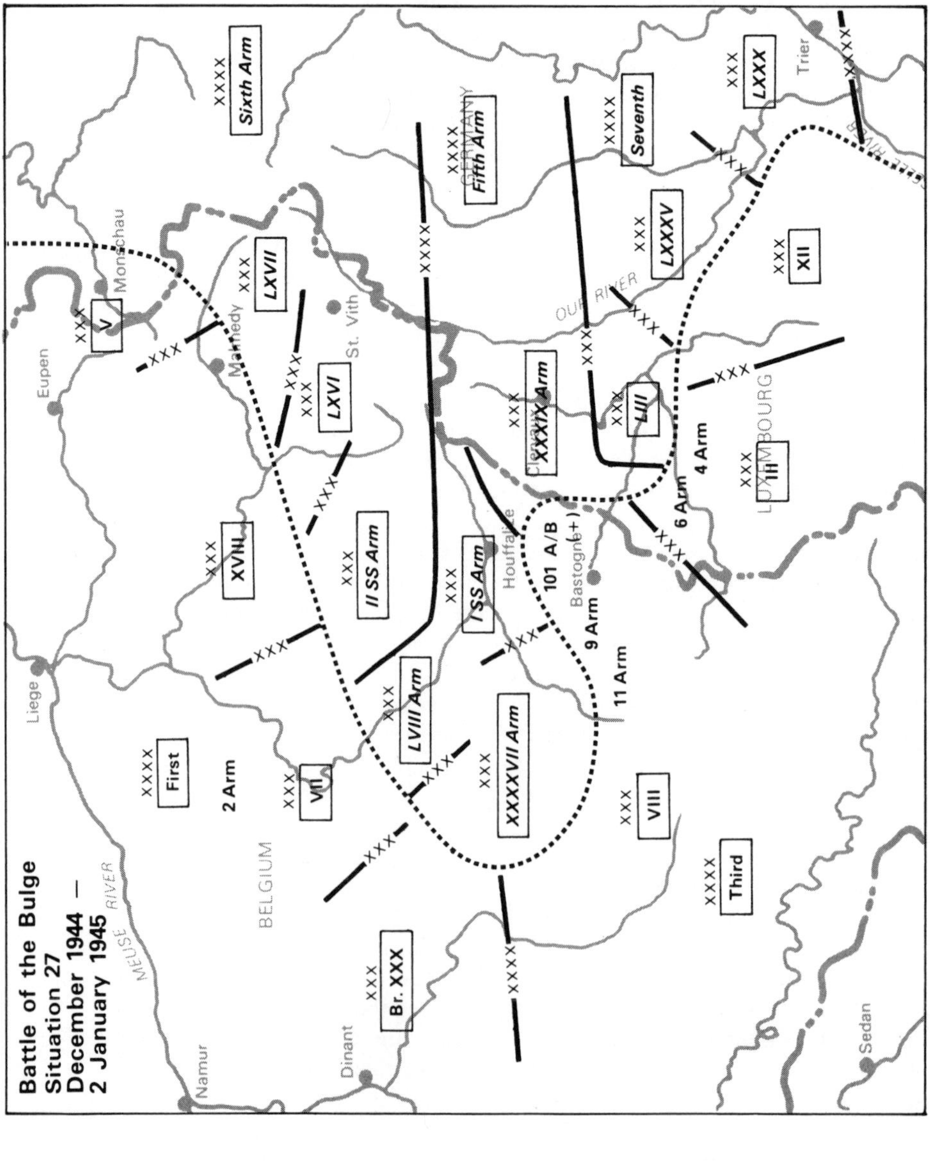

afford to be bogged down by any roadblocks or strongpoints that did not fall on the first attack. Bastogne and St. Vith were two such strong points, and the Germans diverted troops and bogged themselves down trying to knock them out.

In a larger sense, Hitler was right in several of his assessments. He needed to seize the Meuse early. The second day was too ambitious. It presumed no effective opposition. Even if there had been none, the bad weather that Hitler had wanted would have slowed movement enough to prevent that goal. But taking the Meuse by the fourth or fifth day might have done the trick. Once across the Meuse, the Germans could have used their armor. Of course, the Allies would still have had the numerical advantage by the 26th, but it would not have been applied all at one spot, and the Germans could use the terrain of the Ardennes to hold the flanks. In any event, the breakthrough was the key. Without it, Hitler could not succeed.

If he had achieved his goal and taken Antwerp, a curious situation would certainly have arisen. He would have cut off Montgomery. Even if the danger were seen and attempts made to evacuate the 21st Army Group, it all could not have been removed in time. The Americans would have been forced to add about 80 miles to their front lines after having had at least three divisions mauled. They probably could have done this. There were reserves in England and others moving up from western France. The front would not have collapsed. Someone would still have been at the door at the Saar, though the Ruhr would have been safe for the moment. In all probability any attack into the Saar would have been called off. Eisenhower might well have been canned, if only to appease England for the humiliation in the loss of so many units. But, and this is the key point, the alliance would not have collapsed. There is no reason to assume that, having come this far, anything could induce England to pull out. So at best the Western Front would have been quiescent until Spring while the Red Army continued to move.

It probably wouldn't have made one bit of difference in the East. Despite the defeat Hitler pulled *Sixth Panzer Army* out and sent it East. He could have done no more had he won. He couldn't strip the West too much, even in victory, so a major reinforcement of the sagging Eastern Front would not have happened. The net result would probably have been that the Allies would have met at the Rhine rather than the Elbe. The repercussions of that, in terms of post-war Germany, are interesting to imagine. In net terms, had Hitler been successful in his attack, about the only thing he would have done would be to gain some two or three months in the war at best and ensure that more of Germany came under Soviet control than actually did. Of course, Hitler was not concerned about post-war Germany. He felt that if the Germans lost, they deserved whatever fate had in store for them.

Although the Bulge was a spectacular battle, it was not a major one in the sense of being decisive, such as Yorktown or a tactical masterpiece, such as Cannae, or a turning point, such as Stalingrad. It exists as a museum piece. There was no allowance for what Clausewitz calles the "frictions of war." Everything had to go exactly right. In the end, it is simply a monument to the non-productive ends to which a dictatorship can put its armies in the midst of war. How much the losses sustained by Germany hastened the end of the war is hard to say. It had some effect, if only on morale. What it did prove was that by December 1944, the Germans lacked the men, materiel and imagination to continue with the war and that the initiative on all counts had passed to the Allies.

The Hole in the Doughnut: Bastogne

The battle for Bastogne was the pivot about which all other action in the Ardennes revolved. Yet it was a battle that neither side expected nor particularly desired. The German plan for the offensive envisioned a rapid advance to the Meuse. Bastogne lay within the sector of Hasso von Manteuffel's *Fifth Panzer Army,* specifically the area assigned to *XXXXVII Panzer Corps.* Manteuffel planned to by-pass Bastogne with his main force, leaving the *26th Volksgrenadier Division* to take it. On the American side, Task Force Harper, composed of elements of Combat Command Reserve (CCR) of 9th Armored Division, was sent to block the road east of Longvilly, one of the principal approach roads. Behind them were three teams from CCR of 10th Armored Div., sent to cover the direct approaches from the city. Named for their commanders, Team O'Hara held the road to Warden; Team Cherry the road to Longvilly and Team Desobry the road to Neville. The final move on the American side which brought this battle into being was the decision to send the 101st Airborne Division to Bastogne despite the fact that the division commander, MG Maxwell Taylor, was in Washington pushing for more strength in the airborne divisions. The command at that time was held by the division artillery commander, BG Anthony C. McAuliffe. An additional critical factor, though this took somewhat longer to influence the course of events, was the decision to send elements of Patton's Third Army into the flank of the German penetration. At the time that decision was made, Bastogne was not seriously threatened, though it lay in the apparent route of advance.

Moving on the city were the German *2nd Pz. Div., Panzer Lehr Division* and *26th VG Div.* Against these German units were pitted the equivalent of a division and a half of Americans, with the half being armor.

Bastogne was ultimately essential to the German plans, even if Manteuffel felt he could by-pass it initially. The Ardennes is a forest coupled with rough terrain. Steep ravines, most of them running north and south, and a poor road system for the type of traffic the Germans proposed to put on it, made major road junctions vital. Bastogne was the junction of seven major roads.

First blood in the battle went to the Germans on the night of December 18. The *2nd Pz. Div.* was on the road to Longvilly and it stumbled on Task Force Harper. In the fighting that followed, TF Harper was practically destroyed. However, following their orders, the Germans began to by-pass Bastogne to the north. *Panzer Lehr,* following the *2nd,* received reports from the local inhabitants that a second American blocking position lay to the east of Bastogne with over fifty tanks on hand. The division commander, MG Fritz

Bayerlein, made the mistake of believing the report, rather than checking it out. He halted for the night. In fact, there was nothing to stop him from going right into Bastogne. By dawn, however, the 501st Parachute Rgt. barred the way.

On Dec. 19th, Team Desobry was reinforced by a platoon of tank destroyers, which was a piece of good fortune, because the team lay directly in the path of *2nd Pz. Div.* The first clash was repelled on the 19th, at heavy cost. Similarly, the 501st took a beating from advance elements of *Panzer Lehr.*

Now Bayerlein was less cautious and urged a full-blown attack on Bastogne, judging correctly that the force holding it wasn't very strong. The corps commander, LG Heinrich von Luttwitz, stuck by his original orders, however.

On December 20th, *2nd Pz. Div.* attacked Team Desobry again. A second platoon of tank destroyers was sent in, but the situation was made more serious by determined German efforts to cut the road from Neville, around which town the team was deployed. Faced with the prospect of having the whole team cut off, McAuliffe directed that they withdraw, which was just as well as it was, by then, down to four tanks.

Having taken Neville, Lauchert, the *2nd Pz. Div.* commander, also wanted to turn on Bastogne. Once again, Luttwitz stuck by his plans and tried to swing the *26th VG Div.* to the south of the city, hoping to have more luck there.

At this juncture, MG Troy Middleton, commanding VIII Corps, proposed abandoning Bastogne. McAuliffe dissuaded him, pointing out that, aside from the morale problems which that would pose, the German position was sto strong that the division would probably take more losses trying to pull out than if it stayed. So, in that sense, the die was cast.

By December 21st, Bastogne was surrounded, though that day was otherwise a day of respite. The 22nd saw the renowned exchange of notes between the Luttwitz and McAuliffe, in which the former demanded the latter surrender, only to receive the reply "Nuts!". This was also the day Patton launched his Third Army into the German flank.

It was not until the 23rd that the Germans made their first real efforts to take the city. Elements of the *26th VG Div.* attacked from southwest, northwest and east. The going was slow, and well-timed American counterattacks repelled the few gains. Most importantly, the weather finally broke on the 23rd, allowing American ground support aircraft and supply planes to get up for the first time since the offensive started.

The following day saw another lull, but the Germans planned a new push on Christmas Day. Luttwitz was to be reinforced by *15th Pz. Gren. Div.*, though in the event it turned out to be only a regimental *kampfgruppe* from the division. The Christmas attack failed at heavy cost. Two panzergrenadier columns were destroyed wtih all of their infantry and seventeen tanks. The *26th VG* was so depleted that it could not launch large-scale attacks any longer.

On the afternoon of December 26, the lead elements of the Third Army, Creighton Abram's 37th Tank Battalion, reached the 326th Airborne Infantry's position in Bastogne. The following afternoon Taylor was able to rejoin his command. On the 30th of December, Eisenhower assigned 11th Armored and 87th Divisions to widen the corridor leading into Bastogne. At the same time, having lost their chance for victory in the whole offensive, the Germans planned to throw in everything they could to at least reduce this thorn in their side. *1st SS Pz.* and *67th Divisions* attacked the flank of Third Army, primarily in its 35th and 26th Infantry Divisions' sectors. The Germans lost 55 tanks in the operation. The next day, Third Army reported *seventeen* separate German attacks. During the period January 1 to 4, 1945, the Germans kept attacking, even though Manteuffel felt he could no longer take the city. Prisoners from eight separate German divisions were taken during this period, but the attacks were launched in piecemeal fashion, not a coordinated one.

By January 9th, the 101st was able to launch its first offensive operation, and the battle for Bastogne was over.

Without a doubt, the nerve of the men in the pocket was a major factor in the American success. More significant, however, was a curious failure of initiative on the part of the German commanders, men who had been known for their tactical skill in the past. The Germans could have won at Bastogne with initiative. By the time they launched a determined attack, the Americans were so well dug in that they needed far more force. They could have readily taken the town on the 18th or 19th, and their greatest attacks were made at the time when the Third Army had linked up and substantially reinforced the elements around Bastogne.

Perhaps the Germans had been stalled in fighting for too many cities in Russia and the lesson had finally been driven home to the point where they now shied away from anything that looked like a city fight when on the offensive. Whatever the reason, this, coupled with solid resistance by those American troops trapped in the city, ensured that Bastogne would remain the hole in the German doughnut.

Malmedy

No account of the Bulge would really be complete without touching on the events of 17 December 1944 near Malmedy—the so-called Malmedy Massacre. For many Americans, it underscored the moral reasons for their involvement in World War II. However, it also demonstrates, ironically, Germany's own patriotic or moralistic beliefs in what Germany was fighting for.

Kampfgruppe Peiper was an *ad hoc* strike force commanded by Joachim Peiper, Lt. Col. of the Waffen SS. It was a highly mobile armored/mechanized force, composed of elements of *1st Panzer Division,* and was to be one of the spearheads in the drive to the Meuse. During the Bulge the *kampfgruppe* has been accused of killing some 300 American prisoners of war and 100 Belgian civilians. Its most infamous episode occurred in the town of Baugnez, several miles from Malmedy, near a cafe known by its owner's name—Cafe Bodarwe.

On 17 December 1944, Peiper's force captured Battery B, 285th Field Artillery Observation Battalion, consisting of about 150 men. The prisoners were formed up in a field next to the cafe. There is some dispute as to exactly what happened next, but apparently as the main body of the *kampfgruppe* moved up, someone fired a pistol into the prisoners, then another fired a pistol, and finally, machine guns opened up. Some prisoners escaped by running into the nearby woods. Others played dead while the Germans went around shooting anyone who seemed to be alive. About 70 were killed.

Peiper's men moved on. Later that afternoon, a patrol from the 291st Engineer Battalion discovered the massacre. By nightfall, word had spread to the upper echelons where it was decided to give the incident wide publicity. The net result, in the immediate context of the battle, was to make it harder for German soldiers, particularly Waffen-SS, to surrender.

After the war, a large number of people were tried for the massacre, at Dachau, appropriately. They included Dietrich, the commander of *Sixth Panzer Army,* and Peiper himself. The verdicts included death by hanging for 43, including Dietrich and Peiper, life imprisonment for 22 and prison terms of 10 to 20 years for another eight. Most of the sentences were commuted, on the grounds that some confessions were coerced and some witneesses less than stable mentally, nor could evidence be produed indicating that either Dietrich or Peiper knew of the incidents. Both spent some time in prison. After the War Dietrich became head of an SS veterans organization and claimed former members of the SS were "discriminated" against. Peiper eventually, and surprisingly, retired to France, where, in a still unresolved incident, he was blown up in his chateau one day in the late 1970s.

In terms of casualties sustained in the battle, Malmedy was a minor event. However, it was the first direct experience that Americans had had with the mentality that produced the concentration camps, the *Sonderkommandos* of the Eastern Front, and Oradour-sur-Glan in France. If the Americans wondered why they were fighting, Malmedy provided some of the answers.

150th Panzer Brigade

One aspect of the Bulge which has particularly captured popular fancy was the *150th Panzer Brigade* of Otto Skorzeny—the Germans in Allied uniforms.

Skorzeny was one of the most dramatic figures of the war. He had freed Mussolini from captivity in September 1943; had played an active role in Berlin in keeping order for Hitler while the 20 July 1944 bomb plot was being put down; had forced the abdication of Admiral Horthy, the regent of Hungary, and kept Hungary in the war. On 21 October 1944, when he reported to Hitler on his latest effort in Hungary, he was advised of his role in the forthcoming attack in the Ardennes. He was to organize a unit with the primary mission of capturing one or more bridges over the Meuse between Liege and Namur. The key was that Skorzeny's men were to wear captured British and American uniforms. In addition, he was to have these men give false orders and generally disturb Allied rear areas. The brigade included a combined arms force to seize the bridges and small commando teams, called *Einheit Steilau,* which were to spread the confusion.

The issue of appearing in enemy uniforms was a delicate one. The Hague Convention prohibited improper use of enemy uniforms. Exactly what constituted "improper use" was not defined, and Skorzeny tried to find out by consulting several legal sources. He reached the conclusion that as long as they didn't open fire while in Allied uniforms,there would be no violation. The risks run by being in Allied uniforms were deadly. The improper use of enemy uniforms would mean that the soldier could be shot as a spy. In fact, three of his commandos were shot for just that reason after being captured by the Americans.

This secret effort was promptly compromised by the high command circulating a secret request for all English speaking officers and men who wanted to volunteer for a special mission. The wide circulation of the order ensured that it would fall into Allied hands. In any event, Skorzeny managed to assemble a 3,300 man unit. That is actually small for a brigade. The main force, to seize the bridges, consisted of two tank companies, three recon companies, three panzergrenadier battalions and anti-aircraft and fire support elements. Since the brigade would not be used for true combat, but only for a short spurt to the bridges, combat service support elements, such as supply trains, were kept to a minimum. The commando units of the *Einheit*

Steilau would be in nine teams of about four men each. The plan was to send the *Einheit Steilau* through the Allied lines on the first day. The main body would follow the lead elements of the *Sixth Panzer Army,* which was scheduled to be *1st SS Panzer Regiment.* Assuming that this lead force achieved its breakthrough by the second day, *150th Panzer Brigade* would then "sprint" from behind their cover to get the bridges intact and hold them until the main force arrived. Of course, the plan for *Operation Greif* read better on paper than it came out. The English speaking volunteers were a mixed lot. Most of them were fluent enough but had readily recognizable accents and little grasp of slang, particularly American slang. The brigade was supposed to be outfitted with captured American equipment but came up short in critical areas, such as Sherman tanks. They decided to disguise German tanks to look like Shermans. Anyone who has seen the limited success movie makers have disguising American tanks to look like German tanks will know why Skorzeny commented that these disguised tanks would only fool very young Americans, at night, from far away.

One of the most beneficial aspects of the whole operation arose out of a chance remark during the preparation period. A lieutenant remarked to Skorzeny that he had determined their real mission. They were not involved in a prosaic attempt to capture bridges. That was merely their cover. In fact they were to capture Eisenhower and other key Allied generals. Skorzeny made no effort to stop the rumor.

When the attack began, Skorzeny was ready to move. However, he saw early that the attack was not achieving its breakthrough. In fact, he found himself fighting a monumental traffic jam. *Kampfgruppe Peiper* was to be committed on the night of 16–17 December. This, Skorzeny felt, was the last chance to get the necessary breakthrough early in the attack. When, by the night of 17 December 1944, it was clear that Peiper was doing little better than the main attack, Skorzeny persuaded Dietrich, the *Sixth Panzer Army* Commander, that it would be futile to continue with his proposed mission because if they reached the Meuse, it would only be after a long, hard drive. Dietrich agreed and *150th Panzer Brigade* became a standard combined arms combat unit.

The *Einheit Steilau* had gone out on schedule. Probably six to eight teams actually got behind Allied lines. Two were captured. The teams did their job of ripping up telephone wires and removing sign posts erected by

American units to direct supply efforts. One team even reached the Meuse. The greatest impact was generated merely because these men were about. The secret message sent out for recruits had been compromised and the Americans knew that English speaking Germans would be sent in. Von der Heydte's parachute drop, otherwise a failure, became linked in American minds with Skorzeny's mission. As a result, they began to see English-speaking parachutists behind every bush. The now famous spot identification checks were set up whereby everyone had to identify Betty Grable's husband or which position who played with the Brooklyn Dodgers. This, in itself, slowed progress of messages and relief forces to the front and back. Montgomery was forced to get an American ID card because Americans weren't familiar with the British form. BG Bruce C. Clarke was held prisoner by MPs for five hours because he thought the Chicago Cubs were in the American League.

The most far-reaching impact came from the capture of one of the commando teams. One of them decided to save his life by telling the interrogators everything; the other three were shot as spies. Among the things he told the Americans was the rumor Skorzeny didn't quash: their main mission was to capture Eisenhower, Bradley and Montgomery. Personnel at Eisenhower's headquarters in Paris began to look for Germans marching up the road. Eisenhower was for several days a virtual prisoner in his headquarters due to security precautions. He only escaped it by laying down the law to his staff and insisting that the precautions be relaxed. Things had reached the stage where a double in Eisenhower's uniform and staff car was driven around Paris in hopes of trapping the Germans. Of course, none got near Paris since they weren't headed there anyway.

As for *150th Panzer Brigade,* on 21 December 1944, it was sent in as a regular combat unit under Skorzeny. It atacked in the vicinity of Malmedy and was badly handled by the 30th Infantry Division. Skorzeny was wounded and evacuated and the attack called off. On 28 December, the brigade was taken out of the line permanently.

Despite remarkable success in innumerable cinematic versions of the Battle of the Bulge, the *150th Panzer Brigade* failed in virtually all aspects. Its most formidable accomplishment were the rumors that were stirred up. If nothing else, the curious history of this brigade points up the disorder that can occur in a fluid situation and how it can be properly exploited.

The Battle of the Bulge: A Brief Chronology

16 Dec. The Germans launch a general offensive against American forces in the Ardennes region. Allied High Command believes the assault is purely local.

17 Dec. Sixth Panzer Army makes small gains in its sector. Allied High Command recognizes that the German offensive is general.

17–18 Dec. XXXXVII Panzer Corps of *Fifth Panzer Army* tears a wide breach in the American front, inflicting 90% casualties on 110th Infantry Regiment, which had been holding the Germans since the attack began.

19 Dec. Patton's Third Army is ordered to disengage and shift front roughly 100 miles northwards to help halt the German assault. British XXX Corps is ordered to back up the Americans by assuming positions on the Meuse. *12th SS Panzer Division* out of fuel for 12 hours.

19–20 Dec. The Germans continue to make insignificant gains in *Sixth Panzer Army* sector. *Fifth Panzer Army* makes little progress against St. Vith, but tears a wide hole in VIII Corps and drives westwards. 101st A/B Division (+) occupies Bastogne just as *Fifth Panzer Army* sweeps past it. Siege of Bastogne begins. 3rd Armored Division mops up remnants of *Kampfgruppe Peiper.*

21–22 Dec. Weather turns freezing cold. *2nd SS* and *2nd Panzer Divisions* run out of fuel, preventing the former from isolating St. Vith and the latter from reaching the Meuse. Allies have no troops between the Germans and the Meuse. British XXX Corps arrives north and west of the Meuse. Americans evacuate fortified "goose egg" at St. Vith.

23–24 Dec. Weather clears. Allied air power begins to assert itself. *2nd Panzer Division* comes within five kilometers of the Meuse, but is halted by 2nd Armored Division and fuel shortage.

25–26 Dec. Spearhead of *2nd Panzer Division* surrounded and destroyed. Patton's 4th Armored Division breaks into Bastogne, the siege is lifted.

27–28 Dec. Allied High Command proposes a deep penetration to pinch off the entire German salient and pocket the spearhead units. Proposal is rejected. Heavy fighting east of Bastogne.

29–30–31 Dec. Armored forces from *Sixth Panzer Army,* having been shifted southwards, attack towards Bastogne and make small gains in an effort to comply with Hitler's orders to take Bastogne at all costs.

1–2 Jan 1945. III Corps counterattacks around Bastogne with limited success. VIII Corps attacks against the southwestern face of the German salient with considerable success.

3–4 Jan. German command believes that retreat is necessary but is afraid to bring the subject up with Hitler. XVIII and British XXX Corps attack against the northwestern face of the German salient.

5–6 Jan. Germans continue attacks around Bastogne. Allies continue steady pressure against all sides of the German penetration.

7–8 Jan. Hitler finally realizes that the offensive has failed and orders the most exposed position of the penetration evacuated.

• • •

The Battle of the Bulge gave the Allies a healthy dose of caution. Although an Allied victory could no longer be doubted, it could nevertheless prove a tough and costly business. The German Army, though weakened, still had lots of fight left. And the physical obstacles to victory were potent as well, for the Rhine yet remained to be crossed.

Operation Grenade: The Battle for the Rhineland,
23 February–5 March 1945

By Joseph Balkoski

Lt Alexander Mckain, 329th Combat Engineer Battalion, American First Army, could just hear the rushing waters of the nearby Roer River as he approached his battalion's command post. Mckain and two other young lieutenants from C Company entered the frigid,dark CP, carbines slung over their shoulders and faces blackened in preparation for a mysterious evening mission. The 329th was attached to VII Corps, the command of the renowned MG J. Lawton "Lightning Joe" Collins.

Once inside the CP Mckain and his comrades found themselves face-to-face with seven senior officers standing on the far side of a candle-lit table. The lieutenants came to attention and saluted rigidly. As the salutes were returned, Mckain looked over the assembled generals in the dim light. He recognized none of them except "Lightning Joe" himself. Collins had been in charge of VII Corps since Normandy, and Mckain recognized his Irish face from photos that he had seen in *Stars and Stripes.* He had never conversed with a general before, and the fact that he was being personally briefed by one immediately before a mission left him tense. Quickly, Mckain understood that Collins's presence in this CP indicated that his impending task was going to be of the utmost importance to the corps and perhaps to the army as a whole. And missions of extreme importance, Mckain reluctantly surmised, were usually dangerous.

Mckain snapped out of his reverie when he realized that Collins was addressing the assembled group with a smooth, soft voice. The other generals were poring over the array of maps spread before them on the briefing table and pointing to various locales as Collins referred to them in his talk.

"There have been a number of dramatic changes in the strategic stuation during the past 24 hours, gentlemen," Collins began. "I'll summarize them before I explain to the lieutenants the importance of their mission tonight."

Collins's tone was already beginning to relax Mckain slightly. He found himself fascinated with the general's terse account of the corps' role in the upcoming operations. Until now, he had never grasped the "big picture" with such clarity.

"As you know, VII Corps was to have participated in Ninth Army's major offensive this morning," Collins continued. "However, this attack has been indefinitely postponed. Yesterday, General Huebner's V Corps—just to the south of us—seized the Schwammenaguel and Urfttalsperre dams on the headwaters of the Roer. Unfortunately, the Germans just had time to blow the dams as they were being captured."

Collins paused for a moment, looking straight into Mckain's eyes. "I'm sure all of you people know what this means," he resumed.

"Sir, was the destruction of the dams complete or were only the discharge valves blown?" asked one of Mckain's compatriots.

"I was just getting to that, lieutenant," replied Collins. "The destruction was definitely only partial. It looks as if we will *not* have a major flood on our hands for the next day or two. Instead, the dams will discharge water for a long period of time—perhaps two weeks—and there is absolutely nothing we can do about it. I am told by the Corps Engineer that the velocity of the Roer has now reached ten feet per second, and it has already risen by five feet. I have personally noticed a considerable increase in width opposite Dueren as well. I am also told that the abnormal amount of rain and snow that we have had over the past weeks will probably made this situation even worse."

Collins paused again to gather his thoughts. Mckain thought to himself that the rest of the talk would probably be directed at him and his fellow engineers.

"Now, I must stress that our offensive will still take place in the foreseeable future," Collins proceeded. "First Canadian Army is attacking towards the Rhine to the north of us and is having quite a difficult time of it. It is imperative that our attack jump off soon so as to relieve the pressure on our friends. The only question is, when do we attack? Gen Simpson's Army Engineer has stated that the Roer will be back to normal on 24 February—two weeks from now. But an attack before that date is not being ruled out, and in fact is considered desirable because of its potential surprise value."

Before Collins even began the next sentence, Mckain had fully comprehended what his upcoming mission was intended to prove.

"Ninth Army's Photo Interpretation Department and Engineer Survey Liaison Detachment will be keeping constant readings on the Roer for the next few days," Collins continued. "However, it is mandatory for General Allen and General Moore to comprehend the capabilities of their divisions' assault boats in this torrent. For this reason, Colonel Young, the Corps Engineer, has assigned each of you lieutenants an assault boat and nine men to attempt a crossing of the Roer tonight. One of you will cross near Dueren, another opposite Kreuzow, and the last near Birkesdorf. When you return, you will report back to us as soon as possible. Action is to be avoided—if it is impossible to cross without being fired upon, turn back immediately."

Colonel Young interceded. "It is important for you men to realize that the purpose of this mission is to determine if assault boats can be handled in the Roer by infantry who are fully equipped and very probably have had no training in amphibious operations. Remember that they will probably be crossing under fire in daytime. If you don't think it's possible to cross at this point in the flood, just say so."

"Also remember that now the Roer dams have been burst, the Germans will never be able to play this trick again," Collins added. "Once the river goes down, it will go down for good, and we will never have to worry about it again for the remainder of the campaign. I want an honest and frank appraisal of the river from you men. Should we wait until the river has completely receded, or is an attack now—or in the next several days—feasible?

Another hour went by as procedural details of the mission were ironed out. As the briefing concluded, Mckain left the CP and walked toward the riverbank and his assigned rendezvous. Here, he encountered the nine shadowy members of the squad that were going to accompany him in his boat.

"What the hell is the point of this crazy mission anyway, lieutenant?" his sergent whispered angrily. "You know that there are Germans on the other side of this thing?"

Mckain thought of rehashing Collins's talk for the men, but he realized that he could never succeed in summarizing it clearly and concisely without sounding ridiculous to them. "We have to see what effect the Roer is going to have on our boats," Mckain said meekly.

"What? Just look, lieutenant," the sergeant replied. "It doesn't take much brains for anyone to see that the Roer is a roar."

All the men laughed at this remark, which seemed to ease the tension a little. "All right, let's shove off," whispered Mckain.

The men pushed the boat together into the icy torrent and leaped inside. They started paddling furiously with their short, stubby paddles. Mckain immediately noticed that the boat was being swept by the current. It seemed to be making more progress downstream—to the engineers' left—than across. It was so dark that Mckain could see no features when he stared across the water toward the far bank. He just hoped that there were no German machine guns waiting for him there. "Paddle faster!" he hissed helplessly.

In the center of the Roer, the current got even faster and stronger. Mckain's boat began to spin and bob crazily, making the men's paddling efforts appear to be completely futile. The boat was rapidly being swept downstream. Freezing water was being splashed into the boat and all over the engineers' uniforms. The lieutenant realized that his craft might capsize if this kept up much longer. His hands and feet were utterly frozen and he wanted to turn back, but he thought of Collins and re-doubled the paddling efforts.

Finally, Mckain could dimly make out a few bushes and tree stumps about 20 yards away from the bow of the boat. With the way the boat had been spinning in the center of the river, he realized that he wasn't absolutely sure that this *was* the German side, but he pretended to his men that he was certain. "OK, let's turn back," he said confidently.

The return trip was just as difficult, but not as tense, because everyone in the boat knew that if they kept up their efforts for just ten more minutes, they would be on solid, friendly ground again. When the boat's keel scraped bottom, the engineers leaped out and dragged it ashore. Then, they all promptly collapsed on the river edge, completely exhausted. Mckain propped himself up against a tree and carefully prepared a report mentally for Collins.

With some difficulty, Mckain again located the 329th's CP and reported to the same group of generals that he had left a few hours before. He was the first officer back with his boat, so he found himself stared at with expectant glances. After reporting completion of the mission Mckain began his carefully-rehearsed report.

"There is very little doubt in my mind that a boat-load of inexperienced infantry troops with a full combat load would have very little chance of crossing the river in assault boats at its present stage," Mckain began. "If a boat is tipped, which almost happened to us on this mission, the men would have a very difficult time reaching shore due to the cold and turbulent water, even if wearing life belts. We ended up about 250 yards downstream from our starting point when we were about to reach the German bank."

"A 250 yard drift?" echoed Colonel Young. "That makes an attack now pretty much impossible."

"What about cables and ferries?" Collins queried. "Do you think that they could be employed?"

"Well, sir, a five-eighths inch cable that was securely anchored probably would hold an assault boat ferry," Mckain replied after a moment's thought. "However, you'd have to be pretty careful when ferrying or else the boats would swamp due to the rapid current."

"Lieutenant, did you notice any German obstacles on the far shore that would impede our boats from crossing?" asked MG Terry Allen, commander of the 104th Infantry Division.

"Well, I can't be too sure because of the darkness, sir," Mckain responded. "But I did see some barbed wire on the eastern bank that looked pretty thick. I also saw some tree stumps that were partially obscured by the flood. These probably would cause damage to our boats if they hit them."

"Thank you, lieutenant," Collins said after a moment's silence. "You've done an excellent job. Please make a quick written report of your findings and give it to your commanding officer. General Simpson and General Hodges will both read your report by tomorrow."

Mckain exited the hut to the strains of a strategic discussion among Collins and his subordinates concerning the significance of Mckain's journey across the Roer. He heard a few recognizable geographical names, but understood little else.

The Ninth Army

Operation Grenade, probably the most successful American set-piece offensive of the Second World War, was conducted by the Ninth Army. This had become operational on 5 September 1944 under the command of the highly respected, taciturn, 57-year-old infantryman LG William H. Simpson. It was an efficient organization. Most of the army's staff officers had been with Simpson since its activation as a training unit in September 1943 as part of the Western Defense Command in the United States.

Ninth Army's first combat mission had been to contain or subdue all of the German formations isolated in Brittany following the dramatic campaign in the summer of 1944 that liberated most of France. In addition, Simpson was responsible for preparing all American divisions arriving on the continent for eventual combat. The capture of the deep water port of Brest—Simpson's first important goal—was accomplished on 18 September after a bitter battle. A number of other Breton ports, such as St. Nazaire and Lorient, were carefully contained by Simpson.

By this time, the western front had reached the German frontier, and Simpson and his staff fervently desired to be present for the impending battle of the West Wall. Ninth Army got its wish on 3 October when it became an operational formation situated between FM Montgomery's 21st Army Group to the north and LG Courtney Hodges's American First Army to the south, manning a narrow sector of the western front near Maastricht in southern Holland.

In November, Simpson's Army participated in a series of desultory mini-offensives north of the German city of Aachen, fighting slowly eastwards towards the Roer River against determined Nazi opposition and rough terrain. The line of the Roer was reached by the time Hitler had made his last desperate gamble to regain the initiative in the west by striking against the First Army's thinly-held line in the Ardennes forest on 16 December 1944. Ninth Army responded to this threat to its southern flank by doubling its frontage and assuming a purely defensive posture. By doing so, two corps, V and VII, were freed for employment against the north face of the "bulge" that was seriously denting the American front to the breaking point. These two corps were instrumental in restraining and finally repelling the German offensive. By mid-January, after the Battle of the Bulge had ended, the Ninth Army returned to its former frontage near Aachen and prepared for offensive operations towards the Rhine.

The Western Front, Post-Ardennes Offensive

The progress of the Allied campaigns on the western front after the defeat of the German offensive in the Ardennes was influenced by two strategic decisions, one Allied and the other German. The first was Eisenhower's conclusion in early February 1945 that "one more great campaign, aggressively conducted on a broad front, would give the death-blow to Hitler's Germany." In order to deliver this knockout-punch, the Supreme Commander declared that "before attempting any operations east of the Rhine, it was essential to destroy the main enemy armies west of the river."

Meanwhile, Adolf Hitler had decided upon a policy of tenacious defense along the West Wall and other defensive lines well to the west of the Rhine. He permitted no strategic withdrawal of German forces behind the natural defensive barrier of Germany's greatest river, even in the face of direct pleas from the aged, although highly-respected FM Gerd von Rundstedt. "I want him to hang onto the West Wall as long as is humanly possible," Hitler said to his staff. "A strategic withdrawal would merely mean moving the catastrophe from one place to another."

Most German officers disagreed. "Well-tried experiences came into conflict with this theory, which called for holding out to the last man," a German general said after the war. "This kind of combat—due to the unequal distribution of forces on both sides in the open terrain—made it impossible for us to regain the chance of taking the initiative. Rather, the result was that there were only greatly depleted units available for the Rhine front later on, which necessarily also made that battle hopeless from the first."

The stage for the impending battle was set. The Allies sought to decisively defeat the German armies before lunging into Germany and racing for Berlin. Hitler complied by maintaining virtually all of his available strength on the western front west of the Rhine River. Only one question remained: Where would the Allies strike?

Much to the disgust of his British allies, Eisenhower's plan for the upcoming battle of the Rhineland reaffirmed his implicit faith in the strategy of the *broad front* advance all along the western front. The Supreme Commander insisted upon an almost equal share of provisions for each of his three army groups and seven armies. In turn, when the great offensive began, all would play at least some offensive role.

Eisenhower's broad front advance was to be conducted by successive hammer-blows against the German line, from Strasbourg on the upper Rhine to Nijmegen, on the lower. The first major offensive would be Montgomery's *Operation Veritable,* launched from Nijmegen and intended to break through the heavily fortified Reichswald forest. After accomplishing this mission, Canadian First Army was to drive to the Rhine and then turn south, clearing the river's west bank from Wesel to Dusseldorf and linking up with Simpson's army, driving northeastwards from Aachen.

Simpson's offensive, *Operation Grenade,* was intended to be launched almost simultaneously with Montgomery's. Ninth Army's operational directive required it to assault over the Roer River (a mission made difficult by the enemy's control of a series of dams near its source), drive across the "Cologne Plain" to the Rhine, and link up with British and Canadian forces participating in the *Veritable* offensive. It was hoped that substantial German forces could be pocketed by this envelopment before they could escape eastward over the Rhine.

The third phase of the Allied offensive, labeled *Operation Lumberjack,* was to be commenced after *Veritable* and *Grenade* had united on the Rhine. At this point, LG Omar Bradley's 12th Army Group was to attack directly eastward through the rough Eifel region and along the fertile Moselle River valley. If everything went according to plan, *Lumberjack* would secure the west bank of the Rhine from Cologne to Coblenz within ten days.

Operation Undertone was the last element of Eisenhower's Rhineland plan. Jumping off a few days after the start of *Lumberjack, Undertone* was primarily intended to support Bradley's right flank south of the Moselle as it attacked towards the Rhine. LG Jacob Devers's 6th Army Group was assigned to bring *Undertone* to a successful conclusion.

After the Rhine's west bank was cleared, Eisenhower tentatively planned to make the primary crossing of this great river in the north—near the Ruhr, and within Montgomery's operation sphere of influence. "This route offered the most suitable terrain for mobile operations . . . and the quickest means of denying the Germans the vital Ruhr industries," Eisenhower stated. Additionally, the Supreme Commander envisioned a crossing further south in Bradley's sphere in order to create "a massive double envelopment of the Ruhr to be followed by a great thrust to join up with the Russians."

At the moment his great offensive was about to be launched. Eisenhower could count on 72 Allied divisions on the western front: 50 American, 10 British, eight French, three Canadian, and one Polish. Rundstedt possessed 85 divisions, although not one was at full strength; most, in fact, were at one-third to one-half

WESTERN FRONT: Situation and Plans: 8 February 1945

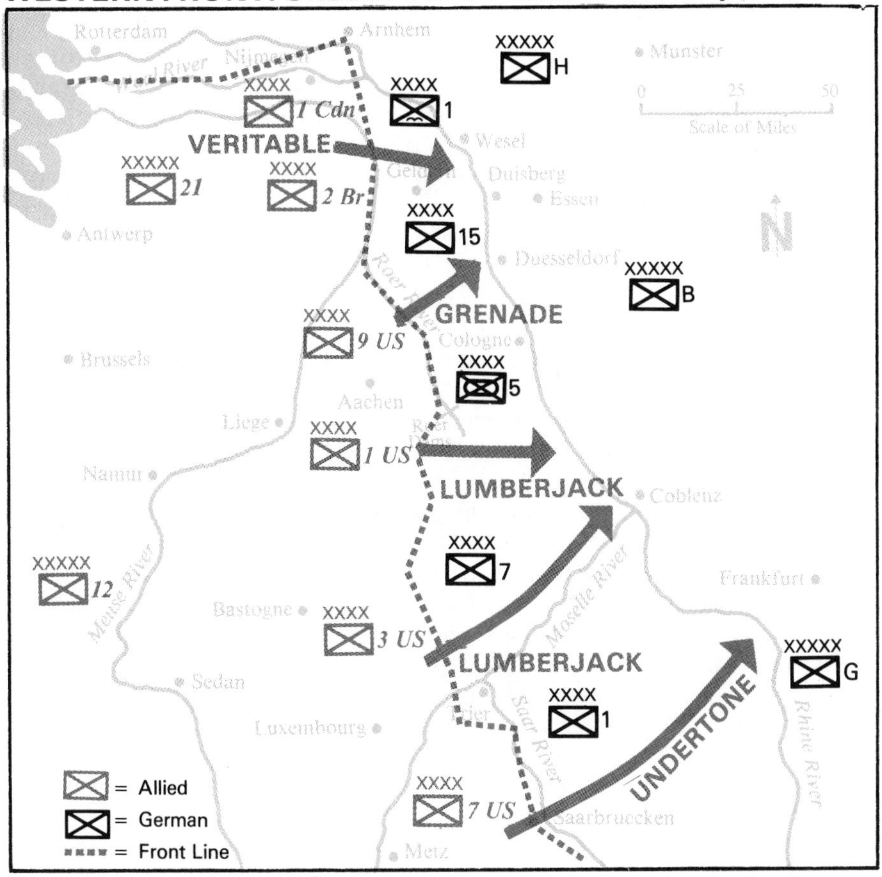

normal effectiveness. As one German general stated, it was the beginning of a "corporal's war" for the Nazis. "There were no big plans—only a multitude of little fights."

As in the post-Normandy period of the campaign on the western front, Montgomery and the British chiefs of staff objected strenuously to the broad front advance. "We will never had enough strength to mount more than one full-blooded attack across the Rhine," said Sir Alan Brooke, Chief of the Imperial General Staff. And because of the North German Plain's suitability for mobile operations, the British insisted, the Rhine crossing should be made in the north while other sectors passed over to the defensive.

However, as in the autumn, Eisenhower's will predominated despite acrimonious debate between the contending parties. The Supreme Commander insisted that the Allies' huge superiority of force, growing larger every day, permitted offensives in all sectors and, in fact, made the broad front strategy all the more certain of success. But the British were not pacified. "We did not advance on a broad front," Montgomery insisted after the war. "We advanced to the Rhine on several fronts, which were uncoordinated."

Grenade: Background

The Ninth Army was familiar with the ground it was to attack over in February 1945—some formations, such as the 29th and 102nd Infantry Divisions, had been occupying stable positions near or on the Roer since December. Therefore, it is not surprising that Simpson and his staff quickly realized that an offensive over this normally-placid river faced one distressing problem: German control of the seven dams situated at the headwaters of the Roer and its tributaries. This state of affairs made any realistic and final plans well-nigh impossible, for German destruction of the dams could cause disastrous floods throughout the Roer River valley. In the middle of offensive operations, such a flood could be catastrophic to American efforts. Huge lakes would be created over former dry land, bridges would be washed out, and troops on the Roer's east bank could be isolated from normally accessible supply sources. For these reasons, the Allied command concluded that an attack over the Roer was only possible after the Americans had seized control of the dams or, alternatively, a few weeks after the Germans had blown the dams and the resultant inundations had subsided.

The source of the Roer is the hilly and forested Eifel region of Germany. Here, the river gathers force as numerous tributaries join it amid the beautiful wilderness near Monschau. It flows in a northerly direction and soon leaves the broken countryside for the flatter, open Rhine plain. As it flows a few miles to the east of Aachen, it enters the operational area that was occupied by the Ninth Army in February 1945.

At no point during its course is the Roer a major river. It averages about 125 feet in width and is even fordable by military units in a number of locations. It has a fairly rapid current on its upper reaches—it drops 14 feet per mile near Aachen—but it slows down considerably near the Ninth Army front near its confluence with the Meuse at the Dutch city of Roermond.

At the Roer's headwaters, there were two major dams and a number of smaller "check" dams which regulated the river's flow. The largest dam was the *Schwammenauel.* It was constructed with built-up earth and had a capacity of 3.5 million cubic feet of water. The other major dam was the *Urfttalsperre,* which was concrete and masonry, and could store up to 1.6 million cubic feet of water at its highest level.

A number of captured German documents indicated that the German high command fully recognized the destructive military potential of the Roer River dams. It was clear that the Germans would fight tenaciously to retain control of these strucures in order to deter Allied offensive operations throughout the extensive Roer valley. On the other hand, Eisenhower recognized that the dams had to be taken or destroyed in order to carry out unhindered assaults over this terrain.

The Germans had two means of flooding the Roer. The first was the outright destruction of the dams, which would create a destructive flash flood throughout the entire valley. A US engineer study stated that this would "produce a short but high flood wave estimated at 15,000 cubic feet per second. . . . Such a wave would probably not last more than eight hours, but it would inundate the Roer River valley to an estimated height of 15 feet above the normal stream level. . . . It is estimated that 30% of the town of Dueren could be flooded in such a manner. As a precautionary measure, it is recommended that large bodies of troops and heavy equipment be kept above the 10-meter line." American engineers determined that *Grenade* could commence approximately five days after the flash flood's initiation.

The other method the Germans could employ in flooding the Roer was the simple destruction of each dam's outlet valve—leaving the structure itself unharmed. This would create a flow of only 650 cubic feet per second into the Roer. As a result, the velocity of the river would initially rise to about 12 miles per hour and the water level would ascend about four or five feet. In addition, some flatter areas of the valley could witness an increase in the river's width to as much as 1,200 feet. The engineers calculated that it would take at least 12 days for the river to regain its normal proportions.

There was only one positive aspect of the Roer River sitution to Allied planners—once the Germans had destroyed the dams, or the valves, they could never play this card again. Once the flood had subsided, the Allies could take the offensive without fear of further inundations. For this reason, bombing strikes were directed against the dams during the first two weeks in December. These raids were unsuccessful, but managed to lower the water level in both dams a small degree. It soon became evident that the Germans could only be forced to play their hand by a direct infantry assault against both major dams.

As early as October 1944, Bradley had ordered a determined offensive toward the Roer dams. In one major effort in early November, the 28th Division of V Corps was bloodily repulsed at a cost of more than 6,000 casualties in six days of attack. Throughout the rest of November, heavy fighting continued in the nearby Hurtgen Forest, although another direct attempt against the dams was not launched until 13 December. This particular attack was just beginning to make headway when the Germans struck the American front in the Ardennes, about 15 miles to the south. The 2nd Infantry Division—spearhead of the American offensive—was immediately pulled back in order to contain the German stroke. Eisenhower did not consider the Germans checked in the Ardennes until mid-January 1945. At this time, he formulated his plans for the upcoming Rhineland campaign and instructed his subordinates to prepare for yet another try against the dams.

The final attack toward the dams was ordered just as *Grenade* and *Veritable* were ready to commence. The 78th Infantry Division, supported by tanks of the 7th Armored Division, fought against ferocious German resistance—including a Hitler Youth Camp—but finally succeeded in overrunning *Urfttalsperre* on 8 February. However, the GI's discovered to their dismay that German engineers had already blown the outlet valves. On 9 February, the far larger and more important *Schwammenauel* was attacked successfully and captured. A team of special engineers from the 303rd Combat Engineer Battalion raced into the dark tunnels underneath the huge structure, fully expecting to be blown up by demolition charges at any moment. However, as at *Urfttalsperre,* the valves had long since been blown, leaving the sappers, and Simpson, completely frustrated.

Within a few hours, American formations on the lower Roer were beginning to witness the effects of the dams' demolition. The water level rose steadily, completely washing out a number of smaller dams along the course of the Roer. The river's velocity and width both increased markedly. *Grenade* was immediately postponed, and corps commanders were instructed to keep a constant eye on the river, testing the feasibility of an assault crossing on each succeeding day. On the VII Corps front, General Collins called for the engineers of the 329th Combat Battlion to test the Roer on the evening of 10 February.

Grenade: Planning

General Simpson was convinced that once the dilemma of the Roer dams had been solved, his army was in the most desirable position of all the Allied armies on the western front to penetrate the German lines and strike for the Rhine. Just east of the Roer lay the cologne Plain—excellent terrain for the employment of his highly-mobile armored formations. Beyond the Rhine in this sector lay the vital Ruhr industries, and beyond that the North German Plain—more ground suitable for tanks. Simpson's plan for his offensive over the Roer was presented to Montgomery, his immediate superior, for eventual consideration.

Within a week, Simpson received a favorable response from Montgomery. The Field Marshal realized that an American offensive along the Roer would fit together nicely with *Veritable,* the British-Canadian offensive in the Reichswald, which Montgomery had been building up for weeks. "The enemy is in a bad way," Montgomery wrote to Simpson. "He has had a tremendous battering and has lost heavily in men and equipment. On no account can we relax or have a 'stand-still' in the winter months; it is vital that we keep going so as not to allow him time to recover and so as to wear his strength down still further. . . . The main objective of the armies on the western front is the Ruhr; if we can cut it off from the rest of Germany, the enemy capacity to continue the struggle must gradually peter out."

Montgomery wrote that he intended "to carry out a converging attack with Canadian and Ninth Armies. Canadian Army to attack southeastwards with its left on the Rhine *[Operation Veritable],* Ninth Army to attack northeastwards with its right on the general line Julich-Dusseldorf *[Operation Grenade).* Once *Veritable* and *Grenade* are launched, the situation will call for continuous and sustained operations. Good management will be vital. . . . Only this way will we be able to keep up the momentum of the attack and thus force the battle to swing relentlessly our way."

Simpson immediately began careful preparations for his upcoming assault. "We will have some tough fighting, but I think we are going right through," he concluded.

Ninth Army possessed 15 divisions in four separate corps, including Collins' VII Corps, on loan from First Army, all poised on extremely narrow frontages along the Roer in preparation for D-day. The total strength was approximately 357,000 men. Despite the army's junior standing among Allied armies on the western front, Simpson's divisions and commanders were all professional and experienced. Only one of the divisions under Simpson's control—the 8th Armored—was new to combat. Most other divisions had been occupying positions along the Roer for extensive periods, and one—the 29th—had been in action since D-day. All in all, Simpson controlled one of the most powerful concentrations of American force yet seen on the western front.

Simpson had to deploy his 15 divisions along a 40-mile frontage, the northern quarter of which was almost totally unsuitable for offensive operations. In the south, about ten miles to the east of Aachen, Collins' 75,000-strong VII Corps lined the Roer. He controlled four divisions, two of which prepared to make the initial river crossing. The remainder, including the elite 3rd Armored, were held in reserve. Just to the north of VII Corps, directly opposite the German-held town of Julich, was MG Raymond McLain's XIX Corps, of four divisions. McLain prepared two divisions for the initial crossing, holding the two others back for an eventual exploitation role—including the 2nd Armored.

North of XIX Corps was MG Alvan Gillem's XIII Corps, parallel with the Roer near the town of Linnich. Gillem possessed two infantry divisions in his front line and an armored division in reserve. Finally, holding the northern sector of the front was MG John B. Anderson's new XVI Corps, occupying positions along the Roer up to its confluence with the Meuse at Roermond. XVI Corps consisted of three divisions, including the 8th Armored. Simpson retained a single infantry division, the 95th as an Army reserve. He made it clear that if any corps commander requested the use of this division after the commencement of operations, he would have to yield another division to Army reserve immediately.

In terms of support from the air, Ninth Army could rely on the XXIX Tactical Air Command, under the command of BG Richard Nugent. XXIX had 300 fighter bombers in five groups. Simpson gave these aircraft the primary responsibility of interdicting the enemy approches to the potential battlefield from the north, south, and east. In mid-February, an intensive bombing campaign against bridges, railroad lines, and suspected German headquarters was initiated. In a massive attack on 22 February by 9,000 aircraft, XXIX TAC, IX Bombardment Division, and all the heavy bombers of the US 8th Air Force and RAF's Bomber Comand participated. On some particularly successful days, German rail lines in the Rhineland were cut in as many as 100 places. In addition, more than 40,000 air photos of German positions along the Roer were taken by XXIX TAC in the month of February alone.

The German *Fifteenth Army,* under the command of Gen Gustav von Zangen, had little with which to face this imposing array of American power in the Roer Valley. Zangen could count on no more than 30,000 men along the river with only a modest amount of artillery and small amounts of ammunition. "It is considered that a quick breakthrough of the enemy's Roer River line, followed by a vigorous exploitation of every enemy weakness, could enable the U.S. Ninth Army to accomplish its mission with rapidity," stated an American report in early February. "The corps operating on the Roer were certainly in no position to prevent the American advance to the Rhine," echoed a German divisional commander later.

Fifteenth Army possessed three corps along the Roer, totalling six tired and battered *volksgrenadier* divisions. In the environs of Dueren was the *LVIII Panzer Corps,* LG Walter Kruger, with no mobile formations under command. The *LXXXI Corps,* LG Friedrich Kochling, held positions near Julich. And the northern third of Zangen's front was held by the *XII SS Corps* under MG Eduard Crasemann. Just north of *Fifteenth Army,* the 180th and 190th *Volksgrenadier Divisions* of the *First Parachute Army* covered the Meuse.

Despite the enormity of the odds, Zengen vigorously prepared for the defense of the Rhineland. American intelligence experts reckoned that *Grenade* would encounter a number of fortified lines throughout the Cologne Plain. Given the fact that the Germans had almost three months to prepare these fortifications between the Roer and the Rhine, it was fully expected that these positions would be elaborate and strong. Of particular worry to Simpson was the German line of entrenchments lining the east bank of the Roer, since the initial American attack would have to jump-off against these fortifications.

Ninth Army staff officers also knew that the Germans had constructed two or three more belts of anti-tank obstacles, minefields, and barbed wire, protecting the large industrial centers of the Cologne Plain, such as Rheydt, Munchen-Gladbach, and Neuss. However, American concern over these rear-area defensive belts was not great since it was recognized that the Germans did not possess enough manpower to fully occupy them. Instead, it was assumed that the Germans would make strongpoints out of the numerous villages and towns that dotted the Plain.

The German command recognized the defensive potential of the Roer position. "The Roer sector, with the exception of a few positions, was favorable for the defense," a German corps commander stated after the war. "Due to the marshy adjacent terrain, possibilities for enemy attacks were confined to certain localities. Organization of the defense adapted itself to these terrain conditions. On the other hand, the partly marshy terrain resulted in some disadvantages for the defender too. The construction of a continuous position was impossible. The troops had over-exerted themselves throughout their stay in the wet terrain. The uneven terrain was difficult to survey and restricted the spotting of heavy weapons." All in all, another German general concluded, "The prerequisites for a defense were not as yet achieved to a decisive effect."

In February 1945, the Luftwaffe was in the process of a minor renaissance on the western front. XXIX TAC reckoned that it might face over 400 German fighters and fighter-bombers on D-day if the weather was clear and the German airmen were prepared. To make matters worse for the Allies, over 75 of these aircraft were jets. Simpson and Nugent recognized the vulnerability of the American bridges that were to be thrown over the Roer to German aircraft and warned the anti-aircraft gunners to be prepared to defend them vigorously.

Both the terrain of the Cologne Plain and the weakness of the enemy forces situated there indicated to Simpson that the potential for a complete breakthrough of the German lines and a resultant rapid, mechanized exploitation in the manner of the Normandy breakout was strong. Nevertheless, a winter attack across a flooded river valley faced obstacles that did not exist in the previous summer *Blitzkrieg* across France. Thus, Ninth Army planned its upcoming offensive to be as flexible as possible. The army Chief-of-Staff, BG James Moore, prepared a directive to corps and divisional commanders to this effect: "*Operation Grenade* will be executed in accordance with one of two general plans. Plan I will require a rapid advance, including maximum exploitation by armored units. The conditions favoring such an operation are firm (dry or frozen) ground, a general deterioration of enemy forces opposing our advance, and the advance eastward of the First US Army units on our right flank. The existence of all three of these conditions will not necessarily be required for staging the rapid advance. Plan II will call for a slower, more methodical advance made necessary by wet, muddy ground, very strong enemy resistance, and threatened flanks. . .

"Measures to insure the secrecy of concentration of additional troops involved in the operation will be included in plans. Contact with the enemy prior to the attack will be maintained substantially stable so that no indications of a build-up for an attack will be apparent."

Due to the destuction of the outlet valves on the Roer dams on 9 February 1945, *Grenade's* 10 February jump-off date was immediately postponed. Careful study of the river by Army engineers indicated that the attack could be scheduled at its earliest one week from the original D-day. The army commander concluded that an early attack—perhaps 17 or 18 February—would achieve surprise, but face forbidding river conditions. An attack in two weeks time—say on 24 or 25 February—would not be hindered by the receded river, but by that time the enemy would be fully prepared to receive the attack.

Also, because of the slugfest Montgomery's *Operation Veritable* was developing into in the north, Simpson realized that the earlier *Grenade* got underway, the more it would draw German attention away from the attacking British and Canadian forces in the Reichswald.

Upon pondering these considerations, Simpson decided to jump-off on 23 February, one day before the Roer's expected return to normal. Although this was almost a two-week delay from the original D-day, some small degree of surprise would still be obtained in the attack. In addition, huge stockpiles of supplies would be building-up in depots during the respite, permitting the offensive—once it got underway—to proceed smoothly and with liberal quantities of all necessary forms of provisions for all attacking troops.

Zangen's situation was made all the more perilous by his almost complete lack of reserves—virtually his entire force was up front in anticipation of the American assault. *Army Group B,* which controlled *Fifteenth Army,* did have a number of mobile panzer or panzergrenadier divisions in the vicinity of the Ruhr, including the *9th, 11th, 116th, 10th SS,* and *Lehr Panzer Divisions,* but most of these were committed to the Reichswald when Montgomery launched *Veritable* on 8 February. "After releasing its only mobile units at the beginning of the British offensive, Zangen later noted, "*Army Group B* had no chance to influence in time—and perhaps decisively—the impending battles of *Fifteenth Army.* "

At the time Simpson was ready to undertake *Grenade,* the Cologne Plain was virtually denuded of troops. All that remained in reserve were the weak *9th* and *11th Panzer Divisions.*

Further exacerbating Zangen's already difficult situation was the activity of Allied air power. With the Luftwaffe virtually annihilated, Allied airmen were free to roam over Germany at will. "The railroads ahead of the Rhine were heavily damaged by the enemy air forces and were also almost completely destroyed in the rear of the foremost battle zone by the beginning of February," a German general lamented. "This could only partially be remedied by motor vehicle transport, as equipment was lacking as well as fuel."

Grenade: Initial Assault

At 2:45 A.M. on 23 February 1945, well over one thousand guns of the Ninth Army, ranging from small infantry support cannon to huge 240mm howitzers, commenced a 45-minute barrage of German defenses, headquarters, and supply depots east of the Roer. *Operation Grenade* was finally beginning, and all of the army's pent-up energy could now be applied to the definitive purpose of reaching the Rhine.

Primarily because the initial attack had to deal with the unsettled Roer as well as the Germans, *Grenade's* D-day preparations were complex. Since a precision bombardment of suspected German strongpoints was required, a short but furious artillery bombardment was decided upon instead of a massive preparatory attack from the air. Following this barrage, six attacking infantry divisions would launch their assault battalions across the Roer by boat. Because an insufficient number of these flimsy craft were available, attacking waves would have to shuttle their companies across the river—a task made extremely difficult by the fact that the paddle-driven boats drifted considerably downstream on both their assault crossing and the return trip. However, some lucky divisions planned to employ motor-driven boats or cable ferries. Typically, each assaulting rifle company was assigned 16 boats and a single platoon of combat engineers. Each boat would cross with ten infantrymen and three engineers for the return trip.

Following the seizure of the Roer's east bank by the assaulting infantry, engineers were to immediately commence the construction of foot-bridges over the river in order to allow second-wave infantry units to cross intact. In preparation for the crossing of heavy equipment on the next day, the sappers were to begin building heavier treadway, pontoon, and Bailey bridges as soon as possible on D-day. It was expected that about five bridges of all types would be built for each attacking division by the end of 23 February.

In order to shield attacking infantrymen and laboring engineers on the Roer, there was widespread use of smoke at the outset of *Grenade*, either through chemical mortar delivery or by generators. Some divisions kept up a continuous smokescreen for 33 hours at their crossing sites, aiding the generally successful assault crossings and quick completion of all projected bridges. Others maintained a screen for only two or three hours due to problems with the wind or blockage of friendly artillery observation. Only in VII Corps was the use of smoke made optional for divisional commanders and it was not, in the event, employed.

Despite setbacks from swamped assault boats, swept-away bridges, and German artillery and small-arms, all six divisions gained footholds on the Roer's eastern bank by the evening of 23 February at a total cost of 1,447 casualties. Twenty-eight battalions of infantry had crossed, although with almost no heavy equipment. However, seven sturdy treadway and pontoon bridges were completed by dusk, allowing the passage of vehicles and artillery to the east bank during the night. Particularly successful were XIII Corps' 84th Division and XIX Corps' 30th Division, both of which secured the eastern shore almost immediately and drove a wedge over two miles deep into the German lines.

Some American infantry divisions, particularly the 8th of VII Corps, ran into more severe problems with the still-raging river and the German defenders than they had expected. This division lined the upper reaches of the Roer where the current was extremely rapid and the riverbanks steep. Sometimes over 50% of company assault waves were swept hundreds of yards downstream or capsized. In one company, 12 of 16 boatloads of infantry were almost annihilated by four hidden

German machine guns. Pre-registration of German artillery fire was extremely accurate all along the front. A number of bridges were destroyed by this fire despite the employment of smokescreens.

In the VII Corps sector, German artillery fired with direct observation from nearby commanding heights for over 50 hours on bridge sites. Out of 400 VII Corps engineers engaged in bridge-building, 153 were casualties, 38%. By the morning of 24 February, only one bridge capable of supporting 8th Division's heavy equipment was ready for use.

"Circumstances similar to those we faced in crossing the Roer constituted probably the one problem they omitted from our assault crossing training at Fort Belvoir," said one engineer colonel. "It was an engineer's nightmare. And, if a year ago, anyone had said that this Roer crossing was possible, I'd have considered him mad." Another engineer officer stated, "The most difficult order I have ever had to give was to start immediate reconstruction of a destroyed treadway bridge, because I knew the men were out on their feet due to the tremendous effort they put into the initial construction."

Despite the obstacles from both nature and the enemy, the crossing of the Roer on 23 February was highly successful. For all intents and purposes, German small-arms fire from the east bank was negated by American artillery and smoke, and no assault battalion was fully repulsed. Most faced more hardships from the Roer than from the enemy. In spite of the effectiveness of German artillery fire on the crossing sites, it was clear that Ninth Army was finally on the Roer's east bank to stay.

Grenade: Build-Up

Zangen quickly realized that he had nothing with which to counterattack—in fact, that he would be hard pressed just to maintain a continuous defensive front. Most German mobile reserves were further north coping with *Operation Veritable.* The reserve formations remaining, *9th* and *11th Panzer Divisions,* were pitifully weak: the *9th* had only 29 tanks! As soon as the battalions and regiments of these divisions were ready to move, they were thrown into the fray piecemeal. The weak *338th Volksgrenadier Division* was also moved into the defensive line from the south, though it lacked artillery. That exhausted Zangen's reserves.

Simpson was aware of the lamentable situation his German counterpart found himself in, but still was somewhat apprehensive on 24 February, *Grenade's* second day. Ten more infantry battalions crossed into the compact east bank bridgeheads on that day, supported by seven tank and tank destroyer battalions and eight of field artillery. More importantly, about 20 secure bridges were constructed by the evening of 24 February, assuring the constant flow of supplies to the attacking spearheads and permitting unceasing offensive operations to continue unabated. Meanwhile, the units that had crossed on D-day made considerable progress in their attacks, particularly the 30th, 84th, and 102nd Divisions.

By the end of D + 1, Simpson concluded that the weakness of the German resistance and the expanding east bank bridgeheads made the American attack ripe for mechanized exploitation—"Plan I" of the pre-offensive study. Only in the south, in General Collins' VII Corps sector, was armored commitment not yet feasible. In fact, the 8th Division spent most of *Grenade's* second day fighting through the streets of Duren directly on the east side of the Roer. However, in the XIX and XIII Corps sectors, both the 2nd and the 5th Armor were given orders to prepare to move into the battle.

Simpson's plan for the fulfillment of *Grenade* was simple. VII Corps was to attack directly eastward, securing Ninth Army's right flank while crossing the Erft River and capturing Cologne if the opportunity presented itself. XIX and XIII Corps were to make almost a 90° pivot to the north, striking toward the major cities of Munchen-Gladbach and Neuss with the ultimate objective of meeting Montgomery's forces near Geldern. Simpson's uncommitted XVI Corps was to attack in the north on D+2 in order to clear the Meuse River Valley of German forces belonging to the *First Parachute Army*.

Grenade: Exploitation

On 25 and 26 February the American infantry divisions vigorously attacked northeastward, advancing a methodical two to three miles per day. Zangen's forces were tenuously holding a continuous front, giving ground grudgingly. However, all German soldiers in the army knew that without considerable reinforcement, a major American breakthrough was inevitable. In fact, by the end of 25 February, signs of this catastrophe to the German cause were already recognizable. In the south, the US 3rd Armored Division had crushed the *12th Volksgrenadier* and *9th Panzer Divisions,* advancing ten miles in one day and capturing the town of Elsdorf—only about 12 miles from Cologne.

On 27 and 28 February, the army's armor came into battle with a vengeance. 2nd Armored Division of XIX Corps achieved an advance of eight miles in one day towards Neuss, almost within sight of the Rhine. 5th Armored of XIII Corps attacked towards Munchen-Gladbach and Rheydt. Even the inexperienced 8th Armored of XVI Corps crossed the Roer and engaged in battle south of Duelken and Viersen. To all observers, it was rapidly becoming clear that *Grenade* was developing into a pursuit rather than a battle.

The Rhine Bridges

The situation in the Rhineland was fast becoming intolerable for Rundstedt, the German commander-in-chief in the west. It was clear to the elderly Field Marshal that total disaster confronted him should Simpson's Ninth Army unite on the banks of the Rhine with Montgomery's forces, which were just beginning to break out of the Reichswald during the last days of February. Most of the *II Parachute Corps* was still on the banks of the Meuse River in defensive positions at this time and, though not attacked, was generally threatened with annihilation in the event of a Ninth Army-Canadian link-up.

Rundstedt pleaded with Hitler for permission to withdraw *II Parachute Corps,* despite the Furher's well-known policy of rigid defense of all German-held territory. Remarkably, Hitler agreed to this proposal, though "With a heavy heart," on 28 February, almost too late to matter.

The first days of March saw Simpson's policy of maintaining a large mobile reserve finally pay off. Three fresh infantry divisions, the 75th, 79th, and 95th, were released for battle, while the Ninth Army's armored divisions, by now fully committed, pursued the defeated German forces. The huge stockpiles of provisions and munitions accumulated in advance were brought up and constant replenishment of manpower was undertaken, which enabled the Ninth Army to press its offensive both day and night without stopping. Simpson himself insisted that the pursuit be vigorous so as to allow the Germans no chance to regroup, or to blow the vitally needed bridges across the Rhine.

The first bridges encountered by Simpson's forces were the four at Dusseldorf on 1 March. The 83rd Division had cleared Neuss and reached the Rhine early on that day, forcing the Germans to immediately blow the three most southerly bridges. A single span joining Dusseldorf with the town of Oberkassel was left intact in order to withdraw the few German forces remaining in the vicinity to the east of the Rhine.

In the XVI Corps the 35th Division, with 784th Tank Battalion, performed the most spectacular advance of 1 March by rushing almost 15 miles to seize the fortress city of Venlo on the Meuse. On the same day, XIII Corps neared Krefeld and Uerdingen on the Rhine, while the 175th Infantry Regiment (29th Division) captured the city of Munchen-Gladbach single-handedly. In General Collins' VII Corps, the 3rd Armored Division attacked toward Cologne, the fourth largest city in Germany, and seized the *Vorgebirge*— a commanding ridge west of the city. Much to the Americans' surprise, they could see that the Cologne factories were still operating when they ascended the ridge for a glimpse of the historic city. On 2 March, the Rhine River was reached by a number of different units under Simpson's command!

With the accomplishment of most of *Grenade's* original goals by early March, the seizure of intact bridges over the Rhine by a daring *coup de main* appeared to be a distinct possibility. Most American planners realized that the speed of recent operations, coupled with the fact that substantial German forces still remained *west* of the river, must have left the German high command in confusion over the fate of each of the ten spans over the Rhine in 9th Army's area of operations. Four of these bridges were located in the Duisberg area, near the confluence of the Rhine and the Ruhr Rivers. Another was situated at Uerdingen, and four more connected Neuss and Oberkassel with Duesseldorf. The last bridge—the famous *Hohenzollern* span—was located in Cologne.

As darkness fell on 1 March, an American task force drawn from the 330th Infantry, 736th Tank Battalion, and the 643rd Tank Destroyer Battalion (self-propelled) moved northward in order to attempt a seizure of this bridge by an unusual deception. All US tanks were painted in German colors and markings, while German-speaking GI's marched alongside the vehicles in German uniforms to deceive any enemy forces that were encountered on the approach to the bridge. Confusion reigned in the German camp, and the imposters easily passed through German lines and outposts—sometimes marching directly behind or ahead of German columns heading for the same bridge without being recognized! Oberkassel was reached without incident, but dawn was breaking and the fresh sunlight took away the GIs' cover.

A German soldier on a bicycle recognized the tanks as American and warned the bridge commander of the impending danger. Sirens immediately wailed and firing broke out on all sides. The American column, with all subtlety lost and guns

Situation: 1 March 1945 ⊠ = Allied ⊠ = German ▪▪▪▪▪ = Front Line

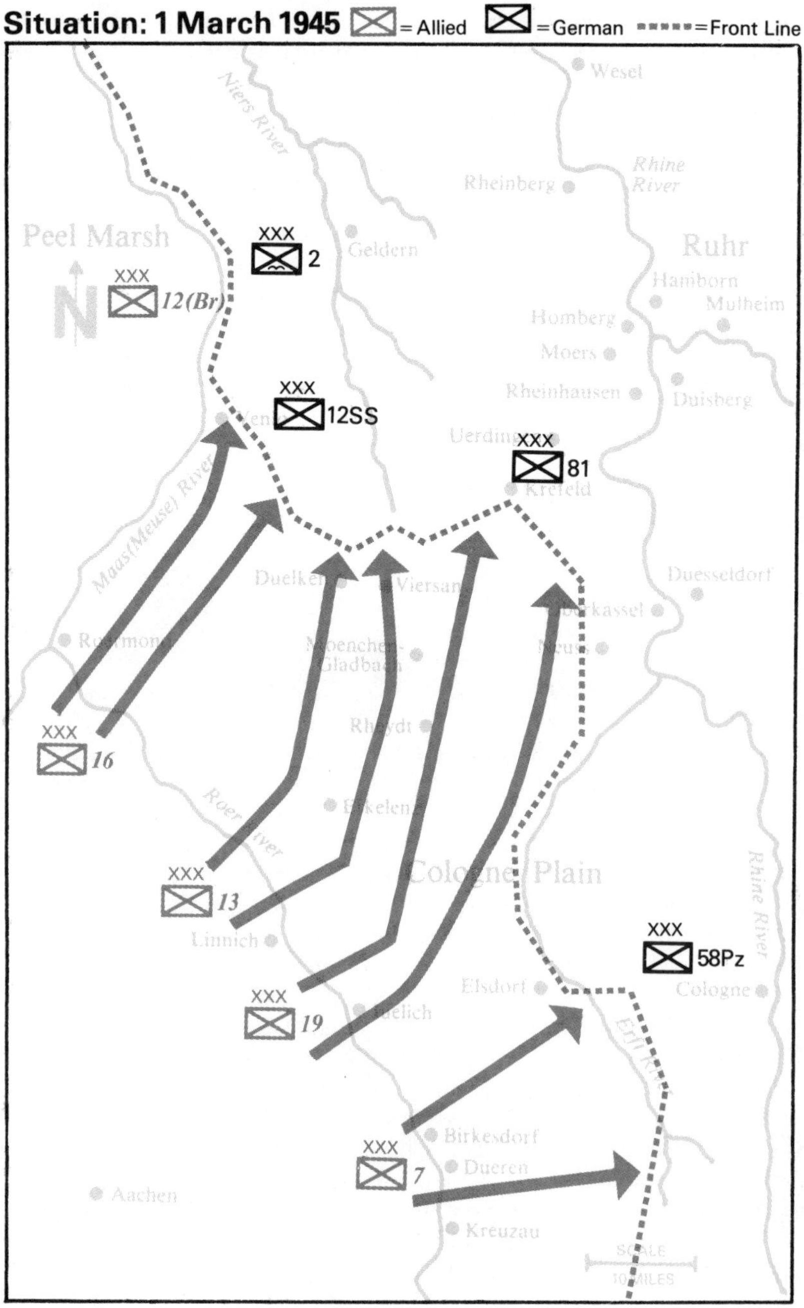

blazing, rushed the bridge. However, as the first two or three tanks drove up its ramp, it was successfully blown sky-high. The American column withdrew as quickly as it had come, its mission a failure, but giving the German high command quite a a scare.

Simpson launched his next drive to capture a Rhine bridge 24 hours later—this time, the 1,640-foot *Adolf Hitler* bridge at Uerdingen, about ten miles north of Dusseldorf. Tanks from Combat Command B of the 2nd Armored Division and two battalions of infantry from the 379th Infantry Regiment, 95th Division, attacked directly into Uerdingen against determined opposition from German paratroopers. The bridge was reached and successfully crossed by a six-man engineer patrol after nightfall. Despite the engineers' efforts to cut demolition wires, the bridge was blown up by the Germans early on the morning of 4 March.

By the beginning of 5 March, American forces of XIX Corps were attacking northwards directly alongside the Rhine's west bank against almost no organized opposition. It was obvious that all Germans in the vicinity had already withdrawn to the east side of the river. This theory was proved valid when American observation aircraft noted that the two most southerly bridges at Duisburg were already blown by the Germans before McLain's forces even got close to them. Clearly, the *Wehrmacht* was prepared to prevent what had occurred at Oberkassel and Uerdingen from happening again.

The last two bridges in Ninth Army's sector were those connecting the west bank city of Homberg with the Ruhr. Gillem's XIII Corps attempted to seize these two structures on 5 March, but was again frustrated by successful German demolition. Now, no bridge stood over the Rhine between the Ruhr and Cologne.

Although the Americans had failed in their efforts to snatch a Rhine bridge, the speed of their advance and the vigor of their attack had left the enemy in complete disarray. Disorganized masses of Germans crossed over to the Rhine's east bank, almost totally demoralized and unable to exert further effort. In addition, thousands of Germans were trapped on the west side of the river with no possible escape route. The VII Corps alone captured 13,000 Germans during its one and one-half week campaign in the Rhineland. *Grenade* was reaching its culmination.

Link-Up

Anderson's XVI Corps, covering Simpson's left flank, had the longest route to the Rhine of any Ninth Army formation. Although this Corps had only commenced its attack on 26 February, it quickly had captured the cities of Roermond and Venlo, while pushing northward in order to clear the east bank of the Meuse. In the early days of March, XVI Corps made dramatic daily advances. The 35th Division finally linked up with the British 53rd (Welsh) Division of Canadian First Army at Geldern on the 3rd, while the 8th Armored Division captured Rheinberg after a stiff fight on the 5th.

Some 50,000 Germans of dozens of different divisional formations now remained on the Rhine's west bank around a 20-mile perimeter under the control of *First Parachute Army.* Behind them, two intact bridges over the Rhine remained at Wesel—a tempting target for the Allies and the last remaining escape route for the Nazis. The German forces in the "Wesel Pocket" fought tenaciously for four more days, managing to blow both bridges on 9 March, while successfully withdrawing most of their beleaguered troops to the east side of the Rhine.

With the departure of the last German soldier from the Rhine's west bank, Operations *Grenade* and *Veritable* were terminated. Both offensives had taken a total of 52,000 German prisoners (30,000 by Ninth Army alone), while suffering 24,000 casualties (7,300 in Ninth Army). The Rhineland had been successfully cleared from Wesel to Cologne, bringing the Allies to the last great barrier on the road to Berlin—the Rhine River. Even while *Grenade* was still being undertaken, a major crossing of the Rhine was being planned by both Montgomery and Simpson, an offensive which the Allies hoped would be Germany's deathblow. Perhaps the greatest success achieved by both *Grenade* and *Veritable* was the near-destruction and demoralization of the vast majority of German forces *west* of this river, so that the Rhine crossing, when it came, was quickly and successfully achieved at very small cost.

Flexible Allied strategic planning, combined with utterly rigid German defensive responses, made the American victory in *Operation Grenade* inevitable and complete. J.F.C. Fuller, the great British military theorist of the inter-war period, once wrote: "A physician who is slave to a doctrine ends up by killing his patients; a general who is under some shibboleth as the oblique-order, envelopment, penetration, or the *offensive a l'outrance,* ends up by destroying his army. There is no difference. If there is a doctrine at all, it is *common sense*— that is, action adapted to circumstances." Hitler would have been wise to heed these words in 1945.

Logistics

The logistical considerations that were faced by American planners for the *Grenade* offensive were truly monumental—as is the case in any major attack involving mechanized armies. In order to support a continuous assault, huge stockpiles of ammunition (particularly for artillery), rations, and fuel had to be accumulated in army and corps-level depots, as close as possible to the front line in order to insure quick delivery during the ensuing battle. General Simpson's Army faced a particularly vexing problem of transporting sufficient supplies over the widely-swollen Roer River into the waiting hands of assault battalions on D-day and D + 1, usually under direct German fire.

These two Tables illustrate the intense accumulation and expenditure of supplies that were required prior to and during a major offensive. Note the tremendous consumption of artillery rounds on D-day (23 February), especially in comparison with the previous day—the firing rate on the day of the assault was usually *ten* times greater than normal—and in some cases, for standard weapons such as the 105mm howitzer, it was far greater. Also note that the army employed a number of British 25-pounder guns and captured German 105mm howitzers. These weapons required special, non-American ammunition.

In terms of supply build-up for *Grenade*, it is interesting to consider that the vast majority of logistical tonnage was delivered to Ninth Army by rail—a sure sign that the front line had been stable for a considerable period of time. In addition, note that the week in which *Grenade* was launched required the accumulation of two and one-half times the normal weekly supply tonnage that was required for non-active operations.

9th Army Supply Delivery February-March 1945

	Supplies (tons) Delivered by . . .			
Period	*Rail*	*Truck*	*Air*	*Total*
1-7 February	17,435	2,491	9	19,935
8–14 February	34,924	3,472	0	38,396
15–21 February	44,555	3,745	10	48,310
22–28 February	27,091	2,870	32	29,993
1–7 March	32,237	4,502	2	36,741

9th Army Artillery Ammunition Expenditure 22–24 February 1945

Gun Type	*XIII Corps*	*XVI Corps*	*XIX Corps*	
25 pdr.	-/-	545/23	-/-	22 Feb
	-/-	187/8	-/-	23 Feb
	-/-	2600/109	-/-	24 Feb
105 (Ger)	-/-	565/57	-/-	22 Feb
	-/-	-/-	-/-	23 Feb
	-/-	-/-	-/-	24 Feb
105	764/4	466/3	481/2	22 Feb
	13715/67	1497/10	21049/95	23 Feb
	19588/96	9016/63	30056/135	24 Feb
4.5" (g)	39/3	35/2	-/-	22 Feb
	646/54	412/17	604/50	23 Feb
	340/28	789/33	847/71	24 Feb
155	861/9	129/3	795/7	22 Feb
	6488/71	582/12	7042/65	23 Feb
	8142/85	2500/52	12222/113	24 Feb
155 (g): M1	162/7	49/2	49/2	22 Feb
	1385/56	380/16	1435/60	23 Feb
	1183/49	704/29	2572/107	24 Feb
155 (g): M12	81/7	-/-	24/2	22 Feb
	692/58	-/-	443/347	23 Feb
	723/56	-/-	634/53	24 Feb
8"	72/6	-/-	88/3	22 Feb
	369/31	-/-	1204/52	23 Feb
	375/31	-/-	2172/91	24 Feb
8" (g)	-/-	-/-	-/-	22 Feb
	-/-	-/-	-/-	23 Feb
	-/-	-/-	-/-	24 Feb
240	-/-	-/-	-/-	22 Feb
	-/-	-/-	-/-	23 Feb
	-/-	-/-	-/-	24 Feb

Notes: All pieces are howitzers unless otherwise noted (g = gun). Calibers are in millimeters unless otherwise noted. The number to the left of the slash is the total number of artillery rounds of the indicated caliber expended by the corps on the indicated day. The number to the right of the slash is the *average* number of rounds expended by each artillery piece of the indicated caliber on that particular day.

The collapse of the Rhine defensive signalled the end of Hitler's Reich. As the Allies pressed in from the West, the Russians launched their final drives from the East. And Germany was crushed between the two in April of 1945. It was an ending that had been inevitable for many months. Yet Germany's efforts in the final six months of the war were nothing short of remarkable.

Battle for Germany: The Destruction of the Reich, December 1944–May 1945

By Stephen B. Patrick

The inability of the Allies to resolve their logistical problems in the Autumn of 1944 gave Germany a brief, desperately needed respite from the onslaught of her enemies as their armies ground to a halt in October and November. In the West, the Allies stood everywhere on the German frontiers or the Rhine itself. In the East the Russians had cleared central Poland and were knocking at the gates of Budapest. As Winter set in, Hitler regrouped his forces and once again unleashed them on his enemies, resuming the offensive on a grand scale for the first time since the disaster at Kursk in July 1943.

Germany's situation was precarious at best. The Western Allies stood at the frontiers of the Reich, indeed Aachen, Charlemagne's ancient capital, was in American hands. Here terrain favored the defense. Before pressing further into Germany, the Americans and British would have to cope with the extensively fortified West Wall, the rugged terrain of the Rhineland, and the great barrier of the Rhine itself. In the east, the Soviets were in East Prussia, heartland of the German state, and on the Vistula. Here terrain was less favorable to the defense. Between the Soviets and Berlin there was only the Oder to present a serious natural obstacle.

Internally, Germany was cracking. Her cities lay shattered beneath massive American and British aerial bombardments; her people war-weary and increasingly hungry; her generals no longer confident in victory or Hitler; *Der Furher* himself showing increasing signs of deterioration. But Hitler was still at the helm, and the *Gestapo* insured the loyalties of the people and the army with draconian efficiency in the wake of the abortive assassination plot of 20 July 1944. So Hitler planned his offensives.

Resuming the offensive would have a number of benefits. It would restore luster to Hitler's rather tarnished image as "the greatest Field Marshal" in history. Moreover, it would give the German people a badly needed boost in morale. And most importantly it would gain time. The "secret weapons" were in preparation which would totally reverse the military situation once produced and introduced into combat, a process which would require time. But even above this consideration there was the fact that while Germany may have a future in a world in which the Allies and the Soviets were the victors, her leaders did not. Having turned Europe into a slaughterhouse, their future would last only so long as Germany resisted.

December 1944

Hitler's first blow came in the west, even as the Allies were preparing to resume the offensive. Breaking through the thinly held American lines in the Ardennes, the Germans attempted to drive on Antwerp, thereby cutting off and destroying an entire army group. Allied efforts to halt, contain, and drive back the German offensive upset their time-table, as first FM Sir Bernard Law Montgomery and then Gen George S. Patton had to be diverted to cope with the threat. The German offensive, launched on 16 December, achieved initial surprise, even unto the destruction of most of an American division. But the heroic resistance of small pockets of American troops and the bastion of Bastogne blunted their drive. Within ten days it was over, as massive elements of Patton's Third Army drove up from the south. By the beginning of January the Allies were poised to erase the last German gains in the Battle of the Bulge.

January

On January 3, Montgomery attacked the north flank of the German salient and Patton the south. By January 8 things had reached the stage where Hitler permitted *Sixth Panzer Army* to pull back, and by January 16 the Bulge was considered eliminated.

Meanwhile, US Seventh Army in Lorraine was attacked in the *Nordwind* offensive. This offensive was stopped on January 21. The Americans had already begun their counterattack the day before, so that by February 9, the Colmar Pocket had been eliminated and the southern Allied wing was on the Rhine.

On January 17, General of the Army Dwight D. Eisenhower resumed his main offensive. His first goal was to clear the Rhineland north of the Mosel. Montgomery's 21st Army Group attacked in the Roermond area while Bradley's 12th Army Group seized the upper reaches of the Roer River. Ultimately Eisenhower wanted to clear the entire west bank of the Rhine before attempting any crossing, since he felt it would be best to destroy as much of the German army west of the Rhine as Hitler would allow. Further, once the Rhine was secured, he could thin out certain sectors more easily in order to beef up the forces to make the crossing.

In the east, on January 12, the Soviets, under FM Georgi Zhukov and others, began their long-feared attack in Poland, taking Warsaw on the 17th. On January 20, they entered Silesia and were thus inside the Reich proper. By the start of February they had occupied almost all of East Prussia and were on the Oder in Silesia, in front of Breslau and Glogau. More seriously, they were on the lower Oder in front of Kustrin and Frankfurt-am-Oder, not 50 miles from Berlin, where the drumfire of their artillery could be heard daily. The Soviet drive had taken them through five hastily erected defensive lines, the Germans having nothing better since Hitler forbade extensive preparations lest they encourage retreat. The cream of the Red Army had been committed to this offensive, FM Ivan Konev's First Ukrainian and FM Konstantin Rokossovky's Second Belorussian Fronts, along with the First Belorussian Front under Zhukov himself, who was also in general overall command of the operation. And it was during this campaign that the names of certain Polish villages were forever carved on the record of Man's inhumanity to Man as the advancing Red Army uncovered the death camps at Auschwitz, Treblinka, and other places.

January was also the month that the Soviets tightened their grip on Budapest. On January 4 the Germans tried to break out but were unsuccessful, the Soviets had encircled the city and were slowly widening the belt between the city and the main German lines. The sort of German strength that broke into Stalingrad was no longer available. The units trapped in Budapest were left to play out their hands to the bitter end.

The Yugoslavs advanced slowly during this period and in Italy the Allies planned for clear weather.

February

Budapest fell to the Red Army on February 13. Gen Feodor Tolbuchin's Third Ukrainian Front was now free to turn its attentions upon Vienna. But German resistance solidified west of Budapest and an offensive was planned. Tolbuchin postponed his own attack and prepared to meet the enemy's.

In the north, Gen Heinz Guderian's Pomeranian offensive, begun on February 16, soon spent itself against determined Soviet resistance. But it did succeed in forcing the Soviets to re-evaluate their plans. Rather than drive on Berlin on a narrow front, they felt they had to clear the east bank of the Oder-Neisse system to preclude a flank attack from that area, either north or south, which could force them to divert troops from their main effort. Zhukov laid plans to accomplish this as soon as his supply permitted.

By and large, February was a month for the Red Army to resupply. Not so in the west. Eisenhower planned three operations to clear the Rhineland. First was *Veritable*. This was Montgomery's show and was to turn the left flank of the West Wall and move down behind it. Meanwhile, Gen William H. Simpson's American Ninth Army was to conduct a subordinate attack, *Operation Grenade*, to cross the Roer River, reach the Rhine at Dusseldorf, and swing north to meet *Veritable*. As a prelude to this, the Roer River dams had to be taken. This was done by February 9, but not before the Germans had opened them, flooding the land below and forcing *Grenade* to wait until the floods went down. Simpson waited two weeks and attacked—the Germans did not think he could move that fast after the flooding—and caught the Germans off guard.

Further south, First Army had *Operation Lumberjack*, a two-pronged operation. One wing was to link up with *Grenade* and the other with Patton's push up the Mosel.

The third operation, *Undertone*, was to await the completion of the first two.

Veritable had tough going at first, but by February 11, the Canadians were in Cleves and by the 28th *Grenade* had broken out to link up with the Canadians on March 3.

Meanwhile, First and Third Armies worked their way through the West Wall. Patton had a mission of active defense but, typically, he chose to emphasize the "active" part.

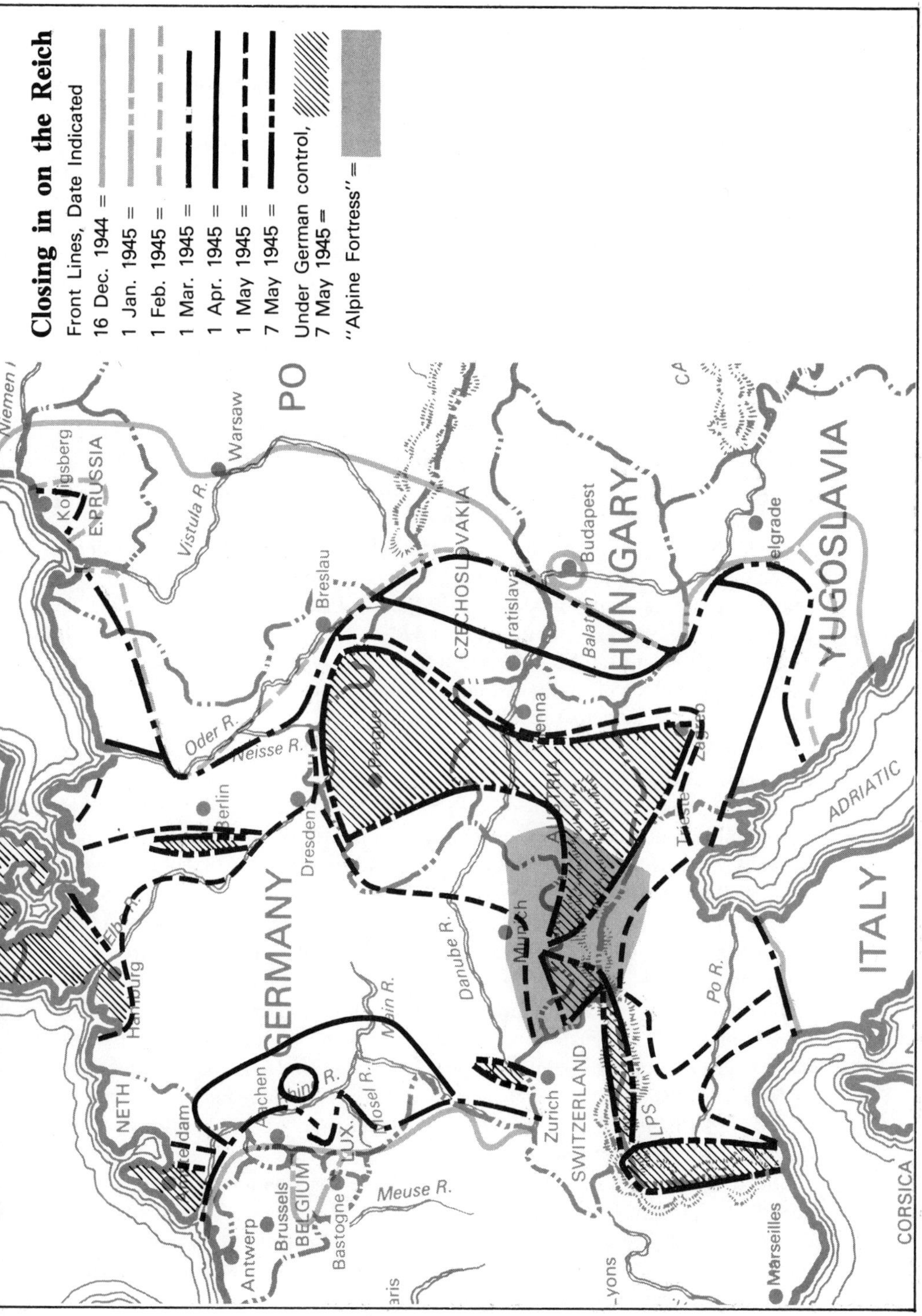

Closing in on the Reich
Front Lines, Date Indicated
16 Dec. 1944 =
1 Jan. 1945 =
1 Feb. 1945 =
1 Mar. 1945 =
1 Apr. 1945 =
1 May 1945 =
7 May 1945 =
Under German control, 7 May 1945 =
"Alpine Fortress" =
Königsberg
E. PRUSSIA
Warsaw
Vistula R.
Breslau
Oder R.
Neisse R.
Berlin
Dresden
Prague
CZECHOSLOVAKIA
Bratislava
Vienna
Budapest
HUNGARY
Balaton
Belgrade
YUGOSLAVIA
Zagreb
Trieste
ADRIATIC
AUSTRIA
Munich
Danube R.
GERMANY
Hamburg
Elbe R.
Main R.
Mosel R.
Rhine R.
Aachen
NETH.
Rotterdam
Antwerp
Brussels
BELGIUM
LUX.
Bastogne
Meuse R.
Zurich
SWITZERLAND
ALPS
Po R.
ITALY
Marseilles
CORSICA

March

By March 5, *Veritable* was over and the Rhine was clear north of Dusseldorf. A general advance now began in the west. By March 7, elements of Third Army were on the Rhine. Cologne had fallen and, more importantly, a task force of the American 9th Armored Division's CCB had found the Ludendorf railroad bridge over the Rhine at Remagen intact. They crossed on March 7 and established a toe-hold on the east bank. By the time the bridge finally collapsed, the Americans had a lodgment nine miles deep.

By March 10, the Rhine was in Allied hands north of the Mosel and *Undertone* was now launched. Originally *Undertone* involved nothing more than Seventh Army slugging through the West Wall. But with Patton on the Rhine north of the Mosel, a new option was exercised: Patton moved south along the Rhine, behind the German resistance. He made 100 miles in ten days, clearing the west bank down to Mannheim, while Patch's Seventh Army advanced 25 miles along its entire front. By March 22, the west bank Rhine was fully in Allied hands. More important, in fighting west of the Rhine, Germany had lost more than 300,000 men.

The next step was crossing the Rhine. The Germans had held the Remagen bridgehead fairly well, but if the Allies crossed at several points, Eisenhower believed the German line would collapse. The plan called for Montgomery to cross near Wesel on the night of March 23–24 while Patton resumed the defensive. Needless to say, Patton was not about to let Montgomery steal a march on him. He put troops across at Mainz on March 22. Montgomery crossed on schedule, using major airborne elements in the last big drop of the war, so that by the night of the 24th, the Allies were across in three places.

They now attacked out of these bridgeheads, Montgomery's British and Canadians heading north and east, with the Ninth Army on his right. The First Army pressed eastwards to link up with Patton's Third Army at Giessen and, more importantly, sending columns northwards in an effort to encircle the Ruhr, strongly held by FM Walther Model's *Army Group B* and 600,000 of the best remaining German troops.

On the eastern front, the Soviets were busy reducing East Prussia, Silesia and Pomerania so that, with a few exceptions (notably Breslau and Konigsburg), all of Germany east of the Oder-Neisse line was in Soviet hands on April 1, 1945.

Further south, the Red Army had to deal with the German offensive around Lake Balaton. This offensive was planned as a two-phase operation, with the first phase to protect the Lake Balaton oil fields and the second to retake Budapest. But by March 17, the offensive had been contained by Tolbuchin and he promptly regained, in 24 hours, all that the Germans had taken in the whole offensive, and then headed west into Austria.

March was again a quiet month in Italy. Time was running out on the "soft underbelly" approach. In part this was because the eastern and western fronts were moving much faster than anticipated. It was also due to the slow movement up Italy during the previous year followed by the bad weather which accompanies Italian winters, turning the ground into a quagmire.

April

On April 9, the Allies began their offensive in Italy. By April 20 they were advancing on the Po River and the following day Bologna fell. At this point Germany could no longer anchor its defensive line on the sea. Lacking sufficient troops to do that, the line began to crack and the tempo pick up. Verona and Parma fell on April 26. Finally, on April 29, the German commander, Vietinghoff, announced that all German forces in Italy would surrender May 2. At the same time the British took Venice and raced toward Trieste, a race lost to the Yugoslavs on May 1.

In the west, Eisenhower had to choose whether or not to go for Berlin. He was aware of the planned zones of occupation. He was also aware of the rumors of a National Redoubt in the Alps. This certainly smacked of the type of thing Hitler would do. He knew that Hitler and the high command were in Berlin. Weighing all these factors, he felt it better to drive into the south, to cut Berlin off from the south and hopefully crush any Alpine Fortress before it was manned.

Meanwhile, British troops pushed slowly forward in Holland, while they were able to take advantage of the flat lands to race toward Hamburg. By April 19 the British were on the Elbe.

Further south the Americans had pocketed *Army Group B* and they proceeded to drive inward on it. On April 14 the pocket was split in two and four days later all resistance ceased.

Meanwhile, Patton was in his element pursuing the broken German forces. These were the very operations for which Eisenhower thought Patton so suited that he refused to get rid of him after some of Patton's more notorious outbursts. In the process of Patton's charge across Germany, he overran Buchenwald, the first concentration camp to fall into western hands. He reached the Elbe on April 11.

At the same time, Seventh Army also drove east. By April 17, they were at the gates of Nurnberg. The French First Army, on the south, moved on Stuttgart, which they took on April 26.

Further south, the Red Army moved into Austria and Slovakia. On April 7, they entered Vienna. At the same time, they pressed on to Linz and Graz. Vienna held out for six days. Since *Sixth Panzer Army* was the principal force defending it, Hitler declared that they had disgraced themselves by failing. From then on, the *Sixth Panzer Army* was primarily interested in getting west.

On April 16, the other shoe dropped on Hitler. The Soviets came across the Oder north of Frankfurt am Oder and south of Furst. On April 25, they completed the circle around Berlin and were on the Elbe at Torgau. They had also crossed just south of Stettin. By the end of the month they were driving westward on a broad front. As the western Allies had halted on the Elbe, it was simply a matter of time before the Soviets crushed what few troops remained between them and the western front.

Psychologically, the most important moment of the war since D-Day occurred on April 25, when troops of the Red Army and the American Army met at Torgau on the Elbe. The Third Reich was cut in two. And even as this occurred, Red Army pincers closed about Berlin.

In Berlin were Hitler and all of his important aides except Goring. As a result, the Red Army had to fight as hard for Berlin as they had for any city in the past year. There were no real defensive positions, but Hitler had declared Berlin to be the front. The SS was out hanging every man who looked old enough to carry a rifle and couldn't give a good account of why he wasn't, or, if he was, where his unit was. The Soviets moved slowly into Berlin but by April 30 the Red Flag was flying over the Reichstag, little more than a stone's throw from the Chancellery.

April was the month that Germany literally fell apart. Accordingly, the tempo of advance picked up more and more as German units were overrun and crushed. The end of the month found Adolf Hitler dead, the capital transferred to Flensburg, the Furher now a navy man named Donitz, and troops surrendering in droves.

May

May was anti-climactic. Germany was finished. Hitler was dead. The Allies were busy consolidating their respective positions. In Austria and Czechoslovakia, little was done prior to the surrender. In Germany proper, the Red Army accepted the formal surrender of Berlin on May 2, and completed its move to the Elbe.

The British pressed on to the Baltic, taking Hamburg and Lubeck in the process. Patton continued his drive eastward, moving across the occupation line into Czechoslovakia and taking Pilsen before being halted by Eisenhower on May 6. The Czechs in Prague, believing that American liberation was at hand, rebelled against the Germans on May 4 and took control of the city. But Patton never came because, as he put it, "I wasn't ordered to."

In Bavaria, the US Seventh Army moved south and east into Austria, linking up with the US forces coming from Italy at the Brenner Pass and taking Linz, Hitler's hometown.

By the time of the armistice, the center section of Austria, the northwest of Yugoslavia and most of Bohemia and Moravia were all that remained in German hands outside of Scandinavia, which had remained untouched by the Allies.

The Red Army spent the first week of peace reducing the German pockets in Czechoslovakia. Tito, for his part, completed the defeat of German troops in Yugoslavia, which actually involved some fighting since the Germans were pretty certain of the treatment they would get at the hands of Tito's partisans. In the west, there were a number of pockets left to be mopped up, such as the Channel Islands, which had been bypassed and blockaded these many months.

All of that done, the Allies then turned to the German government. Donitz was an embarrassment. He had only a tenuous claim to authority and no real ability to exercise it. Moreover, he was slated for trial as a war criminal, as were several of his staff. It would not look good to deal with this government for a prolonged period and then arrest its head. Yet, there was no viable means for appointing a successor government and there was a need for certain nation-wide services, such as rail and telephone, which could best be controlled by a central government.

The Allies finally decided that they would worry about providing services later and cut the Gordion Knot by arresting Donitz and his whole government on May 23, 1945, thereby bringing to a formal end the Third Reich. The war against Hitler was over.

Werwolves and Redoubts

The werewolf, as any horror film fan knows, is a man who turns into a wolf by the light of the full moon. Actually, European folk lore is filled with all sorts of were creatures, but the werewolf has stuck in public imagination. And it was because of the mythic power of the werewolf that the word, in its German form, *Werwolf,* was chosen for a proposed guerrilla resistance movement which would carry on the war after the Allied and Soviet armies occupied all of Germany.

Steps were taken to organize cells of the *Werwolf* program in the latter part of 1944, when the Allies finally began to enter the Reich. They were to be under the control of the Wehrmacht, but fight in occupied areas. The head of *Werwolf,* however, was an SS officer named Prutzmann.

On April 1, 1945, *Radio Werwolf* began broadcasting. While the *Werwolf* organization, such as it was, was Himmler's idea, *Radio Werwolf* was Goebbels'. They were quite separate, though they both exhorted resistance behind Allied lines and, of course, shared a similar name. The Allies were not aware of this difference and assumed that it was just a second step in the overall plan to organize partisans behind their lines.

The *Werwolf* organization entered a new phase when the situation in Berlin became tenuous. Prutzmann decided to decentralize the training camps. One was set up in Austria, in an area which was to be called the Alpine Fortress *(Alpenfestung)* or the National Redoubt.

The Alpine Fortress was another Goebbels propaganda plan. He actively fabricated and leaked stories of a build-up of supplies and fortifications in the Southern Bavaria-Western Austria-Northern Italy area. Once started, the plan gained a life of its own. Switzerland made plans to defend itself against a last-minute seizure of Swiss lands by the Germans to augment their Alpine Fortress.

For the Allies, the Alpine Fortress was considered one of those things which, while not fully believed, could not be totally disregarded. As more and more rumors circulated about the National Redoubt, Eisenhower became more concerned since it had the ring of Nazi logic. It became one of the reasons why he refused to go along with Montgomery and insisted on a broad front strategy.

One of the few who apparently put no credence in the plan was Patton. Perhaps he had good reason since he was meeting none of the resistance which would be anticipated in such a build-up. As he and Patch moved into Bavaria, the *Alpenfestung* was seen for what it was: the last big lie by the master of Big Lies.

In fact, there was *Werwolf* activity. The British encountered two *Werwolf* pockets, one of which was actually reduced by the German *8th Airborne Division!*

On May 5, Donitz, by then Hitler's successor, ordered *Werwolf* to cease activities. With the end of the war, *Werwolf* did just that. There was simply nothing left to fight for.

The Wonder Weapons

During the last months of the war, Goebbels promised that a series of wonder weapons would be forthcoming which would turn the tide and bring victory quite literally from the jaws of defeat. Germany's technological experimentation in this period has become almost legendary, running the gamut from rifles which could shoot around corners to rockets. Had they been available in greater quantities and earlier in the war, several of them might, in fact, have made a significant difference. For every one which became operational, there were a dozen more in prototype or merely in plans. No sphere of activity was ignored; land, sea and air were all involved in an attempt to get a technological jump on the Allies.

On land, the major development was in the area of tanks. As early as 1942 Porsche had begun work on his 188 ton *Maus.* The Army weapons department had their own pet project which they started soon after, called *Lowe* or *Tiger Maus,* running between 110 and 120 tons. Finally, there was an entire new series of tanks planned, beginning in mid-1943, as replacements for the range of tanks then in being.

In addition to tanks, the Germans made somewhat less dramatic efforts to develop various types of recoilless rifles, succeeding with the *panzerfaust,* and a wide variety of specialized small arms, such as rifles which fired around corners. Few of these reached production.

In the air, the most dramatic program was the *Me 264V-I,* a four-engined bomber designed to reach the United States. Called the *Amerika-Bomber,* it was to carry a 3960 lb. bomb load to New York and have a ceiling of 44,000 feet.

More direct to Germany's needs was fighter development. The excellent *Fw 190* was upgraded into a more powerful version, the *Ta 152,* but only 67 reached production. A more important development was the jet fighter. The first operational jet actually flew in 1939, but this jet, the *He 280,* was abandoned, apparently for political reasons, in 1943. In its place the unready *Me 262* was pushed into development. The *Me 262* project was stalled by Hitler demanding that it carry two 550 lb. bombs. This required reworking the design so that it was not delivered to the front until April, 1944, and did not actually see combat until July, 1944. It was not until September that the first all-jet unit was formed. By that time the fuel crisis in Germany was becoming acute and more and more of the jets' time was spent on the ground. Still, it was a successful plane with 22 men becoming aces in the *Me 262.* In the meantime, Messerschmitt was also working on a rocket plane. This plane, the *Me 163 Komet,* flew in 1941 and was operational in mid-1944. It had a speed of 593 mph, a radius of 22 miles and a ceiling of 39,000 feet. It was actually too fast for the pilots of the time to control against the piston planes. In terms of speed, the *HE 172 Volkslager* has to set a record on development. The first plane flew 69 days after the specifications were issued. In the area of jets, Germany made several significant design breakthroughs.

They had a flying wing, *Go 229* and the *Me P1101*, which was only in prototype, a precursor of the *MiG 15* and the *F86* in shape.

Popular imagination has always been fired by the *V2*. The notion of push-button warfare in 1945 has a certain awesomeness to it. The fact is that the *V2* was potentially a very successful system. It was cheaper to make than a bomber and could deliver a 2150 lb. warhead.

Less dramatic, but more important in warfare, were the tactical missiles. The first tactical guided missile was the *Schmetterling*, begun in 1941. It was radio controlled with an infra-red lockon as it reached its target. Most successful in the surface to air field was the *Rheintochter*, a radio-controlled missile with a 330 lb. warhead. These were surprisingly effective but available in too few numbers to make any significant impact. The Germans also developed a hand-held surface to air system called the *Fliegerfaust*, which was a multi-barrelled weapon, but looked much like the modern US Redeye in operation.

The Navy was also pursuing innovation, particularly in submarines. While fairly good surface speed had always been available, the vulnerability of submarines to surface ships made this of little value. The first breakthrough was the *Type XXI* submarine. It mounted eighteen 21 inch torpedo tubes, could made 16 knots underwater and could go six days at six knots, all without having to recharge batteries or even put a *schnorkel* above the surface. The first of these submarines, *U 2511*, didn't get to sea until April 1945. Even more important was the *Type XXVI Walter* U-Boat, under development at the end of the war. It was to be powered by hydrogen-peroxide and could make 24 knots while submerged at full speed for six hours. Many of the prototypes fell into Soviet hands and are generally considered the basis for the big jump the Soviets made in their submarine program after the war.

These are only a few of the projects under way in the last months of the war. The more bizarre have been omitted. But they should not be forgotten because the time spent on developing these, when coupled with the time spent on trying out every crack-pot scheme that hit someone's fancy (and that was virtually what it came to) was time and money and materiel not available for the tried and true equipment. The Soviet Union and the United States basically fixed on one tank design and turned it out by the gross. The Germans developed three different entrants in the main battle tank area when most would agree that a lot more Panther tanks would have been more beneficial than the Tiger II. Similarly, the upgrading of the *Fw 190* into the *Ta 152* was a more valuable contribution to the German war effort than the many bomber prototypes which they toyed with for the purpose of making a run at the United States. Added to this, of course, was the tampering which had come to be expected in the weapons system, such as holding up *Me 262* production to adapt the jet to carry bombs. The combination of events meant that those weapons which might in fact have had an impact on the war arrived too late and in too few numbers to help.

Four Counteroffensives

One of the few controversies surrounding the last six months of the war in Europe was the value of the counter-offensives launched during the three months between December 16, 1944 and March 6, 1945. Since the war was effectively lost before December, none of the attacks could have saved Germany. The debate is over the questionable results which might have been achieved versus the effect of prolonging the war, which might have occurred had the German strength been husbanded for defense.

Wacht am Rhein

The first, both in time and force, was the Ardennes Offensive, *Wacht-am-Rhein,* begun December 16, 1944. Its goal was to take Antwerp and cut off the entire 21st Army Group under Montgomery. To this attack Germany committed some of its best forces, such as the *1st Panzer Division,* and some of its best generals, such as Manteuffel. Hitler sought to strike through the Ardennes and achieve the same surprise achieved in 1940. However, in 1940 the Germans had moved virtually unopposed through the Ardennes and fought the main battles to the west of the region. Now he proposed to fight the crucial battles in the forests and mountains of the Ardennes. The attack was well planned in that it hit the weakest point in the Allied line, the thinly held American First Army lines. But it set an impossible timetable. It was an insoluble problem. The road system of the Ardennes simply could not support a *Blitzkrieg.* The Germans attacked in the First Army area with the cream of the German tank forces in the west. Hitler expected to reach the Meuse in two days. He didn't reach it in ten days and was forced, on that tenth day, to pull back his spearheads. The result was a major loss for the Germans. Although it upset the Allied timetable by a month, it expended badly needed tanks and materiel for an attack which didn't really change things that much.

Nordwind

First Army was not the only thinly held area. South of Patton's Third Army were US Seventh Army and French First Army, holding the Alsace-Lorraine area. When Patton pulled out to take care of the Bulge, Seventh Army had to extend further north. Hitler decided to take advantage of this by a secondary attack with the dual mission of taking Strassburg and forcing the Allies to re-divert Patton away from the Bulge. As it turned out, by the time *Nordwind* got going, the Bulge was well in hand and the need to divert never arose.

The main attack was begun on January 1, 1945, on the left wing of Seventh Army, breaking through the Maginot Line near Hagenau, with an initial goal of Saverne, west of Strassburg. Eisenhower, seeing how thinly held the American positions were, wanted to pull back to the Vosges Mountains. This would have let the Germans have Strassburg, a loss which would have hurt DeGaulle's position badly. After several days of argument, during which it was apparent that the main German drive was being held better than anticipated, Eisenhower agreed to try to hold Strassburg.

At the same time, Himmler, by now commander of *Army Group Oberrhein,* attacked out of the Colmar pocket, a bulge across the Rhine around Colmar, with the objective of meeting the main German push toward the south. The Germans got within a few miles of Strassburg, but the American lines held until, on January 20, the Allies were able to counterattack, ending the last German offensive in the west.

The Pomeranian Offense

After the Soviet attack in January had carried their front line to the Oder, Guderian, then Chief of the General Staff, persuaded Hitler to make a counterattack with the hope of cutting off Zhukov's spearheads. He wanted a two-pronged attack, from Pomerania and Silesia. The *Sixth Panzer Army,* pulled out of the Ardennes, was to be the southern prong. Hitler refused to accept that as he had other plans for *Sixth Panzer Army.* So Guderian had to make do with plans for a one-pronged "pincer." The attack was in the hands of *Third Panzer Army.* Guderian had managed to get Gen Wenck in as chief of staff for Himmer (by this time commander of *Army Group Vistula*) and Wenck was managing the whole affair. The attack jumped off on schedule on February 16, 1945, but that night Wenck was injured in an automobile accident and his successor lacked Wenck's imagination. The attack foundered. It did achieve one goal. To prevent a repetition, the Soviets held off their drive on Berlin to clear the Oder from the Baltic to the Sudeten Mountains.

Frulungserwachen

Budapest had been encircled and cut off early in the year. By the end of February the oil fields around the Nagy-Kanioza area, near Lake Balaton, were threatened. These were the last natural oil fields in German hands and with the Saar on the verge of being taken by the western Allies and Silesia by the Soviets, the sources of coal-derived ersatz oil were in danger.

Hitler called on *Sixth Panzer Army,* commanded by his stalwart, Sepp Dietrich. Rather than sending them against the main Soviet drive on Berlin, he sent them to Hungary to protect the oil regions there.

The plan called for three prongs to drive into the positions of the Third Ukrainian Front, pin it against the Danube and destroy it. One wing, the *XCI Corps,* with three divisions, was to attack over the Orave toward Mohacz. The second wing, *Second Panzer Army,* with five or six infantry divisions, was to go between the Drave and Lake Balaton. The main attack, by *Sixth Panzer Army,* was to go north of Lake Balaton toward Dubafoldvor and destroy the main Soviet force. Once these phases were accomplished, Budapest was to be retaken.

The attack began on March 6. Six days later, *Sixth Panzer Army* had gone only 30 km. and was still 25 km. from the Danube. Tolbuchin, the Soviet Commander, had anticipated the attack, given ground grudgingly, and was prepared to counterattack. The Soviets stuck on March 19 and in 24 hours regained all of the ground lost, thereby ending the last German offensive on an ignominious note.

Reprise

These four attacks bled off what remained of the German reserves. Not spending the reserves in these attacks would have prolonged the war, though it is impossible to say how much longer it could have gone on. The Germans could not have fallen back indefinitely. Psychologically, some form of counterattack was necessary.

The attacks in the Ardennes and in Pomerania did throw off the Allied timetable to some extent and in that regard were of some value. Germany may have bought as much as a month by these attacks. Lake Balaton was even more essential due to the necessity of keeping the oil fields as long as possible. The only attack which was of no real value was *Nordwind.*

No matter what the possible gains from these attacks and the actual delays they imposed on the Allies, the most important result was to remove the last German reserves and prevent the Germans from having the initiative again. After the Lake Balaton attack, the SS units in *Sixth Panzer Army* could no longer be used in their old "fire brigade" role, being shuttled from critical point to critical point. All they could do was fall back toward Vienna. All that was left when these offensives were done was for the German forces to try to avoid suffering too many deaths and, for those in the east, to get to the West as fast as possible.

Organization and Reorganization

War inevitably forces changes on the the organizations with which an army fights. There are special demands imposed by the particular war being fought which lead to *ad hoc* changes in organization and these, in turn, often become formalized in official organization changes. Sometimes a major change is forced by the inability of the previous system to cope with the demands being made on it.

By 1943 the Allies had all hit upon systems of organization which worked for their purposes. For the remainder of the war the armored and infantry organizations in the US, Britain and the USSR did not change.

Germany followed the opposite course. One reason was Hitler's refusal to disband units. Rather than have one strong unit, he chose to have two somewhat weak units. Special interests, such as the Waffen-SS and the later *Volksgrenadier* units had their own organizations. Germany had the most varied range of units, including armored divisions, panzergrenadier divisions, regular infantry divisions, mountain divisions, jager divisions, and Luftwaffe field divisions. The Waffen-SS units usually had a different organization from their regular army counterparts, normally being somewhat stronger. The accompanying chart shows the organization of armored and infantry divisions in Allied armies during the last year of the war. The French, who reappeared as a substantial force with the invasion of Europe, had identical organizations to the United States.

More interesting are the various German systems. The steady decline of the tank strength in an armored division is particularly apparent. The Germans varied between decreasing the number of tanks in a company and altering the number of companies in a battalion, or battalions in a regiment. Thus, in 1941 they had, in their line companies, a total of 153 tanks in a division; in 1943 they had increased the companies in a battalion, and cut battalions to the division, so they fielded 136 tanks among the line companies of the armored division. But in 1944, they were down to 84 and under the 1945 organization they had only 50 tanks, yet the tank battalion had actually acquired a fifth company. The Waffen-SS panzer division had more tanks per line company, so it had 102 tanks in the line companies.

The importance of this lies in the fact that it is the company which is the basic command element. When considering command control problems, it is preferable to deal with fewer leaders. To control 100 tanks in 1943, six companies were needed; in 1944, slightly more than seven; ten companies in 1945.

Faster than they were lost, the number of German divisions and units actually grew until the last few months. However, this was a matter of appearance versus reality. Many units had been reduced to mere cadres during the last months of 1944, with few officers and men. They remained numbers on the rolls, but little else. Rather than let these units disappear, they were al-

German Divisional Reorganization, 1941–1945

Year		**1941**			**1943**		
Type		*Inf*	*Pzr*	*PzGr*	*Inf*	*Pzr*	*PzGr*
Tanks			163			136	
AGs				48			48
Bns:	Tank		3			2	
	AG			1			1
	Inf	9	4	6	4	4	6
	Art	4	6	5	4	5	5
	Recon	1	1	1	1	1	1
	Engr	1	1	1	1	1	1
	Sigs	1	1	1	1	1	1

lowed to remain as shadow divisions, to be filled by reserves as well as by dissolving fortress and other static and security units.

A more basic way of keeping so many units in the field was to change the organization of the unit. The large-scale organization of the divisions changed little in the last year or so of the war—the same number of battalions and the same number of regiments were in each division. It was at the lowest levels that economies were made. An expedient was simply not maintaining units at full strength. If a battalion had three companies nominally, only two would actually be fielded.

Yet another way of keeping the "traditional" divisions around was to combine several *Kampgruppen*—*ad hoc* units formed after a division was badly battered in combat—into a new division. In the end the Germans were not even so subtle as to merely omit a company or battalion. Divisions were raised by fixing a location for a headquarters, assigning a commander (they had spare generals after 1944), and sending out a few troops. This was the ultimate in instant divisions and was the way in which Wenck's *Twelfth Army* and *Group Steiner* were "raised." It is also the reason why they never did anything of merit. They were only a fraction of their nominal strength, but were assigned missions which only an army of full strength could do. Nothing of real value was accomplished by fielding these phantom units. Numbers of units do not replace the lack in numbers of troops. They do provide more flags on situation maps. Hitler seems to have enjoyed that, if nothing else.

1944				**1945**		**Br 1945**		**US 1945**	
Inf	*Pzr*	*SS-Pzr*	*PzGr*	*VG Inf*	*Pzr*	*Inf*	*Arm*	*Inf*	*Arm*
	84	102			52		126		195
		22	48						
	2	2			1		3		3
		1	1						
6	4	3	6	6	5	10	4	9	3
4	5	7	5	4	5	5	4	4	3
1	1	1	1	1	1	1	1	.3	1
1	1	1	1	1	1	1	.6	1	1
1	1	1	1	1	1	1	1	1	1

Panzer Regiment Reorganization, 1938–1945

Year	*Bns*	=	*Coys*	@	*Tanks*
1938	2		4		17
1940	2–3		4		17
1941	2–3		3		17
1943	2		3–4		17
1944	2		3		17
1945	1		5		10

Not only were Tables of Organization reduced on a divisional level, but regiments, battalions, and even companies were considerably reduced in strength during the war, as illustrated by the changes in panzer regiment organization and strength during the war. SS units were not so seriously affected by such reductions as Regular Army ones. The 1944–1945 SS-panzer regiment was essentially a three-battalion 1943 style regiment. The 1945 Army panzer regiment contained a battalion of mechanized infantry making it a theoretically better combat team by promoting even greater integration—*einheit*— than had ever been achieved before, but the ability to undertake blitzkrieg operations was long gone by the time this change was effected.

Volkssturm, Hitlerjugend, and "Stomach" Battalions

In the period June-August 1944, Germany sustained horrendous casualties: 149,000 dead and 749,640 captured, with perhaps an equal number wounded. The wounded aside, this was a net loss of almost a million men in just three months, out of a total ground force of little more than three million. A further 120,000 were killed and 216,000 captured in the last quarter of 1944, along with an enormous number of wounded. Nevertheless, in the same period 1,427,000 men were put *back* into the ranks, and in the first quarter of 1945 a further 1,626,000. Thus, in nine months, over three million men were added to the ground forces. Where they came from is a study in how much manpower can be scraped together when a nation puts its mind to it.

The primary source, at once both the most logical and the least unusual, was simply tightening up on the numbers previously exempt from service. When Germany could still build passenger cars in 1943, it is not surprising that many had been passed over for service. In 1944 they closed art and music schools and cut back on non-essential phases of such industries as radio and movies. More interesting, however, were the less orthodox sources.

One of the best-known German armored divisions, *Panzer Lehr* was the precursor of these last large levies. *Panzer Lehr* was raised at the end of 1943 and became fully operational the following summer. Its troops were the demonstration troops from the armored schools. After *Panzer Lehr* proved successful, similar units were raised from the artillery, parachute, and SS demonstration troops. A further combing of the schools in early 1945 sent the actual cadres, or *Schuletruppen,* to the front, there being no one left for them to train. In this fashion were raised such usually ignored formations as the *Clausewitz, Holstein,* and *Munchenberg Panzer Divisions* and the *38th SS Panzergrenadier Division Nibelungen.*

The air force and navy were also drawn upon for ground combat personnel. With the Luftwaffe fast becoming a name rather than a reality, enormous numbers of surplus airmen were formed into parachute divisions, though these had no parachute training and were ordinary ground divisions. The navy yielded up men to form several marine infantry divisions, so-designated from the origins of their manpower rather than for any amphibious capabilities.

Then there was the *Volkssturm.* This militia-type organization arose out of a Furher decree of 25 September 1944 to the effect that all men between the ages of 16 and 60 were liable for service. Although organized by the Nazi Party and partially officered by party functionaries and fanatics, the *Volkssturm* served under Wehrmacht control. It was generally ill-trained and ill-equipped. Often lacking helmets, the men were frequently armed with captured small arms, a few machine guns, and some anti-tank weapons, mostly commonly the *panzerfaust.* When *Volkssturm* units had heavy equipment, such as artillery, they usually lacked adequate amounts of ammunition or any means to move the stuff.

In March 1945 Germany called up the Class of 1929, the 15-year-olds. Former members of the *Hitlerjugend*, or Hitler Youth movement, were especially sought after in the hope that they had been sufficiently well inculcated with Nazi fervor as to make them tough customers in a fight. Many did fight as expected, and they died in droves, as anyone would without adequate training and equipment in the face of the battlehardened Allied and Soviet armies. The pool of youthful manpower was tapped repeatedly: they eventually began taking boys of 12.

Yet another major source of replacements was, in theory, the source best suited for fighting. These were the soldiers disabled in the war. In other circumstances they would have been out for the duration. Now they were sent back to the front if they could physically do so under their own steam. Because many had stomach problems, they were all jocularly known as "stomach soldiers."

The *Lehr* and other school troops were soldiers by training; the returning wounded, veterans; some of the older *Volkssturm* were World War I veterans. The rest were green and untrained. All were thrown into the breach.

This mixed bag was the means by which Germany fielded so many new troops. For the able-bodied, training was scanty, at best. For the no-so-able-bodied, they were often mustered with only the most perfunctory training. The image of Germany's last levies remains one of young boys and old men lugging Panzerfausts for a lost cause in which they no longer believed.

German Manpower Losses, World War II

Period	*Number*	*%POW*
9/39 – 4/40	100,000	0.0
6/40 – 6/41	100,000	3.0
6/41 – 6/42	600,000	5.0
6/41 – 6/43	900,000	20.0+
6/43 – 6/44	1,600,000	20.0+
4/44 – 9/44	600,000	30.0+
9/44 – 5/45	9,800,000	80.0+
TOTAL	**13,700,000**	**c. 65.0**

This table includes *absolute* manpower losses: men killed, permanently disabled, or made prisoner. Approximately 2,000,000 men were killed, roughly 3,000,000 more permanently disabled, and about 8,500,000 made prisoners during the war. Many of the latter never returned to Germany. Of some 90,000 men captured at Stalingrad, fewer than 10% were repatriated.

The Last Strategies

Germany

By December 1944, the Axis existed only in Hitler's mind. Accordingly, all strategies were Hitler's.

Germany was fighting on four fronts by this time: the west, Italy, Poland and the Balkans. The last two were nominally one front, but, because the two Soviet drives were basically independent, they had to be treated separately.

Hitler's strategy, such as it was, was one of desperation and wishful thinking. He was convinced that the Anglo-American alliance with the Soviets could not endure. Subsequent events proved him right. What he failed to recognize was that the mutual hatred they bore for Nazism was sufficient to hold the alliance together for the duration of the war.

Hitler seemed to have few illusions about Germany's chances to win the war. He now wanted to settle for destroying Communism. Hitler convinced himself that he could work out an alliance with the Anglo-Americans and the three would then crush the Bolshevik menace.

To "encourage" the British and American governments to see things his way, Hitler felt he needed a major victory in the west. He may not have seriously believed he could rout the western Allies, but he did expect to deliver a blow that would seriously upset the western timetable. He also hoped to so upset morale at home in the western alliance that the respective citizenry would be receptive to his offer. The result of all of this wishful thinking was the Ardennes Offensive: the Battle of the Bulge.

With the failure of the Bulge, Hitler had to do something about the renewed Soviet attacks. This resulted in the last two major attacks on the Eastern front: Guderin's mini-offensive in Pomerania was agreed to reluctantly. His major attack was around Lake Balaton, in Hungary.

The failure of these attacks left Hitler no cohesive plan, aside from the discredited "stand-fast" policy. In April there was the tragi-comedy plan for the relief of Berlin, to be accomplished by Gen Walter Wenck's *Twelfth Army,* which actually existed primarily on paper, SS LG Felix Steiner's *Group Steiner,* another paper outfit, and LG Theodor Busse's battered *Ninth Army.*

In Italy Hitler had no plan other than to hold the line.

The Allies

Allied strategy was based on the agreement formalized at Yalta, that Germany would not be partitioned, but would be occupied and the zones of occupation were laid out.

In the west, Eisenhower was still wrestling with Montgomery, who favored a single drive on Berlin, led, coincidentally, by himself. Eisenhower favored a broad front advance, pressing the German line at all points so that it would break in several places, rather than just one or two. Eisenhower did agree to give Montgomery priority in getting over the Rhine since Montgomery would have the clear terrain of northern Germany as his area of operation. However, once cross the Rhine, any strategy was of little meaning since the broad front strategy finally proved its worth and the German front disintegrated into groups of fleeing soldiers.

In Italy the goal had been to charge through the Po Valley into Austria and up the back way into Germany. It was to be a vindication of Britain's "soft underbelly" idea. As it turned out, Italy was never cleared prior to the surrender.

The Soviet strategy is difficult to discuss since their histories generally take the position that the strategy which worked was the one they had planned all along.

Basically, there were two prongs. The main one went through Poland, toward Berlin. Their goal was not gaining ground, but taking Berlin. In the south they dove on the two major Axis capitals still in German hands—Vienna and Budapest. Czechoslovakia, between the two prongs, was left more or less alone, though eastern Czechoslovakia was cleared.

The net result of the strategies based on the Yalta decisions was that the western advance was actually halted before the end of the war because they had advanced beyond the demaracation line at all points. As the Yalta agreement put Berlin in the Soviet zone, no serious attack was ever mounted from the west on that city. One of the interesting questions, then, is what result would have occurred if the occupation zones had been based on the fronts at the end of the war and not predetermined at Yalta.

Opening the Death Camps

The existence of German concentration camps had been known in the West before the war. These were the ones inside Germany, such as Dachau. But even their pre-war reputations as brutal means of suppressing dissent, left the Allies unprepared for what these camps became during the war. Even the Russians, daily in contact with the evidence of German barbarism during the brutal struggle in the East, were shocked by what they found.

The Nazis, under the aegis of the SS and, particularly, Adolf Eichman, embarked on their "final solution" to the Jewish "question." They set up their largest operations outside Germany. The camps inside Germany remained labor camps. People were worked, brutalized, beaten and starved to death. But the wholesale murder of humans was reserved for the extermination camps outside Germany.

So it was that the Red Army was ill-prepared when they entered the small Polish town of Treblinka and found the first of the extermination camps. They quickly advised the western Allies. Himmler, not wishing any more "bad press," proceeded to move the inmates of other camps toward the center of the Reich, away from the fronts. Many more died on this senseless trip.

What the Red Army found at Treblinka was something that even they had not really expected of the Nazis: piles of bodies; mass graves; ashes in the crematoria; stacks of hair, glasses, rings, and clothes. And over it all the sickly-sweet smell of burned flesh mixed with the noxious stench of death and decomposition.

Nor did it end with liberation. Just as the breaking of the human body by starvation takes time, so it takes time to recover from the effects of starvation. Many were already too far gone. These added to the problem of health and sanitation for those who survived. Many more went into mass graves just to avoid plague sweeping the camps.

In the west, the problem was a little different. First, the western camps were not devoted to extermination. Thus, the condition of the inmates was far more precarious on liberation. In the extermination camps the sickly had been quickly disposed of. In the work camps, the Nazis had allowed them to linger. Moreover, because they were not death camps, per se, they became more notorious for the brutalities perpetrated there: Buchenwald with Ilse Koch and her human skin lampshades; Josef Kramer, the Beast of Belşen; Irma Grese, who liked to tie the legs of pregnant women together as they went into labor. The difference was that those in the west often lived to tell the tale of what went on.

The western Allies decided to make a point and quickly. They trooped all of the citizens of the neighboring towns through the camps. It was an insignificant penalty to inflict compared to the enormity of the crimes. All of the camps had been put up well away from the big cities. The towns whose names they bore were usually pleasant little towns. The citizens of the towns were not rabid Nazis. They basically adhered to the notion that if they went their way and kept out of trouble, the government wouldn't bother them. It is unlikely that they were totally unaware of what went on in the camps. Often prisoners left the camps to work and the townspeople could see them. But since the prisoners had to be physically well enough to walk and since they were forced to sing and act happy as they passed by the towns, it is unlikely that the people of the towns were able to gain a good appraisal of the true conditions in the camp from what they saw of the prisoners. Certainly the prisoners going to work were not recommended objects of attention and the camps themselves were not high on the list of local tourist sights. The Germans also had to content with the fact that if they inquired too closely as to what was going on, they might find out first hand. Questions were not encouraged.

Consequently, while they all knew the camps were there, and may have suspected something of what was going on, it is unlikely that they even imagined the true horror of it all. Even those who ran the camps were affected. Many guards, brutal and brutish as they were to the masses of inmates, nevertheless developed perverse friendships with some of them. In the war crimes trials after the war, scarcely a guard was not found to have some witnesses to the fact that they had saved lives in the camps.

In the final analysis, however, the camps were what the war was all about. They were the culmination of the essence of Nazism.

Bringing the War Home

No one who has been raised in an English speaking country can really grasp the magnitude of what the Germans faced in December 1944. By that time all but the most optimistic knew the war was lost. They faced not only defeat, but occupation. Defeat, while hard to bear, was endurable. Occupation, particularly by the Soviets, was intolerable.

Nothing the Germans had experienced prepared them for this. To many, Hitler and the Nazis were the people who had brought them out of the chaos of the Weimar Republic, with its galloping inflation and depression. To them, Nazism's direct impact was generally beneficial and its excesses remote. It meant a strict government, but one the people could respect. It might also mean a knock on the door for some neighbors, but these were enemies of the state—at least that's what the Germans were told and who knew different? Through the first nine years of the Nazi regime, including three years of war, Hitler had made promise after promise and delivered on all of them. That something had gone wrong was obvious. But Goebbels had told them that this was because of shirkers, traitors and lack of hard work.

It is not so incredible that the Germans believed this. People are generally unwilling to believe that their government can do anything genuinely wrong. It is therefore not so surprising that the average German tended to discount rumors and believe them to be merely Allied propaganda. The Germans were promised miracle weapons to turn the tide. They had already heard about the *V1* and *V2*. More were promised and the tide would turn.

Yet it didn't. The start of the new year saw the Americans in Germany itself, at Aachen, and the Soviets in East Prussia. Bombing had become a way of life as cities which were important for the maintenance of the German military machine were slowly turned into rubble, their main products, homeless families, and the dead. The greatest terror before the advent of the nuclear age, firestorm, was a constant threat to the future of all German cities. A firestorm is produced by a concentration of incendiary bombs on a city. The fire draws air from the outside and actually creates a giant blast furnace which melts the steel of the buildings. Hamburg, Kassel, and Darmstadt had all been firestormed. In a matter of months the ancient city of Dresden was to have its turn. But firestorms aside, the people had learned to endure bombing. This very fact belied one of the major theories behind strategic bombing—that it would break the morale of the people.

Goebbels took full advantage of the coming disaster. He portrayed the western Allies as barbarians for their terror bombing. He warned of the *Morgenthau Plan,* a proposal to divide Germany into several small states, to bar any heavy industry in those states, and to make the Germans a pastoral people. For the Soviet forces he had few kind words. The image of the Red Army as a force of half-Mongol, semi-civilized rapists struck terror into the hearts of those who lived in their path.

It is no surprise, then, that the Germans dreaded what the next months would bring. Nor is it surprising that they clung to each thread of hope held out to them, no matter how slender.

The image of *Gotterdammerung* has often been used to describe the last months of the Third Reich. It is an apt image. The old Nordic myths held their gods to be mortal. In a final battle, *Gotterdammerung,* the forces of evil would fight the gods. Both sides would be destroyed in this battle, but out of the chaos would arise a new and more perfect world. The Germans, however, were not anxious to enact one of their folk myths.

During the last five months of the war, the Germans endured regular bombing. In addition to learning to live with the wail of air raid sirens, the sounds of flak and the crash of bombs, slowly, but steadily, they came to learn new sounds. First that of field artillery, then the sound of small arms as the front moved close. Being a part of the front lines was a new terror. For most Germans, knowing that the two fronts were getting closer left only one question: where to go?

For those in East Prussia, Pomerania and Silesia, there was only one choice: go west. The sure threat of the advancing Red Army overpowered the Nazi threats to those leaving their homes. They packed what they could into carts and wheelbarrows and walked west during the winter of 1944–45. Those who lived in the east had little to look forward to under Soviet occupation. If nothing else, Goebbels' portrait of the typical Soviet soldier made that clear.

Nor were their fears unjustified. The Red Army had stored up its resentment since 1941. The excesses of the German army had been compounded by the atrocities of the SS and the *Sonderkommando* death squads. Accordingly, the Red Army was not especially concerned with observing the niceties of dealing with civilians in occupied Germany. Germans were all the same. If they weren't Nazis, they were Nazi sympathizers. Tales of widespread rape and looting may have been exaggerated, but there was more than a grain of truth in them. The Red Army noticeably relaxed discipline when dealing with civilians once the Reich's borders were crossed.

So, not only did Germany have before it the prospect of losing the war, but also that of continuing occupation. Both were awesome prospects, but occupation was the greater fear. When Germany had sent its troops to occupy, they had come as conquerors. The Allies were not only coming as conquerors, but with vengeance in mind, and what that might mean was anyone's guess. But some knew, and many more suspected what treatment Germany had meted out to her conquered subjects over the last five years. The war would soon be over, but who knew when the occupation would end, or what it would mean to Germany? This is what the Germans had to face during the last six months of the war—and to fear.

Recommended Reading

The literature of the Second World War is voluminous. Over 4500 works are listed in one bibliography which treats only of works in English up to 1965. Sorting through this mass of materials can be difficult. For persons interested in pursuing some aspect of the war at greater length, the items listed below may be of value. Note that listings loosely follow the table of contents.

General Accounts and Background

Peter Calvocoressi and Guy Wint, *Total War.*
Winston Churchill, *The Second World War.*
Frederick W. Deakin, *The Brutal Friendship.*
Vincent J. Esposito, editor, *The West Point Atlas of American Wars*, Vol. II.
Joachim Fesch, *Adolph Hitler.*
B. H. Liddell Hart, *History of the Second World War.*
John Toland, *Adolph Hitler.*
Chester Wilmot, *The Struggle for Europe.*
Peter Young, *Atlas of the Second World War.*

The German Army and Military System

Gordon A. Craig, *The Politics of the Prussian Army.*
Heinz Guderian, *Panzer Battles*
David C. Isby, "Panzer Battles," *Strategy & Tactics* #73, March-April 1979.
Albert A. Nofi, "Mechanized Warfare: Experiment and Experience, 1935–1940," *Strategy & Tactics* #41, November-December 1973.
Staff of *Strategy & Tactics* Magazine, *War in the East.*
Telford Taylor, *Sword and Swastika.*
John Wheeler-Bennett, *The Nemesis of Power.*

The Fall of France

Guy Chapman, *Why France Fell.*
L. F. Ellis, *The War in France and Flanders, 1939–1940.*
Alistair Horne, *To Lose a Battle.*
Vivian Rowe, *The Great Wall of France.*
William O. Shirer, *The Collapse of the Third Republic.*
Telford Taylor, *The March of Conquest.*

The Battle of Britain and Operation Sealion

Peter Fleming, *Operation Sealion.*
Telford Taylor, *The Breaking Wave.*
Ronald Wheatley, *Operation Sealion.*

The War at Sea

Marc'Antonio Bragadin, *The Italian Navy in World War II.*
Samuel Eliot Morison, *The Battle of the Atlantic.*
The Atlantic Battle Won.
Jurgen Rohwer, *Chronicle of the War at Sea.*
W. S. Roskill, *The War at Sea, 1939–1945.*
White Ensign.
Friedrich Ruge, *Der Seekrieg: The German Navy's Story, 1939–1945.*

North Africa and the Mediterranean

Correlli Barnett, *The Desert Generals.*
George F. Howe, *Northwest Africa.*
David Irving, *The Trail of the Fox.*
B. H. Liddell Hart, editor, *The Rommel Papers.*
Gavin Long, *To Benghazi.*
Donald Macintyre, *The Battle for the Mediterranean.*

Bernard Law Montgomery, *El Alamein to the River Sangro.*
Alan Morehead, *African Trilogy.*

Sicily and Italy
Martin Blumenson, *Anzio: The Gamble that Failed.*
Mark W. Clark, *Calculated Risk.*
Albert Garland and Edward McG. Smyth, *Sicily and the Surrender of Italy.*
Eric Linklater, *The Campaign in Italy.*
Fred Majdalany, *The Battle of Cassino.*
Samuel Eliot Morison, *Sicily-Salerno-Anzio.*

The Air War
Cajus Bekker, *The Luftwaffe War Diaries.*
Warner Brumbach, *The Life and Death of the Luftwaffe.*
Martin Caidin, *Black Thursday.*
The Night Hamburg Died.
Noble Frankland, *Bomber Offensive: The Devastation of Europe.*
Adolph Galland, *The First and the Last.*
Arthur Harris, *Bomber Offensive.*
R. J. Overy, *The Air War.*

Northwestern Europe: D-Day to V-E Day
Martin Blumenson, *Breakout and Pursuit.*
Hugh M. Cole, *Ardennes: Battle of the Bulge.*
The Lorraine Campaign.
Napier Crookenden, *Dropzone Normandy.*
Dwight David Eisenhower, *Crusade in Europe.*
L. F. Ellis, *Victory in the West.*
Gordon A. Harrison, *Cross-Channel Attack.*
Trumbull Higgins, *Winston Churchill and the Second Front.*
Charles B. MacDonald, *The Siegfried Line Campaign.*
Bernard Law Montgomery, *Normandy to the Baltic.*
Frederick Morgan, *Overture to Overlord.*
Samuel Eliot Morison, *The Invasion of France and Germany.*
Cornelius Ryan, *A Bridge too Far.*
The Longest Day.
C. P. Stacy, *The Victory Campaign.*
Russell F. Weigley, *Eisenhower's Lieutenants.*

Other Theaters
Christopher Buckley, *Greece and Crete.*
Mario Cervi, *The Hollow Legions.*
T. Kingston Derry, *The Campaign in Norway.*
Gavin Long, *Greece, Crete, and Syria.*
Robert M. Kennedy, *The German Campaign in Poland.*
John F. MacDonald, *Abyssinian Adventures.*

The Holocaust
Lucy S. Dawidowicz, *The War Against the Jews, 1933–1945.*
Eugen Kogon, *The Theory and Practice of Hell.*
Quentin Reynolds *et al.*, *Minister of Death.*

The Secret War
Anthony Cave Brown, *Bodyguard of Lies.*
John Masterman, *The Double-Cross System.*
Joseph E. Persico, *Piercing the Reich.*
F. W. Winterbotham, *The Ultra Secret.*